D0918364

THE NEUROPSYCHOLOGY
OF SLEEP AND DREAMING

THE NEUROPSYCHOLOGY
OF SLEEP AND DREAMING

Edited by

John S. Antrobus
City College of the City University of New York

Mario Bertini
University of Rome, La Sapienza

 LAWRENCE ERLBAUM ASSOCIATES, PUBLISHERS
1992   Hillsdale, New Jersey   Hove and London

(SCI)
QP
426
.N48
1992

Copyright © 1992 by Lawrence Erlbaum Associates, Inc.
All rights reserved. No part of the book may be reproduced in any form, by photostat, microform, retrieval system, or any other means, without the prior written permission of the publisher.

Lawrence Erlbaum Associates, Inc., Publishers
365 Broadway
Hillsdale, New Jersey 07642

Library of Congress Cataloging-in-Publication Data

The Neuropsychology of sleep and dreaming / edited by John S.
Antrobus, Mario Bertini.
    p.   cm.
    Includes bibliographical references and indexes.
    ISBN 0-8058-0925-2
    1. Dreaming. 2. Sleep. 3. Neuropsychology.   I. Antrobus, John
S.   II. Bertini, Mario.
    [DNLM: 1. Dreams. 2. Neuropsychology. 3. Sleep.   WL 108 N4955]
QP426.N48 1992
154.6′3 — dc20
DNLM/DLC
for Library of Congress   91–41252
                                         CIP

Printed in the United States of America
10 9 8 7 6 5 4 3 2 1

WITHDRAWN

Dedicated to
William Dement, Allan Rechtschaffen, and David Foulkes

Contents

IV. Lucid Dreaming

Preface

Ever since the discovery by Aserinsky and Kleitman in 1953 of the relation between dreaming and the electrophysiological measures derived from the electroencephalogram and electro-oculogram, a small band of scientists has pursued the search for the functional links between the cognitive and neurophysiological characteristics of dreaming sleep. In the early 1960s, as many as 200 full-time investigators, graduate students, and psychiatric residents were active in the field and the National Institute of Mental Health devoted about ten percent of its research budget to research on sleep and dreaming.

Much of the credit for developing this exciting new field goes to William Dement, Allan Rechtshaffen, and David Foulkes, three enormously creative and dedicated scientists who began their careers in the 1950s and 1960s as graduate students at the University of Chicago. Like Eugene Aserinsky, Bill Dement was a student of Nathaniel Kleitman in the Department of Physiology at the University of Chicago, but unlike Aserinsky's concern with traditional physiology, Bill's interests extended to mind–brain relationships, particularly as they changed with states of sleeping and waking. Bill became an indefatigable champion of research on sleep neurophysiology and dreaming. His early experiments on the incorporation of external stimuli into the dreams of sleeping subjects, including the duration of dream events, on the eye movement scanning hypothesis of dreaming, and on the consequences of dream deprivation, examined with expert precision questions that most people thought were beyond the reach of experimental science. He communicated his excitement about sleep research to large and small audiences all over North America and Europe both through his lectures and in 1972 with his succinct survey of the field in *Some must watch while some must sleep*. He has travelled constantly, encouraging and advising investigators in every aspect of sleep research.

Although it is difficult to appreciate from our contemporary perspective, experimental psychologists were, in the 1950s, strongly discouraged from using any kind of description of one's private experience as research data. The publication of experiments that used dream "reports" as data in the *Journal of Experimental Psychology* by Dement and Kleitman, both of whom were physiologists, pretty much marked the end of that taboo for psychologists.

Although Al Rechtshaffen, the first psychologist at the University of Chicago to dedicate his career to the new field, entered the university shortly after Bill Dement left to take a position in New York City, the two of them subsequently collaborated to help found the Association for the Psychophysiological Study of Sleep (APSS). Because sleep research is painstakingly slow, they encouraged investigators to present the results of work in progress. As a result, the annual meetings of the APSS were filled with excitement as laboratories on each side of the Atlantic presented their latest (often incomplete and partially analyzed) findings.

Al Rechtschaffen was also a tireless researcher. If he had an exciting new idea at lunch, Al had a sleep subject and a small group of students or colleagues ready for a laboratory test by the same evening. He studied the threshold for visual stimuli during dreaming sleep by taping open the eyes of his subjects. He pioneered research on sleep talking and dreaming, on dreaming in nonREM (NREM) sleep, on the effects of presleep stimuli on dream content, on the relation between phasic events and dream novelty and bizarreness, and on the brightness, hue saturation, and visual clarity of dreams.

Coming somewhat later to Chicago, David Foulkes entered the field when it had already reported a number of laboratory findings and made a number of strong psychophysiological claims. Among David's major accomplishments are the qualifications that he placed on several of these claims. For example, he showed that dreaming occurred at sleep onset and in NREM sleep as well as in REM sleep, and, moreover, that dreamlike fantasy commonly occurred in the waking state when conditions were similar to those of a sleeping person. He continued the work of Dement on the effects of external stimuli on dreaming, and worked with Rechtschaffen on the effects of presleep determinants, but he used these procedures to test the features of psychoanalytic theory. In 1966, he reviewed the status of the field in *The psychology of sleep* which remains today one of the best introductions to the early laboratory research on dreaming.

At the time, no one had been able to establish a bridge between dream psychophysiology and the major areas of psychological inquiry. In this theoretical vacuum, David took an early lead in using laboratory dream research to evaluate psychoanalytic conceptions of male development. When he found the conceptions wanting, he pursued a demanding series of laboratory investigations of dream development, some of which are described in *Children's dreams: Longitudinal studies.*

Eventually, David turned to cognitive psychology, particularly psycholinguistics, for a theoretical foundation upon which to build a cognitive model of dreaming. To accomplish this he had to develop the sophisticated set of cognitive scale and grammatical rules that he described in *The grammar of dreams* and *Dreaming: A cognitive-psychological analysis*. His active research program continues to be theory driven as demonstrated by his work with Kerr on the dreams of the blind, and the role of the nonverbal cortical hemisphere in dreaming.

The ranks of investigators in dreaming sleep have thinned in recent years as funding has been moved to more applied research problems. However, the field has benefitted greatly from the enormous advances in the neighboring fields of neurophysiology on the one side, and cognitive psychology on the other. A major consequence of these advances has been the realization that the relations between sleep, neurophysiology, and dreaming can only be studied and understood within the larger context of waking neurophysiology and cognition. *The Neuropsychology of Sleep and Dreaming* is the first book on dreaming that clearly presents this point of view.

Considerable credit for the book goes to the organizers of the European Sleep Society meetings in Zurich, Bologna, and Copenhagen, and the International meetings of the Association for the Psychophysiological Study of Sleep, in Seattle, who through colloquia and informal meetings facilitated the exchange of ideas among North American and European investigators. Most of the contributors to this volume have benefitted greatly from these interactions and many of us have found warm and lasting friendships among our transatlantic colleagues.

We thank Christiano Violani for his constant help and advice, and Nadia Antrobus, Ed Davis, and Edgar Spand who helped us in the preparation of the manuscripts. Finally, we want to express our appreciation to Larry Erlbaum for his support of the book, and to his editorial and production staff, Chava Casper, Kathleen Dolan, and Linda Eisenberg, who have done so much to bring this manuscript to the light of day. Also, we give special thanks to Maria Casagrande and Piero Vereni for preparation of the Author and Subject Indexes.

John Antrobus
Mario Bertini

REFERENCES

Dement, W. C. (1972). *Some must watch while some must sleep*. San Francisco: Freeman.

Foulkes, D. (1966). *The psychology of sleep*. New York: Scribners.

Foulkes, D. (1978). *The grammar of dreams*. New York: Basic Books.

Foulkes, D. (1982). *Children's dreams: Longitudinal studies*. New York: Wiley.

Foulkes, D. (1985). *Dreaming: A cognitive-psychological analysis*. Hillsdale, NJ: Lawrence Erlbaum Associates.

1 Introduction

John Antrobus
City College of the City University of New York

Mario Bertini
University of Rome, La Sapienza

The theories, reviews, and research findings presented in this volume, together with their supporting evidence, describe our current views of how the rhythmic oscillations in the activation of the sleeping brain are associated with shifts in information processing, and with how the cortex creates the fascinating imagery and thought during sleep that popularly goes by the name dreaming. This chapter introduces the reader to the basic research issues and themes that drive sleep neuropsychologists to monitor sophisticated electronic apparatus and study sleeping subjects in grueling, 12-hour, all-night shifts. The passion that sustains this effort derives from the baffling mystery of the dream experience, from the dramatic changes in neurophysiological states during sleep, and from the high degree of covariation between the two. In no other area of neuropsychology has the search for the links between body and mind been so intense and so sustained. The chapters that follow describe our successes (and some failures) in locating these links. For the reader who is unfamiliar with the technical procedures of EEG and REM recording and the elicitation of imagery and thought reports, the opening pages of Armitage, Hoffman, and Moffitt (Chap. 2) will provide an excellent introduction.

The explanatory value of a theory or model is constrained by how well its concepts or terms can be translated into empirically defined operations. This constraint is particularly apparent in the neuropsychological study of dreaming where characteristics of the dream can only be inferred from the often inarticulate verbal report of a disoriented individual who has just been awakened from sleep. Unlike the report of a visual perception, whose accuracy can be checked against the public visual stimulus, there is no way

1

to check the accuracy of the "public" dream report against the sleeper's private dream experience. For this reason, the discovery of a close relation between the dream report and the cortical EEG by Aserinsky and Kleitman (1953) was welcomed as a potentially more reliable way to determine *when* dreaming was taking place. In 1962, Roffwarg, Dement, Muzio, and Fisher also claimed that measures of eye movement direction under the lids indicated the direction of the dreamer's visual gaze. The strong form of this assertion was not supported by subsequent experiments, but a more modest relationship does appear to exist (see Chapter 14). But despite the technical sophistication of accuracy of the physiological instrumentation used in sleep and dreaming research, it has provided us with little additional indication about the characteristics of the dream experience.

The ability of neurophysiological measures to identify the cognitive characteristics of dreaming cannot be better than the cognitive criteria employed to validate those measures. The description of the relations between the characteristics of the sleeping brain and the cognitive characteristics of the dream are ultimately constrained by the quality of the measurements of the characteristics of the imagery and thought that make up the dream experience.

THE MEASUREMENT OF IMAGERY AND
THOUGHT PRODUCED DURING SLEEP

Although there is general agreement that the term *dreaming* is defined by a cluster of variables such as bizarreness, hallucinatory quality, vivid visual imagery and a story-like quality, it is entirely possible that different neurophysiological processes may be associated with each of these quite different properties. If so, the magnitude of these qualities may vary somewhat independently across different conditions within sleep. But if dreaming is defined as some composite of these qualities, the linkages between cognitive (image and thought) and neurophysiological concepts will be visible only when all of the qualities covary. For example, if bizarreness is high and hallucinatory quality low in condition A, and the reverse on condition B, the value of the dream variable will be the same in both conditions, and the possible relation of A to bizarreness and B to hallucinatory quality will be obscured. Moreover, the visual qualities of spatial relationships, clarity of form, surface texture, and color may be controlled by different neurophysiological sites. Again the relations will be obscured if visual images are scaled on a single variable, such as vividness.

Support for this multivariate conception of sleep mentation from the finding that reports from Stage 1 Rapid Eye Movement (REM) sleep can be distinguished from those of Stage 2 (NREM) sleep 92.5% of the time by their greater length (Total Recall [word] Count: TRC; Antrobus, 1983). On the other hand, the length of the report is no help in discriminating Stage 1 REM from waking reports, where the latter are obtained from subjects lying in bed in a dark room, that is, under identical laboratory conditions. But if the mentation reports are divided into thematic units, the units are significantly longer in Stage 1 REM sleep than they are in awakening. Put another way, there are more, and shorter, thematic units per report in waking, especially in a noisy environment, than there are during REM sleep, despite their similar report length.

In the domain of visual imagery, Antrobus (1983) separated the imagery variable into four word-count variables: visual nouns, verbs, modifiers (adjectives and adverbs), and spatial prepositions. But all four behaved similarly in discriminating REM from NREM reports and so were combined to create a Visual Imagery Count for all further analyses. As with the dreaming variable, when the REM–NREM difference was statistically corrected for differences in TRC, there was no significant residual REM–NREM difference in Visual Imagery Count.

Investigators have long been concerned about the error that is inevitably incurred when the dreamer translates the predominately visual dream into a verbal description or report. In response to the problem, Rechtschaffen and Buchignani (chapter 7) have created several visual scales based on variations on a single photograph. The technique yields measures of independent visual dimensions such as hue saturation, clarity or focus, and brightness. Rechtschaffen et al. show that one set of visual variables may discriminate REM from NREM reports, whereas a second set may discriminate Phasic from Tonic REM reports. The relation between visual imagery scales that are based on the traditional verbal report and those based on a modification of this photograph technique (Antrobus, Hartwig, Rosa, & Reinsel, 1987) is currently being studied in our lab. At this point, the new visual imagery scales developed by Rechtschaffen et al. show considerable promise for identifying semi-independent visual–neurophysiological relationships.

At least three distinct bizarreness classifications have been identified thus far. In the chapter by Reinsel, Antrobus, and Wollman, the authors found that a variable that is the conceptual converse of Topic length, and is commonly considered to be a component of bizarreness, namely temporal Discontinuities, is at least as common in waking as in REM reports. This Waking–REM Sleep similarity was also true for Improbable Combinations of visual attributes, a second subclass of Bizarreness. Only Improbable Identities, the least frequent class of Bizarreness, were more typical of REM than Waking reports. All three classes were more typical of REM than NREM reports, but again, statistical correction for TRC eliminates the REM–NREM distinction in Bizarreness, defined as the sum of the three measures.

In summary, the effort to identify relations between the neurophysiological and cognitive variables within sleep is greatly enhanced when the global variable *dreaming* is separated into components that have potentially different neurophysiological origins. As new and more sharply defined relationships are uncovered it becomes possible to build more precise neurocognitive theories and models of sleep imagery and thought.

MODELS OF SLEEP IMAGERY AND THOUGHT

The theory and research described in this volume is driven by the search for the most direct relationships that link the neurophysiological characteristics of the sleeper to his or her concurrent cognitive experience. The neuropsychology, or more precisely the neurocognition, of dreaming sleep is therefore an example par excellence of a body–mind problem. The search is organized primarily around three sets of theoretical models and the three classes of neurocognitive relationships upon which they are based. For the purposes of this introduction, the three sets of models are (1) the cerebral hemisphere asymmetry models first suggested by Ornstein (1972); (2) the Activation–Synthesis model introduced by Hobson and McCarley in 1977, and Hobson's new Activation level, Input source, and Mode of processing (AIM) model (Chap. 12), and (3) Antrobus' DREAMIT model (Antrobus, 1991; Antrobus, Chapter 10). The empirical domains of inquiry that overlap, but do not coincide, with the models are, Tonic Distributed Activation, Hemisphere Asymmetry, and Phasic Activation.

Tonic Distributed Activation

The tonic activation relationships to dreaming was first introduced by Zimmerman in 1970. He proposed a direct link between cortical arousal and dreaming. His concept of cortical arousal is a mixture of sensory thresholds, motor activity within sleep, and other spontaneous psychophysiological activity during sleep. Most of his measures of cortical arousal, however, are associated more with disturbed than with normal sleep and are not part of the cluster of neurophysiological variables that are now considered typical of the contrast REM and NREM sleep. As evidence for the subcortical control of cortical activity during sleep became clearer, Hobson and McCarley (1977) introduced a neurophysiological Activation–Synthesis model of dreaming sleep in which general cortical activation was associated with general cognitive activation which, in turn, led to the production of dreaming in Stage 1 REM sleep. The cognitive activation side of this model has subsequently been elaborated by Antrobus (1990; in press).

Hobson and McCarley (1977), Hobson, Lydic, and Baghdoyan (1986), McCarley and Massaquoi (1986) and Hobson and Steriade (1986) describe a sleep control model in which pontine centers oscillate back and forth to produce the REM and NREM sleep. The medial reticular formation controls a set of cholinergic/cholinoceptive neurotransmitter pathways that activate the association and motor cortex during REM sleep. This activation is characterized by a tonic desychronization of the cortical EEG, a defining criterion of REM sleep, so that the REM EEG is quite similar to that of the waking state. This similarity has persuaded a broad consensus of opinion that the cerebral cortex is similarly activated in REM sleep and waking.

Additional support for this position is provided by two measures that respond to changes in cerebral metabolism. Townsend, Prinz, & Obrist (1973), Sakai, Meyer, Derman, Karacan, and Yamamoto (1979), and Meyer, Ishikawa, Hata, and Karacan (1987) found that cerebral blood flow during REM sleep was higher than during NREM sleep, and equal or higher than during waking. Franck et al. (1987) reached similar conclusions using positron emission tomography (PET).

The concept of cortical activation is derived in part from the concept of cognitive activation, and both concepts rest on the testable assumption that performance on a broad class of perceptual- > cognitive- > motor tasks is associated with a widespread shift in cortical state. There is, however, no simple relationship between any measure of cortical neuronal activity and information processing within the cerebral cortex. The neural activity that is identified by the cortical EEG is produced by the outermost layer of cortical cells, which do not themselves participate directly in information processing (Hobson & Steriade, 1986). Nor does an increase in cerebral metabolism, or total neural metabolic rate, necessarily identify a state of increased cognitive activity. Information processing involves a rapid sequence of delicately patterned activity within large networks of neurons. Increased neural metabolism may indicate an increased rate of processing the information represented in the networks, but it is quite possible that metabolic rates either higher or lower than those of the alert waking brain are incompatible with information processing. The assumption that increased cerebral blood flow indexes increased neural metabolism and thus increased cognitive activity is also vulnerable because blood flow is only indirectly related to neural oxygen consumption. Thus, the high rate of cerebral blood flow in REM may be attributed to a relaxation of arterial wall tonus that is quite unrelated to neural metabolic requirements.

The assumption of a cortical to cognitive activation function, therefore, requires empirical support that links the body–mind domains. Conventional measures of information processing are out of reach during sleep because of the high sensory thresholds of the sleeper. This inaccessibility is acute during REM sleep because of the powerful suppression of motor efferent control. The cortex may be active, but it receives relatively little information from the outside world and is incapable of making a motor response without moving marginally out of the REM sleep state. Cognitive measures must, therefore, be obtained in the postsleep state. Bertini, Violani, Zoccolotti, Antonelli, and DiStephano (1984), Bertini and Violani (Chapter 3), and Lavie and Tzischinsky (1984) have reported considerable success with sensory–motor performance tests designed to evaluate hemisphere asymmetry in prior sleep states, although Lavie (personal communication, 1988) has recommended caution in extrapolating from waking performance to prior sleep states.

Even the assumption that mentation reports obtained following awakening from sleep describe imagery and thought that occurred *during* the prior sleep interval has been questioned from time to time. In 1896, Goblot (Hall & Raskin, 1980) proposed that the production of the dream report begins at the moment the sleeper begins to awaken and ends after the report is completed. The hypothesis was discredited when Dement and Wolpert (1958) found that the time between the presentation of an external stimulus, such as a spray of water, and the time of being awakened from sleep matched the duration of the dream report, which in turn, equaled the time required to act out the narrative. But in an unpublished, privately circulated, critical review of the evidence for and against the Goblot hypothesis, Hall and Raskin (1980) pointed out that the duration of the stimulus interval in the Dement and Wolpert experiment was a constant 30 s in all cases. Evidence against the Goblot hypothesis would require a design where the stimulus-to-awakening interval was varied over some range and that the time to act out the narrative covaried with the duration of the stimulus-to-awakening interval. They argued that the Dement and Wolpert findings were equally compatible with the Goblot hypothesis. To date, no one has carried out such a study.

Closely related to the Goblot hypothesis is the question of whether the greater amount of information in the REM relative to NREM report is a cognitive production or an attention–memory–retrieval effect. Rosenblatt, Antrobus, and Zimler (Chapter 11) showed that the increased cognitive activation of REM sleep carries over to the postawakening mentation report period. Their subjects were presented with six brief audiovisual cartoon sequences just prior to going to bed. Upon subsequently being awakened from REM and NREM sleep and given a brief audiovisual cue, they were able to recall significantly more information following REM than NREM awakenings. Therefore the cortical activation of subjects is greater upon awakening from REM than NREM sleep. But the effect was small relative to that of the extremely large REM-NREM mentation report effect. Therefore, only a rather small part of the REM-NREM mentation report difference may be attributed to an improved ability of the subject to retrieve and translate into words the sleep mentation of REM sleep. The major part the REM-NREM mentation difference must be attributed to the subject's ability, while asleep, to generate actually more thought and imagery in the REM interval. In this sense, the advantage from REM versus NREM cognitive activation is much greater during sleep than upon awakening.

Cerebral Hemisphere Asymmetry

The hemisphere asymmetry models of sleep mentation rest on the activation assumptions that have been described. They assume that the characteristics of cognitive processing that produce dream mentation follow from an asymmetrical pattern of cortical activation that alternates with successive changes in sleep stage. Various forms of the model share the notion that, inasmuch as visual imagery is a salient characteristic of the dream, the right cerebral hemisphere (RH), putatively specialized for spatial information processing, must be the neural structure that contributes most to dream production. Antrobus (1987) has recently reviewed the tests of these models under four classes: patients with selective brain damage, and those with surgical separation of the hemispheres, performance upon awakening from REM versus NREM sleep on sensory–motor tasks that are known to rely differentially on one hemisphere or the other, and finally, asymmetry in hemispheric activation as inferred from hemispheric differences in EEG power spectra.

Armitage et al. open the first section of the book with a clear, informative introduction to the history of cortical asymmetry research in sleep and its implications for a theory of dreaming. It also provides the reader who is new to this area with a superb introduction to the technology of sleep electrophysiology. This chapter, together with the asymmetry chapters of Bertini and Violani (Chapter 3), and Reinsel and Antrobus (Chapter 4) are concerned with identifying neurocognitive hemisphere asymmetries in activation during sleep and determining whether they are associated with the alternation of the sleep stages. Although these chapters were to varying degrees sparked by the well-established relation of REM sleep to the visual characteristics of dreaming, they have gone on to study more fundamental neuropsychological characteristics of hemisphere asymmetry in sleep and are not necessarily directly concerned with dreaming or visual imagery.

The Armitage et al. (Chapter 2) carries the hemisphere asymmetrical issue well beyond its application to the cortical origin of dreaming. It explores the relation of cortical rhythms to the basic rest activity cycle (BRAC) proposed by Kleitman in 1963, and goes on to suggest a fundamental revision of our traditional REM-NREM sleep stage classification. Within the asymmetry set of papers, Murri et al. (Chapter 5) and Doricchi and Violani (Chapter 6) focus on the relation of dreaming to hemisphere asymmetry. Doricchi et al. present a review of the lateralized brain damage and dreaming literature that is more complete, and more sophisticated with respect to sleep and neuropsychology than the earlier brain damage studies reviewed in the Antrobus (1987) paper.

The main conclusion of these reviews is that there is no consistent support for a dominant role of the RH in the production of any characteristic of dreamlike mentation. Antrobus (1987) concluded that the left hemisphere (LH) is capable of producing such mentation with no assistance from the RH. The conclusion is qualified, however, by possibility that cortical reorganization due to the long period of brain disease preceding surgery renders these LHs atypical (Doricchi & Violani, Chapter 6), and by the observation of Kerr and Foulkes (1981) that unless the subject is specifically queried as to whether the image of a reported person or object was actually "seen," one cannot assume from the response to the question, "Tell me everything that was going through your mind" that a dreamed-of event had the properties of brightness, hue, texture, and so on. The fact that subjects who have been blind from birth report dreams that include a typical proportion of persons and objects that can be seen by the normally sighted person when awake, indicates that the presence of such persons or objects in a dream report is not sufficient evidence that the reported "image" of such items possesses the properties of brightness, hue, and surface texture. Such "images" can apparently be constructed exclusively from nonvisual, spatial information that has previously been acquired from touch, motor, and auditory stimuli. In conclusion, final resolution of the Hemisphere Asymmetry position seems to require further research that carefully distinguishes visual from purely spatial processes. Data interpretation of both EEG and brain damage studies should also be careful to distinguish between the process of dreaming and dream recall. As data from postawakening testing procedures (Bertini & Violani, Chapter 3) suggest, although the RH may make a special contribution to the process of generating a dream, The LH contribution appears decisive for the dream to be encoded and reported upon awakening.

Phasic Events: Eye Movements and PGO Waves

The eye movement (EM) –looking hypothesis, introduced earlier, and described in more detail by Herman (Chapter 14), says that the direction and excursion of the rapid eye movements of REM sleep are coordinated with shifts of visual attention during dreaming similar to EMs associated with looking responses in waking perception. The model is handicapped by the fact that we have little evidence about what parts of the visual system participate in the production of visual imagery in waking or in REM sleep.

In a modular neural network system, any or all of the modules that participate in waking visual perception might participate in the production of visual imagery. In 1965, Rechtschaffen and Foulkes were able to rule out any contribution of the retina to the REM dream, but the role of the remainder of the visual system remains uncharted. Herman (Chapter 14) has demonstrated convincingly that at least some REM sleep EMs are associated with the sleeper's reported experience of the direction of his or her looking behavior. Hobson and McCarley (1977) originally proposed that REM EMs were not initiated by cortical centers and that any such coordination must be achieved post hoc, that is, after the EM had occurred. As noted, Antrobus (1990) concludes that there is insufficient neurological evidence to rule out partial cortical control of the oculomotor system during dreaming sleep.

The Phasic Events model, the central leg of the Activation–synthesis model (Hobson & McCarley, 1977), says that pontine–geniculate–occipital (PGO) spikes, a dramatic, high-frequency, high-voltage characteristic of REM sleep, transmit noncognitive information from the pons to the cerebral cortex, where dream mentation is produced, and in so doing, disrupt the ongoing thematic sequence of the dream. In addition, they insert out-of-context eye movement (EM) information into the mentation sequence. In as much as the temporal pattern of the PGO activity is random with respect to ongoing cortical processes, the Activation–synthesis model proposes that mentation following PGO activity in REM sleep should be more bizarre than mentation during non-PGO, or tonic REM sleep.

A review of this research by Watson (Chapter 13) argues that this Phasic-bizarreness position has sufficient support to warrant further investigation. A review by Antrobus (1991) suggests that whatever relation does exist between PGO activity and bizarre mentation may be accounted for by a general increment in cortical activation during PGO activity. Both Antrobus and Herman review evidence supportive of the position that PGO activity is influenced by cortical processes, quite possibly of a visual or more general cognitive nature. If PGO activity is modified by cortical processes, then, according to Herman, the hypothesis that the temporal pattern of PGO activity is controlled solely by the pons and is therefore a random process, or at least independent of cortical processes, must be discounted.

This conclusion has implication for several neurophysiological models of sleep mentation. To the extent that it conflicts with the explanation for bizarreness proposed in the Activation–synthesis model, we need an alternative model for the production of bizarre mentation (see Fookson & Antrobus, Chapter 10).

Crick and Mitchison's (1983, 1986) suggestion that REM dreaming represents a class of unlearning that facilitates future waking cognitive processes is another model that relies on the assumption that PGO activity is the output of a random generator. If the PGO are not random, their theory also falls.

By contrast, the assumption that REM sleep EMs *are* under the influence, if not control, of the cerebral cortex, is an essential assumption of the EM-looking behavior model of REM sleep proposed by Ladd (1892) and Roffwarg et al. (1962). This alternative position is strongly supported by Herman (Chapter 14).

In the meanwhile, Hobson has moved ahead to develop a new neuropsychological model of dream called AIM, for activation level, input source, and mode of processing (Chapter 12). A welcome feature of this new model is its extension to waking cognitive processes so that dreaming is not represented as an absolutely unique cognitive process. As with the Activation–synthesis model (Hobson & McCarley, 1977), it is strongly grounded in neurophysiological models of subcortical processes that Hobson, et al., (1986) have reviewed elsewhere. The three independent dimensions of AIM, together with their relations to dreaming and other perceptual–cognitive processes, are described both in a simple, clear quantitative model and in a visual model. In quantifying several of the components of his model, Hobson is not only saying that these three variables differ in waking and sleeping cognition but that specific combinations of the three AIM components determine the difference.

Parallel Distributed Processing Models

Antrobus (1990) and Fookson and Antrobus (Chapter 10) have suggested that the concept of bizarreness be examined within the theoretical framework of parallel distributed processes (PDP) or neural networks (Rumelhart & McClelland, 1986). PDP models consist of networks of interconnected units that represent selected properties of cortical neurons and neural networks. A network used in the computer simulation of a model may consist of fewer than 100 units, but its properties are assumed to represent those of cortical neural nets of thousands or even millions of neurons. Neural networks can learn to respond lawfully to regularities in the individual's sensory environment by adjusting the weights of their synaptic-like interconnections in response to the pattern of activation they receive from other neurons in the net or, from neurons in nearby network modules. Once these connections are learned, sensory input to any part of the net initiates activity throughout the net that terminates in a pattern that represents a complete perception, which includes characteristics that may have been missing from the current sensory input.

The ability to "fill in" missing features has traditionally been referred to as a top–down process (Feldman, 1989). That is, within the context of the high sensory thresholds of REM sleep, lower level spatial or perceptual input might consist of a small cluster of perceptual features. The "top" might then plausibly refer to the cognitive processes that reconstruct the objects in long-term, visual–spatial memory that "fit" the imaged perceptual features, and which then go on to construct a context in which the objects occur and an appropriate meaning and temporal sequence for them. If the imaged scene is one's living room, the most probable next scene might include some of the people that normally occupy the living room. Thus a net starts with a particular pattern of nodal activation and proceeds on the basis of the weighted internodal connections to construct a response or output pattern that represents the best overall fit. Since the weights have been learned in the process of interacting with the real waking world, this process explicitly eschews improbable or bizarre constructions whether in perception or imagery. That is, the successive iterations of the network of interrelated items produces a final imaged event that maximally harmonizes all the diverse elements that potentially contribute to its construction. The occasions when the network is unable to reach this harmonious state provide a promising model of how bizarre images are created in dreaming sleep. Fookson and Antrobus (Chapter 10) show how two classes of bizarreness, temporal discontinuities and improbable combinations of visual features, can be simulated with a PDP model.

Contrary to popular opinion, REM sleep imagery is not necessarily more bizarre than waking imagery produced under similar laboratory conditions (see, Reinsel, Wollman, & Antrobus, Chapter 8). Bizarre elements, depending on the criteria used for bizarreness, occur in only 5% to 15% of REM sleep reports. As has been described, the search for neurophysiological events within the REM period that uniquely coincide with these bizarre reports has not been particularly rewarding.

Among the difficulties encountered in proposing a model of bizarre mentation production are relations between the psychological concept of bizarreness or improbability and the statistical concept of randomness, as well as the relation between bizarreness in the production of the mentation versus bizarreness in the verbal report. A model that accounts for bizarreness by means of a random process explains nothing. Rather, a useful model must attempt systematically to isolate the components of the production processes that produce bizarre combinations of elements.

Regardless of how bizarre the relations between different components of a visual image, or the relations between a visual image and the identities and meanings attributed to it by the dreamer, the act of "observing" or noticing the experience while it is occurring and the subsequent act of recalling and verbally describing the experience involve selective attention and memory processes that are not well understood and which may well confound inferences about the bizarreness of the original experience. For example, the longer the verbal report, the higher the probability that any reported element or feature may appear improbable or bizarre in the context of the others (see Reinsel et al., Chapter 8). Indeed, if the REM-NREM mentation report difference is statistically corrected for length of report, the REM-NREM bizarreness difference disappears. One might expect that as the activation of the cortex approaches that of the waking state, the bizarre elements would disappear. But as we have mentioned, Reinsel et al. have found that waking reports, obtained under laboratory conditions that match those of sleep reports, are even more bizarre than REM reports.

PDP models of complex cognitive processes, such as reading, can be constructed in a modular fashion, so that there are modules for identifying visual line and curve features, which feed, in a bottom–up order, into modules that identify angles, which in turn feed to letter detecting, and then to word-detecting network modules, and eventually to central modules, which construct schemata that represent complex meanings. Top–down processes in waking perception strongly influence the processing of lower-level modules. For example, the expectation that the next word is *dog* will bias letter-detection nets to favor *d* rather than *p* as the first letter. In the waking state, this perceptual process may rely on coordination from sensory input that is not available to the sleeper. Does it follow that the entire dream production process is under the consistent control of high-level cognitive processes that dictate the production of visual images by a top–down process? If so, why should imagery ever be bizarre?

Or is the top–down influence limited in magnitude, as it must be in waking? In the event that the lower-level visual imagery production modules have some freedom from top–down control, they may occasionally produce images that are "out of context" with respect to the thematic sequence of the dream. If an image becomes well developed, the top–down cognitive influences may no longer be able to suppress it and may be obliged to "incorporate" the image into the ongoing thematic stream.

Some evidence of the cognitive sophistication of this incorporation process can be seen in experiments on the incorporation of external stimuli during REM sleep. Spraying water on a dreamer has induced dream reports of rain suddenly appearing and of being obliged to use one's umbrella (Dement & Wolpert, 1958). When the experimenter's finger slipped on the bell button he was ringing while a subject was in REM sleep, the subject dreamed of getting up to answer the phone, noticing that it stopped ringing and therefore starting back to his chair, then hearing the ring resume, turned again to answer the phone, whereupon he was awakened. Another sleeper, on hearing a recording of a meowing cat, turned to the friend with whom she was walking and said, "Why are you meowing like that, Sally?"

These examples suggest that the cognitive apparatus is quite capable of rendering entirely plausible to the dreamer, an event that is entirely out of context with respect to the ongoing dream. That is, an activated cortex may be able to render a reasonably coherent temporal–spatial, meaningful event sequence out of any kind of quasirandom neural activity in cortical projection areas. And this capability is precisely that simulated by PDP nets in the exploratory chapter of Rumelhart and McClelland (1986). The few dream elements that do appear bizarre may be, therefore, momentary failures in this process. Further well-focused research is required to identify the reasons for this failure.

Future Directions

The contributions to this volume to the neuropsychology of dreaming sleep, particularly Stage 1 REM sleep, demonstrate that the field has begun to move forward in some of the new directions opened up by the rapid advances in contemporary cognitive science, neuropsychology, and neurophysiology. It is the hope of the contributors and editors that this volume will encourage future students of dreaming and other cognitive processes within sleep to continue to take maximum advantage of the work in these neighboring disciplines. They also hope that the day will soon come when our study of the unique characteristics of cognitive process during sleep will make it possible for us to return the favor.

REFERENCES

Antrobus, J. S. (1983). REM and NEM sleep reports: Comparison of word frequencies by cognitive classes. *Psychophysiology, 20,* 562–568.

Antrobus, J. (1987). Cortical hemisphere asymmetry and sleep mentation. *Psychological Review, 94,* 359–368.

Antrobus, J. (1990). The neurocognition of sleep mentation: phasic and tonic REM sleep. In R. R. Bootzin, J. F., Kihlstrom, & D. L. Schacter (Eds.),. *Sleep and cognition (pp. 3–24).* Washington, DC.: American Psychological Association.

Antrobus, J. (1991). *Dreaming: Cognitive processes during cortical activation and high perceptual thresholds.Psychological Review, 98,* 96–121.

Antrobus, J., Hartwig, P., Rosa, D., & Reinsel, R. (1987). *Sleep Research, 16,* 240.

Aserinsky, E., & Kleitman, N. (1953). Regularly occurring periods of ocular motility and concomitant phenomena during sleep. *Science, 118,* 361–375.

Bertini, M., Violani, C., Zoccolotti, P., Antonelli, A., & DiStephano, L. (1984). Right cerebral activation in REM sleep: Evidence from a unilateral tactile recognition test. *Psychophysiology, 21,* 418–423.

Crick, F., & Mitchison, G. (1983). The function of dream sleep. *Nature, 304,* 111–114.

Crick, F., & Mitchison, G. (1986). REM sleep and neural nets. *Journal of Mind and Behavior, 7,* 229–250.

Dement, W., & Wolpert, E. (1958). The relation of eye movements, body motility, and external stimuli to dream content. *Journal of Experimental Psychology, 55,* 543–553.

Feldman, J. A. (1989). A connectionist model of visual imagery (pp. 49–81). In G. E. Hinton & J. A. Anderson (Eds.), *Parallel models of associative memory.* Hillsdale, NJ.: Lawrence Erlbaum Associates.

Franck, G., Salmon, E., Poirrier, R., Sadot, B., Franco, G., & Manquet, P. (1987). Evaluation of human cerebral glucose uptake during wakefulness, slow wave sleep and paradoxical sleep by positron emission tomography. *Sleep, 16,* 46.

Hall, C. S., & Raskin, R. (1980). *Do we dream during sleep?* Unpublished manuscript.

Hobson, J. A., Lydic, R., & Baghdoyan, H. A. (1986). Evolving concepts of sleep cycle generation: From brain centers to neuronal populations. *Behavioral and Brain Sciences, 9,* 371–448.

Hobson, J. A., & McCarley, R. W. (1977). The brain as a dream state generator: An activation–synthesis hypothesis of the dream process. *American Journal of Psychiatry, 134,* 1335–1348.

Hobson, J. A., & Steriade, M. (1986). The brain as a dream state generator: An activation–synthesis hypothesis of the dream process *American Journal of Psychiatry, 134,* 1335–1348.

Kerr, N. H., & Foulkes, D. (1981). Right hemisphere mediation of dream visualization: A case study. *Cortex, 17,* 603–610.

Kleitman, N. (1963). *Sleep and wakefulness.* Chicago: University of Chicago Press.

Ladd, G. (1892). Contributions to the psychology of visual dreams. *Mind, 1,* 299–304.

Lavie, P., & Tzischinsky, O. (1984). Cognitive asymmetries after waking from REM and NONREM sleep: Effects of delayed testing and handedness. *International Journal of Neuroscience, 23,* 311–315.

McCarley, R. W., & Massaquoi, S. G. (1986). A limited cycle mathematical model of REM sleep oscillator system. *American Journal of Physiology, 251,* R1011–R1029.

Meyer, J. S., Ishikawa, Y., Hata, T., & Karacan, I. (1987). Cerebral blood flow in normal and abnormal sleep and dreaming. *Brain and Cognition, 6,* 266–294.

Ornstein, R. E. (1972). *The psychology of consciousness.* San Francisco: Freeman.

Rechtschaffen, A., & Foulkes, D. (1965). Effect of visual stimuli on dream content. *Perceptual and Motor Skills, 20,* 1149–1160.

Roffwarg, H. P., Dement, W., Muzio, J., & Fisher, C. (1962). Dream imagery: Relationship to rapid eye movements of sleep. *Archives of General Psychiatry, 7,* 235–258.

Rumelhart, D. E., & McClelland, J. L. (Eds.). (1986). *Parallel distributed processing: Explorations in the microstructure of cognition.* Cambridge, MA: MIT Press.

Sakai, F., Meyer, J. S., Karacan, I., Derman, S., & Yamamoto, M. (1979). Normal human sleep: Regional hemodynamics. *Annals of Neurology, 7,* 471–478.

Townsend, R. E., Prinz, P. N., & Obrist, W. D. (1973). Human cerebral blood flow during sleep and waking. *Journal of Applied Physiology, 33,* 620–625.

Zimmerman, W. B. (1970). Sleep mentation and auditory awakening thresholds. *Psychophysiology, 6,* 540–549.

DREAMING AND CORTICAL HEMISPHERIC ASYMMETRY: PRO AND CON

2

Interhemispheric EEG Activity in Sleep and Wakefulness: Individual Differences in the Basic Rest-Activity Cycle (BRAC)

Roseanne Armitage
University of Texas Southwestern Medical Center at Dallas

Robert Hoffmann and Alan Moffitt
Carleton University, Ottawa

INTRODUCTION

There is no doubt that aspects of "dream life" are bizarre, fantastic, or unreal, and sometimes violate the laws of physical reality. Yet there another side to dreaming that bears a marked similarity to waking thought: the ordinary, less fanciful events often characterized as mundane, "thought-like" or boring. It is along these dimensions that the continuity of waking and sleeping cognition may lie.

The view that nocturnal dreams and daydreams are continuous processes is not new to psychology. Although the early psychoanalytic tradition emphasized the wish-fulfilling function of dreaming, several contemporaries of Freud suggested that the similarities between daydreams and night dreams reflected the continuity of thought across sleep and wakefulness (Hollingworth, 1904; Smith, 1928). Unfortunately the onset of the tradition of behaviorism in psychology led to the abandonment of fantasy, imagination, daydreaming, nocturnal dreams, and phenomenology as avenues of scientific inquiry. It was not until some 40 years later, in the mid 1950s that imagery and associated processes moved back into the realm of science. In commenting on the moratorium and subsequent evolution of ideas on imagination, Holt (1964), in an article named appropriately "Return of the Ostracized," has said:

The subjective world of images and the like had progressed from being at first the total subject matter of psychology, then a marshy realm of uninteresting epiphenomena, and now a legitimate output of theoretically constructed psychic apparatus (Holt, 1964, p. 263).

At the same time, the emergence of a new area of research, namely sleep psychophysiology, offered the opportunity to study dreaming under controlled laboratory conditions, with observable physiological correlates. The groundbreaking work of Aserinsky, Kleitman, and Dement in the mid 1950s not only identified possible correlates of dreaming but also the ultradian nature of sleep, suggesting an 80–120-min oscillation between two distinct stages of sleep, later identified as REM and NREM. This early research established scientific interest in dreaming and also provided the basis for an investigation of the continuity of physiological processes across sleep and wakefulness, namely Kleitman's basic rest–activity cycle (BRAC) hypothesis.

The BRAC Hypothesis

Although sleep is circadian, occurring once a day in adulthood, there are 90-min rhythmic variations in physiological activity that occur throughout the night. Rhythmic activity with a periodicity shorter than 24 hr has been termed ultradian by Halberg, Carandente, Cornelissen, and Katina, (1973). One of the most influential sleep studies identified the ultradian characteristics of sleep physiology. Aserinsky, one of Kleitman's graduate students, observed the regular occurrence of periods of ocular motility in hospitalized infants during sleep. This finding prompted an investigation of adult sleep from which Aserinksy and Kleitman (1953) determined that these periods of ocular motility were concomitant with increases in heart rate, changes in muscle tonus, the presence of desynchronous electroencephalographic activity and an increase in the probability of obtaining a dream report following awakenings in the presence of rapid eye movements.

Aserinsky and Kleitman (1955) utilized visual scoring of EEG to evaluate further what was later called rapid eye movement (REM) sleep in neonates. They determined that REM sleep reappeared every 50–60 mins throughout the day and night, coupled with a 3-to-4-hr gastric cycle and suggested that this cycle governed rest and activity in neonates throughout sleep and wakefulness. Fifty-to-60-min cycles were later shown in fetal motility, suggesting an early ontogenetic development of sleep and waking cycles (Granat, Lavie, Adar, & Sharf, 1979).

In observations of sleep cycles in older children, Kleitman (1963) determined that the REM–NREM cycle gradually lengthens to 90–100 mins by early adolescence and remains relatively constant throughout adulthood (80–120 min, Dement & Kleitman, 1957). Based on these observations and the cyclical occurrence of REM periods associated with dreaming, Kleitman (1963) proposed the existence of a basic rest–activity cycle (BRAC) active throughout sleep and wakefulness expressing a 90-min period in adulthood.

He further proposed that the BRAC emerged from a more primitive, phylogenetically older digestive rhythm adjusted to the organism's nutritional needs and environmental supply, hypothesizing that the association between dreaming and the emergence of REM sleep reflected cyclical fluctuations in mental activity, which he believed to display a comparable 90-min rhythm in wakefulness. As evidence for the BRAC, Kleitman (1963) cited the continuation of cyclical sleep–waking patterns in decorticate dogs and the rhythmic occurrence of sleep in anencephalous children.

Kleitman (1963) did not, however, speculate on the nature of mechanisms that control ultradian rhythms. There are several possibilities: (1) A single mechanism controls rhythms in sleep and wakefulness; (2) Several mechanisms control harmonically coupled but independent rhythms in sleep and wakefulness; and (3) Interdependent rhythms in sleep and wakefulness are controlled by separate mechanisms. As yet, none of these alternatives has been fully investigated. Nevertheless, the research conducted by Kleitman and his colleagues led to renewed interest in dreaming, an investigation of ultradian rhythms and a more complete description of the electrophysiological characteristics of REM and NREM sleep.

Visual Scoring of Sleep EEG

Visual scoring of polygraphic sleep records generally follows the criteria outlined by Rechtschaffen and Kales (1968) standardized scoring system. This procedure assigns a single value for each epoch (time segment) identified on the basis of changes in eye movements and muscle tonus and the emergence of phasic EEG events. Epochs are classified as awake, Stages 1, 2, 3, 4, and rapid eye movement (REM) sleep. When the frequency of EEG activity is of interest the amplitude and number of wave from peaks per second are measured and counted, classifying EEG frequencies as delta (.5–2 Hz), theta (4–8 Hz), alpha (8–12 Hz), sigma (12–16 Hz) and beta (16–30 Hz). Rechtschaffen and Kales (1968) describe REM sleep as characterized by relatively low-voltage, desynchronized, mixed-frequency EEG, accompanied by binocularly symmetrical eye movements with low-voltage electromyographic (EMG) activity or muscle tonus. Low EMG indicates a suppression of gross muscle activity or muscle paralysis during this stage of sleep.

Relatively low-voltage EEG in the absence of REMs, coupled with fast-frequency EEG, characterizes Stage 1 sleep, often referred to as sleep onset. Stage 2 is associated with the presence of sinusoidal spindle activity (12–14 Hz) and higher-voltage biphasic wave forms (K-complexes) with low-voltage, fast-frequency EEG activity. Stage 3 sleep is characterized by moderate amounts (20%–50%) of high-voltage, slow-wave synchronous EEG activity (delta), while a predominance (50% or more) of delta marks the onset of Stage 4 sleep. Stages 3 and 4 are often referred to as deep sleep, based on higher auditory thresholds during these stages. Auditory thresholds from REM, Stage 1 and Stage 2 sleep are considered closer to waking thresholds and are therefore referred to as light sleep (Bonnet, 1982). Collectively, Stages 1 through 4 represent nonrapid eye movement (NREM) sleep.

Approximately 5–10 mins after sleep onset (Stage 1) spindles and K-complexes appear marking the onset of Stage 2. Some time later (varying among individuals) delta activity appears and Stages 3 and 4 begin. The first REM period (REMP) usually occurs during the second hour of sleep and subsequent REMPs occur on the average of 90 min from the end of the last REMP in most individuals (Globus, 1966; 1970; 1972). Slow-wave activity predominates in the first half of the night, reappearing infrequently during the later hours. The last half of the night is generally characterized by rhythmic oscillations between REM and Stage 2 and most individuals awaken from REM in early morning.

A major benefit of visual stage scoring is that it does not require expensive materials or equipment once the electrophysiological data have been recorded. Techniques of this type, however, result in a great loss of electrophysiological information by assigning a single label to each epoch, combining information from EEG, EOG, and EMG rather than quantifying each variable independently. Hoffmann, Moffitt, Shearer, Sussman, and Wells, (1979) have pointed out that many tonic electrophysiological events remain undetected by the human eye and that visual scoring techniques do not permit an evaluation of the frequency characteristics of EEG activity. Thus visual scoring systems are more appropriate for rapid or on-line identification of sleep stages required while an experiment is ongoing, for example, during REM deprivation studies and when scheduling the sleep stage of experimental awakenings.

Computer Techniques

Off-line or on-line computer analysis of electrophysiological data provides a more detailed description of bioelectrical activity during sleep and wakefulness. The advances in computer technology over the past two decades have made this a feasible alternative to visual scoring of polygraph records (Hoffmann et al., 1979). With computer analysis, analog EEG activity is digitized at a fast sampling rate through the use of analog to digital (A/D) converters.

After EEG signals are digitized they are subjected to an algorithm, the most common being fast Fourier transforms (FFTs), period analysis, and autoregression. FFTs, frequency domain model-fitting techniques, separate time series into harmonic sine and cosine components, yielding a power estimate (area under the rectified curve) for each frequency. A pure sine wave has a peak in spectral power at one frequency and zero at all others. A random set of data has equal spectral power at all frequencies. A plot of the FFTs at each frequency is called a periodogram or a power spectrum.

Fourier-analytical algorithms are also used in biological rhythm research to quantify physiological and behavioral time series. When the interest is in detecting underlying rhythms, FFTs are generally referred to as spectral analysis. The application of FFT algorithms and the assumption that the underlying distribution of the data is sinusoidal does not differ from its use as an EEG quantification procedure. Rhythms in time series are determined by the largest power values in the spectrum. Put more simply, the spectral frequency with the largest power is said to be the predominant rhythm in the time series. These techniques will often reveal a "hidden cycle" undetectable in real time. Power spectral estimates are often transformed by averaging power values at adjacent frequencies. This procedure reduces the number of spectral frequencies and is particularly useful if multiple power estimates are obtained for a very short time estimate (very high-frequency resolution). The transformed power values are referred to as spectral density. Power spectral density functions are more commonly found among behavioral research although Brillinger (1975) has suggested that since sampling rates (the number of repeated observations per unit time), are quite low under testing conditions, the periodogram (untransformed FFT) may provide a better estimate of the spectral characteristics of these time series.

If rhythms within EEG frequency bands are of interest, spectral analysis may be performed on EEG data quantified with FFTs, period analysis, or some other algorithm.

Period analysis is an alternative EEG quantification technique which yields estimates of power, first derivative, and zero-cross events. Period analysis provides percent time amplitude assessments, measured directly, whereas FFTs involve the application of a sine–cosine transformation. In period analysis, the time interval between successive zero-voltage crossings events is measured for each frequency of EEG activity, yielding percent time zero-cross and power estimates. First derivative values are based on the detection of negative inflections in the EEG signal regardless of whether they cross zero volts, and yield percent time estimates for each frequency band. Period analysis is computationally simpler and faster than FFTs. Recent research has demonstrated that period analysis and FFTs share a large portion of the variance, having a canonical correlation of greater than .90 in sleep and waking EEG (Pigeau, Hoffmann, & Moffitt, 1981). Spectral analysis may also be performed on period analyzed EEG data if ultradian rhythms are of interest.

Although there are several other techniques for quantifying EEG and for the detection of rhythmic events in time series, they are used less frequently than those discussed here. For a complete review of time series analysis, the reader is referred to Gottman (1981) and for EEG procedures to Lindsley and Wicke (1974). With this information in mind, we may now turn to a review of the ultradian rhythm literature relevant to the BRAC hypothesis.

PHYSIOLOGICAL RHYTHMS DURING SLEEP

Mandell et al. (1966) have shown that the urine flow of catheterized patients displays a 90-min rhythm during sleep, and is in phase with REM and NREM cycles. These authors attributed this biological rhythm to the periodical secretion of antidiuretic hormone (ADH). This finding, however, was only partly confirmed by the work of Rubin, Govin, Kales, and Odel (1973), demonstrating an episodic secretion of ADH, but unrelated to the phase of the REM-NREM sleep cycle. Mandell et al. (1966) also failed to provide statistical analyses of their data and their conclusions were based upon a visual inspection of peaks in urine flow in real time.

Gastric activity during sleep, measured through stomach contraction devices, does not appear to display a 90-min ultradian rhythm, nor does it appear to be related in phase to REM and NREM alternations (Lavie, Kripke, Hiatt, & Morrison, 1978). This study measured both duodenal acidity and stomach contractions. Studies in wakefulness have indicated a 100-min cycle in gastric activity (Hiatt & Kripke, 1975), but indicate no relationship between stomach contractions and fantasy or EEG cycles (Hiatt, Kripke, & Lavie, 1975).

Ruckebusch and his colleagues have studied gastric cycles extensively (Bueno, Fioramonti, & Ruckebusch, 1975; Bueno & Ruckebusch, 1977; Grivel & Ruckebusch, 1972; Ruckebusch & Bueno, 1977; Ruckebusch & Fioramonti, 1975) Their results indicate that gut periodicity is intiated in the duodenum and spreads throughout the small intestine, expressing a similar periodicity as REM-NREM sleep cycles in humans. In other species, however, such as rats and monkeys, Ruckebusch and his colleagues claim that sleep cycles and gastric cycles are independent, expressing dissimilar periodicities. In some species, gastric cycles are inhibited by large meals and function only as a means of propelling food through the digestive tract. Their results suggest that if gastric cycles are expressions of the BRAC and are harmonically coupled with sleep cycles it is only among humans.

Studies of heart rate have provided conflicting support for the BRAC hypothesis. Orr and Hoffman (1974) demonstrated an approximately 90-min rhythm in cardiovascular function during sleep, although Wilson, Kripke, McClure, & Greenburg (1977) have been unable to replicate this finding in intensive-care patients.

In general, the sleep physiology studies reported here have not provided strong support for Kleitman's original hypothesis that the BRAC was governed by the gastric and consummatory needs of the organism.

Over the past three decades, considerable effort has been devoted to the study of the cognitive dimensions of sleep. Some of this research has focused on ultradian rhythms in cognition in relation to the BRAC hypothesis.

Rhythms in Sleep Mentation

Aserinsky and Kleitman (1953) proposed that REMs were the electrophysiological correlates of dreaming, and that individuals only dreamed during REM sleep. Initial research tended to confirm this hypothesis, obtaining at least 80% dream recall following awakenings from REM sleep (Dement, 1955; Dement & Kleitman, 1957; Kales, Hoedemaker & Jacobson, 1967; Wolpert, 1960; Wolpert & Trossman, 1958). This research, however, was flawed by a number of methodological problems, such as subject selection, method of awakening, definition of dreaming, and perhaps more seriously, combining NREM stages of sleep (see Armitage, 1980, for a review). Later research that analyzed recall rates from all stages of NREM sleep indicated that dream recall from REM sleep reaches 80%–100%, while Stage 2 and 4 awakenings yield 35%–60% and 15%–30%, respectively (Armitage, 1980). Averaging recall rates from Stage 2 and Stage 4 sleep results in an underestimation of the frequency of NREM dream recall. Clearly, recall rates are higher from REM awakenings but dream generation should not be viewed as a process unique to REM sleep. There are, however, qualitative and quantitative differences in dream content elicited from REM and NREM sleep stages.

NREM dreams are considered more "thought-like," boring, and lacking in vividness, while REM dreams have been described as more visual and more bizarre experiences (Broughton, 1972; Foulkes, 1975). Armitage (1980) has suggested that the differences among REM and NREM experiences may lie along such dimensions as color, the likelihood of the dream experience, and number of people in the dream, as well as vividness of events. However, this study reported variations in dream content with individual differences in usual morning dream recall and stage of sleep. High-frequency dream recallers (those who recall dreams every morning with rare exception) report more color, more people, and less likely experiences from REM sleep. In an unprompted free-recall situation, low-frequency dream recallers do not report color in their experiences. When prompted, however, low recallers do acknowledge the presence of color in both REM and Stage 2 sleep experiences. In general, low recallers report more likely, less vivid dreams than high recallers. The content differences reported here do interact with stage of sleep, whether awakenings took place early in the night or toward morning, and the regularity with which subjects recall dreams. We are not suggesting that the content of REM and Stage 2 dreams is indistinguishable when individual differences and time of night are controlled. We are, however, suggesting that the differences between REM and Stage 2 experiences are reduced when these factors are taken in to account. We are also advocating that REM be contrasted to Stage 2 and Stage 4 (or Stages 3 and 4 combined), separately, not compared with NREM (the average of Stages 2 and 4). There is electrophysiological evidence that is relevant to this issue and will be discussed in detail later.

These variations in dream content with stage of sleep, have led to an investigation of task performance following awakenings from REM and NREM sleep.

PERCEPTUAL PERFORMANCE FOLLOWING SLEEP

Lavie and Giora (1973) have investigated perceptual differences in the spiral aftereffect (SAE) following awakenings from REM and Stage 4 sleep. The duration of the SAE is said to depend on the persistence of visual stimuli and the degree of cortical arousability. Lavie and Giora hypothesized that the duration of the SAE would be greater following REM than Stage 4 awakenings, due to the higher level of cortical arousal in REM. Each of their nine subjects were awakened 5 min after the beginning of the first or second REMP and 5 min after the onset of Stage 4.

Repeated measures analysis of variance (ANOVA) confirmed their hypotheses and revealed no significant differences in the duration of the SAE between REM and wakefulness. Although the authors concluded that perceptual abilities as measured by the SAE are similar in REM and wakefulness, there is limited statistical power in this study. Their data are merely suggestive.

Lavie and Sutter (1975) also investigated perceptual phenomena following awakenings from REM and NREM sleep. Five subjects were awakened 20 min after the end of the first REMP, or 7 min after the beginning of the second REMP, and tested on the phi phenomenon. They were also tested prior to sleeping in the lab. This procedure was repeated on a second nonconsecutive night. Five additional subjects were tested under this procedure with awakenings 10 min after the first REMP and 3 mins after the beginning of the second REMP. The authors reported that there was greater variability in perception of the of the phi phenomenon following Stage 4 awakenings, compared with REM awakenings and wakefulness. Unpublished data from their laboratory demonstrated a significant 95 min rhythm in variability of the phi phenomenon in wakefulness. On the basis of these findings, Lavie and Sutter (1975) concluded that the differences in responding to the phi phenomenon following awakenings from sleep reflected the continuity of an approximately 90-min BRAC in perceptual processes across sleep and wakefulness.

Since spectral analyses were not performed on the perceptual data following awakenings from sleep, this conclusion is unwarranted. Rather, the data indicate that there are differences in perceptual capabilities following awakenings from REM and Stage 4 sleep. Furthermore, the authors obtained significant differences in the phenomena in REM and wakefulness, contrary to Lavie and Giora (1973). Although performance was most similar between REM and wakefulness, Lavie and Sutter (1975) do not provide convincing evidence for a BRAC governing perceptual processes.

Broughton (1968) has shown that visual evoked potentials (VEPs) following REM awakenings are similar to waking VEPs. Potentials from all of the NREM sleep stages resembled more closely, the electrophysiological characteristics of slow-wave sleep. These results, and those from Lavie and Sutter (1975), suggest that performance and brain activity during REM is more closely related to wakefulness than to some stages of NREM sleep (Kripke, 1974, 1982).

INTERHEMISPHERIC DIFFERENCES IN REM AND NREM SLEEP: THEORY

The differences among REM and NREM dream content and the rhythmic oscillation of sleep stages has prompted Broughton (1975) to propose a biorhythmic variation in consciousness, which he claimed to be controlled by BRAC mechanisms. This theory is one of the few extensions of the BRAC hypothesis to be well articulated and to encompass recent advances (at the time of publication) in sleep electrophysiology. This theory is of import as it is representative not only of ultradian rhythm theory but a major school of thought attempting to characterize the nature of variations in consciousness and perceptual awareness in terms of the unique specializations of the two hemispheres (Allen, 1983).

Broughton (1975) has suggested that rhythmic fluctuation in mental activity may be active throughout sleep and wakefulness, and that the phase of REM-NREM sleep cycles may be related to oscillations in the activation or efficiencies of the two cerebral hemispheres. This suggestion is based on the assumption that more visual and bizarre dream experiences, which have been associated with REM sleep, involve right-hemisphere processing strategies. More thought-like content, which Broughton claimed to be characteristic of NREM experiences, involves greater left-hemisphere activation, according to his theory. He proposed that oscillations in REM-NREM sleep are phase-locked to activation of the right and left hemispheres respectively. Extending Kleitman's BRAC hypothesis, Broughton suggested that variations in waking consciousness mirror the rhythmic changes associated with the REM-NREM sleep cycle. Thus a 90-min rhythm in interhemispheric EEG activity should be evident in wakefulness. He proposed that psychologically the waking features of the BRAC should manifest themselves in an oscillation in information-processing strategies associated with the two hemispheres. In his conceptualization, the right hemisphere involves visuospatial and fantasy-intuitive functions while the unique specialization of the left hemisphere is reflected in verbal–analytical information processing.

In addition to the phenomenological features of sleep mentation outlined herein, Broughton also cited interhemispheric EEG amplitude differences during REM and NREM sleep in support of his hypothesis. As this research is pivotal to his argument it requires a close evaluation.

Interhemispheric Differences in REM and NREM Sleep: EEG Data

Goldstein, Stolzfus, and Gardocki (1972) investigated differences in EEG amplitude between homologous areas of the right and left hemispheres during REM and NREM sleep. They used monopolar parietal electrodes with linked ear reference in seven human adult males, four cats, and five rabbits. EEG signals were rectified to yield integrated amplitude values of total EEG (not filtered for frequency) over 2-min epochs. Integrated amplitude is a power estimate or the area under the curve. Asymmetry coefficients were calculated using a left-over-right (L/R) ratio of integrated amplitudes. This ratio was transformed by removing the mean L/R ratio, and comparing individual deviations from the mean. Changes in the L/R ratios occurred concomitant with shifts from REM to NREM sleep in humans, cats, and rabbits. EEG amplitude was significantly lower in the left hemisphere during NREM sleep and higher in the left during REM sleep. The assumption in EEG research is that greater amplitude or power reflects hemispheric deactivation as it is associated with slow-frequency, high-amplitude EEG activity characteristic of deep sleep. It is assumed that the lower auditory thresholds obtained from Stage 3 and 4 sleep are associated with decreased cognition. The inference is then made that deactivation in one hemisphere reflects activation of the opposite hemisphere.

Relying on the this interpretation, Goldstein et al. (1972) suggest that the right hemisphere is associated with REM sleep and that the left hemisphere is more activated during NREM sleep. The failure to produce comparable interhemispheric shifts in wakefulness (Sugerman, Goldstein, Marjerrison, & Stolzfus, 1973) suggests that there was no waking analogue of interhemispheric amplitude shifts.

More recent research has failed to confirm the right-hemisphere-REM, left-hemisphere-NREM electrophysiological relationship (Anthrobus, Ehrlichman, & Weiner, 1978; Bertini, Violani, Zoccolotti, & Antonelli, & Distefano, 1984; Moffitt et al., 1982; Pivik, Bylsma, Busby, & Sawyer, 1982). Furthermore, attempts at replicating Goldstein et al. (1972) have provided conflicting results. For example, Antrobus, et al. (1978) reported that activity in the two hemispheres is balanced during NREM with mixed "dominance" in REM. Rosekind, Coates, and Zarcone (1979) reported greater right hemisphere activity in both REM and NREM sleep stages, while Hirshkowitz, Ware, and Karacan (1980) and Goldstein (1979) replicated Goldstein et al.'s original findings. All of these studies utilized integrated amplitude techniques.

Using Fourier analysis of EEG data, Pivik et al. (1982) failed to find significant hemispheric asymmetries during REM sleep among gifted adolescents in support of Moffitt et al.'s findings (1982). These data, taken together, suggest that the hemispheres are relatively balanced during REM and NREM sleep stages in all EEG frequency bands. Period-analytical and spectral-analytical techniques exemplify the complex electrophysiological macro- and micro-architecture of sleep and the cognitive processes associated with them. The methodological and theoretical difficulties with integrated amplitude techniques may explain the inconsistency among results in this area.

First, there is little convention in which sites are used for electrode placement. Asymmetry studies in wakefulness also report significant differences at one electrode site while no substantial asymmeteries are reported at others (Ray & Cole 1985). It has been demonstrated that even those studies that do support asymmetrical activation of the hemispheres during sleep do not find significant differences in all electrode sites Antrobus et al. 1978; Hirshkowitz, Pivik et al., 1982; Turner, Ware & Karacan, 1979). Also, studies relying on integrated amplitude techniques infer activation of one hemisphere from higher amplitude or power estimates in the opposite hemisphere. The EEG techniques utilized by Moffitt et al. (1982); period analysis and by Pivik et al. (1982); Fourier analysis), measure high and low-amplitude EEG activity in both hemispheres, in separate frequency bands rather than inferring activation from amplitude differences in overall EEG. Furthermore, Goldstein et al. (1972); Goldstein (1979); Hirshkowitz et al. (1979) and Hirshkowitz et al. (1980) all used integrated amplitude of total EEG without filtering specific EEG frequencies. Antrobus et al. (1978) and Rosekind et al. (1979) filtered 2–12-Hz and 9–12-Hz frequency bands, respectively. Relying on integrated amplitude analysis rests on the assumption that higher amplitude reflects cerebral deactivation, an assumption without strong empirical support, especially in relation to within stage variation in EEG. In sleep, detailed dream reports can be elicited from Stage 4 sleep, where high amplitude delta activity predominates, and in wakefulness theta activity (relatively high amplitude) is associated with intense problem solving (Pigeau, 1985), hardly suggestive of cortical deactivation in the presence of high amplitude EEG activity. Utilizing total EEG amplitude values without filtering EEG frequency bands results in a bias against low-amplitude, fast-frequency EEG activity. The technique is dependent on the presence of high-amplitude activity and thus in sleep is biased toward the presence of delta activity. In wakefulness, the technique is biased toward the presence of alpha and theta frequencies. Estimates of the percentage of activity within a frequency band relative to tonic variation within an epoch are not provided by this method of analysis. Hence, the presence of high-amplitude activity in epochs within which low-amplitude, fast frequency predominates will result in an integrated amplitude value not representative of overall EEG activity and may be misleading, especially when hemispheric asymmetries are of interest. One hemisphere may display a predominance of alpha activity, while the other consists of mixed delta and beta activity, yet both produce comparable integrated total EEG amplitude values. These values would be interpreted inappropriately as reflecting hemispheric symmetry. Filtering for specific frequency bands overcomes some of the difficulties that have been mentioned. It is interesting to note that the studies that did filter EEG frequency bands did not support Goldstein et al's (1972) study.

An additional problem in this research and other projects investigating physiological and behavioral differences among sleep stages is the failure to separate stages of NREM sleep. This point was introduced earlier in this chapter but requires reiteration. The convention of combining all NREM sleep stages is based on the implicit assumption that REM sleep is unlike all other sleep stages. We suggest that tonic variation in REM electrophysiology is more similar to Stage 2 EEG than originally believed. Furthermore we suggest that Stage 2 EEG is closer to REM than it is to slow-wave sleep. We are not suggesting that REM activity, and in particular phasic EEG variation in REM, is indistinguishable from Stage 2 sleep. We are however, recommending strongly, that Stage 2 and Stage 4 data not be combined to represent NREM sleep. These stages of sleep are too distinct and we cite the following data in support of this: Tonic variation in REM and Stage 2 is characterized by the presence of desynchronous, fast-frequency activity (Hoffmann et al., 1979). Interhemispheric relationships are more similar in REM and Stage 2 than in Stage 2 and Stage 4 EEG (Armitage, Hoffmann, Loewy, & Moffitt, 1989). Late auditory potentials are more similar between REM and Stage 2 than Stage 2 and slow wave sleep (Campbell & Bartolli, 1986). Tonic variation in delta EEG activity is also more similar between REM and Stage 2 than among NREM sleep stages (Moffitt et al., 1982). Finally, dream recall rates from Stage 4 sleep are substantially lower than REM or Stage 2 recall, especially when individual differences are considered. Thus, we recommend that each stage of sleep be analyzed and compared separately, or at least a comparison between fast-frequency, low-amplitude epochs (REM, Stage 2) *versus* epochs within which low-frequency, high-amplitude activity predominates (Stages 3 and 4).

To summarize the EEG literature, there is almost no support for the notion of right-hemisphere activation during REM sleep and left-hemisphere involvement in REM stages. Thus the integrated amplitude data do not suggest differential activation of the two hemispheres characterizes the sleep cycle, as suggested originally by Broughton. Part of the difficulty in evaluating this hypothesis, however, may stem from a general lack of knowledge about the precise EEG characteristics of REM and NREM sleep. Sleep research has not focused on an investigation of the frequencies of EEG activity that are common across all stages of sleep and which are useful in differentiating between REM and NREM sleep stages. As sleep stages are usually evaluated using Rechtschaffen and Kales's (1968) scoring system, assigning a single score for each of the REM and NREM stages, information concerning the EEG frequency characteristics is lost.

The literature reviewed here has been limited to interhemispheric EEG variations with stage of sleep. There is also a body of behavioral data relevant to the BRAC hypothesis and to the notion that sleep stages are associated with unihemispheric predominance.

BEHAVIORAL ASYMMETRIES DURING SLEEP

Lavie and his colleagues have investigated performance asymmetries and perceptual differences between REM and NREM sleep. Gordon, Frooman, and Lavie (1982) tested 12 subjects on six tasks presumed to reflect differential hemispheric involvement following REM and NREM awakenings. Left-hemisphere tasks included digit span, serial ordering of familiar sounds, and word fluency. Right-hemisphere tasks included dot localization, form recognition, and spatial orientation. Raw scores on the tasks were standardized and a composite was created for the left- and right-hemisphere tasks by averaging scores on each task. Gordon et al. (1982) then calculated a cognitive laterality quotient by subtracting the left composite score from the right. Thus, a negative quotient reflected better performance on the left-hemisphere tasks, while a positive value reflected better performance on the right-hemisphere tasks.

Gordon et al. (1982) tested the difference between the laterality quotients and obtained significantly greater left-hemisphere performance following NREM awakenings with virtually no bias in performance following REM sleep. The data presented in this study are extremely difficult to interpret. The authors present analyses of the composite scores, yet discuss performance on individual tasks for which some of the data are not reported. They report that performance on the dot localization task, considered under right-hemisphere control, was most accurate following REM and significantly worse following NREM awakenings. The serial ordering of environmental sounds, considered left-hemisphere dominant, showed the greatest decrement following REM awakenings but was not significantly different from NREM performance. Data for the other tasks were not provided in the paper.

They concluded that their results reflected a "shift in cognitive profile that appears time-locked to a biorhythm" (p. 100), yet they really do not have the data to support this. Their data indicate task performance differences following awakenings from sleep, but they have not specified from which stage of sleep the subjects were awakened. Thus they may have been contrasting REM and Stage 4 or REM and Stage 2 or REM and Stages 2, 3, and 4 combined. Despite the ambiguities and limitations of this report, the data from Gordon et al. (1982) are consistent with another sleep study discussed later.

Bertini, Violani, Zoccolotti, Antonelli, and DiStefano (1984) have demonstrated a left-hand superiority on tactile tasks upon awakening from REM sleep compared with NREM and waking performance on this task. Bertini et al. interpreted this result as evidence for greater right-hemisphere activation during REM sleep. They also obtained higher dream recall rates from those subjects who displayed small differences in right- or left-hand advantage upon awakening from REM, suggesting that dream recall should not be viewed as a right-hemisphere process and that a pattern of hemispheric balance in EEG mediates the recall of sleep experiences. We will return to the issue of hemispheric balance–imbalance during sleep later in this chapter.

In summary, there is some support for the notion of increased performance on visuospatial and perceptual tasks following REM awakenings and a relative deficit in performance on these tasks following NREM awakenings. While they do provide some support for the right-hemisphere-REM, left-hemisphere-NREM relationship, these studies do not address the continuity of biological rhythms in performance during sleep and wakefulness. Spectral analyses of behavioral data during wakefulness have identified rhythms in performance relevant to both the BRAC hypothesis and Broughton's suggestion that interhemispheric oscillations underly ultradian rhythms.

COGNITIVE RHYTHMS IN WAKEFULNESS

Several researchers have pointed out the similarities between daydreams and night dreams (Armitage, 1983; Csikszentmihalyi 1975; Piaget, 1962; Singer, 1966). In part based on the suggestion by Globus (1966; 1970), among others, that there is a waking analogue of dreaming and Kleitman's BRAC proposal, Kripke and Sonnenschein (1978) investigated ultradian rhythms in waking fantasy and the relationship between alpha activity and eye movements with the fantasy content of daydreams.

Ultradian Rhythms in Daydreaming

In the first part of this study, subjects recorded their daydreams every 5 min while EEG and eye movements were recorded. The subjects were isolated and were not provided with any form of amusement. Each daydream was rated on a fantasy scale by the experimenters, and at a later date by the subjects themselves. The amount of alpha activity and eye movements were scored visually for each 5-min epoch from which time series were constructed. The scores on the fantasy daydream scales were averaged between experimenter and subject ratings and used to construct a time series. Lagged autocorrelations, power spectral density functions, and cross-spectral power were computed between each pair of variables.

Their results indicated significant spectral peaks in fantasy content at 16 cycles/day (90 min). Eye movement spectra also peaked at 16 cycles/day, significantly greater than mean variance at adjacent frequencies, but only marginally different from the average spectra. Alpha activity also showed a significant 90-min rhythm. Increases in fantasy content were associated with increased alpha and a decrease in eye movements. All these correlations were significant. Furthermore, the mean coherence spectra, relating fantasy to alpha and eye movement spectra peaked at 16 cycles/day.

Kripke and Sonnenschein (1978) also investigated rhythms in daydreams in individuals allowed to maintain their normal daily habits, adding further support for the continuation of "dream-like" activity throughout sleep and wakefulness, as suggested by Broughton (1975). It should be noted, however, that Kripke and his colleagues have been unable to replicate this finding (Kripke, 1982).

Ultradian Rhythms in Perceptual Processes

Lavie and his colleagues have conducted several research projects to investigate the persistence of rhythms in the perception of the spiral aftereffect in wakefulness. Lavie, Levy, and Coolidge (1974) tested SAE durations throughout the day in a group of university students. One group of subjects was tested every 5 min from 8 a.m. to 4 p.m. and another from 12 midnight to 8 a.m. Time series were constructed from the durations of the after effect and transformed to z-scores. Lag autocorrelations and spectral analyses were then performed on the transformed data. Highest spectral peaks were obtained at approximately 100 min indicating an ultradian rhythm in the magnitude of the SAE, of a similar periodicity as sleep cycles.

Lavie, Lord, and Frank (1974b) replicated these results in a group of high school students, using a similar paradigm. The SAE was tested every 5 min from 4 p.m. until midnight on 2 consecutive days in the laboratory. Four subjects were tested twice, and four subjects tested three times during each 5-min interval. Time series were constructed on the magnitude of the duration yielding 16 time series. Spectral density and autocorrelational analyses were performed after the data were smoothed. Of interest to Lavie et al. were 66.7-, 83.4-, 100-, 142.8-min cycles, the normal range of the REM-NREM cycle. The authors reported that 62% of the time series (10/16) showed peak power in the 66.7–142.8-min range although there was considerable variability among subjects. The median peak was 100 min. Of the eight subjects, three showed significant peaks in the predicted range on both days, three on the second day alone and one on the first day alone. One subject did not show significant peaks in SAE duration on either day. Analysis of the pooled group data revealed one spectral peak at 100 min. It is unclear from their description whether Lavie et al. (1974b) tested the significance of spectral peaks at frequencies other than the four within the range of the REM-NREM sleep cycle. Had this analysis been performed, significant peaks reflecting circadian variations or additional ultradian rhythms may have been determined. These data nonetheless are suggestive of a BRAC involving perceptual processes.

Lavie (1977) has also investigated ultradian rhythms in the phi phenomenon in wakefulness. In this study, eight high school students were tested every 5 min on the SAE, testing the phi phenomenon every fourth trial (every 20 min). Testing sessions lasted from 4 p.m. to midnight. An additional eight subjects slept in the laboratory and were tested after the morning awakening on both these phenomena every 5 min for eight hrs. Two time series were constructed for each subject, one for the range of the phi phenomenon every 20 min, and one for the duration of the SAE, on the 5-min trials. Autocorrelations and spectral analyses were then performed, yielding significant spectral peaks at 14.4 cycles/day (100 min) in both perceptual phenomena. The 100-min cycle was significantly greater than adjacent frequencies for both tasks using autocorrelational analysis. Lavie (1977) used a one-tailed t-test of significance. Cross-spectral analysis also revealed significant 100-min peaks for both phenomena. Lavie obtained a low positive correlation ($r = .11$) between the SAE and phi phenomenon, from which he concluded that the same oscillatory mechanisms govern performance of these two tasks. The value of this correlation is far too small to make such a conclusion. A correlation of this magnitude is usually interpreted to reflect no relationship. His data indicate ultradian variations in perceptual performance in wakefulness but do not suggest similar oscillatory mechanisms are involved in the phi phenomenon and the SAE. Although Lavie (1977) suggests that the mechanisms that govern these events in wakefulness are related to sleep stage oscillations, he did not test this possibility. There are cognitive task performance studies that provide mixed support for ultradian variation in wakefulness.

Ultradian Rhythms in Cognitive Task Performance

More recently Klein and Armitage (1979) have provided evidence for 90-min ultradian rhythms in performance on tasks presumed to reflect the unique specialization of the two hemispheres. This project tested five females and three males, all right-handed, on verbal and spatial tasks from 9 a.m. to 5 p.m. The verbal task involved deciding whether pairs of letters (one upper-, one lowercase) had the same name. The spatial task required subjects to decide if pairs of random dot patterns were identical. The tasks were presented in booklet form and subjects were tested on alternating booklets every 3 min. Performance was measured as the number of pairs correctly matched in each 3 min period, yielding 32 scores for each task throughout the session. Scores were normalized and subjected to spectral analysis.

Significant spectral peaks were obtained at 4 hrs, 96 min, and 37 min. Performance on the verbal and spatial tasks was 180 out of phase, suggesting that differential processes were include in the regulation of these tasks. These results could be taken as support for Broughton's hypothesis (1975) if one assumes rhythms with the same periodicity are likely to be controlled by the same mechanisms.

Kripke, Fleck, Mullaney, and Levy (1983) attempted to replicate ultradian rhythms in performance, using similar tasks to Klein and Armitage (1979). Eleven subjects were tested for 10 hr on a letter-and-dot-matching task and the Wilkinson Auditory Vigilance Task, adapted for computer presentation. Each subject was tested individually for 3 min on the letter task, 3 min on the dot task, 3 min on the vigilance task, and 1 min completing self-ratings on sleepiness and attention-fantasy scales, throughout the day. From the resulting 60 scores, time series were constructed and spectral analyses were performed on the smoothed data.

Kripke et al. (1983) found no significant 90-min peaks in performance and reported that performance on the letter and dot tasks was positively correlated ($r = .59$), in opposition to Klein and Armitage (1979). Results for the vigilance task were not reported.

SCIENCE
LOYOLA
UNIVERSITY
LIBRARY

There are a number of differences between Kripke et al. (1983) and Klein and Armitage (1979) that may account for the discrepancies among these two studies. First, Kripke et al. provided subjects with feedback on their performance throughout testing, with monetary rewards for high accuracy. This information was displayed after each trial and at the end of each 10-min session. They also provided strong negative auditory feedback for errors. This procedure which Kripke et al. introduced to "control motivation," produced demand characteristics that might reduce variability in performance over time, and which was not a characteristic of the Klein and Armitage procedure. Indeed, Gopher and Lavie (1980) demonstrated that providing subjects with feedback and knowledge of their results suppresses performance cycles. Thus, Kripke et al. may have obscured the rhythms in their data by altering the demand characteristics and motivational features of their study. Their data analysis procedure also utilizes spectral density functions while Klein and Armitage (1979) computed periodograms without averaging spectral estimates. As suggested by Brillinger (1975), periodograms may be more appropriate with behavioral time series, given the low sampling rate.

With these considerations in mind, the results from Kripke et al. may be interpreted several ways. These data may either reflect conditions under which ultradian rhythms may be masked by motivational changes and demand characteristics or that the ultradian variation in performance obtained in the study by Klein and Armitage (1979) was artifactual. Neither Kripke et al. (1983) nor Klein and Armitage (1979) included corroborative EEG data and should therefore be viewed as assessments of ultradian rhythms in cognition rather than hemispheric asymmetries. The tasks employed by Klein and Armitage (1979) and Kripke et al. (1983) share a common information-processing component, which makes it difficult to conceive of these tasks as reflecting unique asymmetry of function. Both the letter and the dot tasks require a same/different comparison. It is probable that processes required to perform a same/different comparison are not unique to one hemisphere. Thus the tasks in these studies differ on stimulus characteristics and they require subjects to name the letters while the visuospatial task requires a pattern comparison in the absence of a linguistic code. There is also an inherent bias in degree of difficulty between these tasks, with the spatial task being considerably more difficult than the letter-matching task. In Klein and Armitage (1979), subjects correctly matched an average of 182 letter pairs and only 115 patterns. Since stimulus characteristics alone are not sufficient to predict functional asymmetries and a number of studies suggest that the right hemisphere can recognize simple linguistic code (cf. Armitage, 1981) it is suggested that these tasks should not be viewed as hemisphere-specific. None of the studies discussed in this chapter ensured lateralization of presentation to the right or left visual fields and do not include corroborative EEG data. Periodicities in behavioral data of the type outlined here should be interpreted as aspects of a performance cycle. The tasks need not be viewed as dependent on processes unique to the two hemispheres. Finally, there are theoretical issues that are relevant to the two studies described, and those introduced earlier, which have attempted to find waking analogues of the REM-NREM cycle. There is an implicit assumption that if rhythms are of the same periodicity than they must be related or controlled by similar mechanisms. This assumption has not been tested in any of the studies presented in the previous section of this chapter. Furthermore, research on REM-NREM sleep cycles has focused on electrophysiological data. Research on potential waking analogues of the sleep cycle has focused on perceptual or cognitive performance. There are electrophysiological data from wakefulness that are suggestive of the frequency bands of EEG activity that may display BRAC oscillations.

Ultradian Rhythms in EEG In Wakefulness

Okawa, Matousek, and Peterson (1984) recorded five seconds of parietal and occipital EEG activity in nine subjects every 20 min for 11 hr. During the recording interval subjects were required to lie down, close their eyes, and relax. In the intervening periods when EEG activity was not being recorded the subjects were permitted to engage in "light" activities such as reading, handicrafts, and writing. This procedure was repeated 1 week later. Okawa et al. analyzed the EEG using a computerized method for "vigilance assessment," a technique for measuring alertness based on the presence of fast-frequency desynchronous EEG and the absence of slow-frequency high-amplitude wave forms. Time series were constructed from the vigilance EEG profile and autocorrelational analyses were performed to determine the sine wave frequency that best approximated the vigilance profile throughout the testing session. The results from their study conformed with the general pattern of performance fluctuations (Kleitman, 1963) indicating more variability in the morning, a large "post-lunch dip" and relative stability in the afternoon. In addition Okawa et al. (1984) reported significant 60–110-min rhythms in 16 of the 19 analyzable vigilance time series with 12 of the 19 recordings displaying significant 80–110-min rhythms. Their results indicated that EEG vigilance displays an ultradian variation in wakefulness but there was very large intra- and intersubject variability obtained in this data set.

Manseau and Broughton (1984) have also investigated ultradian rhythms in waking EEG, focusing on hemispheric differences from frontal and parietal recording sites. The eight subjects in this study were not required to perform tasks during the 8-hr. testing session but were required to write down their thoughts after EEG samples were recorded every 15 min. Every 45 min subjects completed a mood questionnaire and received two personality inventories upon completion of the test session. FFTs were performed on each EEG lead and spectral density functions were computed in addition to cross-spectral analysis comparing left- and right-hemisphere activity at frontal and parietal recording sites. Predominant 16 c/day rhythms (90 min) were obtained in frontal but not parietal theta amplitude measures while the cross-spectral analysis indicated bilaterally synchronous ultradian theta cycles. These results do not support Broughton's (1975) hypothesis of interhemispheric fluctuations in wakefulness but do indicate synchronous rhythms in theta activity of a similar periodicity to the REM-NREM sleep cycle.

More recently, we (Armitage, Hoffmann, & Moffitt, 1987) conducted a study of ultradian rhythms in EEG activity during task performance, including two sets of interhemispheric EEG values: a ratio of the difference between the two hemispheres relative to overall EEG activity and a set of values reflecting the absolute value of the difference between the two hemispheres. The absolute difference measures were interpreted as reflecting hemispheric balance when absolute differences were small and hemispheric imbalance when absolute differences were large. These measures were chosen for several reasons. First, an increasing number of studies have shown few hemispheric asymmetries during sleep (Armitage, Hoffmann, Moffitt, Shearer, 1985; Moffitt et al., 1982; Pivik et al., 1982), suggesting a balance in EEG activity throughout the night. Second, the relative ratio measure of interhemispheric EEG is susceptible to artifact, namely small differences between the two hemispheres can produce large asymmetry coefficients. Although the absolute difference measure is not adjusted for background EEG, including both measures will allow you to assess whether the background information is essential to ultradian rhythms in interhemispheric EEG.

Four female and three male right-handers performed mathematical and visuospatial tasks for 4 hr. while parietal EEG was recorded. The visuospatial task consisted of four random asterisk patterns displayed in one of four quadrants of a video screen. Following a 3-s delay, a single pattern appeared in the center of the screen and the subjects were asked to identify in which quadrant the target had originally appeared. The target task could be rotated 180. The mathematical task consisted of an equation of the form:

$$35 + 15 - 52 + 13 = ?.$$

Subjects were asked to solve the equation as quickly as possible. The equations consisted of either two additions or two subtractions and all solutions were between 10 and 99. Both tasks required a verbal response and the EEG activity was recorded for a 6-s epoch during problem solving but prior to responding. Each task was performed for 3 min, followed by a 4-min rest. Time series were constructed from the percentage of correct estimates and the power spectra were computed for each individual subject on both tasks and a relative ratio performance ratio: (% Correct Spatial − % Correct Math/% Correct Spatial + % Correct Math) × 100.

EEG data were quantified using FFT algorithms and time series were constructed from the relative ratio and balance EEG measures for each EEG frequency band. Spectral analyses were performed on all time series, including both the EEG and performance data. Females showed 80–120-min rhythms in mathematical performance and on the relative ratio performance measure, while males showed 80–120-min variation in the relative performance ratios only. Of the EEG measures, females tended to show strongest ultradian variation among balance EEG measures rather than the relative ratio interhemispheric values. Males showed 80–120-min rhythms in relative ratios of delta power during performance on the mathematical task. Females showed 80–120-min sigma cycles during the visuospatial task and small 80–120-min beta cycles during the mathematical task. Although the sample size was small in this study, data from the individual subjects were very consistent.

To determine the relationship between EEG and performance, correlations were computed among these measures. Females showed negative correlations between absolute difference EEG measures and visuospatial performance, ranging from −.41 for delta to −.81 for beta. These results indicated that hemispheric balance was associated with increased task performance. Males on the other hand showed strong positive correlations between relative ratios of EEG and task performance suggesting greater left-hemisphere activity associated with both tasks. We included this data here as it was relevant to the ultradian performance cycle data discussed earlier in this chapter.

These results did not support the hypothesis that rhythms in unihemispheric predominance are associated with task performance and the unique information-processing capabilities of the right and left hemispheres. Furthermore, the findings suggested that the rhythmic organization of cortical activity differs among males and females. There were only seven subjects in this study and they were not selected on the basis of frequency of dream recall. In a study of the relationship between pre-awakening EEG activity and subsequent dream content Moffitt et al. (1982) found striking differences among high- and low-frequency male dream recallers. For example, high recallers a strong positive correlation between the number of words in the dream report and beta activity averaged across the two hemispheres. Low recallers, on the other hand, showed strong negative correlations between interhemispheric beta and sigma ratios and report length, suggesting an association between the right hemisphere and the number of words in the dream report. Thus if high and low recallers show a dissimilar relationship between EEG and verbal descriptions of dream reports, it is conceivable that they may differ in their relationship between EEG and other cognitive activities, such as task performance, and that the rhythmic organization of cortical activity differs among the two recall groups. We pursued this highly speculative theory.

To test this hypothesis we investigated ultradian rhythms in balance and relative ratio EEG activity during a night of uninterrupted sleep. This "sleep-through" night was preceded and followed by a night during which experimental awakenings took place, as described by Moffitt et al. (1982). Four high-recall and four low-recall male subjects participated in this study. EEG was recorded from central electrode sites and was quantified using digital period amplitude analysis of the type outlined earlier in this chapter (for a more complete description, see Hoffmann et al., 1979).

Of the relative ratio EEG measures, Beta Zero-cross showed ultradian variation in the 80–120-min range, but only among low recallers. High recallers showed 80-min cycles in relative ratio Total Power measures. As obtained in the task performance study, there was stronger evidence of 80–120-min cycles in the balance EEG measures. Specifically, Delta Power, Theta Power, Total Power, Beta First Derivative, Delta Zero-cross showed approximate 90-min rhythms. These cycles were more prominent among high recallers, compared with lows, but provided only marginally significant frequency of recall × periodicity interactions from repeated-measures ANOVA. Again, the hypothesis that oscillations in unihemispheric predominance govern ultradian rhythms in sleep was not supported. We also concluded that period analysis was more informative than FFTs for the study of rhythmic EEG processes. The additional information provided by period analysis, zero-cross, and first derivative measures in addition to power, displayed ultradian variation that would not have been detected by FFTs.

Both of the studies reported here and seven of the eight reviewed earlier in this chapter do provide evidence for waking ultradian variation in physiology and behavior with an 80–120-min period. However, none of these studies addressed the continuity of these processes across sleep and wakefulness. To express the same periodicity is not a sufficient condition to conclude that rhythms in sleep and wakefulness are controlled by the same oscillatory mechanisms. It must be demonstrated that there is high coherence between waking and sleeping cycles. To address this issue a third study was conducted in our laboratory.

Twenty-four subjects, divided equally among groups of high- and low-recall males and females spent one night in the laboratory. Parietal and frontal EEG was recorded throughout the night and during a two-hr task performance session upon awakening. The tasks included in this study were identical to those outlined earlier (Armitage, Hoffmann, & Moffitt, 1987). Both the interhemispheric relative ratios and balance EEG measures were included in this study and the EEG data were quantified using period analysis. Spectral analyses were performed on the EEG data from the last 2 hr of sleep and during task performance and correlations were computed between the power spectra. Only three EEG measures (all balance measures) provided evidence for the continuity of cortico-rhythmic processes across sleep and wakefulness, Beta Power, Alpha Power, and Alpha First Derivative. In general, high-recall females showed the strongest correlations between waking and sleeping EEG cycles at 80 min, (r ranging from .60 to .99) in support of Kleitman's BRAC hypothesis. High-recall males showed strong positive correlations between waking and sleeping Beta Power cycles at 80 min ($r = +.97$). Both low- and high-recall female groups showed moderate negative correlations, ($r = -.40, -.60$ respectively) suggesting that a phase shift occurs in Beta EEG cycles upon awakening. In Alpha Power, high-recall males and both female groups showed peak spectral correlations at 80 min with a range of $+.76$ to $+.99$. In Alpha First Derivative, high-recall females showed peak spectral correlations at 80 min ($r = +.96$). These results suggest that females, and in particular, high-recall females show greater continuity of rhythmic EEG activity in the transition from sleep to wakefulness. Only low-recall males showed no evidence of strongly correlated 80-min EEG cycles in sleep and wakefulness. These subjects did, however, show strong positive correlations at shorter ultradian frequencies in support of Lavie's (1982) multi-oscillatory view of ultradian rhythms.

None of the relative ratio EEG measures showed 80–120-min variation in both sleep *and* wakefulness, supporting the idea that rhythms in hemispheric balance better characterize the ultradian nature of EEG. Recently, Manseau and Broughton (1984) have demonstrated 80–120-min bilaterally synchronous theta cycles in wakefulness, indicating that right- and left-hemisphere EEG cycles were in phase. These findings are consistent with the results presented here, that 80–120-min variation in EEG activity is better described as oscillations in hemispheric balance–imbalance. There is no support from these studies for the hypothesis that oscillations in unihemispheric predominance characterize sleep and wakefulness.

Ray and Cole (1985) have suggested that variations in alpha activity reflects the attentional demands of task performance, while beta activity is associated with the emotional and information-processing components of cognitive tasks. If it is assumed that EEG activity reflects underlying cognitive processes, then the correlations between waking and sleeping beta and alpha cycles obtained in our laboratory may reflect the continuity of cognition across sleep and wakefulness. The positive correlations between waking and sleeping EEG cycles at 80 min suggest a strong basis for Kleitman's BRAC hypothesis among beta and alpha EEG frequency bands.

It should be noted that Broughton et al. (1985) have suggested that unless a sampling period of at least five complete cycles is included, spectral estimates may not be reliable. Although they present no data to demonstrate the unreliability when shorter sampling periods are used, multiple cycle observations are preferred. This represents an ideal, where a test of the BRAC hypothesis could be conducted over 24 hr. of continual recording, but it is not feasible. Given the average of 3 to 4 REM periods in 8 hr of sleep, it would be impossible to meet the criterion specified by Broughton et al. (1985). Further, to provide cross-spectral analyses or cross-spectral correlations the sampling intervals in sleep and in wakefulness must be equal. Their paper suggests that the spectral estimates provided in the BRAC study and perhaps the daytime performance study reported here do not provide stable spectral estimates. Given that all three studies conducted in our laboratory not only provide evidence of 80–120 min variation in EEG activity but also of individual differences that are consistent from one study to the next. We suggest that although the sampling interval in these three studies is not ideal, it is reliable. Recording and analyzing EEG and performance throughout a 24-hr period is a labor-intensive effort that often requires a tradeoff between the sampling interval and the number of subjects in the experiment, due to the massive amounts of EEG data generated. For case studies it is feasible to meet the sampling criterion of at least five cycles but not if groups of individuals are included in the study.

In addition to providing evidence for the continuity of rhythmic EEG processes across sleep and wakefulness, we feel research in this area will contribute to our understanding of hemispheric asymmetries and ultradian rhythms in physiology and behavior. From the studies described in this chapter we can provide little support for the view that oscillations in unihemispheric predominance characterize either sleep or waking EEG cycles. Rather our results suggests that it is a rhythm in hemispheric balance–imbalance that better describes rhythmic cortical activity. Although seemingly simplistic, the idea that similar patterns of EEG activity in both hemispheres gives rise to increased task performance and better dream recall, has intuitive appeal. According to our notions of lateralization and hemispheric specialization a central nervous system that has access to the specializations of both sides of the brain at the same time would be expected to excel at a variety of tasks. In preliminary analyses we have found a strong positive relationship between pre-awakening measures of hemispheric balance and success or failure of obtaining a dream report postawakening. We have, since the preparation of this chapter, evaluated the relationship between hemispheric balance and stage of sleep. We confirmed that the hemispheres are balanced during REM with small asymmetries present during Stage 2 sleep. Predominant asymmetries were only found in slow-wave sleep (Armitage, et al. 1989). This has also been demonstrated in the amplitude of late auditory evoked potentials during sleep (Armitage, Bell, Campbell, & Stelmack, 1989; Campbell, Bell, & Armitage, 1987).

These findings, coupled with the data presented earlier in this chapter suggest a few revisions to Kleitman's BRAC hypothesis, and the later extensions. Foremost is the replacement of REM-NREM comparisons with fast frequency, low-amplitude sleep *versus* slow-frequency, high-amplitude sleep. The fast-wave–slow-wave distinction is a more conceptually appealing dichotomization of sleep stage differences, that is not unlike the distinction of quiet sleep–active sleep that appears in the animal literature.

Second, a unihemispheric model of sleep and potential BRAC rhythms should be abandoned in favor of a model of the degree of hemispheric synchronization. There is ample evidence to suggest that REM is not a right-hemisphere phenomenon and NREM is not associated with activation of the left hemisphere.

Third, we suggest that oscillations in electrophysiology in sleep and in wakefulness are best described by 80–120-min rhythms in hemispheric balance. Integrating the perceptual and cognitive performance literature introduced in this chapter, it appears that rhythms in EEG activity are more prominent and perhaps more replicable than rhythms in information processing. If, as Kleitman has suggested, the BRAC is phylogenetically old, than electrophysiological indexes would be expected to show stronger oscillations than newly acquired cognitive skills.

In summary, there is no evidence that unihemispheric EEG activity characterizes ultradian rhythms in sleep or wakefulness. It may be the degree of hemispheric balance or symmetry that displays an 80–120-min cycle. These rhythmic hemispheric processes appear to be continuous throughout sleep and wakefulness and support Kleitman's BRAC hypothesis. The evidence for the BRAC is stronger in electrophysiological measures than it is in performance or cognitive processes.

REFERENCES

Agnew, H., & Webb, W. (1973). The influence of time course variables on REM sleep. *Bulletin of Psychonomics Society 2*, 131–133.

Allen, M. (1983). Models of hemispheric specialization. *Psychological Bulletin, 93*, 73–104.

Antrobus, J., Ehrlichman, H., & Weiner, M. (1978). EEG asymmetry during REM and NREM: Failure to replicate. *Sleep Research, 7*, 24.

Armitage, R. (1980). *Changes in dream content as a function of time of night, stage of awakening and frequency of recall,* master's thesis, Carleton University; Ottawa.

Armitage, R. (1981). *Functional asymmetrics in the human brain: Methodological, theoretical and empirical consideration.* Unplublished paper, Carleton University, Ottawa.

Armitage, R. (1983). *Play, fantasy, dreams and the steam of consciousness.* Unpublished paper, Carleton University, Ottawa.

Armitage, R., Hoffmann, R., Loewy, D., & Moffitt, A. (1989). Variations in period-analysed EEG asymmetry during REM and NREM sleep. *Psychophysiology, 26,* 329-335.

Armitage, R., Hoffmann, R., & Moffitt, A. (1987). The continuity of rhythmic EEG synchronization across sleep and wakefulness. *Sleep Research, 16,* 593.

Armitage, R., Hoffmann, R., Moffitt, A., & Shearer, J. (1985). Ultradian rhythms in interhemispheric EEG activity during sleep: A disconfirmation of the GILD hypothesis. *Sleep Research, 14,* 283.

Armitage, R., Moffitt, A., Hoffmann, R., & Pigeau, R. (1985). Ultradian rhythms in interhemispheric EEG during task performance. *Sleep Research, 14,* 287.+ Aserinsky, E., & Kleitman, N. (1953). Regularly occurring periods of motility and concomitant phenomena during sleep. *Science, 118,* 273-274.

Aserinsky, E., & Kleitman, N. (1955). A motility cycle in sleeping infants as manifested in ocular and gross body motility. *Journal of Applied Physiology, 8,* 11-18.

Bertini, M., Violani, C., Zoccolotti, P., Antonelli, A., & DiStefano, L. (1984). Right cerebral activation in REM sleep. Evidence from a unilateral tactile recognition test. *Psychophysiology 21,* 418-423.

Bonnet, M. (1982). Performance during sleep. In W. Webb (Ed.), *Biological rhythms, sleep and performance* (pp. 205-237). Chichester, England: Wiley.

Brillinger, D.R. (1975). *Time series: Data analysis and theory.* New York: Holt, Rinehart, & Winston.

Broughton, R. (1968). Sleep disorders: Disorders and arousal. *Science, 159,* 1070-1098.

Broughton, R. (1975). Biorhythmic variations in consciousness and psychological function. *Canadian Psychological Review, 16,* 217-239.

Broughton, R., Stampi, C., Ramano, S., Ciriginotta, Baruzzi, A., & Lugaresi, E. (1985). Ultradian BRAC rhythms of spike discharges in case of petit mal epilepsy. *Sleep Research, 14,* 289.

Bueno, L., Fioramonti, J., & Ruckebusch, Y. (1975). Rate of flow of digesta and electrical activity of the small intestine in dogs and sheep. *Journal of Physiology, 249,* 69-85.

Bueno, L., & Ruckebusch, Y. (1977). Hormonal factors of the migrating myoelectric complex. *Proceedings of the International Congress on Physiology, 12,* 417.

Bueno, L., & Ruckebusch, Y. (1978). Insulin and jejunal electrical activity in dogs and sheep. *American Journal of Physiology, 230,* 1538-1544.

Campbell, K., Bell, I., & Armitage, R. (1987). Probe-evoked potentials as a test of asymmetric processing within sleep. *psychophysiology 24,* 583.

Campbell, K., & Bartolli, E. (1986). Human auditory evoked potentials during natural sleep: The early components. *Electroencephalography and Clinical Neurophysiology, 65,* 142-149.

Csikszentmihalyi, M. (1975). *Beyond boredom and anxiety,* New York: Academic Press.

Dement, W. (1955). Dream recall and eye movement during sleep in schizophrenics and normals. *Journal of Nervous Mental Disorders, 1955,* 263-269.

Dement, W., & Kleitman, N. (1957). Cyclic variations in EEG during sleep and their relation to eye movements, body motility and dreaming. *EEG and Clinical Neurophysiology,* 673-690.

Foulkes, D. (1972). Nonrapid eye movement mentation. *Experimental Neurology, 19,* 28-38.

Gevins, A. S., Zeitlin, G. M., Doyle, J. C., Schaffer, R. E., & Callaway, E. (1979b). EEG patterns during cognitive tasks II: Analysis of controlled tasks. *EEG and Clinical Neurophysiology, 49,* 704-710.

Gevins, A. S., Zeitlin, G. M., Yingling, C. D., Doyle, J. C., Dedon, M. F., Schaffer, R. E.,

Roumasset, J. T., & Yeager, C. L. (1979). EEG patterns during cognitive tasks I: Methodology and analysis of complex behaviors. *EEG and Clinical Neurophysiology, 47,* 693-703.

Globus, G. (1966). Rapid eye movement sleep in real time. *Archives of General Psychophysiology, 15,* 654-659.

Globus, G. (1970). Quantification of the REM sleep cycle as a rhythm. *Psychophysiology, 7,* 248-253.

Globus, G. (1972). Periodicity in sleep and waking states. In M. H. Chase (Ed.), *The sleeping brain* (pp. 193-238). Los Angeles: Brain Research Institute, UCLA.

Goldstein, L. (1979). Some relationships between quantified hemispheric EEG and behavioral states in man. In J. Gruzelier & P. Flor-Henry (Eds.), *Hemisphere asymmetry of function in psycopathology* (pp. 237-254). Elsevier-North Holland Biomedical Press.

Goldstein, L., Stolzfus, N., & Gardocki, J. (1972). Changes in interhemispheric amplitude relations in EEG during sleep. *Physiological Behavior, 8,* 811-815.

Gopher, D., & Lavie, P. (1982). Ultradian rhythms in the performance of a simple motor task. *Journal of Motor Behavior, 12,* 207-219.

Gordon, C. R., & Lavie, P. (1982). Ultradian rhythms in urine excretion in dogs. *Life Sciences, 31,* 2727-2734.

Gordon, C. R., Frooman, B., & Lavie, P. (1982). Ultradian rhythms in urine excretion in dogs. Role of sympathetic innervation. *Sleep Research, 11.*

Gottman, J. M. (1981) *Time series analysis,* Cambridge, England: Cambridge University Press.

Granat, M., Lavie, P., Adar, D., & Sharf, M. (1979). Short term cycles in human fetal activity I. Normal pregnancies, *American Journal of Obstetrics and Gynecology, 134,* 696-701.

Grivel, M. L., & Ruckebusch, Y. (1972). The propagation of segmental contractions of the small intestine. *Journal of Physiology, 227,* 611-625.

Halberg, F., Carandente, F., Cornelissen, A., & Katina, G. (1977). Glossary of chronobiology. *Chronobiologia Supplement, 1.*

Hiatt, J. F., & Kripke, D. (1975). Ultradian rhythms in waking gastric activity. *Psychosomatic Medicine, 37,* 320-325.

Hiatt, J. F., Kripke, D., & Lavie, P. (1975). Relationships among psychophysiological ultradian rhythms. *Chronobiology Supplement, 1,* 30.

Hirshkowitz, M., Turner, D., Ware, J., & Karacan, I. (1979). Integrated EEG amplitude asymmetry during sleep. *Sleep Research, 8,* 25.

Hirshkowitz, M., Ware, J., & Karacan, I. (1980). Integrated EEG amplitude asymmetry during early and late REM and NREM periods. *Sleep Research, 9,* 291.

Hoffmann, R., Moffitt, A., Shearer, J., Sussman, P., & Wells, R. (1979). Conceptual and methodological considerations toward a computer controlled study of sleep. *Sleep and Waking, 3,* 1-16.

Hollingworth, H.L. (1926). *The psychology of thought: approached through studies of sleeping and dreaming.* New York: Appleton.

Holt, R.R. (1964). Imagery: The return of the ostracized. *American Psychologist, 12,* 254-264.

Kales, A., Hoedemaker, F., & Jacobson, A. (1967). Mentation during sleep: REM and NREM recall reports. *Perceptual and Motor Skills, 24,* 556-560.

Klein, R., & Armitage, R. (1979). Rhythms in human performance: One and one-half hour oscillations in cognitive style. *Science, 204,* 1326-1328.

Kleitman, N. (1963). *Sleep and wakefulness.* Chicago: University of Chicago Press.

Kripke, D. (1974). Ultradian rhythms in sleep and wakefulness. In E. Weitzman (Ed.), *Advances in sleep research,* (Vol. 1; pp. 305-325). New York: Spectrum.

Kripke, D. (1982). Ultradian rhythms in behavior and physiology. In F. M. Brown & R.C. Graeber (Eds.), *Rhythmic aspects of behavior* (pp. 313-343). Hillsdale, NJ: Lawrence Erlbaum Associates.

Kripke, D., Fleck, P., Mullaney, D., & Levy, M. (1983). Behavioral analogs of the REM-nonREM cycle. *Advances in Biological Psychiatry, 11,* 1–8.

Kripke, D., & Sonnenschein, D. (1978). A biologic rhythm in waking fantasy. In K. Pope & J. Singer (Eds.), *The stream of consciousness* (pp. 321–332). New York: Plenum Press.

Lavie, P. (1977). Nonstationarity in human perceptual ultradian rhythms. *Chronobiology, 4,* 38–48.

Lavie, P., & Giora, Z. (1973). Spiral after-effect following awakening from REM and NREM sleep. *Perception and Psychophysics, 1,* 19–20.

Lavie, P., Kripke, D., Hiatt, J. F., & Morrison, J. (1978). Gastric rhythms during sleep. *Behavioral Biology, 23,* 526–530.

Lavie, P., Levy, C. M., & Coolidge, F. L. (1974a). Ultradian rhythms in the perception of the spiral after-effect. *Physiological Psychology, 3,* 144–146.

Lavie, P., Lord, J. W., & Frank, R. A. (1974b). Basic rest–activity cycle in the perception of the spiral after-effect. A sensitive detector of a basic biological rhythm. *Behavioral Biology, 11,* 373–379.

Lavie, P., & Sutter, D. (1975). Differential responding to the beta movement after waking from REM and nonREM sleep. *American Journal of Psychology, 88,* 595–603.

Lindsley, D. S., & Wicke, J.D. (1974). The electroencephalogram: Autonomous electrical activity in man and animals. In R. F. Thompson & M. M. Patterson (Eds.), *Bioelectric recording techniques* (Pt. B). New York: Academic Press.

Mandell, A. J., Chaffey, B., Brill, P., Madell, M. P., Rodnick, J., Rubin, R. T., & Sheff, R. (1966). Dreaming sleep in man: Changes in urine volume and osmolality. *Science, 151,* 1558–1560.

Manseau, C., & Broughton, R. (1984). Bilaterally synchronous ultradian EEG rhythms in awake adult humans. *Psychophysiology, 21,* 265–273.

Moffitt, A. Hoffman, R., Wells, R., Armitage, R., Pigeau, R., & Shearer, J. (1982). Individual differences among pre-and post-awakening EEG correlates of dream reports following arousals from different stages of sleep. *Psychiatric Journal of the University of Ottawa, 7,* 111–125.

Okawa, M., Matousek, M., & Peterson, I. (1984). Spontaneous vigilance fluctuations in the daytime. *Psychopysiology, 21,* 207–211.

Orr, W. C., & Hoffman, H. J. (1974). A 90 minute cardiac biorhythm: Methodology and data analysis using modified periodograms and complex demodulation. *IEEE Transactions Biomedical Engineering, BME-21,* 130–143.

Piaget, J. (1962). *Play, dreams and imitation in childhood.* New York: Norton.

Pigeau, R. (1985). *Psychophysiology and cognition: Some EEG correlates and a new descriptive technique.* Unpublished doctoral thesis, Carleton University, Ottawa.

Pigeau, R., Hoffmann, R., & Moffitt, A. (1981). A multivariate comparison of two EEG analysis techniques: Period analysis and fast fourier transforms. *EEG and Clinical Neurophysiology, 52,* 656–658.

Pivik, R. T., Bylsma, F., Busby, K., & Sawyer, S. (1982). Interhemispheric EEG changes in relationship to sleep and dreams in gifted adolescents. *Psychiatric Journal of the University of Ottawa, 7,* 56–76.

Ray, W. J., & Cole, H. W. (1985). Alpha activity reflects attentional demands and beta reflects emotional and cognitive processes. *Science, 228,* 750–752.

Rechtschaffen, A., & Kales, A. (Eds.), (1968). *Manual of standardized terminology, techniques and scoring system for sleep stages of human subjects.* NIH Publication No. 204, Washington, Superintendent of Documents.

Rosekind, M.R., Coates, T.J., & Zarcone, V.P. (1979). Lateral dominance during wakefulness, NREM stages 2 sleep and REM sleep. *Sleep Research, 8,* 36.

Ruckebusch, Y., & Bueno, L. (1977). Electrical spiking activity of the small intestine as an ultradian rhythm. *Proceedings of the International Congress on Physiology, 2,* 789.

Ruckebusch, Y., & Fioramonti, J. (1975). Electrical spiking activity and propulsion in small intestine in fed and fasted rats. *Gastroenterology, 68,* 1500–1508.

Rubin, R. Gouin, P., Kales, A., & Odell, W. (1973). Leutinizing hormone, follicle stimulating hormone and growth hormone secretion during sleep and dreaming. *Psychosomatic Medicine, 35,* 309–321.

Singer, J. L. (1966). *Daydreaming.* New York: Random House.

Smith, T. L. (1904). The psychology of day dreams. *American Journal of Psychology, 15,* 465–488.

Sugerman, A., Goldstein, L., Marjerrison, G., & Stolzfus, N. (1973). Recent research in EEG amplitude analysis. *Disorders of the Nervous System, 34,* 162–166.

Wilson, D. M., Kirpke, D., McClure, D. K., & Greenburg, A.G. (1977). Ultradian cardian rhythms in surgical intensive care unit patients. *Psychosomatic Medicine, 39,* 432–435.

Wolpert, E. (1960). Studies in psychophysiology of dreams. II: An electrophysiological study of dreaming. *Archives of General Psychiatry, 2,* 231–241.

Wolpert, E., & Trossman, H. (1958). Studies in psychophysiology of dreaming. I: Experimental evolution of sequential dream episodes. *American Association of Neurology and Psychiatry, 79,* 603–606.

3
The Postawakening Testing Technique in the Investigation of Cognitive Asymmetries During Sleep

Mario Bertini and Cristiano Violani
University of Rome-La Sapienza

As knowledge of the cognitive functional specialization of the right cerebral hemisphere has increased, several authors (e.g., Ornstein, 1972; Jouvet, 1973; Galin, 1974; Broughton, 1975; Bakan, 1975; Cartwright, 1977; Cohen, 1979) have advanced the speculative hypothesis, which considers dreaming a function of the right hemisphere (RH). This hypothesis relies mainly on the recognition of some correspondences between dreaming and the cognitive "style" of the RH (prevalence of imagery, alogicity, etc.) and assumed the existence of some shift in hemispheric asymmetry during sleep with greater relative activation of the RH in REM sleep, that is, the state in which dreaming is pre-eminent.

The most extensively used method for investigating cerebral asymmetries during sleep has been the comparison of the relative amplitude (or power) of the EEG recorded from homologous locations on the two hemispheres of human subjects in the different stages of sleep. Since the pioneering research of Goldstein and his coworkers (Goldstein, Burdick, & Lazslo, 1970; Goldstein, Stolzfus, & Gardocki, 1972) at least 16 studies have been reported involving a total of more than 100 normal subjects Angeleri, Scarpino, & Signorino, 1984; Antrobus, Ehrlichman, & Wiener, 1978; Ehrlichman, Antrobus & Wiener, 1985; Goldstein, 1979; Goldstein et al., 1970; Goldstein et al., 1972; Herman, 1984; Hirshkowitz, Ware, Turner, & Karacan, 1979; Gaillard, & Laurian, Le, 1984; Moffitt, et al., 1982; Murri, et al., 1982; Murri, et al., 1984; Rosadini, Ferrillo, Gasperetto, Rodriguez, & Sannita, 1984; Rosekind, Coates, & Zarcone, 1979; Violani, De Gennaro, & Capogna, 1984). Only three investigations out of 16 reported findings confirming Goldstein and coworkers' claims of consistent and significantly greater activation of the RH during REM sleep as compared with NREM (Angeleri et al., 1984; Goldstein, 1979; Hirshkowitz et al., 1979). It may be noticed that at least 5 studies out of 10 have shown greater RH activation both in REM and NREM sleep, compared with waking (Ehrlichman et al., 1984; Goldstein et al., 1970; Moffitt et al., 1982; Murri et al., 1982; 1984; Rosekind et al., 1979). Many studies have enphasized the existence of relevant intersubject variability (Gaillard, Laurian, & Le, 1984; Goldstein et al., 1970; Herman, 1984; Violani et al., 1984).

Relations between dreaming and the RH have been investigated also in brain-damaged patients. Since Paul Broca's (1827–1880) clinical studies, research with patients suffering from lateralized brain damage has greatly contributed to the understanding of functional asymmetries in the human brain; this approach, however, has so far made only a limited contribution to the understanding of the role of the RH in dreaming. Findings by Humphrey and Zangwill (1951) have often been quoted as evidence of the cessation of dreaming following RH damage and as indicative of a special responsibility of that hemisphere in the dreaming process. A closer scrutiny of the literature on this issue reveals a quite different picture. In fact, considering only right-handed patients with unilateral brain lesions, impaired capacity to recall dreams has been found both in RH (Humphrey & Zangwill, 1951, case 1) and in left-hemisphere (LH) damaged patients (Nielsen, 1955: case 2; Basso, Bisiach, & Luzzatti, 1980). A crucial role of the LH for dreaming has been suggested by the findings of Epstein and Simons (1983), who have found that cessation of dreaming is often signaled by aphasic patients, and has been confirmed by recent reviews of cases of patients with unilateral brain damage (Doricchi & Violani, this volume; Greenberg & Farah, 1986).

The idea of a functional asymmetry during REM sleep favoring the RH is extremely appealing to us because it offers a possibility to understand relationships between waking and sleeping cognitive modalities within the psychophysiological model developed by Bertini (Bertini, 1982, 1985; Bertini, Solano, & Violani, 1988). We were not discouraged by the substantial weakness of the empirical evidence yielded by EEG and brain-damaged studies because we felt that both approaches relied on two unjustified assumptions: (a) that during sleep the higher functional involvement of one cerebral hemisphere will be reflected by EEG desynchronization; (b) that absence of dream recall reflects necessarily the cessation of the process of dreaming.

Recognizing correspondences between oneiric mentation and cognitive modalities abscribed to the RH is certainly legitimate, since the stage of sleep in which dreaming predominates is REM; it also seems quite reasonable to hypothesize higher functional involvement of some RH functions during REM sleep. But the hypothesis that the RH EEG activity should be more desynchronized in REM assumes that greater EEG relative activation (i.e., relatively smaller amplitude and higher frequencies) corresponds to a greater contribution of that hemisphere in the production of dreaming. The equation between hemispheric EEG relative desynchronization and hemispheric cognitive activation has been proved as substantially correct during waking (e.g., Bradshaw & Nettleton, 1983) but it may not necessarily be true during sleep. The opposite might even be true: the cognitive peculiarities of REM mentation could be related to a greater involvement of the RH coinciding with a relatively greater synchronization of that hemisphere. As a matter of fact, basic differences exist between the cortical electric activity along the sleep–wake cycle. During waking, most of the EEG power is within the high frequencies while in sleep it is within the low frequencies. In any case the functional specificity of REM sleep is given by a complex pattern of different physiological parameters and cannot be totally described by surface EEG activity. The coexistence of cortical arousal and motor and sensorial inhibition make REM sleep a qualitatively different and complex state, so that it appears rather difficult to identify a single parameter as a reliable indicator of dreaming activity.

Investigations of patients suffering from lateralized brain lesions often rely on a different unjustified assumption. They equate the process of generation of the dream to the process of recall of the experience of dreaming. Possible cessation or reduction in recall of dreaming after unilateral brain damage should be taken as indexing an impairment in any of the processes allowing the production of the dream experience and its recall, and not exclusively in the contribution of the damaged hemisphere to the process underlying the production of the dream.

Once the substantial limitations of current EEG and clinical neurological investigations in revealing functional cognitive asymmetries during sleep are recognized, how advantageous could be the implementation of behavioral methods to draw inferences on the relative efficiency of one hemisphere becames clear. The most widely used methods use the assessment of performances in laterally presented tasks. Dichotic and lateralized tachistoscopic tests are widely used in neuropsychological investigations during waking in normal subjects, but how can one have a sleeping subject perform them?

CARRY-OVER EFFECTS

Hints for solving this problem came from a reconsideration of previous research (Bertini, Torre, & Ruggeri, 1975), in which subjects were first given a special training to produce free mentation reports upon the presentation of a white noise while awake; the same noise was subsequently presented during sleep. When the stimulus was presented in REM sleep it was possible to obtain more dream-like verbalizations than when it was introduced in NREM or in waking. Initial enthusiasm for a procedure capable of "capturing" ongoing oneiric mentation during sleep was constrained by the recognition that the polygraphic records during subjects' verbalizations were definable, with minor variations, as waking. Since the ongoing mentation produced following REM sleep was the most dream-like in character, it was concluded that the process of awakening had not completely canceled all the functional characteristics of the preceding sleep state. It was also clear that this "carry-over effect," originally recognized by Fiss, Klein, and Bokert (1966), could be used for a variety of purposes in the psychophysiological study of the sleep–wake cycle. Unambiguous carry-over effects have been shown in studies where TAT cards were used to prompt mental productions after awakenings from REM and NREM sleep (Fiss et al., 1966). Also perceptual illusions, such as the spiral aftereffect and the beta movement, have been shown to vary as a function of the preawakening sleep stage (Lavie, 1974; Lavie & Giora 1973; Lavie & Sutter, 1975). Lavie (1974) also shown that "carry-over effects" last at least 15 mins following the awakenings. At the electrophysiological level, Broughton (1968) has noticed that visual evoked potentials after REM awakenings are different from those recorded after NREM awakenings, the former being more similar to those obtained in waking. As to the possibility of identifying carry-over effects in EEG asymmetries, Murri and coworkers (Murri et al., 1984) comparing EEG asymmetry coefficients pre- and postawakenings from REM sleep, noticed a significant reduction of asymmetry during the postawakening stage and concluded that this does not favor the idea that a carry-over effect exists at the EEG level. On the other hand, Moffitt and coworkers (Moffitt et al., 1982; Moffitt, Hoffmann, Wells, Shearer, & Armitage, 1985) concluded their papers on the relationships between EEG asymmetries pre- and postawakenings from REM and NREM sleep by stating that "the carry-over effect, that Fiss and others have proposed for the phenomenology of dreams, also occurs on the electrophysiological level as well." These contrasting EEG results could be due to high intersubject variability that Moffitt and coworkers (Moffitt et al., 1985) have suggested is related to individual differences in the ability to recall their dreams. In fact, high dream recallers showed a smaller carry-over effect than low dream recallers. The existence of a carry-over effect is suggested by a conspicuous set of empirical evidences; furthermore it will be easily recognized that chronobiological studies on ultradian rhythms in general show how variations in the physiological phenomena underlying behavioral states are better described by sinusoidal than by square wave functions. In conclusion it seems reasonable to assume that psychophysiological functions characterizing a behavioral state are not readily switched off and on at the transition to another state, but may somehow persist during the following state.

POSTAWAKENING TESTING

The foregoing considerations led us to believe that Postawakening Testing (PAT) could be advantageously used to investigate cognitive asymmetries during sleep. If a state is characterized by a particular asymmetry pattern in the functioning of the cerebral hemispheres, as a consequence of the carry-over effect this pattern should persist in the waking state immediately following the interruption of that state.

In the study of functional asymmetries along the sleep–wake cycle, the PAT method consists basically of awakening subjects either from REM or NREM sleep and administering tasks known to be capable of reflecting differentially the functional efficiency of each hemisphere immediately after the awakening.

In our applications of the PAT only unilaterally presented test stimuli have been used because they should allow a more direct assessment of the level of functioning of the counterlateral hemisphere than what is allowed by nonlateralized tests assessing performances in tasks (verbal or spatial) in which a different contribution of the two hemispheres is assumed on the basis of inferential evidences. Furthermore, the procedures we used are designed in such a way as to introduce only minimal variations in the environmental setting after the awakening: Subjects remain in bed, a very dim light is used, verbal interactions are usually minimal. For testing in the waking state the same experimental settings are used.

So far we have used the PAT in two investigations both aimed at giving answer to two different issues: The first is concerned with the existence of different functional asymmetries in REM and in NREM sleep; the second with possible relationship between the latter and the recall of dreams. Evidence relevant to these issues will be evaluated separately in this chapter.

FUNCTIONAL ASYMMETRIES DURING REM AND NON-REM SLEEP

In the first study (Bertini, Violani, Zoccolotti, Antonelli, & Di Stefano, 1983; Bertini, Violani, Zoccolotti, Antonelli, & Di Stefano, 1984) we used for the PAT a new tactile–tactile recognition test, designed to be given under a very dim light while the subject was still lying in bed. The subject was required to feel an irregular polygon with the top of the fingers of either hand and then, with the same hand, locate the form in a set of three polygons. Preliminary results showed a left-hand superiority ascribed to the superiority of the RH for spatial tasks and for the tactile modality. The test was administered during waking and upon awakenings from REM and NREM stages of sleep, to 16 right-handed healthy young subjects. The hypothesis was that the expected functional asymmetry favoring the RH in REM sleep should be reflected by an enhancement of the differences in performance between the two hands and in the superiority of the left hand upon awakenings from that stage.

Results (Fig. 3.1) support the hypothesis of a RH superiority during REM sleep. In fact left-hand superiority was significantly greater after REM PAT than after NREM or in waking, the superiority being due both to a decrease in the performance of the right hand (left hemisphere, LH) and in an increase in that of the left hand (RH). The interesting findings of increased performance of the LH and decreased performance of the RH observed after awakenings from Stage 2 NREM were not predicted.

About the same time Gordon, Frooman, and Lavie (1982) and Lavie, Matanya, and Yehuda (1984), working independently of our laboratory, obtained results with the PAT method that were fully compatible with those of our laboratory, that is, better performance in a set of three nonlateralized RH (mainly spatial) tasks after awakenings from REM sleep, and better performance in (mainly verbal) LH tasks after NREM awakenings. It is worth noting that in the Haifa laboratory, effects were obtained with a

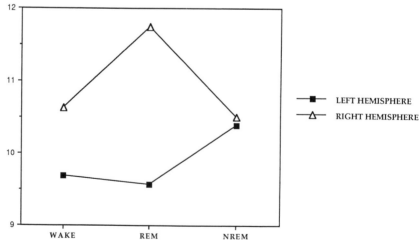

FIG. 3.1. Performance scores of the right hemisphere (left hand) and of the left hemisphere (right hand) in a tactile–tactile spatial recognition test administered during waking and after awakenings from REM and NREM sleep (Bertini et al. 1984).

procedure in which tests were administered for a rather long period of time (about 30 min) in a room different from that in which subjects had slept. This seems to indicate that carry-over effects must be strong and persistent. Subsequently, Lavie and coworkers (Lavie et al., 1984; Lavie & Tzischinsky, 1984) have presented data concerning right- and left-handed males and females confirming the effect for right-handers and showing it to be bigger in females and absent in both male and female left-handers. A second investigation from our laboratory (Bertini et al., 1985) had the following aims: (1) To extend the findings from the tactile test to a different sensory modality (i.e., visual); (2) To ascertain whether shifts in hemispheric asymmetries in REM and NREM could be shown both in spatial (RH) and verbal (LH) tasks. For the PAT two tachistoscopic unilateral tests were used: a verbal task requiring the recognition of vertical arrays of four letters and a spatial task requiring the enumeration of the dots presented in patterns containing from 5 to 12 dots. Tests were given to subjects lying in bed, required verbal answers and could be completed in less than 15 min. Sixteen right-handed young healthy male subjects served as subjects in this investigation; each subject slept for 3 consecutive nights in the sleep lab, Night 1 being for adaptation; procedures were identical to those of the previous experiment; tests were given upon arrival in the laboratory in Night 1 and upon awakenings from REM and Stage 2 NREM in Nights 2 and 3. For the spatial task, as in the previous study, the largest RH advantage was found upon awakenings from REM sleep (see Fig. 3.2). At variance with the tactile test, however, the superiority of the RH in the point enumeration task in REM was not due to an increase in the performance of the RH and to a decrease in the performance of the LH, but to a dramatic drop of the latter alone.

For the verbal task a consistent superiority of the LH was found, which did not show variations across the states considered (Fig. 3.3). The absence of variation in verbal task performance across conditions may indicate that state-related effects observed do not reflect a general shift in hemispheric activation but concern specifically spatial tasks (both tactile and visual). This interpretation, however, needs more substantial evidence, since increased verbal performance after NREM awakenings has been reported in nonlaterally presented tasks (Gordon et al., 1982; Lavie, Matanya, & Yehuda, 1984) and we cannot rule out the possibility that our verbal task was not sensitive to state-related variations in hemispheric asymmetries.

At the moment there are five different investigations completed in two different laboratories that have employed the PAT technique in order to reveal state-related shifts in hemispheric asymmetry during sleep. All the studies have yielded consistent results suggesting that the RH increases its superiority in performing spatial tasks upon awakenings from REM sleep. There is little doubt now about the reliability of these effects. It must be also

POINTS ENUMERATION TASK

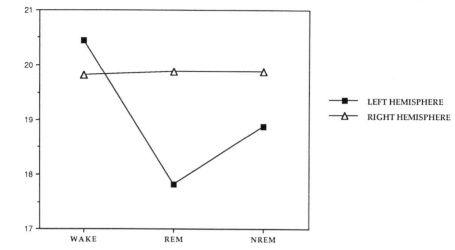

FIG. 3.2. Number of correct enumerations of the dots tachistoscopically presented to the right hemisphere (left visual field) and to the left hemisphere during waking and after awakenings from REM and NREM sleep (Bertini et al. 1985).

recognized that they are strong since they have been consistently shown in relatively small groups of right-handed subjects both through laterally presented tasks (in our laboratory) and through nonlaterally presented tasks (in Haifa's laboratory).

One might wonder whether it is correct to infer from postawakening tests the actual functioning of the pre-awakening state. At the moment no alternative interpretation exists to the one considering the shifts found as the consequence of a "carry-over" effect that reflects the neurophysiological functioning prior to the awakening. In fact the shifts in hemispheric asymmetries found with the PAT method could: (a) Reflect the characteristics of the pre-awakening state through the carry-over effect (b) Reflect ultradian variations in hemispheric asymmetries linked to the BRAC as hypthesized by Broughton (1975) and by Klein and Armitage (1979), (c) Or be specifically linked to the waking state following an awakening. Militating against hypothesis (b) is the fact that when PAT was applied after 35 and 75 min from REM and NREM awakenings (i.e., supposedly at opposite phases of a 90-min ultradian cycle), equal performance by the two hemispheres was found (Lavie & Tzischinsky, 1984). Furthermore, hypothesis (b) is weakened by the fact that ultradian cyclicities in hemispheric asymmetries have not been found by Kripke, Fleck, Mullaney, and Levy (1983) at the behavioral level and by Manseau and Broughton (1984) at the EEG level.

LETTERS RECOGNITION TASK

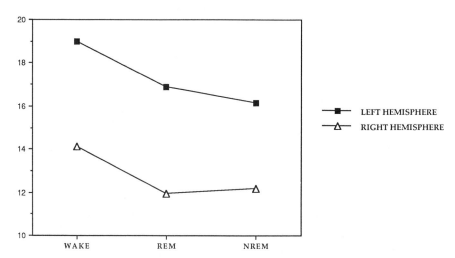

FIG. 3.3. Number of correct recognitions of letters tachistoscopically presented to the right hemisphere (left visual field) and to the left hemisphere during waking and after awakenings from REM and NREM sleep (Bertini et al. 1985).

Opposing hypothesis (c) is the fact that differences have been found in the awakenings from REM relative to NREM sleep.

Now let us consider the overall meaning of the findings obtained through the PAT method that might give important cues to a better understanding of the relationships between cognitive asymmetries during sleep and dreaming.

Two questions may be raised at this moment. First, do our findings confirm the hypothesis of a RH general activation in REM sleep? Second, do our findings support the hypothesis that the RH is the dreamer? The answer to both questions must be cautious and articulated. As far as the first question is concerned, our findings indicate that the RH increases its superiority in performing spatial tasks in the REM state, compared with NREM and even to the wake state, but there is no consistent evidence that the RH is generally more activated during REM sleep. At the behavioral level, this evidence could come from findings of increased performance of the left hand in nonlateralized tasks such as simple reaction time; at the physiological it could be provided by event-related evoked potentials or by measures of regional cerebral blood flow.

We feel quite confident in claiming that in REM sleep the RH seems to become relatively more efficient in the performance of spatial tasks, that is in the tasks more attuned to its more characteristic mode of functioning. Claiming that the RH has relative improvements in tasks for which it is specialized, but that this does not necessarily imply a general activation of that hemisphere, may sound a subtle and finicky distinction. We feel, however, that this qualification must be stated in order to avoid any commitment to a generical model of physiological activation that does not rely on indicators proven as theoretically and methodologically reliable.

As far as the second question is concerned, the answer is that PAT results give us a reliable albeit indirect indication that REM state does increase some modalities of cognitive functioning characteristic of the RH, but does not reveal anything about the physiology of this phenomenon. In a sense, Lavie's claim that "the association of RH dominance after awakening from REM sleep apparently supports the assertion that dreaming is a lateralized function" (Lavie, Tzinshinsky, Epstein, & Frooman, 1984) is legitimate, but how does one reconcile it with evidence of decreased dream reporting in left-brain-damaged patients? By showing an increase in the functional superiority of the RH (at least in spatial tasks implying functions in which a superiority of the RH is recognized in waking) in the very sleep stage in which dreaming becomes prominent, certainly could point to relationships between the RH and the dream-generating processes, but this does not imply a direct responsibility of the RH in the process of recalling and reporting a dream. The view that "the right hemisphere is the dreamer" is misleading because it confounds dreaming and dream recall and because it implies an absolute hemispheric specialization for this complex cognitive product.

It will be noted that findings obtained through the PAT method, while suggesting that the increased relative predominance of the RH in spatial functions should affect the processes generating the dream, in no way assume that recalling the experience of dreaming and its content is a RH function. On the contrary some experimental findings disconfirm the existence of a direct relationship between RH predominance and dream recall hypothesized by other dream researchers (e.g., Cohen, 1977).

FUNCTIONAL ASYMMETRIES IN THE SLEEP CYCLE AND DREAM RECALL

No relationships between both ability to recall the dream and characteristics of the REM report on one hand and cognitive lateral asymmetries characterizing right-handed male subjects during wake (Lavie & Tzischinsky, 1985) have been found.

In addition to studying variations in asymmetry, in both of our experiments, we tried to answer to the question of whether and how dream recall was related to the pattern of hemispheric functional asymmetry observed through the PAT method.

In the first experiment (Violani, Bertini, Zoccolotti, & Di Stefano, 1983) we assigned *a posteriori* our subjects to two dream recall subgroups ("high" and "low") on the basis of the median value of the number of dreams that they reported both in the laboratory after the final morning awakenings and at home through a sleep and dream diary that subjects completed for 15 days. Results (see Fig. 3.4) do not confirm the idea of a direct relationship between dream recall and RH superiority in REM state. Rather they suggest a different relationship. In fact PAT assessed performance while indicating that REM is generally characterized by a heightening of RH efficiency and by its lowering in the LH, indicates also that the subjects who show this pattern in a more pronounced way are those who have less access to dream content.

This pattern was substantially confirmed by results of the point enumeration task of the second investigation (Bertini et al., 1985) in which subjects were preselected as low recallers and high recallers on the basis of the

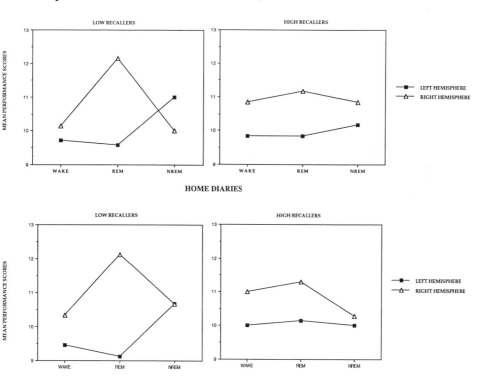

FIG. 3.4. Performance scores of the right hemisphere and of the left hemisphere in the tactile spatial task in low dream recallers and high dream recallers (Violani et al., 1983).

number of dreams reported in a 7-day diary. As shown in Fig. 3.5, greater hemispheric shift was shown by low dream recallers while high dream recallers maintained a steady level of performance across states. It might be worth emphasizing how in both experiments the pattern of low dream recallers is characterized by a marked decrease in LH efficiency.

Results from both our investigations point to the importance of an adequate functioning of the LH for the function of recall of the dream, in that subjects who recall dreams better are characterized by the maintenance of stable levels of efficiency of the linguistic hemisphere. This does not contradict the view that increased relative efficiency of the RH during REM sleep affects the dream generation process. At the same time, findings of decreased recall of dreams following LH damage (e.g., Basso et al., 1980; Doricchi & Violani, this volume; Greenberg & Farah, 1986) do not contradict per se the idea that some special contribution to the generation of dream might be given by the RH.

CONCLUSIONS

At the moment the PAT method has been employed by two independent groups of researchers in (5) different investigations: all of them yielded consistent results revealing strong shifts in hemispheric functional asymmetries as a function of the pre-awakening sleep stage. These shifts are assumed, on the basis of theoretical and empirical considerations, to reflect differences in hemispheric asymmetries during the sleep–wake cycle. At the moment the PAT method has given the most consistent set of results indicating a RH superiority during REM. EEG measures of hemispheric activity during sleep have yielded contrasting results, but their adequacy for the purpose of showing functional asymmetries during sleep is questionable.

Results with nonlateralized tasks suggest that in right-handed individuals RH functions predominate during REM while LH functions predominate during Stage 2 NREM.

Results with lateralized tasks suggest that in right-handed individuals during REM there is a strengthening of the RH superiority for processing spatial information, regardless of the sensory modality by which it is acquired.

Clinical neuropsychological investigations indicate that both hemispheres, and the left more than the right, are implied in the recall of dreaming. However, this does not contradict the idea that the RH gives a special contribution to the processes generating the dream. PAT results suggest that in REM the RH predominates over the LH, at least under certain aspects, but the more this happens in a given subject the less he or

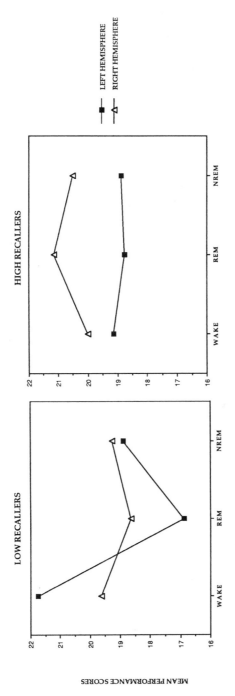

FIG. 3.5 Number of correct enumerations of dots presented to the right and to the left hemisphere in high and in low dream recallers.

59

she will be able to recall dreams. This appear fully compatible with the conclusions of clinical neuropsychological investigations.

A speculative and simplified view stems from the cited results here: In REM sleep, as a consequence of its increased efficiency, the RH will predominate in the processes of generation of certain aspects of the mental content but these cannot be encoded and stored in a retrievable way without the contribution of the LH.

REFERENCES

Angeleri, F., Scarpino, O., & ino, M. (1984). Information processing and hemispheric specialization: Electrophysiological study during wakefulness, stage 2 and stage REM sleep. *Research Communications in Psychology, Psychiatry and Behavior, 9,* 121–138.

Antrobus, J., Ehrlichman, H., & Wiener, M. (1978). EEG asymmetry during REM and NREM: Failure to replicate. *Sleep Research, 7,* 24.

Bakan P. (1975, June). *Dreaming, REM sleep and the right hemisphere: A theoretical integration.* Paper presented at the second International Congress of Sleep Research, Edinburgh, Scotland.

Basso, A., Bisiach, E., & Luzzatti, C. (1980). Loss of mental imagery: A case study. *Neuropsychologia, 18,* 435–442.

Bertini, M. (1982). Sonno, veglia, sogno e dinamica della conoscenza [Sleep, waking and consciousness dynamics]. In M. Bertini & C. Violani (Eds), *Cervello e sogno* (pp. 203–227), Milan: Feltrinelli.

Bertini, M. (1985). Pensiero razionale e pensiero onirico lungo l'arco della veglia e del sonno [Rational thought and oneiric thought along sleep and waking]. *Comunicazioni scientifiche di psicologia generale, 12,* 121–142.

Bertini, M., Solano L., & Violani, C. (1988). Beyond unidimensional views of mental activity along the sleep wake cycle. In W. Koella, F. Obal, H. Schulz & P. Visser (Eds.), *Sleep '86* (pp.123–130). Stuttgart: G. Fischer Verlag.

Bertini, M., Torre, A., & Ruggeri G. (1975). Induced verbalizations during awake, REM and NREM states. In P. Levi & W. Koella (Eds.), *Sleep 1974.* Basel: Karger.

Bertini, M., Violani, C., Zoccolotti, P., Altomare, P., Doricchi, F., Evangelist, L. (1985). Lateralization of verbal and configurational processing during waking and upon awakenings from REM and NREM. In W. Koella, E. Ruther, H. Schultz (Eds.), *Sleep 1984* (pp. 358–370). Stuttgart: G. Fischer Verlag.

Bertini, M., Violani, C., Zoccolotti, P., Antonelli, A., & Di Stefano, L. (1983). Performance on a unilateral tactile test during waking and upon awakening from REM and NREM sleep. In W. Koella (Ed.); *Sleep 1982* (pp. 383–385). Basel: Karger.

Bertini, M., Violani, C., Zoccolotti, P., Antonelli, A., Di Stefano, L. (1984). Right cerebral hemisphere activation in dreaming sleep: evidence from a unilateral tactile recognition test. *Psychophysiology, 21,* 418–423.

Bradshaw, J. C., & Nettleton, N. C. (1983). *Human cerebral asymmetry.* Englewood Cliffs, N. J.: Prentice-Hall.

Broughton, R. (1968). Sleep disorders: Disorders of arousal? *Science, 159,* 1070–1078.

Broughton, R. (1975). Biorythmic variation in consciousness and psychological functions. *Canadian Psychological Review, 16,* 217–239.

Cartwright, R. D. (1977). *Night life: Explorations in dreaming.* Englewood Cliffs, N. J.: Prentice-Hall.

Cohen, D. B. (1977). Changes in REM dream content during the night: Implications for a hypothesis about changes in cerebral dominance across REM periods. *Perceptual and Motor Skills, 44,* 1267-1277.

Cohen, D. B. (1979). *Sleep and dreaming: Origins, nature and functions.* Oxford, England: Pergamon Press.

Ehrlichman, H., Antrobus, J. S., & Wiener, M. S. (1985). EEG asymmetry and sleep mentation during REM and NREM. *Brain and Cognition, 4,* 477-485.

Epstein, A. W., & Simons, S. (1983). Aphasia with reported loss of dreaming. *American Journal of Psychiatry, 140,* 108-109.

Fiss, H., Klein, G., & Bokert, E. (1966). Waking fantasies following interruption of two types of sleep. *Archives of General Psychiatry, 14,* 543-551.

Gaillard, J. M., Laurian, S., & Le, P. (1984). EEG asymmetry during sleep. *Neuropsychobiology, 11,* 224-226.

Galin, D. (1974). Implications for psychiatry of left and right cerebral specialization. *Archives of General Psychiatry, 31,* 572-584.

Goldstein, L. (1979). Some relationships between quantified hemispheric EEG and behavioral states in man. In J. Gruzelier & P. Florhenry (Eds.), *Hemisphere asymmetries of function in psychopathology* (pp. 237-254). Amsterdam: Elsevier.

Goldstein, L., Burdick, J. A., & Lazslo, M. (1970). A quantitative analysis of the EEG during sleep in normal subjects. *Acta Physiologica Academiae Scientiarum Hungaricae, 37,* 291-300.

Goldstein, L., Stolzfus, N. W., & Gardocki, J. F. (1972). Changes in interhemispheric amplitude relationships in EEG during sleep. *Physiology and Behaviour, 8,* 811-815.

Gordon, H. W., Frooman, B., & Lavie, P. (1982). Shift in cognitive asymmetry between waking from REM and NREM sleep. *Neuropsychologia, 20,* 99-103.

Greenberg, M. S., & Farah, M. J. (1986). The laterality of dreaming. *Brain and Cognition, 5,* 307-420.

Jouvet, M. (1973). Essai sur la rêve [Essay on dreaming]. *Archives Italiennes de Biologie, 11,* 564-567.

Herman, J. H. (1984). Experimental investigations of the psychophysiology of REM sleep including the question of lateralization. *Research Communications in Psychology, Psychiatry and Behavior, 9,* 53-75.

Hirshkowitz, M., Ware, J. C., Turner, D., & Karakan, I. (1979). EEG amplitude asymmetry during sleep. *Sleep Research, 8,* 25.

Humphrey, M. E., & Zangwill, O. L. (1951). Cessation of dreaming after brain injury. *Journal of Neurology, Neurosurgery and Psychiatry, 14,* 322-325.

Klein, R., & Armitage, R. (1979). Rhythms in human performance: 1.5 hour oscillations in cognitive style. *Science, 204,* 1326-1328.

Kripke, D., Fleck, P. A., Mullaney, D. J., & Levy, M. L. (1983). Behavioral analogs of the REM-NonREM cycle. In Mendelwitcz & von Praag (Eds.), *Advances in Biological Psychiatry, 11* (pp. 72-79). Basel: Karger.

Laurian, S., Le, P. K., & Gaillard, J. M. (1984). Spectral analysis of sleep stages as a function of clocktime or sleep cycles. *Research Communications in Psychology, Psychiatry and Behavior, 9,* 77-86.

Lavie, P. (1974). Differential effects of REM and non-REM awakenings on the spiral aftereffect. *Physiological Psychology, 2,* 107-108.

Lavie, P., & Giora, Z. (1973). Spiral aftereffects duration following awakening from REM and non-REM sleep. *Perception and Psychophysics, 14,* 19-20.

Lavie, P., & Sutter, D. (1975). Differential responding to the beta movement after waking from REM and non-REM sleep. *American Journal of Psychology, 88,* 595-603.

Lavie, P., Tzishinsky, O., Epstein, R., & Frooman, B. (1984). Cognitive asymmetry, REM sleep and dreaming. In M. Bosinelli & P. Cicogna (Eds.), *Psychology of dreaming,* (pp. 117-129), Bologna; Italy: CLUEB.

Lavie, P., Matanya, Y., & Yehuda, S. (1984). Cognitive asymmetries after waking from REM and nonREM sleep in right handed females. *International Journal of Neuroscience, 23,* 111–116.

Lavie, P., & Tzischinsky, O. (1984). Cognitive Asymmetries after waking from REM and nonREM sleep: Effects of delayed testing and handedness. *International Journal of Neuroscience, 23,* 311–315.

Lavie, P., & Tzischinsky, O. (1985). Cognitive asymmetry and dreaming: Lack of relationship. *American Journal of Psychology, 98,* 353–361.

Manseau, C., & Broughton, R., (1984). Bilaterally synchronous ultradian EEG rhythms in awake adult humans. *Psychophysiology, 21,* 265–273.

Moffit, A., Hoffmann, R., Wells, R., Armitage, R., Pigeau, R., & Shearer, J. (1982). Individual differences among pre and post-awakening EEG correlates of dream reports following arousals from different stages of sleep. *Psychiatric Journal of the University of Ottawa, 7,* 111–125.

Moffit, A., Hoffmann, R., Wells, R., Shaerer, J., & Armitage, R. (1985, July). *Individual differences in the electrophysiological organization and interrelation of state: Stages REM and awake.* Paper presented at the meeting of the Sleep Research Society, Seattle.

Murri, L., Stefanini, A., Navona, C., Dominici, L., Muratorio, A., & Goldstein, L. (1982). Automatic analysis of hemispheric EEG relationships during wakefulness and sleep. *Research Communication in Psychology, Psychiatry and Behavior, 7,* 109–118.

Murri, L., Arena, R., Siciliano, G., Mazzotta, R., & Muratorio, A. (1984). Dream recall in patients with focal cerebral lesions. *Archives of Neurology, 41,* 183–185.

Murri, L., Massetani, R., Siciliano, G., Giovanditti, L., & Arena, R. (1985). Dream recall after sleep interruption in brain-injured patients. *Sleep, 8,* 356–362.

Murri, L., Stefanini, A., Bonanni, E., Cei, C., Navona, C., & Denoth F. (1984). Hemispheric EEG differences during REM sleep in dextrals and sinistrals. *Research Communication in Psychology, Psychiatry and Behavior, 9,* 109–119.

Nielsen, J. M. (1955). Occipital lobes, dreams and psychosis. *Journal of Nervous and Mental Diseases, 121,* 50–52.

Ornstein, R. E. (1972). *The psychology of consciousness.* San Francisco: W. H. Freeman.

Rosadini, G., Ferrillo, F., Gasperetto, B., Rodriguez, G., & Sannita, W. G. (1984). Topographic distribution of quantitative EEG during human sleep. *Research Communications in Psychology, Psychiatry and Behavior, 9,* 43–52.

Rosekind, M. R., Coates, T. J., & Zarcone, V. P. (1979). Lateral dominance during wakefulness, NREM stage 2 sleep and REM sleep. *Sleep Research, 8,* 126.

Violani, C., Bertini, M., Zoccolotti, P., & Di Stefano, L. (1983). Dream recall as a function of individual patterns of hemispheric lateralization. *Sleep Research, 12,* 190.

Violani, C., De Gennaro, L., & Capogna, M. (1984). EEG and EOG indices of hemispheric asymmetries during sleep. *Research Communications in Psychology, Psychiatry and Behavior, 9,* 95–107.

4 Lateralized Task Performance After Awakening From Sleep

Ruth A. Reinsel and John Antrobus
City College of the City University of New York

INTRODUCTION

The Biological State Carry-over Effect

The process of awakening from sleep is not instantaneous. There is reason to believe that the transition to wakefulness is a gradual phenomenon, where the influence of the prior sleep stage may persist for an appreciable amount of time after awakening. These sleep-state aftereffects have been found for fantasy and dream reporting, for perception and memory, and possibly for some EEG measures. In some cases the carry-over effects appear to be stage-specific. This evidence will be summarized here.

Evidence for carry-over effects in the domain of dream reporting and fantasy is quite robust. The superiority of dream recall after stage REM is well known. Whether this represents a difference in mentation production during sleep itself, or whether it reflects a difference between stages in the ability to store and later retrieve sleep mentation in the waking state is not clear. Nevertheless, in the period immediately after awakening from REM the individual appears to have greater access to prior mentation experiences. Retrieval from long-term memory also appears to be enhanced; Rosenblatt (this volume) reports that subjects shown movie clips prior to sleep showed better recall of these clips after REM than Stage 2 awakenings.

Differential carry-over effects on fantasy processes have been demonstrated upon awakening from sleep. Stories given in response to TAT cards were longer, more complex, and more visual and affect-laden after REM awakenings than after Stage 2 (Fiss, Klein, & Bokert, 1966); and after interrupted as opposed to completed REM periods (Fiss, Ellman, & Klein, 1969). The fantasy and affect of the TAT stories given after REM awakenings showed similarities to dreams recalled on the same awakenings. The authors suggested that the waking TAT stories reflected a continuation of the cognitive processes that are involved in dreaming. Conceptualizing dreaming as a drive state, these authors feel that "if a drive state continues to be active as a person passes from one state of consciousness to another, schemata associated with this drive will continue to be recruited" (Fiss et al., 1966, p. 550).

The process of visual perception seems to be influenced especially by carry-over effects. Here, evidence suggests that the brain state after awakening from REM sleep is somehow different from other stages. Lavie (1976) reports studies on the spiral after-effect (SAE) and the beta movement or phi phenomenon, conducted after awakening subjects from either REM or NREM sleep. Susceptibility to both of these visual illusions was greater after REM sleep, as shown by the duration of the SAE and the increased range of frequencies yielding the phi phenomenon.

Several investigations of short-term and long-term memory upon sleep interruption have found stage-specific carry-over effects that may be reflected in both immediate and delayed recall of materials given for learning upon awakening from sleep. Stones (1977) gave subjects word lists to learn after REM, NREM, or a Waking Control. Immediate memory was poorest after NREM awakenings, but was as good after REM as in Waking. Delayed recall was tested after a 20-min interval filled with an interference task (Ravens Progressive Matrices) to prevent verbal rehearsal of the material. After this 20-min interval, NREM recall declined, but REM and Waking maintained their high levels of performance. This suggests that the carry-over effect may dissipate at different rates for REM and NREM.

The effect of depth of sleep on memory after awakening was tested by Akerstedt and Gillberg (1979). Looking at NREM stages only, they compared long-term memory for items presented on arousal from either a baseline night or a night of recovery sleep following 64 hr of sleep deprivation. The increased depth of sleep on the recovery night impaired morning recall for the information presented during the night. Similarly, Bonnet (1983) found that memory was worse after Stage 4 awakenings than after Stage 2, presumably due to the greater depth of sleep in Stage 4. If, however, the subjects were given an additional 8 min awake before beginning the memory task, scores improved. This effect was interpreted as supporting an arousal explanation; in effect, subjects needed more time to wake up after Stage 4.

This interpretation is supported by reaction-time data presented by Feltin and Broughton (1968), who found that reaction times to light flashes after slow-wave sleep were significantly longer than after REM. Arousal from

SWS appeared to be progressive, whereas subjects appeared more alert immediately after REM awakenings. Similarly, Goodenough, Lewis, Shapiro, Jaret, and Sleser (1965) report that time to pick up a telephone and make a verbal response was nearly twice as long after NREM as after REM awakenings (13 s vs. 7 s, respectively). These response times were computed *after* EEG signs of arousal had appeared on the record.

Evidence for EEG carry-over effects is fragmentary. It has been reported that in some normal subjects, upon awakening from slow-wave sleep, the delta waves of the prior sleep state continue to be present in the waking EEG for as long as 20 min in some cases (Broughton, 1968). The same effect, seen in hypersomniacs, has been termed "sleep drunkenness" (Nevsimalova, Roth, Sagova, Paroubkova, & Horakova, 1981). In their study of the visual evoked potential (VEP) in sleep, Myslobodsky, Ben–Mayor, Yedid–Levy, and Minz (1976) found a sleep-specific asymmetry in the VEP alpha after-discharge which persisted for 10 to 20 min after awakening. A similar effect had been previously reported by Broughton (1968). On the other hand, Herman, Roffwarg, and Hirshkowitz (1981) report pilot EEG data (not evoked potentials) indicating that the prevailing RH activation in REM shifts back to LH dominance within 10 s of arousal.

Only two studies to date have attempted to relate EEG measures before and after awakening in the same subjects. With four subjects in each group, Moffitt et al. (1982) found that these correlations are high only for high dream recallers, and low for infrequent dream recallers. Pivik, Bylsma, Busby, and Sawyer (1982), in six subjects, found no consistent relationship in lateralization between pre- and postawakening EEG characteristics. These studies do not provide convincing evidence that the awake-state EEG is strongly influenced by the prior sleep stage; but the hypothesis cannot be definitively rejected, due to the small sample sizes in these studies.

Is the Carry-over Effect Lateralized by Sleep Stage?

Although the difference in cerebral asymmetry between REM and NREM sleep has not been clearly established to date (Antrobus, 1987), the original report by Goldstein, Stoltzfus, and Gardocki (1972) of right-hemisphere dominance in REM aroused great interest, and was widely cited in support of Galin's (1974), Broughton's (1975), and Bakan's (1978) thesis of the unique contribution of the right hemisphere to the dreaming process. As Bakan (1978) put it in his influential formulation,

> There are some striking similarities between REM dream thought and right hemisphere thought. The mentation of both dreaming and the right hemisphere is characterized by reliance on imagery, affect and primary process

thought. . . . The evidence from diverse sources converges to support the theory of a cyclic ascendance in the functioning of a right hemisphere system during sleep (and perhaps in wakefulness) which is manifested by changes at the physiological (REM state physiology) and psychological levels (dreams). (p. 286)

Following up on this lead, Lavie and his colleagues at the Technion Institute in Israel conducted several studies to assess the function of the right hemisphere immediately upon awakening from REM or NREM sleep. They administered a battery of lateralized cognitive tasks to 12 male subjects over 2 nights in the laboratory. While there was no difference in total performance scores between sleep stages, they found that performance of right-hemisphere (RH) tasks was facilitated after REM awakenings, while left-hemisphere (LH) tasks showed better performance after NREM awakenings (Gordon, Frooman, & Lavie, 1982). Replication studies showed that the effect was present in right-handed females as well ($n = 11$; Lavie, Matanya, & Yehuda, 1984), but not in 24 left-handed subjects (Lavie & Tzischinsky, 1984, Experiment 2). Using two groups of nine right-handed males, these same authors also demonstrated that if the onset of cognitive testing was delayed for 35 or 75 min after awakening, the lateralized after-effects were no longer present (Lavie & Tzischinsky, 1984, Experiment 1).

Independent evidence of right-hemisphere facilitation during or after REM sleep, was provided by a group of investigators at the University of Rome. Bertini, Violani, Zoccolotti, Antonelli, and Di Stefano (1984) used a tactile recognition task to assess performance of the contralateral hemisphere after awakenings from REM or Stage 2 sleep. Their findings indicated superior left-hand (i.e., RH) performance overall, reflecting the RH advantage for spatial processing (Bryden, 1982; De Renzi, 1978). Additionally, there was a hand by stage interaction, such that the left-hand (RH) advantage was significantly greater after REM awakenings, while right-hand (LH) performance showed improvement after Stage 2.

Lateralized Carry-over Effects: Summary

The studies reviewed in the preceding sections provide a considerable weight of evidence that, while it is not clearly demonstrated that REM and NREM differ in cerebral dominance,

1. Some differential effect of the previous sleep stage carries over into the waking state and can influence perception and cognitive performance.

2. Awakening from REM sleep has different implications for performance on lateralized cognitive tasks than NREM awakenings.
3. This differential carry-over effect remains fairly stable for at least 15–25 min, and thereafter declines, so that if testing is delayed for 35 or 75 min after awakening, the effect is no longer present.

On the other hand, it must be recognized that the studies on carry-over effects that give rise to these conclusions rely on two major assumptions: (a) that general brain states can be inferred from behavior; (b) that the same brain/behavior relationships exist in waking as were present in the previous stage of sleep. Both of these assumptions require more experimental scrutiny. In the absence of direct measurements of cortical activity in the brain during and after sleep, these two assumptions cannot be accepted as proven.

Rationale for the Present Study

The purpose of the present investigation is to assess the nature of stage-specific carry-over effects on lateralized cognitive tasks. This study was undertaken, in part, to replicate the findings of lateralized performance carry-over effects reported by Gordon et al. (1982), Lavie et al. (1974), Lavie and Tzischinsky (1974), and Bertini et al. (1984). Experimental procedures were designed to be as similar as possible to these prior studies.

To examine the additional hypothesis that time of night may alter or mediate hemispheric asymmetry effects, the present study incorporated a time of night manipulation into the design. Cohen (1977) has proposed that a systematic bias favoring the LH develops over the course of the night. The evidence he has advanced for this proposition is based on content analysis of dreams and on the directionality of eye movements. It is not clearly established that these measures are directly related to hemisphericity (Ehrlichman, Antrobus, & Wiener, 1985; Ehrlichman & Weinberger, 1978). If Cohen's Gradual Increase in Left Dominance (GILD) hypothesis is correct, and if the LH dominance is reflected in carry-over effects, late awakenings should show better performance on LH cognitive tasks. To test the GILD hypothesis further, awakenings were made from REM or Stage 2 sleep either in the first or the second half of the sleep period (defined as the midpoint between the time of lights out and the time of morning wake-up). Previous reports of carry-over effects were generally confined to the first half of the night (awakenings in the second and third sleep cycles). We proposed to investigate whether the carry-over effects would vary in accordance with the time of night when measurements were taken.

Although EEG data during sleep were collected as an integral part of this study, the EEG data will be reported separately. This chapter will focus on the behavioral performance data, which extend the study of lateralized cognitive processing after REM and Stage 2 sleep to both early and late phases of the sleep period.

The major hypothesis of the study was formulated in accordance with the findings of previous investigators (Gordon et al., 1982; Lavie et al., 1984; Bertini et al., 1984). A significant hemisphere by stage of sleep interaction was predicted, wherein RH task performance would be facilitated after REM awakenings, while LH task performance would be improved after Stage 2 sleep.

METHOD

Subjects

Thirty-three right-handed volunteers participated in this study (22 males and 11 females). Handedness was assessed by a modified version of the Edinboro Inventory (Oldfield, 1971). Only 3 subjects had a left-handed relative among their immediate family. All subjects were assessed to be normal sleepers. Ages ranged from 17 to 36. Most participants were college or graduate students, and were paid $20–$30 for their participation in the study.

Procedure

Subjects spent one afternoon or early evening control session in the lab to familiarize them with the tasks and to gather waking control data on all measures. Subjects returned to the lab for 3 nonconsecutive nights, of which the first served as an adaptation night. Sleep EEG, EOG, and EMG were recorded on a Grass Model 78 polygraph and scored by the Rechtschaffen and Kales (1968) criteria. On the two experimental nights, subjects were awakened twice per night, in REM or Stage 2 in counterbalanced order, with awakenings scheduled for early or late in the night (defined as the first or second half of the sleep period, with the first REM cycle omitted from sampling.)

Immediately after awakening, subjects were administered a battery of cognitive tasks chosen to assess the functions of the left and right hemispheres. The order of task administration was completely counterbalanced within subjects using a Latin Square design, so that order and practice effects would not affect any experimental condition more than another. In order to maximize the probability of detecting carry-over effects, and to minimize the influence of the waking state, subjects performed the tasks while remaining in bed, with room lights at low levels, and verbal interaction with subjects was kept to a minimum. Each task required about 1-2 min, with the exception of the tactile task, which took about 4 to 5 min. The entire testing procedure was generally completed within 20–25 min and the subject was then allowed to return to sleep.

Tasks

Tasks were chosen to assess cognitive functions specialized to the left or right cerebral hemisphere. Rather than employing a single measure, multiple tasks were used to assess the extent of the performance carry-over effects. By using several tasks, it was hoped to generalize the carry-over tasks to the functions of an entire hemisphere, rather than to isolated cognitive abilities. Additionally, the variety of tasks used allowed the assessment of asymmetries in the visual, auditory, tactile, and motor modalities. Considered in task selection were (1) The need for sufficient items to make several independent versions of the task for use on the different awakenings; and (2) Use of several trials on each task so as to yield reliable scores.

In order to replicate the Gordon et al., (1982) study as closely as possible, several tasks from the Cognitive Laterality Battery (CLB) used in their study were retained for use. The CLB has been validated as reliably measuring lateralized cerebral function in brain-damaged and normal adults (Bentin & Gordon, 1979; Gordon, 1986) and in learning-disabled children (Gordon, 1983). The CLB tasks are marked with an asterisk in the descriptions that will be given. These tasks included *Serial Numbers (a modified digit span) and Anagrams as measures of LH function; and *Form Completion (a Gestalt picture recognition task) and *Point Localization, a spatial orientation task, as measures of RH functioning. The latter task is scored as millimeters of deviation of reported from actual location; thus a lower score indicates better performance. In a pilot study with 10 subjects (Reinsel, 1985) the *Form Completion task significantly discriminated between REM and Stage 2 awakenings, with better performance after REM sleep.

The Tactile Recognition task was included to replicate the results of Bertini et al. (1984). On a movable plastic belt are affixed Plexiglas shapes, which the subject is asked to explore with the first two fingers of each hand, without looking at the stimuli. A matching-to-sample response is required, by choosing the correct stimulus from three response alternatives. The task is performed with alternate hands for seven trials with each hand, in counterbalanced order. This task is considered lateralized, since when tactile stimulation is received from the index and middle fingers of each hand, the sensory input is processed entirely by the contralateral hemisphere (Brinkman & Kuipers, 1972; Ghez, 1981, p. 283). Previous work presenting tactile stimuli and requiring selection of the identical stimulus from a visually presented array found this task to involve RH abilities in brain-damaged patients (De Renzi, 1978) and in split-brain patients (Nebes, 1978).

While the Tactile Recognition task may be understood to represent processing of sensory input, a Choice Reaction Time (RT) task was also included to assess motor output. These latter two tasks, when performed with the left hand, assess RH function; with the right hand, LH performance. The Choice RT task employed a device that presented the subject with stimulus lights on either side of a central "warning" indicator. After a 2-s foreperiod, the left or right light was illuminated in random sequence. The subject was instructed to press the response button on the same side as the illuminated stimulus light. The subject's response stopped a clock, which indicated reaction time to the nearest hundredth of a second. Six trials were conducted with each hand, of which the last five were averaged to provide a mean score for each hand. The order of starting hand was counterbalanced across trials. RT scores were log-transformed and averaged to remove skew before being entered in the data analysis.

Thus, four measures are designated Left-hemisphere Tasks: Anagrams, *Serial Numbers, right-handed Tactile Recognition (TAC-rh), and right-handed Reaction Time (RT-rh). The Right-hemisphere Tasks consist of *Form Completion, *Point Localization, left-handed Tactile Recognition (TAC-lh), and left-handed Reaction Time (RT-lh). Further details on the administration of the individual tasks, and justification of their lateralization in the human brain, have been presented elsewhere (Reinsel, 1988).

Stanford Sleepiness Scale (SSS). The SSS is widely utilized in sleep research when a subjective rating of sleepiness is desired (Herscovitch & Broughton, 1981; Hoddes, Zarcone, Smythe, Phillips, & Dement, 1973). In order to determine if there is any systematic variation in subjective sleepiness as a function of time of night or stage of sleep, the SSS was administered to each subject immediately upon awakening and prior to the administration of any other task. The scale consists of seven statements, where 1 is the most alert end of the scale, and seven is the sleepiest. In pilot work (Reinsel, 1985) the SSS significantly discriminated between Waking, REM, and Stage 2 awakenings and showed significant time-of-night effects over repeated arousals within the night.

RESULTS

Tasks

Performance on the left and right hemisphere tasks is presented graphically in Figures 1 and 2, respectively. The between-subject variability in perfor-

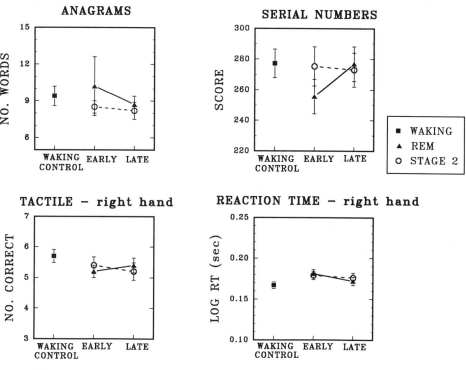

FIG. 4.1. Results of left hemisphere tasks (mean ± standard error of mean) by stage and time of night. Solid lines = REM awakenings, dashed lines = Stage 2 awakenings.

mance, as indexed by the standard deviations, was generally quite comparable between the waking control and the nocturnal awakenings, regardless of sleep stage or time of night (see Table 1).

Repeated-measures analysis of variance tests were computed for each task individually to examine the main effects of stage of sleep (REM vs. Stage 2), time of night (Early vs. Late), and gender. These results are summarized in Table 4.2. None of these variables was significant, either as a main effect, or as an interaction term. Specifically, these factors did not account for significant differences between REM and Stage 2 awakenings for any task. Due to the ineffectiveness of the time of night manipulation, the means in Table 4.1 are collapsed across Early and Late awakenings within stage.

Time of Night

Table 4.3 presents the mean elapsed time between lights out (LO) and the first and second awakenings of a night. Due to the randomization of conditions, on any given night, both awakenings might fall in the Early

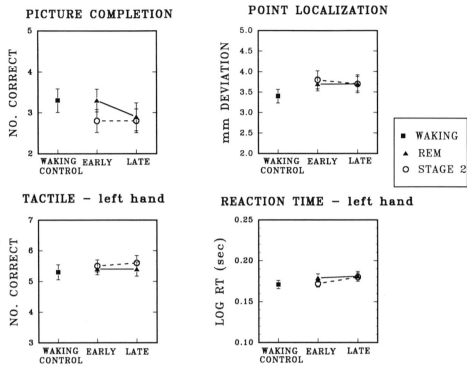

FIG. 4.2.   Results of right hemisphere tasks (mean ± standard error of mean) by stage and time of night. Solid lines = REM awakenings, dashed lines = Stage 2 awakenings.

condition, the Late condition, or consist of an Early followed by a Late awakening. As can be seen in Table 4.2, there was no indication that performance differed consistently between early and late awakenings for any task. This result fails to support the Gradual Increase in Left Dominance (GILD) hypothesis proposed by Cohen (1977), which would have predicted more LH dominance on late awakenings. Pilot work with 10 subjects (Reinsel, 1985) found that performance differed significantly between early and late awakenings; however in the pilot study, subjects were awakened four or five times in a single night, and the accumulated sleep deprivation may have accounted for the performance changes. In the present study, with only two awakenings per night, separated by lengthy intervals, time-of-night effects were not seen.

Sleepiness

The only measure to show significant variation between experimental conditions was the Stanford Sleepiness Scale (SSS). Here, stage of sleep had

TABLE 4.1
Means and Standard Deviations for All Tasks (raw scores) by Condition
(Waking, REM, Stage 2) Collapsed Across Early and Late Awakenings

Variable	Waking	REM	Stage 2
*Serial numbers	277.2 ± 53.7	266.3 ± 64.4	274.1 ± 67.8
Anagrams	9.4 ± 4.8	8.3 ± 3.6	8.4 ± 3.4
*Point loc.	3.4 ± 1.0	3.7 ± 1.1	3.7 ± 1.2
*Form completion	3.3 ± 1.7	3.1 ± 1.9	2.8 ± 1.6
Tactile (rh)	5.7 ± 1.2	5.3 ± 1.3	5.3 ± 1.6
Tactile (lh)	5.3 ± 1.4	5.4 ± 1.2	5.5 ± 1.3
LOG rt (rh)	0.167 ± 0.02	0.176 ± 0.03	0.177 ± 0.03
LOG rt (lh)	0.171 ± 0.03	0.180 ± 0.03	0.176 ± 0.03
SSS	2.7 ± 0.09	5.3 ± 1.2	4.6 ± 1.2

by far the most powerful effect, with REM awakenings resulting in reports of more sleepiness ($F(1,25) = 15.47, p = .0006$). This finding is in contrast to the reports of Feltin and Broughton (1968) and Goodenough et al. (1965), where subjects were more alert after REM awakenings than after non-REM sleep. The main effect of time of night was not significant in itself, but the interaction of Stage of Sleep with Time of Night suggested more sleepiness on early REM awakenings, while Stage 2 did not vary (Stage × Time: $F(1,25) = 3.88, p = .06$).

Tactile Recognition

In the attempt to replicate previous claims of differences between REM and NREM for lateralized tasks, the results of the Tactile Recognition task were of particular interest. Unfortunately our data show no sign of any difference between left and right hands in tactile sensitivity as a function of stage of sleep. Possible explanations for the discrepant results between this study and the Bertini et al. (1984) experiment will be considered in the Discussion section.

Dream Recall

Since Violani, Bertini, Di Stefano, and Zoccolotti (1983) found that individual differences in dream recall were an important factor in modulating the effect of the lateralized tactile task, we also examined this variable. In the Violani et al. study, poor dream recallers showed more RH activation following REM sleep (i.e., better left-hand performance on the tactile task). In the present data, however, no such effect was found. Subjects' self-report of their dream recall frequency was obtained on the initial screening questionnaire. Subjects were divided into groups of High

TABLE 4.2
Results of repeated-measures Analysis of Variance for Individual
Performance Measures: Main Effects of Gender, Stage (REM vs. Stage 2),
Time (Early vs. Late), and Interaction Terms

| | Performance Measures | | | | | |
	ANA	SNUM	LOC	PIC	TAC	RT
Effect						
Gender						
F	0.00	0.98	0.02	0.00	0.56	0.28
p	ns	ns	ns	ns	ns	ns
Stage						
F	0.04	0.62	0.,05	1.52	0.12	0.26
p	ns	ns	ns	ns	ns	ns
Stage * Gender						
F	1.20	2.84	1.10	0.24	1.79	0.02
p	ns	<.11	ns	ns	ns	ns
Time						
F	0.35	1.01	0.40	1.19	0.00	0.01
p	ns	ns	ns	ns	ns	ns
Time * Gender						
F	0.34	0.25	0.09	1.24	0.01	0.53
p	ns	ns	ns	ns	ns	ns
Stage * Time						
F	1.29	1.90	0.27	0.80	0.31	1.20
p	ns	ns	ns	ns	ns	ns
Stage * Time * Gender						
F	0.06	0.23	0.27	0.66	0.24	4.73
p	ns	ns	ns	ns	ns	.037

Note: ANA = Anagrams, SNUM = *Serial Numbers, LOC = *Point
Localization, PIC = *Picture Completion, TAC = Tactile Recognition, RT =
Choice Reaction Time.
Degrees of freedom for all effects are (1,31).

Recallers (n = 16) and Low Recallers (n = 15). High Recallers reported remembering a dream at least once a week. However, this individual difference variable did not account for significant variance for either hand, as a main effect or in combination with other variables.

Standardized Scores

To replicate further the data analysis used by Lavie and his colleagues, data for each task were converted to z-scores. Standardization of the data in this manner has the advantage of reducing the influence of skew in the distribution of scores, and increasing the validity of parametric statistical tests. Additionally, once the scores have been transformed to a common metric (i.e., standard deviation units) data from one study can be more

TABLE 4.3
Mean Elapsed Sleep Time between Lights Out (LO) and the First and Second Awakenings of a Night

	Elapsed Sleep Time to Awakening (in minutes) Type of Awakening		
Interval	Both early	Mixed	Both late
LO–Awak. 1	178	191	307
Awak. 1–Awak. 2	91	215	126
LO–Awak. 2	239	376	403

Note: Times shown do not include the approximately 25–30 minutes required for administration of the task battery.

easily compared with other studies using different measures. Z-score transformation was accomplished using the pool of all scores on that task, for all subjects and all awakenings.

The standardized scores thus derived for each task were then summed and averaged to provide a total score for all LH tasks (ZLEFT), and similarly for all RH tasks (ZRIGHT). Thus, the summary score ZLEFT includes standardized scores for Anagrams, *Serial Numbers, RT-rh, and TAC-rh. The summary score ZRIGHT includes *Form Completion, *Point Localization, RT-lh, and TAC-lh.

These summary variables were then combined in various ways to duplicate the variables used in the Cognitive Laterality Battery described by Gordon et al., (1982). The difference between ZLEFT and ZRIGHT (ZDIFF) approximates the Cognitive Laterality Quotient (CLQ), a measure of asymmetry in performance between these groups of lateralized tasks. The variables ZLEFT and ZRIGHT were summed (ZSUM) to correspond to Cognitive Performance Quotient (CPQ), a measure of total performance for both hemispheres.

The data for these summary z-score variables are given in Table 4.4. Since the time-of-night manipulation was not significant in any of the analyses, scores were averaged over Early and Late awakenings for each stage. For these z-score variables, a positive sign indicates performance

TABLE 4.4
Standardized z-score Means for LH (ZLEFT) and RH (ZRIGHT) Tasks, Their Difference (ZDIFF) and Their Sum (ZSUM)

Variable	Waking	REM	Stage 2
ZLEFT	+0.063	−0.032	+0.0002
ZRIGHT	−0.088	+0.038	+0.004
ZDIFF	−0.151	+0.071	+0.004
ZSUM	−0.026	+0.006	+0.005

above the mean of the distribution, while a negative sign indicates below-average scoring. Inspection of the LH task means (ZLEFT) show that both REM and Stage 2 performance on these tasks falls very close to the mean of the distribution. The RH tasks (ZRIGHT) are performed slightly better in REM than in Waking, but REM and NREM scores are identical. For both sets of tasks, deviations from the mean are on the order of less than one tenth of one standard deviation, and as such are more likely to represent sampling error than any meaningful variation in the data. A repeated-measures ANOVA including ZLEFT and ZRIGHT as a Hemisphere factor found no differential performance of either set of tasks as a function of sleep stage or time of night (see Table 4.5). In particular the predicted Stage × Hemisphere interaction was not present. Gender was not included in this analysis since it did not account for any meaningful part of the variance on the individual tasks.

Next, ZDIFF (ZRIGHT − ZLEFT) was computed as a measure of difference in lateralized performance. In this case, positive values indicate higher scores on the RH tasks; negative values are associated with better performance on LH tasks. Lavie's laboratory has found significant differences between REM and NREM using a similar variable (CLQ). As expected, the LH tasks are performed best in the Waking Control. REM gives a very slight advantage to the RH tasks, but in Stage 2 there is no difference between the two sets of tasks. However, differences between the three conditions are not significant ($F(2,64) = 1.79$, ns). Thus, the present data do not confirm the Technion group's findings of stage-specific performance differences on these lateralized tasks.

If we combine the ZLEFT and ZRIGHT scores into one global measure of performance (ZSUM), we have an index equivalent to the CLB's Cognitive Performance Quotient (CPQ). Lavie and his coworkers found that this total performance score did not vary with stage of sleep. We confirm this finding. There is no evidence of any difference in total

TABLE 4.5
Results of repeated-measures Analysis of Variance on ZLEFT Compared to ZRIGHT: Main Effects of Hemisphere (LH vs RH), Stage (REM vs Stage 2) and Time (Early vs. Late), and Interaction Terms

Effect	$F(1,32)$	p value
Hemisphere	0.24	ns
Stage	0.00	ns
Time	0.02	ns
Hem * Stage	0.44	ns
Hem * Time	0.01	ns
Stage * Time	0.27	ns
Hem * Stage * Time	2.58	<.12

performance between sleep stages, or between early and late awakenings. More surprisingly, there is no difference even between the waking control session and performance after nocturnal awakenings ($F(2,64) = 0.06$, ns). This stability in performance at such widely separated points on the presumed underlying circadian curve is truly remarkable.

DISCUSSION

Lateralized Carryover Effects?

The results of this study fail to support the conclusions of five other studies: (Bertini et al., 1984; Gordon et al., 1982; Lavie et al., 1984; Lavie & Tzischinsky, 1984, Violani et al., 1983). While this failure to replicate does not invalidate the previous investigations, the large sample size in this study argues that if there is a relationship, it should have been detected. According to the power analysis (Cohen & Cohen, 1975) an N of 30 gives an 80% probability of detection of a moderately strong effect (for example, one with an effect size of .5). An effect size of this magnitude is indicated by the significant differences in task performance found between sleep stages by Gordon et al. (1982), Lavie et al. (1984), and Bertini et al. (1984). On the other hand, if the effect size is assumed to be much smaller (for instance, .2) a sample size of 196 subjects would be required to give an 80% detection probability with the standard significance level of alpha = .05. Thus, the failure to find differences between REM and NREM awakenings indicates that the lateralized cognitive effect, if present, is too weak to be considered either robust or reliable.

The present failure to replicate increases the caution with which we view the assumption of RH dominance in REM sleep, and the persistence of this asymmetry into the waking state as lateralized performance carry-over effects. In an attempt to account for these conflicting results, several types of procedural and statistical differences between these studies and the present work will be considered.

Stage of Awakening

In previous studies reporting performance asymmetries, some proportion of awakenings were made in Stages 3 or 4. Also, in the memory studies, the strongest carryover effects were found after Stage 4 awakenings. In the present study with Non-REM awakenings limited to Stage 2 sleep, we do not find any such performance asymmetries.

Testing Conditions

The procedures in this study were chosen to be as similar as possible to those other studies: only two awakenings per night, testing durations of similar lengths, and so on. Wherever possible, the performance tasks used were identical to those used in the previous studies; if they differed (e.g. *Verbal Fluency vs. Anagrams), the differences were not felt to be substantial. Care was taken in selecting subjects to insure that they were right-handed, and normal sleepers, free from excessive use of caffeine, drugs, or alcohol.

One difference between the procedures of the present study and the method used by Lavie and his colleagues involves the order of administration of the individual tasks in the battery. In Lavie's work, all tasks drawing on the abilities of a given hemisphere were presented together; order of hemispheres was counterbalanced between subjects. In this study, tasks were counterbalanced individually, rather than in blocks. The rationale for this was that if the carry-over effect dissipated rapidly, we wanted to have at least one or two tasks given for each hemisphere before the effect disappeared. On the other hand, one might argue that by forcing the hemispheres to alternate in task processing, this procedure may actually have worked against the effect we were trying to demonstrate. To evaluate the effects of task order within the battery, z-scores for each task were derived as a function of task position within the battery. If the carry-over effect is strongest immediately after awakening, then only the first or second task administered would be expected to show significant asymmetry effects. If the carry-over effect remains strong throughout the testing period, then order within the task battery should have no effect on performance. Correlations of the individual z-scores with order of administration on any given awakening were computed separately for the waking, REM, and Stage 2 conditions. These correlations were very close to zero in all but two instances, indicating that for most tasks order of administration within the battery was not an important factor in the results. Of the two exceptions, one was for left-handed Tactile Recognition in Waking only ($r = +0.35$, $p < .05$). Since a similar effect was not seen for right-handed performance on the latter task, the correlation may be considered spurious. The other exception is for *Picture Completion in REM ($r = +0.33$, $p < .05$) when the task appears late in the battery. This finding is contrary to the expectation of greater RH bias immediately after awakening from REM sleep. Thus these analyses do not support the argument that order of task administration within the battery influenced performance after awakening.

Trial Duration and Response Modality

A methodological difference also exists in the procedures used on the tactile task. Subjects in this study had 15 s to perform each trial, and during this time the standard as well as the comparison stimuli were available for palpation. In the Bertini et al. (1984) study, though total trial duration was the same, subjects had only 7 s for tactile palpation of the stimulus, the rest of the trial being devoted to response selection. A comparable increase in the haptic exploration time for the standard stimulus from 4 to 16 s has been shown by Davidson, Abbott, and Gershenfeld (1974) to increase accuracy of response selection significantly. A further difference in the tactile procedure involved response modality; the verbal response used here may be less sensitive to hemispheric asymmetries than the manual pointing response used in the original study (Gardner et al., 1977; Milner & Lines, 1982).

Memory Load

Violani (personal communication, December, 1986) has suggested that this minor difference in task instructions adds a memory dimension to the lateralized processing of the tactile information. Since, in the Bertini et al. (1984) study, subjects were not allowed to go back to the standard stimulus to verify the similarity, they had to maintain a memory representation of the test stimulus while comparing it with the three distractor items. Such memory loads were not imposed in the present work. The ability to recheck the original stimulus while comparing it with the distractor items may have raised accuracy levels to the point where minor carry-over effects were masked.

Certain studies show that laterality effects are most clearly seen when a memory load is imposed on the task (Dee & Fontenot, 1973; Jason, 1983; Oscar–Berman, Rehbein, Porfert, & Goodglass, 1978; Young & Ratcliff, 1983). This hypothesis is also relevant to Lavie's studies, since the two tasks in the CLB that showed the greatest asymmetries with sleep stage both involved a memory load: Point Localization for the RH and nonverbal serial recall for the LH. This interpretation is not supported by the results from the *Serial Numbers (Digit Span) task in the present study. Digit Span is the prototypical short-term memory task, yet the data showed no significant differences between sleep stages. However, Violani (personal communication, July, 1987) has also suggested that the memory factor only becomes relevant when task stimuli are presented to the subject in a lateralized fashion, which was not done in this or the previous studies.

Data Transformation

Other variations in method involve the statistical treatment of the data. In the CLB studies the data were standardized by conversion to z-scores on the basis of normative responses from large numbers of normal individuals. In other words, they derived waking norms from a very large number of adult controls on these same tasks, and then used the waking norms to score the sleep data.

The present data were standardized by computing z-scores from the pool of all available data for each task. This method is preferable to the use of a normative data base collected under waking conditions, inasmuch as the distribution of postsleep scores may lie outside the range of the waking scores. If waking and postsleep performance lie on different portions of the distribution, reference to the waking mean and standard deviation might yield a biased and truncated distribution for the sleep scores. Using the full range of behavioral scores, obtained across states, to generate the normal distribution seems to introduce less possible distortion into the data. In hindsight, this concern was not necessary, since the REM and Stage 2 data fell very close to the waking mean on most tasks.

Subject Variation

Entirely apart from questions of procedural variations and statistical treatment of the data, variability among subjects poses problems for interpretations of laterality in performance. Important sources of variability include gender and handedness. There were no differences between right-handed males and females in this study, which agrees with the finding of Lavie, Metanya, and Yehuda (1984). However, these results conflict with the conclusions of Trotman and Hammond (1979), McGlone (1980) and Bryden (1982) that males are more lateralized than females for verbal and spatial processes.

The original report of Gordon et al. (1982) on stage-specific carry-over effects gives evidence of fairly large individual differences in prevailing patterns of interhemispheric relationships. A careful reading of the Gordon et al. paper tempers the initial impression of an RH advantage after REM and a LH advantage after NREM. In that study, the authors do not claim that REM awakenings, on the average, result in a performance bias for either hemisphere. The difference between the sleep stages is contributed entirely by the NREM awakenings, which lead to a significant advantage for LH tasks. However, there is considerable variability among individuals. In the 12 subjects studied, a variety of patterns of cerebral dominance were shown. Judging by the CLB task performance, 4 subjects were RH-dominant in both stages, but less so after NREM. Another 4Ss were LH-dominant in both REM and NREM, but more so after NREM. Only 3 subjects actually showed LH dominance after NREM and RH dominance after REM, and these asymmetries were of quite small magnitude.

Conclusions

In summary, in a careful attempt to replicate two previous bodies of research, with a larger sample size and very similar procedures, we have failed to demonstrate the performance asymmetries that have been previously reported. One might conclude therefore that these carry-over effects are not as robust and long-lasting as has been previously claimed. Some of the previously reported performance asymmetries may be specific to the individual tasks employed. Additionally, we must bear in mind that apparently minor variations in task instructions and experimental procedures may either obscure behavioral effects, or perhaps even induce effects which are not normally present.

It should be clear from the foregoing discussion that a reassessment of the nature of cerebral dominance during sleep is in order. While shifts in cerebral asymmetry may occur between sleep states and wakefulness, it is not clear that there are any consistent differences in lateralization between REM and NREM sleep (Antrobus, 1987; Ehrlichman et al., 1985). A preliminary report of the EEG data from these same subjects (Reinsel, Antrobus, & Fein, 1989a, 1989b) found EEG asymmetry during sleep only in the delta band, and there was no relationship between EEG measures during sleep and performance on these postawakening laterality measures. This being so, the present failure to document behavioral carry-over effects lateralized by prior sleep stage is not too surprising. The EEG studies have not provided convincing evidence that such lateralized carry-over effects persist in the brain waves for any appreciable time after awakening (Moffitt et al., 1982; Pivik et al., 1982). Thus, if the carry-over effects are not present in the EEG, how then can we expect to find them in postawakening behavioral measures?

The Right Hemisphere and Dreaming

Perhaps it is time to re-evaluate our ideas of the role of the RH in REM sleep and in dreaming. In recent years, the widespread interest in the specialized functions of the two cerebral hemispheres has led to the suggestion that the right hemisphere (RH) plays a special role in dreaming (Bakan, 1978; Broughton, 1975; Galin, 1974). This suggestion is based loosely on the similarity between dreaming and primary process thought, or on the evidence for RH specialization for visual imagery, spatial processing and affect.

However, there is reason to suspect that this hypothesis may be an oversimplified appraisal of the role of the RH in dreaming. Ehrlichman and Barrett (1983) reviewed the literature on the role of the RH in visual imagery, and found very little evidence to support the unique role of the RH as an image generator. Greenberg and Farah (1986) present case studies of patients with localized brain damage, and show that unilateral RH damage does not eliminate the dreaming process. Damage to temporal or parietal cortex seems to be the crucial factor, regardless of left- or right-sided locus; although neurological case studies reviewed by Farah, Gazzaniga, Holtzman, and Kosslyn (1985) suggest that the role of the left hemisphere (LH) in generating mental imagery may be proportionately larger than that of the RH.

The literature on differential hemispheric involvement in dreaming has recently been reviewed by Antrobus (1987), who concurs with the authors just cited in concluding that

> [t]he RH may have a role in producing relatively simple images and sporadically communicating them to the LH during REM sleep. But the LH may be capable of generating all of the imagery qualities that have been associated with REM mentation and of extracting this information and producing, upon awakening, a verbal mentation report. (Antrobus, 1987, p. 366)

Such re-evaluation of the relative roles of the left and right cerebral hemispheres in producing dream imagery and mentation must inform our expectations for performance on tasks that are presumed to tap the differential abilities of the cerebral hemispheres after awakening from sleep states. In a relatively large number of subjects who are neurologically normal, and for whom the task stimuli were not presented exclusively to one or the other cerebral hemisphere, we have been unable to find any evidence that a state of differential hemispheric dominance exists after arousal from either REM or Stage 2 sleep on early or late awakenings. Rather than continuing to focus on minor differences in activation of the two cerebral hemispheres in sleep versus waking, it might be more fruitful in the future to investigate the relative contributions of each hemisphere to the joint processing operations required for performance of complex cognitive functions, and how this processing is affected by changes in cortical activation across varying states of consciousness.

REFERENCES

Akerstedt, T., & Gillberg, M. (1979). Effects of sleep deprivation on memory and sleep latencies in connection with repeated awakenings from sleep. *Psychophysiology, 16,* 49–52.

Antrobus, J. (1987). Cortical hemisphere asymmetry and sleep mentation. *Psychological Review, 94,* 359–368.

Bakan, P. (1978). Dreaming, REM sleep, and the right hemisphere: A theoretical integration. *Journal of Altered States of Consciousness, 3,* 285–307.

Bentin, S., & Gordon, H. W. (1979). Assessment of cognitive asymmetries in brain-damaged and normal subjects: Validation of a test battery. *Journal of Neurology, Neurosurgery and Psychiatry, 42,* 715–723.

Bertini, M., Violani, C., Zoccolotti, P., Antonelli, A., & Di Stefano, L. (1984). Right cerebral activation in REM sleep: Evidence from a unilateral tactile recognition test. *Psychophysiology, 21,* 418–423.

Bonnet, M.H. (1983). Memory for events occurring during arousal from sleep. *Psychophysiology, 20,* 81–87.

Brinkman, J., & Kuipers, H. (1972). Split brain monkeys: Cerebral control of ipsilateral and contralateral arm, hand and finger movements. *Science, 176,* 536–539.

Broughton, R. J. (1968). Sleep disorders: Disorders of arousal? *Science, 159,* 1070–1078.

Broughton, R. (1975). Biorhythmic variations in consciousness and psychological functions. *Canadian Psychological Review, 16,* 217–239.

Bryden, M. P. (1982). *Laterality: Functional asymmetry in the intact brain.* New York: Academic Press.

Cohen, D.B. (1977). Changes in REM dream content during the night: Implications for a hypothesis about changes in cerebral dominance across REM periods. *Perceptual and Motor Skills, 44,* 1267–1277.

Cohen, J., & Cohen, P. (1975). *Applied multiple regression/correlation analysis for the behavioral sciences.* Hillsdale, NJ: Lawrence Erlbaum Associates.

Davidson, P.W., Abbott, A., & Gershenfeld, J. (1974). Influence of exploration time on haptic and visual matching of complex shape. *Perception and Psychophysics, 15,* 539–543.

Dee, H.L., & Fontenot, D.J. (1973). Cerebral dominance and lateral differences in perception and memory. *Neuropsychologia, 11,* 167–173.

De Renzi, E. (1978). Hemispheric asymmetry as evidenced by spatial disorders. In M. Kinsbourne (Ed.), *Asymmetrical function of the brain* (pp. 49–85). New York: Cambridge University Press.

Ehrlichman, H., Antrobus, J.S., & Wiener, M.S. (1985). EEG asymmetry and sleep mentation during REM and NREM. *Brain and Cognition, 4,* 477–485.

Ehrlichman, H., & Barrett, J. (1983). Right hemispheric specialization for mental imagery: A review of the evidence. *Brain and Cognition, 4,* 55–76.

Ehrlichman, H., & Weinberger, A. (1978). Lateral eye movements and hemispheric asymmetry: A critical review. *Psychological Bulletin, 85,* 1080–1101.

Farah, M.J., Gazzaniga, M. S., Holtzman, J.D., & Kosslyn, S.M. (1985). A left hemisphere basis for mental imagery. *Neuropsychologia, 23,* 115–118.

Feltin, M., & Broughton, R.J. (1968). Differential effects of arousal from slow wave sleep versus REM sleep. *Psychophysiology, 5,* 231.

Fiss, H., Ellman, S.J., & Klein, G.S. (1969). Waking fantasies following interrupted and completed REM periods. *Archives of General Psychiatry, 21,* 230–239.

Fiss, H., Klein, G.S., & Bokert, E. (1966). Waking fantasies following interruption of two types of sleep. *Archives of General Psychiatry, 14,* 543–551.

Galin, D. (1974). Implications for psychiatry of left and right cerebral specialization: A neurophysiological context for unconscious processes. *Archives of General Psychiatry, 31,* 572–583.

Gardner, E. B., English, A. G., Flannery, B. M., Hartnett, M. B., McCormick, K., & Wilhelmy, B. B. (1977). Shape-recognition accuracy and response-latency in a bilateral tactile task. *Neuropsychologia, 15,* 607–616.

Ghez, C. (1981). Introduction to the motor systems. In E.R. Kandel & J.H. Schwartz (Eds.), *Principles of neural science* (pp. 271–283). New York: Elsevier/North Holland.

Goldstein, L., Stoltzfus, N.W., & Gardocki, J.F. (1972). Changes in interhemispheric amplitude relationships in the EEG during sleep. *Physiology and Behaviour, 8,* 811–815.

Goodenough, D. R., Lewis, H.B., Shapiro, A., Jaret, L., & Sleser, I. (1965). Dream reporting following abrupt and gradual awakenings from different types of sleep. *Journal of Personality and Social Psychology, 2,* 170–179.

Gordon, H.W. (1983). The learning disabled are cognitively right. *Topics in learning and learning disabilities,* April, 23–39.

Gordon, H.W. (1986). The Cognitive Laterality Battery: Tests of specialized cognitive function. *International Journal of Neuroscience, 29,* 223–244.

Gordon, H.W., Frooman, B., & Lavie, P. (1982). Shift in cognitive asymmetries between wakings from REM and NREM sleep. *Neuropsychologia, 20,* 99–103.

Greenberg, M.S., & Farah, M.J. (1986). The laterality of dreaming. *Brain and Cognition, 5,* 307–321.

Herman, J.H., Roffwarg, H.P., & Hirshkowitz, M. (1981). *Electroencephalographic asymmetries and REM sleep dreaming.* Paper presented at the APSS conference, Hyannis, MA.

Herscovitch, J., & Broughton, R. (1981). Sensitivity of the Stanford Sleepiness Scale to the effects of cumulative partial sleep deprivation and recovery oversleeping. *Sleep, 4,* 83–92.

Hoddes, E., Zarcone, V., Smythe, H., Phillips, R., & Dement, W. (1973). Quantification of sleepiness: A new approach. *Psychophysiology, 10,* 431–436.

Jason, G. W. (1983). Hemispheric asymmetries in motor function: I. Left hemisphere specialization for memory but not performance. *Neuropsychologia, 21,* 35–45.

Lavie, P. (1976). Ultradian rhythms in the perception of two apparent motions. *Chronobiologia, 3,* 214–218.

Lavie, P., Matanya, Y., & Yehuda, S. (1984). Cognitive asymmetries after wakings from REM and NONREM sleep in right-handed females. *International Journal of Neuroscience, 23,* 111–116.

Lavie, P., & Tzischinsky, O. (1984). Cognitive asymmetries after waking from REM and NONREM sleep: Effects of delayed testing and handedness. *International Journal of Neuroscience, 23,* 311–315.

McGlone, J. (1980). Sex differences in human brain asymmetry: A critical review. *Behavioral and Brain Sciences, 3,* 215–263.

Milner, A. D., & Lines, C.R. (1982). Interhemispheric pathways in simple reaction time to lateralized light flash. *Neuropsychologia, 20,* 171–179.

Moffitt, A., Hoffmann, R., Wells, R., Armitage, R., Pigeau, R., & Shearer, J. (1982). Individual differences among pre- and post-awakening EEG correlates of dream reports following arousals from different stages of sleep. *Psychiatric Journal of the University of Ottawa, 7,* 111–125.

Myslobodsky, M. S., Ben-Mayor, V., Yedid-Levy, B., & Minz, M. (1976). Interhemispheric asymmetry of electrical activity of the brain in sleep and "cerebral dominance." *Bulletin of the Psychonomic Society, 7,* 465–467.

Nebes, R.D. (1978). Direct examination of cognitive function in the right and left hemispheres. In M. Kinsbourne (Ed.), *Asymmetrical function of the brain* (pp. 99–137). Cambridge, England: Cambridge University Press.

Nevsimalova, S., Roth, B., Sagova, V., Paroubkova, D. & Horakova, A. (1981). Clinical and polygraphic studies of sleep drunkenness. In W. P. Koella (Ed.), *Sleep 1980* (pp. 394–396). Basel: Karger.

Oldfield, R.C. (1971). The assessment and analysis of handedness: The Edinburgh Inventory. *Neuropsychologia, 9,* 97–113.

Oscar-Berman, M., Rehbein, L., Porfert, A., & Goodglass, H. (1978). Dichhaptic hand-order effects with verbal and nonverbal tactile stimulation. *Brain and Language, 6,* 323–333.

Pivik, R.T., Bylsma, F., Busby, K., & Sawyer, S. (1982). Interhemispheric EEG changes:

Relationship to sleep and dreams in gifted adolescents. *Psychiatric Journal of the University of Ottawa, 7,* 56–76.

Rechtschaffen, A., & Kales, A. (Eds.). (1968). *A manual of standardized terminology, techniques, and scoring system for sleep stages of human subjects.* Washington, DC: U. S. Government Printing Office.

Reinsel, R. (1985). *Lateralized EEG and psychomotor performance after REM and Stage 2 sleep.* Paper presented to the Sleep Research Society, Seattle.

Reinsel, R. (1988). *Performance on lateralized psychomotor tasks after awakening from REM and Stage 2 Sleep.* Unpublished doctoral dissertation, City University of New York.

Reinsel, R., Antrobus, J., & Fein, G. (1989a). Hemisphere differences and sums in sleep and waking: Effects of state of consciousness, time of night, and electrode placement. *Sleep Research, 18,* 21.

Reinsel, R., Antrobus, J., & Fein, G. (1989b). Lack of correlation between pre-awakening EEG and post-awakening task performance. *Sleep Research, 18,* 125.

Stones, M.J. (1977). Memory performance after arousal from different sleep stages. *British Journal of Psychology, 68,* 177–182.

Trotman, S., & Hammond, G.R. (1979). Sex differences in task dependent EEG asymmetries. *Psychophysiology, 16,* 429–431.

Violani, C., Bertini, M., Di Stefano, L., & Zoccolotti, P. (1983). Dream recall as a function of patterns of hemispheric activation. *Sleep Research, 12,* 190.

Young, A. W., & Ratcliff, G. (1983). Visuospatial abilities of the right hemisphere. In A. W. Young (Ed.), *Functions of the right cerebral hemisphere* (pp. 1–32). New York: Academic Press.

5 Neurological Approaches to the Dream Problem

L. Murri, E. Bonanni, and A. Stefanini
Clinica Neurologica, University of Pisa, Italy

L. Goldstein
UMDNJ–Rutgers Medical School

C. Navona and F. Denoth
Istituto Elaborazione Informazione–CNR, Pisa, Italy

Data derived from electrophysiological studies, from performances in right-hemisphere - mediated tasks after REM awakenings, and from brain-lesioned patients, though not always homogeneous, suggest prevalent involvement of the right hemisphere in elaborating mental activity during sleep. This conforms with the hypothesis that the characteristics of dream content — holistic and visuospatial, with many bizarre aspects — express a prevalent right-hemisphere (RH) activity (Bakan, 1976; Broughton, 1975; Jouvet, 1973) or that the RH is more involved only in the visuospatial aspects of dreaming (Kerr & Foulkes, 1981).

The first electrophysiological data were supplied by Goldstein, Stoltzfus, and Gardocki (1972), who observed an EEG asymmetry, with an amplitude reduction on the left during NREM, which shifted to the right during REM. On the basis of the assumption that mental activity is reflected in an EEG power decrease, we can hypothesize that right- or left-side asymmetries reflect the involvement of different hemispheres in cognitive functions elaboration.

Our experience of interhemispheric variations during sleep is based on calculation of total power, from 1.2 to 30.0 Hz, and the power associated with individual frequency bands: 1.2–2.8 Hz, 3.0–4.6 Hz, 4.8–7.8 Hz, 8.0–12.8 Hz, 13.0–19.8 Hz, 20.0–30.0 Hz. The EEG signal was recorded from F4–C4, F3–C3, P4–O2, P3–O1, according to the 10–20 International System, on paper and on magnetic tape and subsequently evaluated with an HP 5451 C Fourier Analyzer. The logarithm of the right/left ratio for 5-s epochs, and then the mean of all epochs considered were calculated. Since one is dealing with this formula, and it is well known that activity corresponds to a decrease in relative power, an increase of the ratio indicates an increase in activity on the left, while a decrease indicates an increase in RH EEG activity.

In 21 all right-handed male subjects (age ranged from 20 to 29) EEG recordings were made during awake while they read a passage from a newspaper for at least 5 min, after which they were free to continue reading, or to relax or fall in sleep. Subsequently, the subjects who fell asleep spontaneously were studied. In most cases the asymmetry observed during reading, which was characterized by prevalent left-side activity, was no longer present during sleep (Stage 1), but in some subjects the trend of lower total power on the left was maintained (see Fig. 5.1). Considering the mean values of all 21 subjects, the R/L ratio reduction during sleep, compared with wakefulness was thus not significant (see Fig. 5.2) (Murri, 1984).

More homogeneous data were obtained from evaluations of all-night sleep in another group. The data were obtained from 16 normal male subjects, of which 11 were right-handed (age ranged from 22 to 30 y) and 5 left-handed (age range 23–29 y). The right-handed subjects showed a general right-side prevalence during sleep, with occasional shifts to the left (see Fig. 5.3) (Murri et al., 1982). The values of R/L log, based on the mean of all epochs for Stages 2 and REM separately, were significantly below 0 for the anterior regions (F4-C4/F3-C3) in both stages 2 and REM in the right-handed subjects (see Fig. 5.4).

The presence of RH activity in NREM and REM sleep does not conflict with the hypothesis that dreaming is an expression of prevalent RH activity. "Dream-like" mental activity can in fact be observed both in the REM stage, to which it was initially considered limited, and in other NREM sleep stages.

The site from which recordings are obtained influences the information

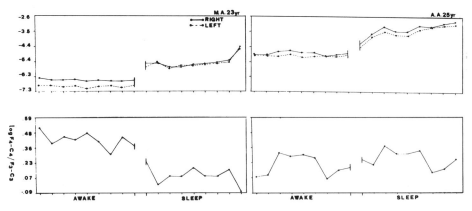

FIG. 5.1. Top: Total power values measured from right and left derivations in two subjects. Bottom: Logarithm of right/left ratio for the same epochs in the same two subjects.

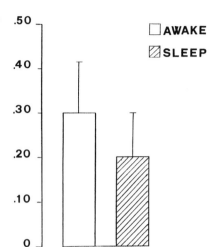

FIG. 5.2. Mean values of total power SEM (log F4-C4/F3-C3) for all epochs, during awake and sleep in all subjects examined.

received. The evaluation of the ratio in posterior regions (P4-O2/P3-O1) showed wide variability among the subjects (see Fig. 5.4) (Bonanni et al., 1987), showing that symmetry variations depend on the area explored — on limited areas rather than whole hemispheres, as also observed using monopolar derivations (Hirshkowitz, Ware, Turne, & Karaenn, 1979). Moreover, the various elaboration techniques should also be considered, since in some cases integrated amplitude is used, and in others spectrum analysis. This could explain the contrasting data reported from the various laboratories.

Some studies have demonstrated a RH prevalence during REM or during both REM and NREM (Barcaro, Denoth, Murri, Stefanini, & Navona, 1986; Goldstein et al., 1972; Hirshkowitz, Ware, & Kavakan, 1980; Murri et al., 1982; Rosekind, Coates, & Zarcone, 1979); in some cases this occurred only in some subjects while others showed a prevalence on the left (Antrobus, Ehrlichman, & Wiener, 1978; Herman, 1984; Violani, De Gennaro, & Capogna, 1984); other studies revealed no consistant prevalence during sleep (Rosadini, Ferrillo, Gaspareto, Rodriguez, & Sannita, 1984). Such differences in findings may be indicative of such a wide individual variability as to contradict the hypothesis of a prevalent right-side activity during sleep, but they could also be at least partly explained by the different methodologies adopted. The various formulas used as an index of asymmetry (R/L, R/L log., R−L/R+L) do not, however, appear to modify the values obtained, as shown in Fig. 5.5, which describes total power asymmetry, from our set of EEGs obtained from the frontocentral regions, calculated according to the three ratios that have been reported in the literature.

Among our subjects, the asymmetry distribution for frontocentral

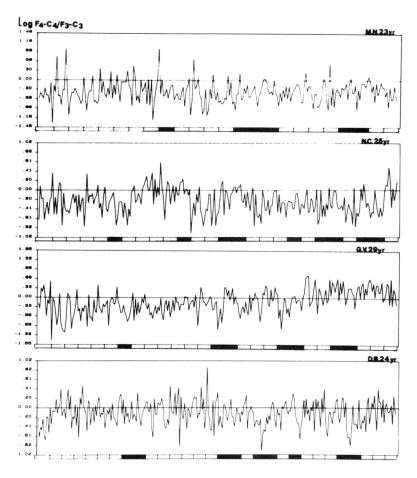

FIG. 5.3. Time course variations of log of right/left total power ratios during sample epochs from the more common sleep trend. White lines = NREM sleep; dark lines = REM sleep.

derivations remained stable in the first, second, and third cycles, but diminished on the last cycle, a trend evident both for total power (see Fig. 5.6) and for the single-frequency bands (Bonanni et al., 1987), while Myslobodsky, Ben Mayor, Yedid Levy, and Minz (1976) and Laurian Le, and Gaillard (1984) described interhemispheric variations not related to the NREM/REM cycles. This could suggest that what is experienced as dreaming derives from a prevalent RH activity during the earlier part of the night while there is an increase in left-hemisphere activity during the later part, necessary for dream recall. Alternatively, both hemispheres may participate at different levels in dream formation and recall. (Bertini et al., 1983; Cohen, 1977).

Handedness appears to be another factor influencing EEG asymmetry

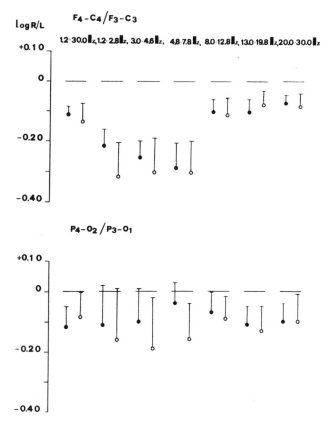

FIG. 5.4. Mean values (SEM) of total and single-frequency bands power from 11 right-handed subjects with bipolar frontocentral derivations (top) and parieto-occipital derivations (bottom). Dark circle = stage 2; white circle = stage REM.

during sleep (Murri et al., 1984a). A small group of left-handed subjects, homogeneous with the right-handed group as regards age and sex, gave mean values of R/L ratio of total power on the anterior regions, which indicate a left-hemisphere prevalence in all NREM/REM cycles, though there was considerable variability among the subjects (see Fig. 5.6). This finding could signify that EEG asymmetry during sleep in left-handed subjects differs from that in right-handed subjects, as occurs during wakefulness with cognitive tasks (Butler & Glass, 1976; Galin, Ornstein, Herron, & Johnstone, 1982; Murri et al., 1984b).

Furthermore, this EEG asymmetry during sleep could explain the finding that movements of the limbs during sleep, both spontaneous and provoked, occur mainly on the left side in right-handed subjects, and vice versa (Jovanovich, 1971; Mueller-Limmroth 1965).

While data resulting from electrophysiological investigations can only

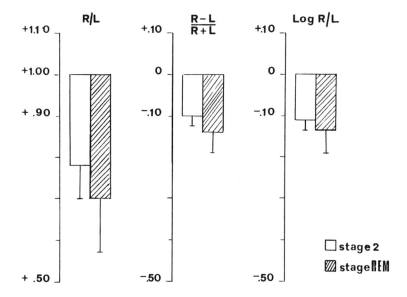

FIG. 5.5.   Mean values from 11 right-handed subjects calculated according to three different formulas.

indirectly support the hypothesis of different hemispheric involvement during sleep, more direct data can probably be obtained by clinical observation of brain-lesioned patients. Although the interpretation of results obtainable using the evaluation of cerebral lesion patients is subject to numerous difficulties, much knowledge relating to human behavior has emerged from observations on patients with destroyed brain tissue.

The existence of a relationship between brain lesion and dream recall (DR) was first hypothesized in 1883 by Charcot, who reported a case in which, following brain damage in an unspecified site, there was loss of DR.

In subsequent decades, rare cases of loss of DR, often associated with posterior area brain lesions and visuoperceptive deficit, were reported (Adler, 1944; Basso, Bisiach, & Luzzatti, 1980; Boyle & Nielsen, 1954; Brain, 1950; Epstein, 1979; Gloning & Sternback, 1953; Humphrey & Zangwill, 1951; Mac Rae & Trolle, 1979; Mueller, 1982; Nielsen, 1955; Tzavaras, 1967; Wilbrand, 1887).

Using a simple questionnaire on 53 patients with unilateral brain lesions in the acute phase, we observed that patients with lesions in posterior areas frequently showed an absence of DR, and among these same patients there was a greater incidence of defective visuoperceptive performances than in patients with damage in anterior regions and in the control group (Murri, Arena, Siciliano, Mazzotta, & Muratorio, 1984c). In 19 of these patients, DR was evaluated following provoked awakenings from Stages REM and 2,

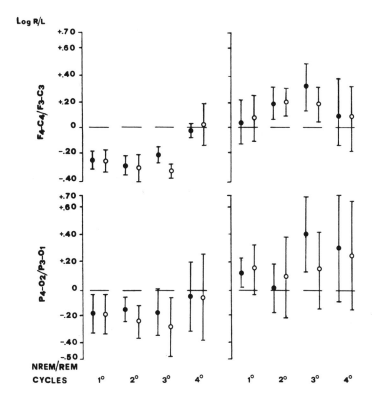

FIG. 5.6.   Total power mean values during Stage 2 (dark circles) and stage REM (white circles) in right- (left) and left-handed subjects (right) for frontocentral and parieto-occipital derivations.

and the results, particularly on awakenings from REM, corresponded reasonably well with reports obtained on spontaneous morning awakening (Murri et al., 1985). A similar relationship was found by Cathala et al., (1984) who, using the provoked-awakening method, noted a lower DR frequency in patients with parietal lesions than in frontal lesion patients.

In a larger sample (69 patients) using the same modalities, we considered five broad regions on the basis of CT scan findings: frontal, anterior and midtemporal, basal ganglia, parietal and temporo-posterior-occipital. The extent of brain damage, defined as localized or broad, did not appear to influence DR ability, while the site of the lesion proved significant. Loss of DR in patients with localized lesions was clearly more frequent when the damage involved the temporo-posterior-occipital and parietal regions, particularly in the RH.

A multiple correspondence analysis showed that the lack of DR was associated with lesions involving these areas and to the presence of visuoperceptive disorders (see Fig. 5.7). The DR deficit, however, appears to be associated with the acute state of the lesion, since the deficit is considerably reduced in the chronic phase. Two to 4 years after the acute phase study, we again investigated 32 of the original 69 patients, and only 5 of these continued to report absence of DR, while a visuoperceptive functions deficit persisted in only one (Murri et al., 1989).

A connection between lack of DR and visuoperceptive disorders was proposed with the earliest observations, owing to the association found with agnosia for objects or faces, or alteration of visual imagery. This could indicate that the absence of DR is strictly secondary to visuoperceptive or visual image abnormalities (Farah, 1984), but the hypothesis that lesions in tempoposterior-occipital or parietal regions provoke both phenomena cannot be excluded. On the other hand, although lesions of these regions are more frequently associated with loss of DR, damage in other sites, such as thalamic or frontal regions, can give rise to the same effect (Gloning & Sternback, 1953; Jus et al., 1973; Partridge, 1949).

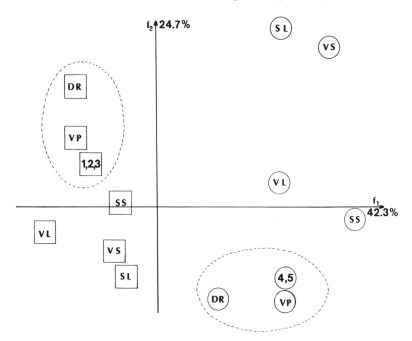

FIG. 5.7. Correspondence analysis. First and second factorial axes concerning dream recall, visuoperceptive and memory functions and site of the lesion. Key to interpretation: DR = dream recall; VP = visuoperceptive functions; VS = verbal short-term memory; VL = verbal long-term; SS = spatial short-term memory; SL = spatial long-term memory; 1, 2, 3, = frontal, anterior midtemporal, and thalamus nuclear areas; 4, 5 = parietal and posterior temporal occipital areas strongly characterized clusters; □ = function maintained; ○ = function lost

Another pathological condition of the CNS that can interfere, in the apposite sense, with DR ability is temporal-lobe epilepsy. The first report of a high frequency of DR in epileptics, with complex partial seizures, came at the end of the last century (De Sanctis, 1896). Later Epstein (1964) observed a high frequency of recurrent dreams of particular content in epileptic patients. We studied 55 epileptic patients and 35 healthy subjects, who compiled a morning diary at home for 2 months, noting the presence or absence of DR. Of these with complex partial seizures, 64% reported DR more than 30 times (means:34 ±2.6(SEM); medians: 36) during the 60 days, while among the 21 patients with primary generalized seizures (*grand mal* type) the figure was 9% (means: 14.7 ±3.1; medians:11), compared with 14% in the control group (means: 18 ±2.8; medians: 12) (see Fig. 5.8). However, DR frequency in patients with temporal-lobe epilepsy did not appear to be influenced by the side of the EEG focus (right or left) or by whether or not the lesion was identifiable on the CT scan. Provoked awakenings during REM sleep in 14 patients with temporal focus confirmed the results obtained with the diary method.

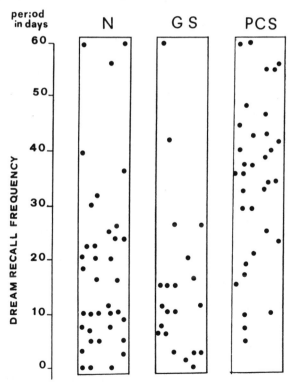

FIG. 5.8.   Distribution of dream-recall frequency in single subjects over a period of 60 days (N = normal subjects; GS = patients with generalized seizures, PCS = patients with partial complex seizures).

The data obtainable with these approaches, electrophysiological and clinical and also from performance studies using RH-mediated tasks after REM awakenings (Bertini, Violani, Zoccolotti, Antonelli, & Di Stefano, 1983; Gordon, Frooman, & Lavie, 1982) though not always consistent as to the sides predominantly involved in dream production, provide stimulating openings in the attempt to understand the neurobiological bases of dreaming.

REFERENCES

Adler, A. (1944). Disintegration and restoration of optic recognition in visual agnosia: Analysis of a case. *Archives of Neurology, 51,* 243-259.

Antrobus, J., Ehrlichman, H., & Wiener, M. (1978). EEG asymmetry during REM and NREM: Failure to replicate. *Sleep Research, 7,* 24.

Bakan, P. (1976). The right brain is the dreamer. *Psychology Today, 9,* 66-68.

Barcaro, U., Denoth, F., Murri, L., Stefanini, A., & Navona, C. (1986). Changes in the interhemispheric correlation during sleep in normal subjects. *Electroencephalography and Clinical Neurophysiology, 63,* 112-118.

Basso, A., Bisiach, E., & Luzzatti, C. (1980). Loss of mental imagery: A case study. *Neuropsychologia, 18,* 453-462.

Bertini M., & Violani C. (1984). Cerebral hemispheres, REM sleep and dream recall. *Research Communications in Psychology, Psychiatry and Behavior, 9,* 3-14.

Bertini, M., Violani, C., Zoccolotti, P., Antonelli, A., & Di Stefano, L. (1983). Performance on a unilateral tactile test during waking and upon awakening from REM and NREM sleep. In W. Koella (Ed.), *Sleep* (pp. 383-385). Basel: Karger.

Bonanni, E., Murri, L., Stefanini, A., Barcaro, U., Denoth, F., & Navona, C. (1987). Topographic variations in EEG asymmetry during sleep. *Functional Neurology, ,* 79-85.

Boyle, J., & Nielsen, J. M. (1954). Visual agnosia and loss of recall. *Bulletin Los Angeles Neurological Society, 19,* 39-42.

Brain, W. R. (1950). The cerebral basis of consciousness. *Brain, 73,* 465-479.

Broughton, R. (1975). Biorythmic variations in consciousness and psychological functions. *Canadian Psychological Review, 16,* 217-239.

Butler, S. R., & Glass, A. (1976). EEG correlates of cerebral dominance, In A. H. Riesen & R. F. Thompson (Eds.), *Advances in Psychobiology, 3,* New York: Wiley.

Cathala, H., Lafont, M., Siksou, M., Esnault, S., Gilbert, A., Minz, M., Morett-Calmin, C., Buzaret, M., & Waisbord, P. (1984). Sommeil et rêve chez des patients atteints de lesions parietales et frontales [Sleep and dreaming in patients with parietal and frontal lesions]. *Revue de Neurologie, 139,* 497-508.

Charcot, J. M. (1883). Un cas de suppression brusque et isolée de la vision mentale des signes et des objets (formes et couleurs) [A case of sudden and isolated suppression of mental vision of signs and objects (shapes and colours)]. *Progres Medicale, 2,* 568-571.

Cohen, D. B. (1977). Changes in REM dream content during the night: Implications for a hypothesis about changes in cerebral dominance across REM periods. *Perceptual and Motor Skills, 44,* 1267-1277.

De Sanctis, S. (1896). *I sogni e il sonno* [Dreams and sleep]. Roma: Dante Alighieri.

Epstein, A. (1964). Recurrent dreams: Their relationships to temporal lobe seizures. *Archives of General Psychiatry, 10,* 25-30.

Epstein, A. (1979). Effect of certain cerebral hemispheric diseases on dreaming. *Biological Psychiatry,* 77-93.

Farah, M. J. (1984). The neurological basis of mental imagery: A componential analysis. *Cognition, 18,* 245-272.

Galin, D., Ornstein, R., Herron, J., & Johnstone, J. (1982). Sex and handedness differences in EEG measures of hemispheric specialization. *Brain and Language, 16,* 19-55.

Gloning, K., & Sternback, J. (1953). Über das Traumen bei cerebralen Herdlesionen, [The dreams of brain-damaged people]. *Zeitschrift für Nerven Heilkunde, 6,* 302-309.

Goldstein, L., Stoltzfus, N. W., & Gardocki, J. P. (1972). Changes in interhemispheric amplitude relationships in EEG during sleep. *Physiology and Behavior, 8,* 811-815.

Gordon, H. W., Frooman, B., & Lavie, P. (1982). Shift in cognitive asymmetry between waking from NREM and REM sleep. *Neuropsychologia, 20,* 99-103.

Herman, J. H. (1984). Experimental investigations of the psychophysiology of REM sleep including the question of lateralization. *Research Communications in Psychology, Psychiatry and Behavior, 9,* 53-75.

Hirshkowitz, M., Ware, I. C., & Karakan, I. (1980). Integrated EEG amplitude asymmetry during early and late REM@NREM periods. *Sleep Research, 9,* 291.

Hirshkowitz, M., Ware, I. C., Turne, D., & Karakan, I. (1979). EEG amplitude asymmetry during sleep. *Sleep Research, 8,* 5.

Humphrey, M. E., & Zangwill, O. L. (1951). Cessation of dreaming after brain injury. *Neurology Neurosurgery and Psychiatry, 14,* 322-325. Jouvet, M. (1973). Essai sur le rêve. [Essay on dreams] *Archives Italiennes de Biologie, 111,* 564-569.

Jovanovich, V. J. (1971). *Normal sleep in man.* Stuttgart, Germany: Hippokrates Verlag.

Jus, A., Jus, K., Villenueve, A., Pires, A., Lachance, R., Fortier, J., Villenueve, R. (1973). Studies on dream recall in chronic schizophrenic patients after prefrontal lobotomy. *Biological Psychiatry, 6,* 275-293.

Kerr, N. H., & Foulkes, D. (1981). Right hemisphere mediation of dream visualization: A case study. *Cortex, 17,* 603-610.

Laurian, S., Le, P. K., & Gaillard, J. M. (1984). Spectral analysis of sleep stages as a function of clocktime or sleep cycles. *Research Communications in Psychology, Psychiatry and Behavior, 9,* 77-86.

Mac Rae, D., & Trolle, E. (1979). The defect of function in visual agnosia. *Brain, 79,* 94-110.

Mueller, F. (1982). Ein Beitrag zur Kenntnis der Seelenblindheit [A contribution to the study of cortical blindness]. *Archives Psychiatrie Nervenarzt, 24,* 655-692.

Mueller-Limmroth, W. (1965). *Der schlaf des menschen* [Human sleep]. Konstanz, Germany: Guden Lomberg.

Murri, L., Arena, R., Siciliano, G., Mazzotta, R., & Muratorio, A. (1984c). Dream recall in patients with focal cerebral lesions. *Archives of Neurology, 41,* 183-185.

Murri, L., Mancino, M., Massetani, R., Canapicchi, R., Puglioli, M., & Rossi, G. (1989). Effect of acute and chronic brain damage on dreaming. *Research Communications in Psychology, Psychiatry and Behavior, 14,* 121-142.

Murri, L., Massetani, R., Siciliano, G., Giovanditti, L., & Arena, R. (1985). Dream recall after sleep interruption in brain-injured patients. *Sleep, 8,* 356-362.

Murri, L., Muratorio, A., Stefanini, A., Navona, C., & Denoth, F. (1984b). Asimmetria EEG e specializzione emisferica [EEG asymmetries and hemispheric specialization]. *Rivista Italiana EEG Neurofisiologia Clinica (Suppl. 1),* 241-265.

Murri, L., Stefanini, A., Bonanni, E., Cei, G., Navona, C., & Denoth, F. (1984a). Hemispheric EEG differences during REM sleep in dextrals and sinistrals. *Research Communications in Psychology, Psychiatry and Behavior, 9,* 109-120.

Murri, L., Stefanini, A., Navona, C., Domenici, L., Muratorio, A., & Denoth, F. (1984). Changes in EEG symmetry during drowsiness. *Electroencephalography and Clinical Neurophysiology, 58,* 79.

Murri, L., Stefanini, A., Navona, C., Domenici, L., Muratorio, A., & Goldstein, L. (1982). Automatic analysis of the hemispheric EEG relationships during wakefulness and sleep.

Research Communications in Psychology, Psychiatry and Behavior, 7, 109–118.

Myslobodsky, M. S., Ben Mayor, V., Yedid Levy, B., & Minz, M. (1976). Interhemispheric asymmetry of electrical activity of the brain in sleep and "cerebral dominance". *Bulletin Psychonomic Society, 7,* 465–467.

Nielsen, J. N. (1955). Occipital lobes, dream and psychosis. *Journal of Nervous and Mental Disease, 125,* 50–52.

Partridge, M. (1949). Some reflections on the nature of affective disorders, arising from the results of prefrontal leucotomy. *Journal Mental Sciences, 95,* 795–825.

Rosadini, G., Ferrillo, F., Gaspareto, B., Rodriguez, G., & Sannita, W. G. (1984). Topographic distribution of qualitative EEG during human sleep. *Research Communications in Psychology, Psychiatry and Behavior, 9,* 43–51

Rosekind, M. R., Coates, T. J., & Zarcone, V. (1979). Lateral dominance during wakefulness, NREM stage 2 sleep and REM sleep. *Sleep Research, 8,* 126.

Tzavaras, A. (1967). Contribution a l'étude de l'agnosie des physionomies [A contribution to the study of prosopagnosia]. *Faculté de Medicine de Paris, 1,* 1–71.

Violani, C., De Gennaro, L., & Capogna, M. (1984). EEG and EOG indices of hemispheric asymmetry during sleep. *Research Communications in Psychology, Psychiatry and Behavior, 29,* 95–107.

Wilbrand, H. (1887). *Die Seeleblindheit und ihre Beziehungen zur homonymen Hemianopsie, zur Alexie und Agraphie* [Cortical blindness and its relationships with homonimous hemianopsia, alexia and agraphia]. Wiesbaden, Germany: J. P. Bergman.

6

Dream Recall in Brain-damaged Patients: A Contribution to the Neuropsychology of Dreaming Through a Review of the Literature

Fabrizio Doricchi and Cristiano Violani
Università degli Studi di Roma

INTRODUCTION

Why a Neuropsychological Approach to Dreaming?

The recent scientific explosion of interest in dreaming has led to the strong consensus that this unique psychological state is the concomitant of rapid eye movement sleep. Investigations in animals have further provided convincing evidence that the cortical activation of REM is basically modulated by the brain stem. But how the REM-activated cortex actually elaborates the dream is still to be understood. Experimental evidence of cortical influences on some REM sleep-related phenomena (e.g., rapid eye movements; Jeannerod, Mouret, & Jouvet, 1965) have been obtained from animal studies, but it is obviously impossible to gain from such studies any information on the higher cognitive processes leading to the production and the retrieval of a dream. An alternative investigative strategy could be to look at experiments of nature in humans. An analysis of the effects of brain damage on the higher neurocognitive processes and on dreaming, could determine what damaged areas and functions are common to clinical cases of dreaming loss, alteration or maintenance.

The Origin of the Neuropsychological Approach: The Controversial Laterality Issue and its Heuristic Limits

Since the first clinical description of the case of one of Charcot's patients who experienced loss of the visual component of dreaming (Bernard, 1883), a number of clinical observations and studies of groups of brain-damaged patients concerning cessation, alteration, or maintenance of dreaming have been reported in the neurological literature. Recently some of these cases have been reconsidered in order to provide evidence concerning the contribution of the two cerebral hemispheres to dreaming. On the basis of brief reviews of the literature, some authors (Bakan, 1978; Galin, 1974) have suggested a right-hemisphere localization for dreaming while others have emphasized that both the hemispheres are indispensable to dreaming, each contributing to different features of the dream (i.e., right-hemisphere-visuospatial features, left-hemisphere-visuoverbal integration; Antrobus, 1987) and both equally involved in the recall of a dream (Bertini & Violani, 1984). The laterality issue has been rendered even more controversial by Greenberg and Farah (1986), who reviewed nine cases of cessation of dreaming and pointed out that in all cases the damage involved the hemisphere dominant for language. Greenberg and Farah concluded that the left hemisphere plays a crucial and perhaps exclusive role in generation of dreaming. In our opinion, the controversy on the laterality issue suggests that a more analytical neuropsychological approach to the study of dreaming could overcome the heuristic limits of a purely dichotomic laterality approach. As recently affirmed by Antrobus (1987) "the global concept of dreaming includes several partly independent cognitive functions . . . carried out in different cortical locations." Since most of the cases reported in the neurological literature provide descriptions of the damaged area and of the concomitant cognitive impairments, a neuropsychological analysis of the cases can provide direct information not only about the lateralization (if any) of the dreaming process but also about relationships between dreaming and distinct higher neurocognitive structures and processes having specific intra and/or interhemispheric locations.

Aims of the Chapter

The aims of the present chapter are as follows:

To provide an analytical description of the cases of cessation, maintenance or alteration of dreaming following cerebral damage reported in the English, French, German, and Italian literature.

To analyze the distribution of the sites of damage along the lateral, anterior–posterior, and intrahemispheric lobe dimensions.

To define the neurocognitive syndromes associated with loss of dreaming.

To integrate data and conclusions drawn from the review of single cases with those drawn from investigations on groups of brain-damaged patients. Most of our conclusions will be necessarily tentative, owing to the relatively limited number of cases reviewed. The exclusive utilization of a quantitative approach implies the loss of much potentially relevant information concerning functional aspects of the neurocognitive disorders associated to the damage. By reporting the most relevant neuropsychological data for each individual patient we have tried to compensate for this loss. The appendix is meant to allow other investigators to assess the consistency of our tentative conclusions and to advance further hypothesis.

Review of Single Cases

Since 1883, to our knowledge, 104 cases relevant to the relationship between dream recall and brain lesions have been published in the neurological literature. The present review concerns only cases in which maintenance or loss of dream recall, either complete or of the visual component only, was clearly reported (spontaneously, on REM awakenings, or upon direct inquiry) to clinicians by patients who described themselves as frequent or usual dream recallers before the onset of illness. The following have not been considered: (1) Autobiographical anecdotal reports (Farrel, 1968; Moss, 1972); (2) Cases in which it is not possible to state whether the patient was indeed capable of recalling dreams before the accident (Hecaen and De Ajuriaguerra, 1956); (3) Cases in which it is unclear whether the patient was able to recall dreams after the onset of illness (MacRae, & Trolle, 1956); (4) Cases in which patients affirmed that they were incapable of recalling dreams before the accident (Deleval, De Mol, & Noterman, 1983; Hecaen, Goldblum, Masure, & Ramier, 1974; Rubens, & Benson, 1971). Observations concerning 12 split-brain patients described by Hoppe (1977) were excluded from the present review because the report lacked any individual neuropsychological information. Three commisurotomized patients studied by Greenwood, Wilson, and Gazzaniga (1977) and two similar cases reported by Montplaisir, Cote, Laverdiere, and St. Hilaire (1985) have not been considered because several factors (e.g., preoperative seizures, duration of the neurological disease, medications) may have determined a neurological reorganization (Mendius & Engel, 1985) obscuring the effects due to surgical disconnection per se. For similar reasons, four brain-damaged patients suffering also from general cortical atrophy (Schanfald, Pearlman, & Greenberg, 1985b; 2 cases) or of brain stem damage (Schanfald, Pearlman, & Greenberg, 1985a; 2 cases) have not been considered. Also a group of chronic schizophrenic patients who underwent prefrontal lobectomy (Jus, et al, Vil, 1974), four investigations concerning groups of patients with chronic brain syndromes (Greenberg & Pearlman, 1967; Greenberg, Pearlman, Brooks, Mayer, & Hartmann, 1968; Kramer, Roth, & Trinder, 1975; Torda, 1969) and the case of a patient suffering from Huntington's chorea (Starr, 1967) were excluded from the review. We have also considered 65 patients with unilateral focal brain damage reported in an unpublished dissertation (Corda, 1985). This study, besides providing reliable neurological (CAT scans) and neuropsychological informations for each patient, considered only patients who used to recall their dreams before illness and who were not affected by severe language and gnosic disorders. All these patients were asked about the quantity and quality of their dreaming and were interviewed twice in the early morning; those who did not recall any dreams were interviewed five times at weekly intervals. Outlines of all the individual cases considered in our review, together with available basic neuropsychological information, are reported in the Appendix. The Appendix consist of three sections. The first reports cases of total dream cessation, the second cases of dream persistence, and the third cases with loss of the visual component of dreaming. For each case we have provided the reference, the subject's sex, age, handedness, the time interval between the onset of illness and clinical examination, the etiology of the damage, the localization (lobe and hemisphere), the method by which localization was defined, summaries of the neurocognitive deficits, and of the spared cognitive functions when available. Other relevant information, for example, the follow-up length of dream deficit, have been added as final notes. The set of cases reviewed can be considered as a sample on which the contingency of cessation, persistence, or alteration of dreaming on the localization of the lesion and on the concomitant cognitive syndrome can be statistically analyzed. Due to the bibliographical nature of this sample, the presence of several potential sources of bias must be acknowledged. The first identifiable source of bias concerns cases drawn from samples of patients and depends on the selection criteria adopted by the original authors. This bias applies to cases No. 14–20, which were drawn from a sample of aphasic (i.e., LH-damaged) patients (Epstein & Simmons, 1983), and to cases No. 4–12 (Corda, 1985), which were drawn from a sample in which patients with bilateral damage were not considered. In a bibliographical sample there are also sources of bias which are difficult to assess; the first is linked to the clinical relevance of the disorders associated with the damage. Cases showing language disorders (i.e., LH disease) may have received more clinical attention, especially in the less recent literature; in fact, strokes with language impairment are more obvious to the layperson and more likely to reach the clinic. Conversely, a corresponding tendency of "frequent dismissal of minor hemisphere symptomatology by patient (and occasionally clinician)" has been noted (Bradshaw & Nettleton, 1981). Both these factors may have been responsible for the greater proportion of LH damage in the cases reported in the literature and included in our sample. A second source of bias is linked to historical changes in the scientific interest in specific neuropsychological pathologies. For example, observations by Brain (1941b) renewed the interest in the study of visuoperceptive and visuospatial deficits (e.g., Paterson & Zangwill, 1944) often associated with right parietal disease. Later, split-brain animal studies by Myers and Sperry (1953) and by Myers (1956) gave impetus to the reconsideration of the human disconnective syndrome (Geschwind, 1965), a disease mostly associated with left occipitotemporal vascular damage. Therefore, cases with a given anatomical location of damage may have been more or less frequently reported in the literature at different points in history. This factor may therefore have additionally altered the balance of distribution of damage among the cerebral hemispheres and lobes in the sample of cases that we reviewed. The presence or absence, in each case reported, of information concerning the follow-up of the length of dream cessation, the methodology by which patients' dream reports were obtained (through spontaneous report, REM awakening, inquiry), and more generally the extensiveness of neuropsychological clinical evaluation, is also relevant to this investigation. On these methodological premises the frequency distribution analysis of site of damage has been repeated in two subsamples from which cases introducing the assessable confounding effects that have been mentioned (first subsample), and cases with primary subcortical involvement and/or lacking relevant information (second subsample) were excluded.

RESULTS

Dream Cessation

Cases of dream cessation are outlined in the first section of the Appendix. Differences in the distribution of the lobe of the lesion (frontal, parietal, occipital-temporal) and the hemisphere (left, bilateral, right) have been analyzed by chi-square and binomial tests. For bilateral damage the lateral predominance of the lesion has not been considered. Considering all the 43 cases of cessation of dreaming reviewed (see Fig. 6.1), the test reveals a significant relation between the site of the lesion and cessation of dreaming (chi square, 4 df = 10.298, p = .036). Although there is no significant difference between the lobes (chi square, 2 df = .88) cases of dream cessation are more frequent among patients with posterior (parietal, temporal, occipital) lesion than among anterior (frontal) patients (chi square, 1 df = 8.39, p = .004). Cessation of dreaming is more frequently associated with LH than with bilateral or RH lesions (chi square, 2 df = 7.86, p = .02). Considering the three different lobes separately, this laterality effect is significant only in occipitotemporal cases (chi square, 2 df = 10.7, p = .005). The same analyses have been repeated, excluding seven cases reported by Epstein and Simmons (1983) and nine cases reported by Corda (1985) because drawn from "biased samples" (see Fig. 6.2).

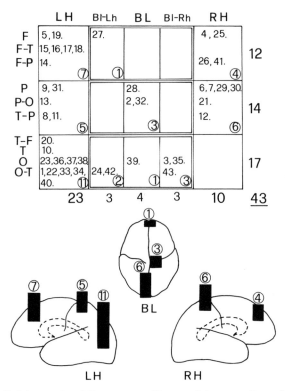

FIG. 6.1. Total sample of the cases with complete cessation of dreaming. Frequency distribution of the anatomical localization of the damage (lobe and side). In each cell is shown the frequency (in circlet) and the reference number given to each case in the Appendix. Histograms of the cell frequencies are depicted in the lower part of the figure. F = Frontal; P = Parietal; T = Temporal; O = Occipital; LH = Left Hemisphere; RH = Right Hemisphere; BL = Bilateral; BL - LH = Bilateral with left hemisphere predominance; BL - RH = Bilateral with right hemisphere Predominance.

Within this subsample cases with frontal lobe damage are significantly less frequent than cases with parietal or occipital damage (chi square = 6.88, 2 *df*, *p* = .031). Only within occipital - temporal patients is there an association between loss of dreaming and hemisphere of the lesion (chi square = 8.40, 2 *df*, *p* = .015), RH lesions are absent while there is no difference in the frequency of LH and bilateral lesions. The same analyses were repeated for the subsample where also all the cases with damage involving subcortical structures (cases No. 23, 41) and cases lacking relevant information about length of illness and neuropsychological assessment (cases No. 37–39) were excluded (see Fig. 6.3).

Chi-square tests confirmed greater frequency of posterior lesions (chi square = 11.63, 1 *df*, *p* = .001) and the association between loss of

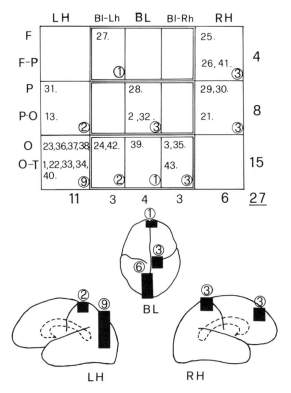

FIG. 6.2. First subsample of the cases with complete cessation of dreaming. Frequency distribution of the anatomical localization of the damage. Cases drawn from biased samples are not included in this subsample.

dreaming and laterality of the lesion was confirmed only within occipital - temporal patients (chi square, 2 *df* = 5.63, *p* = .06).

Dream Persistence

Persistence of dreaming has been reported for 18 unilaterally damaged patients (UBD) (cases No. 1, 2, 4–8, 12, 15,–24; see Appendix, Sec. 2) and for 56 UBD patients studied by Corda (1985) not reported in the Appendix. The only case with a bilateral damage (No. 25), cases with primary subcortical involvement (No. 9–13, 14) and a case in which damage was not specifically localized (No. 3) were not included in the analysis. A chi-square test on the distribution of the sites and hemisphere of damage reported in Table 6.1. 6.1 Total sample of cases with maintainance of dream experience. Frequency distribution of the anatomical localization of the damage reveals no significant differences (chi square, 3 *df* = 5.18, *p* = .16). No

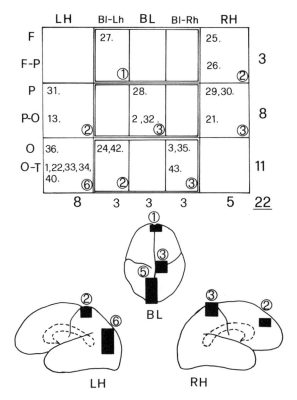

FIG. 6.3. Second subsample of the cases with complete cessation of dreaming. Frequency distribution of the anatomical localization of the damage. Cases drawn from biased samples, cases with predominant subcortical involvement and cases lacking relevant informations are not included in this subsample.

significant association to the persistence of dreaming is shown considering separately both the laterality and the anterior–posterior localization of damage. There are significant differences in the distribution of the lesions in the different lobes (chi square, 3 df = 22.97, p < .001), dream persistence being more frequently associated with frontal and temporal damage. Within parietal and occipital groups of cases, no significant difference was found in the laterality of damage (Parietal : binomial test, p = .0805 ; Occipital : binomial test, p = .0937).

Loss of the Visual Component of Dreaming

A total of nine cases with selective loss of the visual component of dreaming have been outlined in the third section of the Appendix. Such cases are of

TABLE 6.1
Total sample of cases with maintainance of dream experience. Frequency
distribution of the anatomical localization of the damage.

	F	P	T	O	
LH	⑰	③	⑭	⑤	39
RH	⑭	⑧	⑫	①	35
	31	11	26	6	74

great potential interest for the neuropsychology of dreaming, because they
could indicate that the visual component of dreaming (or even some of its
aspects; see cases No. 8 and 9) can be disrupted independently from other
sensorial-cognitive components. Unfortunately the limited number of cases
available does not allow any statistical analysis and the variety of etiologies
and locations of damage prevent any further comment on this group.

Investigations on Groups of Patients

Beside reports concerning clinical descriptions of single cases there are a few
investigations that have analyzed dream recall in groups of brain damaged
patients. Cathala and coworkers (Cathala et al., 1983) have studied dream
reports from REM awakenings in nine nonacute patients with parietal
lesions (six patients were right-handed, three had a RH and three LH lesion;
three were left-handed and all had RH lesions), and in seven with frontal
lesions (4 right-handed with bilateral lesions, one with unilateral right, one
with unilateral left, and an ambidextral with left damage). All patients had
a first adaptation night in the sleep laboratory with no awakenings. During
the second night, subjects were awakened in each REM period. Each group
of patients was matched with a control group of normal subjects. Instances
of absence of dream report were significantly greater in parietal patients
(69.4%), compared with their controls (14.3%; chi square, 1 $df = 19.93$ p
$< .001$), while between frontal patients (34.6%) and controls (17.6%) no
significant difference was found. In three reports Murri and coworkers
(Arena, Murri, Piccini & Muratorio, 1984; Murri, Arena, Siciliano, Mazzotta, & Muratorio, 1984; Murri, Massetani, Siciliano, Giovanditti, &
Arena, 1985) have evaluated dream recall in a progressively extended group
of UBD patients in the acute stage (within 30 days of the onset of damage);
a re-evaluation of dream recall in a subgroup of 32 patients in the chronic
stage (2–4 years after the accident) has been reported in a fourth study
(Murri et al., in preparation). All patients were right-handed and used to
recall at least one dream per week before damage; all patients with global

aphasia and clinically detectable visual–agnosic defects were excluded. Although the same subjects have been considered in more than one investigation, the results of each study will be reanalyzed and summarized separately. The first report (Murri et al., 1984) showed that only for patients with posterior lesions was the proportion of dream loss (14 over 21) greater than for matched controls ($\frac{4}{28}$; chi square, 1 df, $= 14.167\ p <$ .001), and for anterior patients ($\frac{4}{32}$; chi square, 1 $df = 16.587$, $p < .001$). The latter groups showed no difference from the control group in dream loss. For both the anterior and posterior patients, the laterality of the lesions did not affect the probability of dream loss; which for the posterior patients was 75% ($n = 8$) for RHD and 62% ($n = 13$) for LHD. For the left posterior group only, however, patients with language defects had a higher rate of dream loss ($\frac{6}{7}$) than controls ($p < .006$). A second paper (Arena et al., 1984) was mainly concerned with the lateralization issue and disregarded comparisons on the anterior–posterior dimension. For acute patients with UBD, they found that there were more cases of dream loss ($\frac{33}{52}$) than within matched controls ($\frac{4}{18}$). Dream was absent in 15 out of 19 RHD patients (chi square, 1 $df = 11.9$, $p < .001$) and in 18 out of 33 LHD patients (chi square, 1 $df = 4.96$, $p < .03$). Moreover, in the latter group only patients with language defects ($\frac{13}{20}$) differed from the controls (chi square, 1 $df = 7.01$, $p = .008$). In LHD patients without language defects the rate of dream absence ($\frac{5}{13}$) did not differ with respect to that of the control subjects ($\frac{4}{18}$; $p = .32$). At variance with Murri's conclusions, a lateralization effect is suggested by the authors with a higher rate of dream loss 78.9% ($n = 19$) for the RHD, compared with 54.5% ($n = 33$, $p = .075$) for the LHD subjects. In fact, this difference was significant only with respect to LHD patients without language deficits ($p < .02$). The use of REM awakenings and of careful interviewing necessary in order to assess the total absence of dream recall has been recommended by Schanfald et al., (1985a). In a group of eight unilateral brain-damaged patients they found an absence of dream recall in only two but these patients had suffered extensive damage, including to the brain stem. Percent of report in the other patients ranged from 9 to 33, over a mean number of 7.3 (SD $= 3.5$) awakenings. With regard to this issue a third investigation (Murri et al., 1985) has demonstrated a substantial correspondence between the classification of patients as recallers and nonrecallers based on the 10 days of dream diary and REM awakenings, and confirmed that posterior lesions are more frequently associated with dream loss. Loss of dream was found in REM awakenings of $\frac{7}{11}$ posterior patients versus $\frac{2}{8}$ anterior patients. The right–left dimension did not appear related to dream recall either in anterior or posterior patients, dreams being reported by two left-posterior patients out of five. A more recent report (Murri et al., in preparation) has evaluated dream recall, visuoperceptive functions, and long-term and short-term memory for visual and verbal materials in a subsample of 32 patients re-examined 2 to 4 years after the first neuropsychological assessment. Out of 22 patients originally classified as nonrecallers, only 5 showed total absence of dream recall in a 10-day dream diary. All these 5 patients had a lesion confined to the RH : 2 in the temporal-occipital area, 1 in the thalamic area, and 2 in the parietal and posterior occipital-temporal area. At a cognitive level, the whole group of patients originally classified as nonrecallers showed a significant improvement only in the visuoperceptive task and a marginal improvement of the long-term verbal memory functions. Within a study on visual mental imagery, Vera De La Puente (1987) gave a questionnaire on the presence and vividness of visual dreams to 25 brain-damaged patients with lesions limited to either right-posterior, left-posterior, right-frontal or left-frontal area, and to 25 matched controls. A preliminary report (Vera De La Puente, 1987) states that "an absence or diminuition in the vividness of visual dreams was found more frequently in both right and left brain-damaged patients than in controls. The lesions were both in right and left temporal lobes" and also in a patient with right parietal damage.

DISCUSSION

Frontal Lobe Lesions and Dream Loss: An Apparent Lack of Relationship

Findings from the group of single cases reviewed in this chapter and from investigations on groups of brain-damaged patients suggest a consistent pattern of association between loss or maintainance of the dreaming experience, on the one hand, and the localization of brain damage and the associate cognitive deficits on the other. Localization of the lesion along the anterior–posterior dimension is relevant; in fact, damage to the frontal lobes does not seem to play a critical role in the loss of the subjective experience of dreaming. Both in the individual reports of patients with loss of dreaming and in all the groups of brain-damaged subjects studied by other investigators, cases of frontal damage are significantly fewer than cases with damage in the posterior lobes. Conversely frontal cases are significantly more frequent among patients who maintained the experience of dreaming. A notable exception are the cases with LH anterior damage associated with language impairments (cases No. 14–20) described by Epstein and Simmons (1983), which will be discussed later with reference to the connection between loss of dreaming and aphasic disorders.

Parietal Lobes Attention and Dreaming: A Double Function for Parietal Lobes? Producing REMs, Generating, and Inspecting the Dream Scene

In patients who reported dream cessation following parietal damage, the laterality of the lesion seems irrelevant: Among the single cases of cessation of dreaming reviewed in this chapter there are two patients with LHD, three with RHD and three with damage involving both hemispheres. One may notice that even in the total sample (see 6.1), including parietal unilateral BDP drawn from Corda's group (1985), the laterality of parietal damage is unrelated to dream loss (LHD $n = 5$, RHD $n = 6$). Consistent with classical neuropsychological notions (e.g., Hecaen, 1972), all cases presented some degree of visuospatial and visuoconstructive deficit and notably deficits in spatial judgments and orientation in addition to attentional deficits. In four patients transitory (case No. 13) and permanent (cases No. 28, 29, 32) disphasic symptoms complicated the typical parietal-attentional symptomatology that was present in cases No. 2, 21, 30, 31; in cases No. 2 and 30 visual recognition problems were particularly severe. Besides cases of complete cessation of dreaming following parietal damage, cases of alteration of the dreaming experience have been studied. Two cases of bilateral parietal damage with loss of the visual component of dreaming (No. 1, 3; Sec. 3) have been reported but in both cases, because of etiology and diagnostic method, it is unclear if damage was confined to the parietal lobes.

Parietal Lobes, Waking Oculomotion, and REMs

Since parietal lobes subserve neuropsychological processes at different levels of functional complexity, it is difficult to individualize the neurocognitive subfunctions that could be more critical for the maintainance of the dream experience. However, the results of three recent studies suggest that during REM sleep the parietal-occipital system (Ungerleider & Mishkin, 1982) could be implicated both in the sequence of neurophysiological events that lead to the production of rapid eye movements (REMs) and in the elaboration of the cognitive information which, according to the activation–synthesis hypothesis (Hobson & McCarley, 1977), is conveyed to the cortex through the corollary discharge or which, according to the most recent version of the scanning hypothesis (Herman, this volume), could parallel the ocular inspection of the dream scene. McCarley, Winkelman and Duffy (1983) found a large spike potential immediately preceding REMs, which had its maximal intensity over the parietal area controlateral to the direction of REMs and suggested that it could represent the human equivalent of animal PGO waves. Two subsequent studies have confirmed the presence of this potential (Miyauchi, Takino, Fukuda, & Torii, 1987; Niiyama, Shimizu, Abe, & Hishikawa, 1988) and emphasized its resemblance (also noted by McCarley and coworkers) to presaccadic wake potentials; furthermore they showed the existence of large parieto-occipital potentials following the REMs. Both Miyauchi and coworkers and Niiyama and coworkers suggested a functional relationship between these tardive potentials and the ongoing processing of dreaming visual imagery. In light of these recent findings it is therefore suggested that in humans a parietal damage could influence the dream production process by interfering on : (1) the production of eye movements; (2) the internal production and inspection of the dreaming visual imagery. Neurophysiological and neuropsychological studies have confirmed the relevance of parietal lobes for the regulation and promotion of environmental visual inspection (Lynch, 1980; Mesulam, 1983), and covert orienting (i.e., displacements of the attentive focus without eye movements; Posner, Walker, Friedrich, & Rafal, 1984). Alterations of oculomotor behavior concomitant with parietal damage have been described, among others, by Gassell and Williams (1963), Sundqvist (1979) and Pierrot–Deseilligny and Rivaud (1987), and the relevance of posterior areas in oculomotor control is also suggested by the significantly higher occurrence of gaze paresis in stroke patients with posterior damage when compared with those with anterior damage (De Renzi, Colombo, Faglioni, & Gibertoni, 1982). In the single cases reviewed by us, disturbances of waking oculomotor attentive scanning were shown by two patients who reported a complete cessation of dream experience (No. 2, 32); both cases were reported as having normal REM periods, but only for case 32 the normality of REMs was reliably assessed. Relationships among parietal oculomotor attentive disturbances (as, for example hemi-inattention, Holmes's Syndrome or Balint's Syndrome), abnormalities in REMs, and dream experience are still unclear. Greenberg's (1966) finding of a strong quantitative reduction of REMs in patients with parietal damage may suggest a relationship between attentional scanning and dreaming; however, dreaming was not assessed in these patients. Further research is needed to determine whether in order to cause a disruption of the dream experience a parietal damage must be associated with alterations in the frequency or the morphology of REMs and to clarify the influence of these alterations on the phenomenological features of the dream. In a noteworthy study, Starr (1967) reported that a patient affected by Huntington's Chorea (a neurological pathology in which a general cholinergic depletion plays an essential role) showed total absence of rapid eye movements and reported only one dream upon awakenings from 25 REM episodes.

Inspecting, Generating and Shifting the Dream Scene

Parietal lobe damage affects also generation and/or inspection of waking mental imagery originating from long-term memory and, as suggested, this could be another locus of functional influence of parietal damage on dream-recall ability. Bisiach and coworkers (Bisiach & Luzzatti, 1978; Bisiach, Luzzatti, & Perani, 1979; Bisiach, Capitani, Luzzatti, & Perani, 1981) have repeatedly showed that right-parietal hemi-inattentive patients are affected by a left hemi-inattentive imagery deficit when describing places from memory, and that this deficit is significantly greater in patients with both left hemianopia and left hemi-inattention when compared with left hemianoptic patients without hemi-inattention (Bisiach et al., 1981). This finding suggests the existence of a functional link between eye movements and imagery functioning since (when compared with hemi-anoptics) only hemi-inattentive patients show lack of compensatory saccadic inspection of the blind visual hemifield (Ishiai, Furukawa, & Tsukagoshi, 1987). However, a causative link between impaired oculomotricity and the hemi-inattentive imagery deficit is rejected by Bisiach and coworkers, who interpreted the experimental evidences as favoring a fundamental hemirepresentative defect (Bisiach & Berti, 1987). The existence of an equivalent attentional bias in the description of the dream scene, though of great potential interest in the understanding of the functional relationships between waking and dreaming imagery, has never been assessed while the specific influence of parietal damages on spatial imagery functions has also been recently showed by Levine, Warach, and Farah (1985), who found a dissociation between deficits of spatial imagery and imagery for objects or animals, the former being linked to bilateral parietal damage and the latters to a right occipitotemporal damage; unfortunately in both the cases dreaming was not assessed. Some clinical evidence on the influence of parietal damage on the qualitative aspects of the dream visual content are provided by Cathala and cooworkers (1983), who analyzed reports from REM awakenings and responses to questions evaluating several qualitative aspects of dream experience in nine parietal patients. Their result showed a quantitative reduction in dreaming and an impoverishment of the spatial organization of the dream scenery, including a complete lack of shifts in the dream scene. The predominance of PGO-like electrophysiological activity concomitant to REMs over the parietal area and the findings of Cathala et al. (1983) could be taken as converging evidences favoring the claim that PGO waves (or their equivalents in humans) are the basic events producing spatial–temporal discontinuities in the dream plot (Mamelak & Hobson, 1989).

Aphasia and Dreaming: Does Language Subserve Dream Production, Dream Recall, or Both?

There are several pieces of evidence suggesting a relationship between loss of dream recall and language disorder. The first two cases of receptive aphasia in which the dream experience was lost have been mentioned by Grunstein (1924), who unfortunately did not give any other information about the neuropsychological condition of these patients. Cessation of dreaming in aphasic patients has also been investigated by Epstein and Simmons (1983), who described seven patients who "emphatically" affirmed the loss of their dreaming experience. Aphasic disorders with loss of dreaming experience were also found in some of the posterior LHD patients in the groups of acute patients studied by Murri (Arena et al., 1984; Murri et al., 1984). It will be recalled that these patients were the only LHD patients who had a rate of dream recall lower than control patients. Since patients with severe receptive deficits were excluded both in Epstein and Simmons's (1983) sample and in studies on groups, it is unlikely that these findings were due to defective understanding of the questions concerning dreaming posed by the clinician. The neuropsychology of aphasic disorders can clarify the relationship between loss of dreaming and language deficits. Following earlier suggestions (e.g., Bay, 1962), research on aphasia has recently provided evidences showing that the appearance of language disorders is frequently associated with deficits in nonlinguistic functions such as the full recognition of the semantic and functional properties of visual percepts and the retrieval of visuo-imaginal, picture-like information. On the perceptive level aphasics are notoriously impaired in the interpretation of the meaning of pantomimes (Duffy, Duffy, & Pearson 1975; Duffy & Watkins, 1984; Gainotti & Lemmo, 1976; Varney, 1982), in the choice of conceptually associated pictures (Gainotti, Miceli, & Caltagirone, 1979), in pointing out objects named by the experimenter among semantically related distractors (Butterworth, Howard & McLoughlin, 1984; Gainotti, Ibba, & Caltagirone, 1975; Pizzamiglio & Appicciafuoco, 1971) and in integrating perceptual and contextual–functional visual information (Caramazza, Berndt, & Brownell, 1982; Wayland & Taplin, 1985a, 1985b; Whitehouse, Caramazza, & Zurif, 1978). Aphasic patients also show deficits in tasks that involve some form of visuo-imaginal memory, such as in drawing objects from memory (Bay 1962; Gainotti, Silveri, Villa, & Caltagirone, 1983; Piercy, Hecaen, & De Ajuriaguerra, 1960), and in associating color to object form (Basso, Faglioni, & Spinnler, 1976; Cohen & Kelter, 1979; De Renzi, Faglioni, Savoiardo & Vignolo, 1972). Although the relationships between the nonlinguistic deficits and the type of aphasia are still debated (Butterworth et al., 1984; Gainotti et al., 1975; Gardner, Albert & Weintraub, 1975; Goodglass & Baker, 1976; Kosslyn, Berndt & Doyle, 1985; McCleary & Hirst, 1986; Pizzamiglio & Appicciafuoco 1971), the majority of the aphasiological studies cited have clearly suggested that, independently from the type of aphasia, the degree of disruption of the semantic–conceptual organization highly correlates with a deficit in the semantic guided parsing of visual information and, more importantly, with respect to the issue of loss of visual dreaming imagery, it is directly related to the inability to perform a test requiring generation and use of imaginal information such as the drawing from memory test (Gainotti et al., 1983). It has been suggested that the deficit in drawing from memory could be explained assuming that "perceptual properties are represented as part of the concept of an object, either directly or in verbal terms." A slightly different view of the role of language in the retrieval of imaginal information has been proposed by Kosslyn (1987), who views the component-parts of a visual image as stored separately from the linguistic system which should be merely implicated in accessing nonlinguistic categorical–propositional information for arranging the different parts of the visual image in their appropriate locations. Considering the production and the recall of the dream experience as tasks in which respectively perceptual–semantic and semantic–imaginative processes (both sharing a common storage of semantic knowledge) play a significant role, the observed relationship between semantic impairment and perceptual–imaginative deficits could hypothetically explain the concomitance of aphasic disturbances and dream loss observed in some of the cases reviewed in this chapter. Indeed, not all the aphasics experience loss of dreaming as showed by the presence of LHD temporal and frontal patients with persistence of dreaming (see 6.1). It might be of interest to assess whether those who don't lose dreaming do maintain abilities, such as drawing from memory, indirectly suggesting intact coding and retrieval of visuo-imaginal information and integrity of semantic–lexical structures. The cases reviewed in this chapter do not allow this analysis, but it may be mentioned that in the study of Schanfald et al. (1985a), aphasic patients who claimed to experience dreaming, though with a relevant reduction in recall (see Appendix, Sec. 2), were capable of drawing from memory the dream scene. Available neuropsychological evidences suggest that language and more in particularly semantic functions are functionally involved both in the decoding of a dream and in its later recall.

Visual-verbal Disconnection, Occipitotemporal Lesions and Dream Recall Failure: Getting Closer to How Language and Vision Interact in Creating Dream Sense

Considering the sample of single cases of patients who reported complete cessation of dreaming, lateralization of damage appears to be related to dream loss only for damage within the occipital area, left or bilateral cases being more frequent than right cases. The latter were virtually absent both among patients experiencing dream cessation (zero cases) and among those who continued to dream (only one case, No. 12). A closer inspection of cases with cessation of dreaming that were classified as having occipital damage and for which an extensive neuropsychological description was available (see 6.3), revealed the presence of a highly homogeneous group with respect to localization of damage and syndromic pattern of the associated cognitive deficits. Patients No. 1, 24, 33, 34, 36, 40, all suffered from associative agnosia. In all cases the anatomical area predominantly involved was the left-infero-mesial, occipitotemporal cortex, with the exception of case No. 34, who suffered from a tumor of the left forceps of corpus callosum, and patient No. 36, who underwent left occipital lobectomy. The latter cases closely resemble other cases of surgically produced associative agnosia as those reported by Hecaen and De Ajuriaguerra (1956), and Hecaen et al., (1974). All patients reported a right homonimous hemianopia, alexia without agraphia and signs of visual associative agnosia such as object or picture anomia and color anomia. It is well known that this symptomatology characterizes the most typical and frequent human vascular disconnective agnosic–associative syndrome (Rubens, 1979), which is classically explained by assuming that the visual information processed by the intact RH fails to reach the speech area because of the presence of a left-infero-mesial occipital-temporal damage usually involving the LH posterior callosal fibers. In the group of BD patients reviewed in this chapter there are also three cases of patients with damage to the left infero-occipital lobe who maintained the experience of dreaming (cases No. 2, 8, 17; sec. 2). This suggests a more precise definition of the deficit associated with dream loss. All these patients reported some disconnective symptoms (alexia without agraphia, right homomimous hemianopia, etc.) but none was reported as suffering from anomic associative defects. It is noteworthy that one patient (No. 8) had a transient anomia with concomitant loss of dreaming for 3 months after an accident and recovered dream experience when the associative anomic deficit disappeared. A similar phenomenon occurred in a patient who experienced total loss of dreaming for 7 months (No. 40; Sec. 1) and who was reported as having had one dream when visual confrontation naming improved, but no more since. Two other cases of left occipital damage with persistence of dreaming activity are reported by Corda, both had traumatic etiology and absence of disconnective symptoms. The foregoing cases could therefore suggest a close functional link between disruption of visual naming and loss of dream recall; a possible exception is the case No. 22 (Sec. 1), who showed visuoverbal agnosia only during the acute phase. In this patient total dream loss persisted despite improvement in object naming. It has, however, to be remarked that some residual verbal receptive and visual perceptual disconnective deficits, which did not escape clinical notice (Farah, Levine, & Calvanio, 1988), were still present at the time of the investigation on his dream-recall ability.

Naming and Dreaming

Different cognitive models of object naming have been proposed to account for the visual anomic deficit showed by agnosic patients. Based on observations showing that these patients often fail to perform tasks requesting utilization of semantic knowledge (such as the functional matching or the semantic categorization of pictures or objects; Ferro & Santos, 1984; Hecaen et al., 1974; Lhermitte, Chedru, & Chain, 1973; Pillon, Signoret, & Lhermitte, 1981) it has been proposed that access to the phonological form of objects names depends on the prior access to semantic information about the object to be named (for a review of the naming models, see Riddoch & Humphreys, 1987, and Coslett & Saffran, 1989). The existence of cases of anomia and visual anomia with intact access to semantic storage (Coslett & Saffran, 1989; Gainotti, Silveri, Villa, & Miceli, 1986; Riddoch & Humphreys, 1987) has, however, confirmed the existence of a "non-semantic route to naming," (Ratcliff & Newcombe, 1982), directly linking the visual structural representation of an object to its associated phonological representation. In the recent literature, four cases have been described that could provide interesting suggestions about the nature of the relationship between the visual naming problem and the dreaming imagery deficits. Coslett and Saffran (1989) and Riddoch and Humphreys (1987a) have described two cases of visual anomics patient in which both access to semantic knowledge, and performance in imagery-based tasks (such as object–color matching and drawing from memory) were unimpaired. In contrast, Riddoch and Humphreys (1987b) and Beauvois and Saillant (1985) have described two cases of visual agnosia in which in correspondence with an impaired access to semantic storage in the first case and with a disconnection between visual and verbal representation of colors in the second case, drawing from memory and object to color matching (first case) and object to color matching (second case) were severely impaired. Only one of the disconnective cases reviewed in this chapter provides sufficient evidence in relation to this topic: case No. 40 (Pena-Casanova, Roig-Rovira, Bermudez, & Tolosa-Sarro, 1985) showed, in fact, visual anomia, total loss of dreaming, and severe deficits in the generation of visual images in association with severe problems of functional and semantic categorization of visual stimuli. These observations suggest the visual–semantic interactive nature (Gainotti et al., Miceli, 1986) of the concomitant naming, dreaming, and imagery deficits showed by some disconnective patients. Loss of dreaming in these cases could be explained by a basic cognitive disorder similar to that previously proposed for receptive aphasic patients. However, at variance with those patients (who suffer from a central disruption of the semantic storage) in disconnective cases, the locus of damage could be located in the neural route subserving both the access to the semantic knowledge from the visual modality and, in the opposite sense, the access to perceptual-like information from a verbal command (as in tasks such as recalling a dream or generating a mental image). Basing on present converging evidences, it is possible therefore to hypothesize that unilateral LH infero-occipito-temporal (IOT) damage, when associated with a visuoverbal disconnection producing failure to access to semantic knowledge of visually perceived inputs and to anomic deficits, is sufficient per se to cause cessation of dreaming. The visual recognition deficit could be due either to the fact that the "extraction of semantic values from visual informations" is disrupted (Gil et al., 1985; Lhermitte & Beauvois, 1973) or to the fact that visual semantic information is still provided by the RH but is not sufficient to produce the correct response (Coslett & Saffran, 1989; Michel, Schott, Boucher, & Kopp, 1979), while in the opposite sense imagery and dream-recall deficits could be ascribed to the fact that preserved semantic–visual links are not sufficient for reactivating visual–imaginative memories.

The Ventral Visual System: Discriminating Basic Visual Features and Linking Dreaming to Memory

Cases No. 3, 24, 35, 42, 43 were patients with bilateral infero-occipital damage who reported loss of dreaming. Three of them (cases No. 3, 42, 43) differed markedly in symptomatology from disconnective cases and showed a predominance of visual–perceptive deficits due probably to a more general damage of the IOT visual system, which is known to be critical for form discrimination (Fuster & Jervey, 1981; Van Essen & Maunsell, 1983). Wilson DeBauche, 1981; In case No. 24, damage to the RH was probably very limited; in fact, his agnosia evolved from an initial apperceptive type to a typical associative type. Similar symptomatological evolution has been observed in other patients (e.g., Larrabee, Levin, Huff, Kay, & Guinto, 1985). Case No. 35 suffered from a predominantly RHD and displayed agnosic–associative defects. Her hand preference, however, was unknown and in addition she was illiterate; therefore no solid assumption of her functional cerebral organization can be made (Tzavaras, Kaprinis, & Gatzoyas, 1981). In case No. 42 the association between predominantly LHD and strong visuoperceptive symptomatology (accompanied by proso-pagnosia) was probably due to the fact that the patient was left-handed. The absence of RH infero-occipital-temporal-damaged patients, both within dream loss and dream maintenance single-case samples, together with the lack of a more precise description of location of damage in group patients reported to be RHD does not allow firm conclusions about the role played by this area in the dreaming process. In patients with bilateral IOT damage cessation of dreaming could be linked both to a primary lesion of cortical areas subserving visual perceptive and storage processing (Ross, 1980) and to a bilateral interruption of visual–limbic connections (i.e., the inferior longitudinal fasciculi; Albert, 1980; Albert, Soffer, Silverbeg, & Reches, 1979) causing a disruption of the mechanism responsible for memory matching and storage of visual information. The role played by middle temporal area in the two temporally separated stages of formation and retrieval of visual memory traces is also suggested by the finding that electrical stimulation of this area can independently disrupt both processes preventing a subsequent re-retrieval of the memory trace (Halgren, Wilson, & Stapetlon, 1985).

GENERAL DISCUSSION

Dream Cessation and Localization of Damage

Although investigations on groups of patients agree in pointing out that cessation of dreaming is a relatively frequent consequence of brain damage, few case reports of patients with cessation or alteration of dreaming have been reported in the literature. This is probably due to a scarce clinical relevance attributed to dreaming both by clinicians and patients. Notwithstanding the relatively limited number of cases reviewed and the nonsystematic character of much of the information provided by different reports, a few tentative conclusions can be advanced. The most robust and consistent conclusion supported by the quantitative consideration, both of single cases and of groups of subjects with UBD, is that frontal lobe integrity is not critical for the maintainance of the experience of dreaming. The relationships between localization of damage in the RH or in the LH and the maintenance or loss of the dreaming experience appears more complex. With respect to frequency of cases, patients who report a loss of dreaming tend to have damage in the LH. However, the hypothesis of a LH specialization of dreaming advanced by Greenberg and Farah (1986) cannot be reconciled both with findings from the group of single cases with maintainance of dreaming and with findings from studies on groups of patients. In patients with cessation of dreaming damage is no doubt predominantly localized in the LH only within the occipital cases, and the consistency of the neurocognitive deficits associated with this localization of damage points to a precise relationship between loss of dreaming and visuoverbal disconnection. The total absence of reports of cases with damage confined to the occipitotemporal area of the RH both among patients who lost and among those who maintained dreaming does not allow to draw any conclusion on the relevance of the lateralization of this damage. The general lack of RH occipitotemporal cases points to the existence of a strong bias of "clinical relevance" in our bibliographical sample. The same bias is probably responsible of the fact that an ambidextrous parietal RHD patient showing language disorders (case No. 29) underwent clinical observation and entered in the sample of single cases: It could be, questionable therefore, to consider similar cases as unbiased and supportive of a predominance of the language-dominant hemisphere for dreaming as claimed by Greenberg and Farah (1986). Moreover, in unselected groups of patients no difference in loss of dream recall was found between RHD and LHD posterior patients. As shown by Arena et al. (1984), in a group of 33 UBD patients with damage in the LH, 15 subjects were able to report at least one dream over 10 days, and in the report by Murri et al. (1984) there were 5 patients, 4 of whom were without language disorders, with damage in the posterior LH still capable of recalling their dreams. Furthermore in their last paper, Murri and coworkers (in preparation) found that the only 5 patients in which complete dream cessation persisted in the chronic phase were all RHD.

More on Language and Dreaming

Several findings point to a relationship between language disorders and cessation of dreaming. Studies on groups of subjects with UBD show that for patients with damage confined to the LH, only the subgroup with language disorders showed a significant reduction in the frequency of dreaming relative to control subjects. Virtually all patients with damage in the LH who experienced loss of dreaming suffered from some aphasic disorder, a notable exception being patients with disconnective symptoms. Among patients with visuoverbal disconnection the symptom more closely associated with the loss of dreaming was visual anomia. This symptom was absent in disconnective cases with maintainance of dreaming or disappeared in concomitance with recovery of dream experience. Future investigations should determine: (a) what degree of disconnection, along the dimension "pure visuo-verbal agnosia-general associative agnosia," is sufficient to produce a dream-recall deficit; (b) if impaired access to semantic knowledge from visual modality must be accompanied by visual anomia in order to disrupt dreaming. On the bases of available knowledge it is hypothesized that when aphasic or anomic difficulties are purely due to problems in accessing the phonological form of an object name (Gainotti et al., 1986) dream recall (as well as imagery generation) will not be affected. The disconnective cases reviewed seem to indicate that a defective interaction between visual information elaboration and the long-term semantic memory storage (Tulving, 1972) could be a disrupting factor in the depth of encoding of the dream experience (Craik & Lockart, 1972; Craik & Tulving, 1975) and consequently in dream retrieval. Similarly, aphasic disturbances producing a damage more selectively limited to semantic memory storage could influence the quality and/or quantity of dream encoding and retrieval by altering the semantic top–down parsing of endogenously generated informations.

Are Dreaming and Imagery Generation Deficits Selective?

The strong association between language disorders and disconnective symptoms, on one hand, and loss of the dreaming experience on the other, suggests a direct relationship between visual–semantic functions and dreaming imagery. A direct relationship between loss of dreaming and a selective imagery deficit has been claimed by Farah et al. (1988) who, however, have not completely substantiated their claim through an evaluation of the visual–semantic abilities of the patient (No. 22; Sec. 1). Also Grossi, Orsini, Modafferri, and Liotti (1986) have recently claimed the selective nature of an imagery deficit reported by a patient with a circumscribed ischemic lesion of the left IOT area, a right superior quadrantanopia and no anomia. However, it must be mentioned that in the neuropsychological evaluation of this patient the Lesser test was administered in a visuovisual version (i.e., matching of a picture with the corresponding object placed among distractors); this method, by providing morphological cues, could not allow an adequate evaluation of the functioning of the visual–verbal semantic system, which, in fact, was at least in part disrupted since the patient showed striking problems in the interpretation of complex pictures (a soldiers' parade) or bizarre pictures (a jacket-dressed centaurus), a task requiring the correct integration of pictorial and semantic information. The claim of the selectivity of imagery generation function (Farah, 1984), when based on clinical cases with damage confined to the hemisphere dominant for language, needs therefore to be substantiated by a careful evaluation of the integrity of the interaction between visual and semantic processes. Given the constant concomitance of dream recall and imagery deficits found in the present review it is possible to suggest that the LH contribution to the dreaming experience relays at least in part on the same psychological processes that it subserves for waking mental imagery. Needless to say, however, the sequence of cognitive operations requested for the voluntary evocation of perceptual-like information cannot be assumed as identical to the basically authomathical processing of the inner cognitive events of the REM sleep. Looking at the striking consequences of semantic disorders on dream recall one is also led to the apparently paradoxical conclusions that the appearance of the visual–semantic incongruities that so often characterize dreaming is strictly conditioned to the perfect and complete functioning of the processes subserving meaning recognition during waking.

Right Occipitotemporal Lesions and Dreaming: An Unsolved Neuropsychological Issue

As repeatedly noticed present data do not allow any definition of the nature of the contribution of the RH occipitotemporal area to dreaming. However, on the functionally realistic assumption that the RH during sleep will continue to subserve the same functions for which it is responsible during waking, and given its greater ability in decoding percepts characterized by low-stimulus energy (Sergent & Hellige, 1986) and its competence of the RH occipital-temporal areas in test of perceptual closure (Gur & Reivich, 1980; Wasserstein, Zappulla, Rosen, & Gerstman, 1984; Wasserstein, Zappulla, Rosen, Gerstman, & Rock, 1987), it can be hypothesized (in agreement with Antrobus, 1987) that the RH provides the perceptual "large grain" basis, which is probably indispensable for the sensorial vividness of the dream experience.

CONCLUSIONS AND PERSPECTIVES

Findings from the present review point out that the disruption of specific hemispheric areas can lead to cessation of dream experience. It has been suggested that the extension of the lesion is the critical factor in producing a dream deficit (Schanfald et al., 1985a). The fact that dream persistence is shown by LHD patients without language disorders could support this hypothesis, since it is known that in these patients damages are confined to smaller areas. However, in contrast to the view of Schanfald and coworkers, our review shows that: (a) The frequency of cases with bilateral damages (which, at least for the patients considered in the present review, can be assumed as wider than unilateral damages) is not higher than the frequency of left or right unilateral damage; (b) Damage to specific lobes (frontal) is not associated to loss of dreaming while damage in precise and limited areas of one hemisphere (those associated with disconnective syndrome) is linked to total cessation of dreaming. The fact that a precise area subserving a specific function plays a critical role in the dreaming experience casts doubt on the appropriateness of the hypothesis linking dreaming to a generic asymmetry in "hemispheric activation" during sleep. This notion has to be recognized as too generic and potentially misleading though it has had an unquestionable heuristic value, stimulating a large number of EEG. studies yielding contradictory results (see for review, Bertini & Violani, this volume). If any asymmetry in activation exists it should be detected by careful cerebral blood flow studies (Stirling Meyer, Ishikawa, Hata, & Karacan, 1987) in those cerebral regions subserving neuropsychological functions that are more likely to be primarily involved in dreaming. Further research on brain-damaged patients enlarging the present data base is needed in order to confirm and extend our conclusions. Such research could consider, for example, an accurate follow-up of the eventual functional and cognitive recovery preceding or concomitant to the recovery of the experience of dreaming. Also studies on normal subject can contribute in confirming (or disconfirming) some of our hypothesis. These investigations could ascertain whether performance level and/or pattern of hemispheric lateralization of neuropsychological functions critically implicated in the dream experience are different in habitual dream recallers, compared with those subjects who are usually incapable of recalling their dreams. At present the neuropsychological nature of damages more seriously compromising dream recall indicates that lack of dreaming could depend not only on a mnemonic deficit or on a defective verbalization of dream experience, but also on deficits in cognitive decoding of the dream during its actual nocturnal development, since these damages, beside affecting linguistic functions, also affect cognitive processes that are nonlinguistic but functionally linked to language and probably indispensable to the full perceptual–cognitive processing of internally generated information. In the interpretation of the scattered neuropsychological evidences concerning dreaming we deliberately did not rely on any of the existing theories of dream production (scanning hypothesis, activation–synthesis hypothesis, cortical activation hypothesis) and by contrast we chose a microheuristic approach consisting in the consideration of circumscribed empirical and theoretical nodes that appear to be central to the formulation of any theory of dream production and recall. We think that a complete and exhaustive interpretative frame of reference for the available neuropsychological data will be provided only by a future empirically grounded definition of the flow of neurocognitive information within the "dreaming human nervous system." Our review was primarily intended at promoting and help anyone interested in the realization of such an ambitious and exciting scientific project.

ACKNOWLEDGMENTS

The chapter is dedicated to Patrizia Sirianni Doricchi who provided continuous support during the preparation of the manuscript.

REFERENCES

Adler, A. (1944). Disintegration and restoration of optic recognition in visual agnosia. *Archives of Neurology and Psychiatry, 51,* 243–259.

Adler, A. (1950). Course and outcome of visual agnosia. *Journal of Nervous and Mental Disease, 111,* 41–51.

Albert, M. L. (1980). The anatomic basis of visual agnosia: Letter to the editor. *Neurology, 30,* 110.

Albert, M. L., Soffer, D., Silverberg, R., & Reches, A. (1979). The anatomic basis of visual agnosia. *Neurology, 29,* 876–879.

Antrobus, J. (1987). Cortical hemisphere asymmetry and sleep mentation. *Psychological Review, 94,* 359–368.

Arena, R., Murri, L., Piccini, P., & Muratorio, A. (1984). Dream recall and memory in brain lesioned patients. *Research Communications in Psychology, Psychiatry and Behavior, 9,* 31–42.

Bakan, P. (1978). Dreaming, REM sleep, and the right hemisphere: A theoretical integration. *Journal of Altered States of Consciousness, 3,* 285–307.

Basso, A., Bisiach, E., & Luzzatti, C. (1980). Loss of mental imagery: A case study. *Neuropsychologia, 18,* 435–442.

Basso, A., Faglioni, P., & Spinnler, H. (1976). Non-verbal colour impairment in aphasics. *Neuropsychologia, 14,* 183–192.

Bay, E. (1962). Aphasia and nonverbal disorders of language. *Brain 85,* 411–426.

Beauvois, M. F., & Saillant, B. (1985). Optic aphasia for colours and colour agnosia: A distinction between visual and visuo-verbal impairments in the processing of colours. *Cognitive Neuropsychology, 2*(1), 1–48.

Benson, D. F., & Greenberg, J. P. (1969). Visual form agnosia. *Archives of Neurology, 20,* 82–89.

Bernard, D. (1883). Un cas de suppression brusque et isolée de la vision mentale des signes et des objets (formes et couleurs) [A case of sudden and selective suppression of mental vision of signs and objects (forms and colors]. *Le Progres Medicale, 2,* 568–571.

Bertini, M., & Violani, C. (1984). Cerebral hemispheres, REM sleep and dream recall. *Research Communications in Psychology, Psychiatry, and Behavior, 9,* 3–14.

Bisiach, E., & Berti, A. (1987). Dyschiria. An attempt and its systematic explanation. In M. Jeannerod (Ed.), *Neurophysiological and neuropsychological aspects of spatial neglect.* Amsterdam: North Holland.

Bisiach, E., Capitani, E., Luzzatti, C., & Perani, D. (1981). Brain and conscious representation of outside reality. *Neuropsychologia, 19,* 543–551.

Bisiach, E., & Luzzatti, C. (1978). Unilateral neglect of representational space. *Cortex, 14,* 129–133.

Bisiach, E., Luzzatti, C., & Perani, D. (1979). Unilateral neglect, representational schema and consciousness. *Brain, 102,* 609–618.

Botez, M. I., Olivier, M., Vezina, J. L., Botez, T., & Kaufman, B. (1985). Defective revisualization: dissociation between cognitive and imagistic thought case report and short review of the literature. *Cortex, 21,* 375–389.

Botez, M. I., Serbanescu, T., Vernea, I. (1964). Visual static with special reference to literal agnosic alexia. *Neurology, 14,* 1101–1111.

Boyle, J., & Nielsen, J. M. (1954). Visual agnosia and loss of recall. *Bulletin of the Los Angeles Neurological Society, 19;* 39–42.

Bradshaw, J. L., & Nettleton, N. C. (1981). The nature of hemispheric specialization in man. *Behavioral and Brain Sciences, 4,* 51–91.

Brain, W. R. (1941a). Visual object agnosia with special reference to the gestalt theory. *Brain, 64,* 43–62.

Brain, W. R. (1941b). Visual disorientation with special reference to lesions of the right cerebral hemisphere. *Brain, 64,* 224–272.

Brain, W. R. (1954). Loss of visualization. *Proceedings of the Royal Society of Medicine, 47,* 288–290.

Butterworth, B., Howard, D., & McLoughlin, P. (1984). The semantic deficit in aphasia: The relationship between semantic errors in auditory comprehension and picture naming. *Neuropsychologia, 22*(4), 409–426.

Caramazza, A., Berndt, R. S., & Brownell, H. H. (1982). The semantic deficit hypothesis: Perceptual parsing and an object classification by aphasic patients. *Brain and Language, 15,* 161–189.

Cathala, H. P., Laffont, F., Siksou, M., Esnault, A., Gilbert, M., Minz, M., Moret-Chalmin, C., Buzare, M. A., & Waisbord, P. (1983). Sommeil et rêve chez des patients atteints de lesions parietales et frontales [Sleep and dreaming in patients with parietal and frontal lesions]. *Revue Neurologique, 139,* 497–508.

Cohen, R., & Kelter, S. (1979). Cognitive impairment of aphasics in a colour-to-picture matching task. *Cortex, 15,* 235–245.

Corda, F. (1985). *Esperienza onirica in pazienti portatori di lesioni cerebrali unilaterali* [Oneiric experience in patients with unilateral brain damage]. Unpublished dissertation, University of Rome.

Coslett, H. B., & Saffran, E. M. (1989). Preserved object recognition and reading comprehension in optic aphasia. *Brain, 112,* 1091–1110.

Craik, F. I. M., & Lockart, R. S. (1972). Levels of processing: A framework for memory research. *Journal of Verbal Learning and Verbal Behaviour, 11,* 671–684.

Craik, F. I. M., & Tulving, E. (1975). Depth of processing and the retention of words in episodic memory. *Journal of Experimental Psychology: General, 1104,* 268–294.

Deleval, J., De Mol, J., & Noterman, J. (1983). La perte des images souvenirs [Loss of memory images]. *Acta Neurologica Belgica, 83,* 61–79.

De Renzi, E., Colombo, A., Faglioni, P., & Gibertoni, M. (1982). Conjugate gaze paresis in stroke patients with unilateral brain damage. *Archives of Neurology, 39,* 482–486.

De Renzi, E., Faglioni, P., Savoiardo, M., & Vignolo, L. A. (1972). Impairment in associating colour to form concomitant with aphasia. *Brain, 95,* 293–304.

Duffy, J. R., & Watkins, L. B. (1984). The effect of response choice relatedness on pantomime and verbal recognition ability in aphasic patients. *Brain and Language, 21,* 291–306.

Duffy, R. J., Duffy J. R., & Pearson, K. (1975). Pantomime recognition in aphasics. *Journal of Speech and Hearing Research, 18,* 115–132.

Epstein, A. W. (1979). Effect of certain cerebral hemispheric disease on dreaming. *Biological Psychiatry, 14,* 77–92.

Epstein, A. W., & Simmons, N. N. (1983). Aphasia with reported loss of dreaming. *American Journal of Psychiatry, 140,* 108–109.

Ettlinger, G., Warrington, E., & Zangwill, O. L. (1957). A further study of visual-spatial agnosia. *Brain, 80,* 335–361.

Farah, M. J. (1984). The neurological basis of mental imagery: A componential analysis. *Cognition, 18,* 245–272.

Farah, M. J., Levine, D. N., & Calvanio, R. (1988). A case study of mental imagery deficit. *Brain and Cognition, 8,* 147–164.

Farrell, B. (1969). *Pat and Roald.* New York: Random House.

Ferro, J. M., & Santos, E. M. (1984). Associative visual agnosia: A case study. *Cortex, 20,* 121–134.

Fuster, J. M., & Jervey, J. P. (1981). Inferotemporal neurons distinguish and retain behaviorally relevant features of visual stimuli. *Science, 212,* 952–954.

Gainotti, G., Ibba, A., & Caltagirone, C. (1975). Perturbations acoustiques et semantiques de la comprehension dans l'aphasie [Acoustic and semantic comprehension deficits in aphasia]. *Revue Neurologique, 131,* 645–659.

Gainotti, G., & Lemmo, M. (1976). Comprehension of symbolic gestures in aphasia. *Brain and Language, 3,* 451–460.

Gainotti, G., Miceli, G., & Caltagirone, C. (1979). The relationship between conceptual and semantic–lexical disorders in aphasia. *International Journal of Neuroscience, 10,* 45–50.

Gainotti, G., Silveri, M. C., Villa, G., & Caltagirone, C. (1983). Drawing objects from memory in aphasia. *Brain, 106;* 613–622.

Gainotti, G., Silveri, M. C., Villa, G., & Miceli, G. (1986). Anomia with and without lexical comprehension disorders. *Brain and Language, 29,* 18–33.

Galin, D. (1974). Implications for psychiatry of left and right cerebral specialization. *Archives of General Psychiatry, 31,* 572–583.

Gardner, H., Albert, M. L., & Weintraub, S. (1975). Comprehending a word: The influence of speed and redundancy on auditory comprehension in aphasia. *Cortex, 11,* 155–162.

Geschwind, N. (1965). Disconnection syndromes in animals and man. *Brain, 88,* 237–294.

Gil, R., Pluchon, C., Toullat, G., Micheneau, D., Rogez, R., & Lefevre, J. P. (1985). Disconnexion visuo-verbale (aphasie optique) pour les objects, les images, les couleurs et les visages avec alexie "abstractive" [Visual-verbal disconnection (optic aphasia) for objects, pictures, colours and faces with "abstractive alexia"]. *Neuropsychologia, 23,* 333–349.

Gloning, K., & Sternbach, I. (1953). Über das Traeumen bei zerebralen Herdlaesionen [Dreaming in patients with focal brain lesions]. *Wiener Zeitschrift für Nervenheilkunde und deren Grenzgebiete, 6,* 302–329.

Goodglass, H., & Baker, E. (1976). Semantic field, naming and auditory comprehension in aphasia. *Brain and Language, 3,* 359–374.

Greenberg, M. S., & Farah, M. J. (1986). The laterality of dreaming. *Brain and Cognition, 5,* 307–321.

Greenberg, R. (1966). Cerebral cortex lesions: the dream process and sleep spindles. *Cortex, 2,* 357–366.

Greenberg, R., & Pearlman, C. 91967). Delirium tremens and dreaming. *American Journal of Psychiatry, 124,* 133–142.

Greenberg, R., Pearlman, C., Brooks, R., Mayer, R., & Hartmann, F. (1968). Dreaming and Korsakoff's psychosis. *Archives of General Psychiatry, 18,* 203–209.

Greenwood, P., & Wilson, D. H., & Gazzaniga, M. S. (1977). Dream report following commisurotomy. *Cortex, 13,* 311–316.

Grossi, D., Orsini, A., Modafferi, A., & Liotti, M. (1986). Visuoimaginal constructional apraxia: On a case of selective deficit of imagery. *Brain and Cognition, 5,* 255–267.

Grunstein, A. M. (1924). Die Erforschung der Traeume als eine Methode der topischen Diagnostik bei Grosshirnerkrankungen [The analysis of dreams as a method of diagnostic localization in severe head injuries]. *Zeitschrift für die gesamte Neurologie und Psychiatrie, 93;* 416–420.

Gur, R.C., & Reivich, M. (1980). Cognitive task effect on hemispheric blood flow in humans: Evidence for individual differences in hemispheric activation. *Brain and Language, 9;* 78–92.

Halgren, E., Wilson, C. L., & Stapetlon, J. M. (1985). Human formation and retrieval of recent memories. *Brain and Cognition, 4;* 287–295.

Hecaen, H., (1972). *Introduction à la neuropsychologie* [An introduction to neuropsychology]. Paris: Larousse.

Hecaen, H., & de Ajuriaguerra, J. (1956). Agnosia visuelle pour les objects inanimes par lesion unilaterale gauche [Visual agnosia for inanimated objects due to left unilateral brain damage]. *Revue Neurologique, 94;* 222–233.

Hecaen, H., Goldblum, M. G., Masure, M. C., & Ramier, A. M. (1974). Une nouvelle observation d'agnosie d'objet. Deficit de l'association ou de la categorization specifique de la modalité visuelle? [A new case observation of object agnosia. Associative or categorization deficit of the visual modality?] *Neuropsychologia, 12;* 447–464.

Herman, J. H. (in press). Transmutative and reproductive properties of dreams: Evidence for cortical modulation of brain stem generators. In J. Antrobus, & M. Bertini, (Eds.), *The neuropsychology of dreaming sleep,* Hillsdale, NJ: Lawrence Erlbaum Associates.

Hobson, J. A., & McCarley, R. (1977). The brain as a dream state dream generator: An activation-synthesis hypothesis of the dream process. *American Journal of Psychiatry, 134;* 1335-1348.

Hoppe, K. D. (1977). Split brains and psychoanalysis. *Psychoanalytic Quarterly, 46;* 220-245.

Humphrey, M. E., & Zangwill, O. L. (1951). Cessation of dreaming after brain injury. *Journal of Neurology, Neurosurgery, and Psychiatry, 14;* 322-325.

Ishiai, S., Furukawa, T., & Tsukagoshi, H. (1987). Eye-fixation patterns in homonymous hemyanopia and unilateral spatial neglect. *Neuropsychologia, 25*(4); 675-679.

Jeannerod, M., Mouret, J., & Jouvet, M. (1965). Étude de la motricité oculaire au cours du sommeil chez le chat [A study of sleep oculomotor behavior in the cat]. *Electroencephalography and Clinical Neurophysiology, 18,* 554-566.

Jus, A., Jus, K., Villeneuve, A., Pires, A., Lachance, R., Fortier, J., & Villeneuve, R. (1974). Studies on dream recall in chronic schizophrenic patients after prefrontal lobotomy. *Biological Psychiatry, 6;* 275-293.

Kerr, N. K., Foulkes, D. (1981). Right hemispheric mediation of dream visualization: A case study. *Cortex, 17;* 603-610.

Kerr, N. K., Foulkes, D., Jurkovic, G. J. (1978). Reported absence of visual dream imagery in a normally sighted subject with Turner's syndrome. *Journal of Mental Imagery, 2,* 247-264.

Kosslyn, S. M. (1987). Seeing and imagining in the cerebral hemispheres: A computational approach. *Psychological Review, 94*(2), 148-175.

Kosslyn, S. M., Berndt, R. S., & Doyle, T. J. (1985). Imagery and language processing: A neuropsychological approach. In M. S. Posner & O. S. Marin (Eds.), *Attention and performance* (Vol. 11, pp. 319-334). Hillsdale, NJ; Lawrence Erlbaum Associates.

Kramer, M., Roth T., & Trinder, J. (1975). Dreams and dementia: Laboratory exploration of dream recall and dream content in chronic brain syndrome patients. *International Journal of Aging Human Development, 6,* 169-178.

Larrabee, G. L., Levin, H. S., Huff, F. J., Kay, M. C., & Guinto, F.C. Jr. (1985). Visual agnosia contrasted with visual-verbal disconnection. *Neuropsychologia, 23,* 1-12.

Lesser, R. (1974). Verbal comprehension in aphasia: An English version of three Italian tests. *Cortex, 10,* 247-263.

Levine, D. N., Warach, J., & Farah, M. (1985). Two visual systems in mental imagery. *Neurology, 35,* 1010-1018.

Lhermitte, F., & Beauvois, M. F. (1973). A visual speech disconnexion syndrome. *Brain, 96,* 695-714.

Lhermitte, F., Chedru, F., & Chain, F. (1973). A propos d'un cas d'agnosie visuelle [On a case of visual agnosia]. *Revue Neurologique, 128,* 301-322.

Lynch, J. C. (1980). The functional organization of posterior parietal association cortex. *Behavioral and Brain Sciences, 3,* 485-534.

Lyman, R. S., Kwan, S. T., & Chao, W. H. (1938). Left occipito-parietal brain tumor with observations on alexia and agraphia in Chinese and English. *Chinese Medical Journal, 54,* 491-516.

Mamelak, A. N., & Hobson, J. A. (1989). Dream bizarreness as the cognitive correlate of altered neuronal behavior in REM sleep. *Journal of Cognitive Neuroscience, 1*(3), 201-222.

MacRae, D., & Trolle, E. (1956). The defect of function in visual agnosia. *Brain, 79,* 94-110.

McCarley, R. W., Winkelman, J. W., & Duffy, F. H. (1983). Human cerebral potentials associated with REM sleep rapid eye movements: Links to PGO waves and waking potentials. *Brain Research, 274,* 359-364.

McCleary, C., & Hirst, W. (1986). Semantic classification in aphasia: A study of basic, superordinate, and function relations. *Brain and Language, 27,* 199-209.

Mendius, J. R., & Engel, J., Jr. (1985). Studies of hemispheric lateralization in patients with partial epilepsy. In F. D. Benson, & E. Zaidel (Eds.), *The dual brain* (pp. 263-273). New York: Guilford Press.

Mesulam, M. M. (1983). The functional anatomy and hemispheric specialization for directed attention. *Trends in Neuroscience,* September, 384–387.

Michel, F., Jeannerod, M., & Devic, M. (1965). Trouble de l'orientation visuelle dans les trois dimensions de l'espace [Deficit of visual orientation into the three spatial dimensions]. *Cortex, 1,* 441–466.

Michel, F., Schott, B., & Boucher, M., & Kopp, N. (1979). Alexie sans agraphie chez un malade ayant un hemisphere gauche deafferenté [Alexia without agraphia in a patient with left hemisphere deafferntation]. *Revue Neurologique, 135,* 347–364.

Michel, F., & Sieroff, E. (1981). Une approche anatomo–clinique des deficits de l'imagerie onirique, est elle possible? [An anatomo–clinical approach to oneiric-imagery deficits, is it possible?]. *Sleep: Proceedings of an International Colloquium.* Milan: Carlo Erba Formitalia.

Miyauchi, S., Takino, R., Fukuda, H., & Torii, S. (1987). Electrophysiological evidences for dreaming: Human cerebral potentials associated with rapid eye movements during REM sleep. *Electroencephalography and Clinical Neurophysiology, 66,* 383–390.

Montplaisir, J., Cote, J., Laverdiere, M., & St. Hilaire, J. M. (1985). Dream recall before and after partial commisurotomy. In W. P. Koella, E., Ruther, & H. Schultz (Eds.), *Sleep.* Stuttgart; New York: Fischer Verlag.

Moss, C. S. (1972). *Recovery with aphasia: The aftermath of my stroke.* Urbana, IL: University of Illinois Press.

Muller, F. (1892). Ein Beitrag zur Kenntnis der Seelenblindheit [A contribution to the study of cortical blindness]. *Archives psichiatrie und Nervenarzt, 24,* 856–917.

Murri, L., Arena, R., Siciliano, G., Mazzotta, R., & Muratorio, A. (1984). Dream recall in patients with focal cerebral lesions. *Archives of Neurology, 41,* 183–185.

Murri, L., Arena, R., Mancino, M., Canapicchi, R., Puglioli, M., & Rossi, G. (in preparation). *A neurological approach to the anatomofunctional correlates of dreaming.*

Murri, L., Massetani, R., Siciliano, G., Giovanditti, L., & Arena, R. (1985). Dream recall after sleep interruption in brain injured patients. *Sleep, 8,* 356–362.

Myers, R. E. (1956). Function of the corpus callosum in interocular transfer. *Brain, 79,* 358–363.

Myers, R. E., & Sperry, R. W. (1953). Interocular transfer of visual form discrimination habit in cats after section of the optic chiasma and corpus callosum. *Anatomical Record, 115,* 351–352.

Nielsen, J. M. (1955). Occipital lobe dreams and psychosis. *Journal of Nervous and Mental Disease, 121,* 50–52.

Niiyama, Y., Shimizu, T., Abe, M., & Hishikawa, Y. (1988). Phasic EEG activities associated with rapid eye movements during REM sleep in man. *Electroencephalography and Clinical Neurophysiology, 70,* 396–403.

Paterson, A., & Zangwill O. L. (1944). Disorders of visual space perception associated with lesions of the right cerebral hemisphere. *Brain, 67,* 331–358.

Pena-Casanova, J., Roig-Rovira, T., Bermudez, A., & Tolosa-Sarro, E. (1985). Optic aphasia, optic apraxia and loss of dreaming. *Brain and Language, 26,* 63–71.

Piercy, M. F., Hecaen, H., & De Ajuriaguerra, J. (1960). Constructional apraxia associated with unilateral cerebral lesions. Left and right sided cases compared. *Brain, 83,* 225–242.

Pierrot-Deseilligny, C., & Rivaud, S. (1987). Cortico–nuclear circuitry controlling lateral visually guided saccades in man. In J. K. O'Regan, A. Levy-Schoen (Eds.), *Eye movements: From physiology to cognition.* New York: Elsevier (North–Holland).

Pillon, B. G., Signoret, L., & Lhermitte, F. (1981). Agnosie visuelle associative. Role de l'hemisphere gauche dans la perception visuelle [Associative visual agnosia. Role of the left hemisphere in visual perception]. *Revue Neurologique, 137,* 831–842.

Pizzamiglio, L., & Appicciafuoco, A. (1971). Semantic comprehension in aphasia. *Journal of Communication Disorders, 3,* 280–288.

Posner, M. I., Walker, J. A., Friedrich, F. A., & Rafal, R. D. (1987). How do the parietal lobes direct covert attention? *Neuropsychologia, 25*(1), 135–145.

Ratcliff, & Newcombe (1982). Object recognition: Some deductions from clinical evidence. In A. W. Ellis (Ed.), *Normality and pathology in cognitive function*. London: Academic Press.

Riddoch, M. J., & Humphreys, G. W. (1987a). A case of integrative visual agnosia. *Brain, 110*, 1431–1462.

Riddoch, M. J., & Humphreys, G. W. (1987b). Visual object processing in optic aphasia: A case of semantic access agnosia. *Cognitive Neuropsychology, 4*(2), 131–185.

Ross, E. D. (1980). The anatomic basis of visual agnosia: Letter to the editor. *Neurology, 30*, 109.

Rubens, A. B. (1979). Agnosia. In K. M. Heilman & E. Valenstein (Eds.), *Clinical neuropsychology*, New York: Oxford University Press.

Rubens, A. B., & Benson F. (1971). Associative visual agnosia. *Archives of Neurology, 24*, 305–316.

Schanfald, D., Pearlman, C., & Greenberg, R. (1985a). The capacity of stroke patients to report dreams. *Cortex, 21*,

Schanfald, D., Pearlman, C., & Greenberg, R. (1985b). Focal brain damage and dream recall. *Sleep Research, 14*, 116.

Sergent, J., & Hellige, J. B. (1986). Role of input factors in visual fields asymmetries. *Brain and Cognition, 5*, 174–199.

Shuttleworth, E. C., Syring, V. Jr., Allen, N. (1982). Further observations on the nature of prosopagnosia. *Brain and Cognition, 1*, 307–322.

Starr, A. (1967). A disorder of rapid eye movements in Huntington's chorea. *Brain, 90*, 545–564.

Stirling Meyer, J., Ishikawa, Y., Hata, T., & Karacan, I. (1987). Cerebral blood flow in normal and abnormal sleep and dreaming. *Brain and Cognition, 6*, 266–294.

Sundqvist, A. (1979). Saccadic reaction-time in parietal-lobe dysfunction. *Lancet*, April 21, 870.

Torda, G. (1969). Dreams of subjects with loss of memory for recent events. *Psychophysiology, 6*, 358–365.

Tulving, E. (1972). Episodic and semantic memory. In E. Tulving & W. Donaldson, (Eds), *Organization of memory*. New York: Academic Press.

Tzavaras, A. (1967). Contribution a l'étude de l'agnosie des physionomies: memoire pour le titre d'assistant entrager [A contribution to the study of prosopagnosia]. *Faculté de medicine de Paris, 1*, 1–71.

Tzavaras, A., Kaprinis, G., & Gatzoyas, A. (1981). Literacy and hemispheric specialization for language: Digit dichotic listening in illiterates. *Neuropsychologia, 19*(4), 565–570.

Ungerleider, L. G., & Mishkin, M. (1982). Two cortical visual systems. In D. J. Ingle, R. J. W. Mansfield, M. S. Goodale, (Eds.), *The analysis of visual behavior*. Cambridge, MA: MIT Press.

Van Essen, D. C., & Maunsell, J.H.R. (1983). Hierarchical organization and functional streams in the visual cortex. *Trends in Neurosciences, 6*, 370–375.

Varney, N. R. (1982). Pantomime recognition defect in aphasia: Implications for the concept of asymbolia. *Brain and Language, 15*, 32–39.

Wapner, W., Judd, T., & Gardner, H. (1978). Visual agnosia in an artist. *Cortex, 14*, 343–364.

Wasserstein, J., Zappulla, R., Rosen, J., & Gerstman, L. (1984). Evidence for differentiation of right hemisphere visual–perceptual functions. *Brain and Cognition, 3*, 51–56.

Wasserstein, J., Zappulla, R., Rosen, J., Gerstman, L., & Rock, D. (1987). In search of closure: Subjective contour illusions, gestalt completion tests, and implications. *Brain and Cognition, 6*, 1–14.

Wayland, S., & Taplin, J. E. (1985a). Feature-processing deficits following brain injury. I.

Overselectivity in recognition memory for compound stimuli. *Brain and Cognition, 4,* 338–355.

Wayland, S., & Taplin, J. E. (1985a). Feature-processing deficits following brain injury. I. Overselectivity in recognition memory for compound stimuli. *Brain and Cognition, 4,* 338–355.

Wayland, S., & Taplin, J. E. (1985b). Feature-processing deficits following brain injury. II. Classification learning, categorical decision making, and feature production. *Brain and Cognition, 4,* 356–376.

Whitehouse, P., Caramazza, A., & Zurif, E. B. (1978). Naming in aphasia: Interacting effects of form and function. *Brain and Language, 6,* 63–74.

Wilbrand, H. (1892). Ein Fall von Seelenblindheit und Hemianopsie mit Sektionsbefund [A case of cortical blindness and hemianopia with pathological verification]. *Zeitschrift für Nervenheilkunde, 2,* 361–387.

Wilson, M., & DeBauche, B. A. (1981). Inferotemporal cortex and categorical perception of visual stimuli by monkeys. *Neuropsychologia, 19,* 29–41.

Zaidel, E. (1976). Auditory vocabulary of the right hemisphere following brain bisection or hemidecortication. *Cortex, 12,* 191–211.

Zurif, E., Caramazza, A., Myerson, R., & Galvin, J. (1974). Semantic feature representations for normal and aphasic language. *Brain and Language, 1,* 167–187.

APPENDIX

Section 1

Cases with total cessation of the dreaming experience.

Table caption: No = Case number, Ref = Reference, S = Sex, A = Age in year, Hd = Handedness (R = right, L = left, R+L = ambidexterous), Id = Investigation delay from the accident (in months or years),E = Etiology (Cg = Congenital, S = Surgical, Tu = Tumoral, Tr = Traumatic, Tx = Toxic, V = Vascular), Loc = Localization (F = Frontal, O = Occipital, P = Parietal, Post = Posterior, T = Temporal, Thal = Thalamic, R = Right, L = Left, BL = Bilateral, Pred. = Predominantly), Dm = Diagnostic methodology (a = autopsy, bs = brain scan, ct = computerized tomography scan, S = Surgical, sympt. = symptomatologic, r = X ray)

No. Ref., S, A, Hd, Id, E, Loc., Dm.

1 Basso ea 80, M, 63, R, 4m, V, O-T. L. + left sup. cerebellum, ct.

Deficit: Right homonymous hemianopia, picture naming, transitory dysphasia, alexia, mild color gnosis, color-figure matching, visual imagery, topographical memory, topographical agnosia, hypnagogic imagery, prosopanomia, poor drawing from memory.

Intact: Writing on dictation, object recognition, calculia, praxia, recent and ancient memories, topographical orientation.

2 Benson & Greenberg 69, M, 25, -, 7m, Tx, P-O. BL, eeg+bs *Deficit:* Oculomotor patterns during object inspection, object and picture matching and recognition, letter recognition, geometrical figures matching, body recognition, total copying, drawing from memory, prosopagnosia.

Intact: Visual fields, language, recent and ancient memory, comprehension, repetition, color recognition and identification, ocular fixation, slow foveal pursuit, tactile–olphactive–auditive identification, somesthesia, REMrems, luminance and wavelength perception, facial and limb movements on verbal command.

Note: EOG study in wake, REM awakenings, bilateral posterior ventricular dilatation, carbon monoxide poisoning.

3 Boyle & Nielsen 54; Nielsen 55. M, 31, -, 5m, S, O.R. + L. opt. radiation, S.

Deficit: Left homonymous hemianopia, right superior hemianopia, restriction of visual fields, visual object agnosia, prosopagnosia, mild animate object visual agnosia, temporal and spatial disorientation, color identification, visual imagery.

Intact: Language, calculation (algebra), writing, acoustic–tactile–olphactive identification.

Note: Introduction of a drainage tube in right occ. lobe producing a lesion of left optic radiation, Mathematician.

4 Corda 85. M, 66, R, 4m, V, F. R., ct.
Deficit: Left leg paresis, LTM Verb. *Intact:* STM Verb., STM Vis., LTM Vis., *Note:* Previously poor dream recaller.

5 Corda 85. M, 74, R, 3m, V, F. L., ct.
Deficit: Right hemiparesis, slight motor aphasia, LTM Verb. *Intact:* STM Verb., STM Vis., LTM Vis., Token test $^{27}/_{36}$.
Note: Previously poor dream recaller.

6 Corda 85. F, 56, R, 2m, V, P. R., ct.
Deficit: Left homonymous hemianopia, left hemiplegia, LTM Verb. *Intact:* STM Verb., STM Vis., LTM Vis.
Note: Previously poor dream recaller.

7 Corda 85. M, 53, R, 1m, V, Internal Capsule R. Parietal, ct.
Deficit: Left hemiparesis, left homonymous hemianopia, Slight LTM Verb., Slight LTM Vis
Intact: STM Verb, STM Vis.

8 Corda 85. F, 48, R, 27m, V, T-P. L., ct. *Deficit:* Right hemiplegia, fluent aphasia, LTM Verb., slight LTM Visual.
Intact: STM Verb., STM Vis., Token Test: $^{26}/_{36}$.
Note: Previously poor dream recaller.

9 Corda 85. M, 63, R, 6m, V, P. L., ct.
Deficit: Right hemiparesis, Wernicke aphasia, LTM Verb., Token test $^{23}/_{36}$.
Intact: STM Verb, STM Vis, LTM Vis. *Note:* Previously poor dream recaller.

10 Corda 85. M, 67, R, 6m, V, T. L., ct.
Deficit: Right hemiplegia and hypoesthesia, Right homonimous hemianopia, Wernicke aphasia, LTM Verb.
Intact: STM Verb., STM Vis., LTM Vis., Token test $^{24}/_{36}$.

11 Corda 85. F, 51, R, 2m, -, T-P. L., ct.
Deficit: Right hemiplegia, LTM Verbal.
Intact: STM Verb., STM Vis., LTM Vis.

12 Corda 85. M, 52, R, 4m, -, T-P. R., ct. *Deficit:* Left hemiplegia, left homonimous hemianopia, sensorial aphasia, LTM Verb., Token test $^{21}/_{36}$.
Intact: STM Verb., STM Vis., LTM Vis.

13 Epstein 79. F, 56, L+R, 5m, V, P-O. L., -.
Deficit: Right homonymous hemianopia, mild dislexia (i.e., misidentifications + transpositions), color agnosia, poor visual imagery, prosopagnosia, slight dysphasia in acute phase.
Intact: Object identification, language.
Note: recovery of dreams 19 months after illness onset.

14 Epstein 83. F, 59, R, 2m, V, F-P.L., ct. *Deficit:* Transitory right hemiparesis, mild reading and writing impairment, mild dysnomia.
Intact: Visual fields, verbal fluency, auditory comprehension.
15 Epstein 83. F, 47, R, 6m, V, F-T. L., -.
Deficit: Expressive aphasia, transitory right hemiparesis.
Intact: Visual fields, auditory comprehension.
16 Epstein 83. M, 33, R, 2m, V, F-T.L., ct.
Deficit: Mild expressive aphasia, right sensory-motor.
Intact: Visual fields.
17 Epstein 83. F, 52, R, 4m, V, F-T. L., -.
Deficit: Severe expressive aphasia, right hemiparesis.
Intact: Visual fields.
18 Epstein 83. M, 43, R, 2y6m, V, F-T. L., -.
Deficit: Severe expressive aphasia, right sensory-motor.
Intact: Visual fields.
19 Epstein 83. F, 35, R, 4m, V, F. L., ct.
Deficit: Dysnomia, dysgraphia, dyslexia, transitory right hemiparesis, right-hand sensory impairment.
Intact: Visual fields.
20 Epstein 83. F, 56, R, 9m, V, T-F. L., -.
Deficit: Right homonymous hemianopia, transitory right hemiparesis, anomia, alexia, dysgraphia, auditory comprehension.
Intact: Verbal fluency.
Note: Mild and transitory of frontal symptoms
21 Ettlinger ea 57. M, 57, R, 5w, Tu, P. R. + Mesial O-T. R.,a.
Deficit: Left hemi-inattention, visuo-constructive tasks, dressing dispraxia, loss topographical memory, evaluation of spatial coordinates and spatial relationships, perception of sagittal movements, spatial thought.
Intact: Language, abstract orientation, Weigl test.
22 Farah ea 86. M, 64, R, 3m, V, O-T. L., bs.
Deficit: Right homonymous hemyanopia, alexia, verbal memory loss, rare verbal errors, verbal comprehension, copy and memory drawing, imagery, color-form matching, graphic completion, mild colour anomia.
Intact: Object denomination, phoneme reading, comprehension of verbal three-steps command.
Note: Initial associative agnosia.
23 Gloning & Sternbach 53. M, 57, R, 3y, V, Thal. R. + O.L., sympt.
Deficit: Left superior homonymous hemianopia, right inferior scotoma, left central facial paresis, left spastic hemiparesis, left hypoesthesia, slight spatial orientation, apathy.
Intact: Central visual fields, nystagmus, visual gnosis, visualization, time orientation.
Note: Dream interruption for 3y.

24 Gloning & Sternbach 53. M, 64, -, 18m, V, O.B.L. + Inf-O.L.Pred., a.

Deficit: Right homonymous hemianopia, right nystagmus, alexia, associative agnosia (initially apperceptive type), mild chromatognosia, revisualization, and description of faces and buildings.

25 Gloning & Sternbach 53. M, 52, -, 6w, V, F.R., r.

Deficit: Central facial paresis, Left hemiparesis, prehension and retroflexion reflex, akinesia.

Intact: Psychic orientation, social interaction.

26 Gloning & Sternbach 53. F, 32, -, 6y, Tu, F-P.R., S.

Deficit: Left hemiplegia, central facial paresis, left spastic hemiparesis.

Intact: Sensory functions.

27 Gloning & Sternbach 53. F, 56, -, 4w, Tu, F.Bl. Left Pred., S.

Deficit: Deep apathy, deep sleepiness.

Note: Extremely vivid dreams at illness onset.

28 Humphrey & Zangwill 51. M, 21, R, 6y, Tr, P.BL., S + r.

Deficit: Left homonimous hemianopia, visual disorientation, topographical disorientation, mild visual memory, mild dyspraxia, mild dysphasia, hypnagogic imagery, visual imagery.

Note: Not a single dream after 6y.

29 Humphrey & Zangwill 51. 52, M, 32, L+R, 6m, Tr, P.R., r.

Deficit: Hemi-inattention, block design, block counting, verbal analogies, verbal reasoning, calculia, visual imagery, spatial perception, slight residual dysphasia, mild topographical loss, slowness in reading (parietal dyslexia).

Note: Recovery from total loss of dreaming after 5y, familial dextrality, right-handed in writing.

30 Humphrey & Zangwill 51. M, 26, R, 1m, Tr, P.R., S+r.

Deficit: Left homonymous hemianopia, topographical loss, visual recognition, visualization, spatial judgments.

Note: 6y later: left homonimous hemianopia, topographical loss, mild deficit of visual memory. Almost no dreams.

31 Lyman ea. M, 42, -, 10m, Tu, P.L., S.

Deficit: Right homonymous hemianopia, dyscalculia, topographical memory, slowed but correct color denomination, parietal dysgraphia in English, alexia and agraphia for ideograms, visual construction, drawing from memory, visual imagery.

Intact Language fluency (English and Chinese), verbal comprehension (English and Chinese), reading in English (words and texts), color recognition, copy drawing.

Postoperative Conditions (2 months)

Deficit: Right homonymous hemianopia, dyscalculia, mild dyslexia and dysgraphia for ideograms, mild visual imagery.

Intact: Topographical memory, visual construction, drawing from memory, English reading.
Note: Bilingual (Chinese, English), Surgical resection: Sup. Par. Lob. -Inf. Par. Lob. -partial Supramarg. Gyrus. -partial Angul. Gyrus., general postoperative improvement. Previously poor dream recaller.
32 Michel ea 65. M, 51, R, 6m, V, P-O.BL., a.
Deficit: Right hemiparesis, semantic and phonetic paraphasias, mild syntax, right–left confusion, topographical memory, topographical disorientation, temporal disorientation, visual disorientation, visuomotor incoordination, stereopsis and oculomotor coordination, attentional and intentional ocular behaviour (Holmes's Syndrome), simultanagnosia, inability to tell tales, sequential movements upon command, recent and ancient personal memory, mild general mental deterioration.
Intact: Elementary calculia, visual fields, vocabulary, recognition of objects and faces, map recognition, slow eye pursuit movements, unintentional eye movements, REM rems, vigilance, somatognosis, autotopognosis, finger-gnosis, stereognosis.
Note: EOG study (wake and sleep), consciousness of visuoperceptive and paraphasic defects.
33 Michel ea 81. M, 59, R, -, V, O-T.L. Inf-Med., bs.
Deficit: Right homonymous hemianopia, alexia without agraphia, visual anomia, memory, imagery
Intact: Graphia
Note: REM awakenings.
34 Michel ea 81. F, 18, R, -, S, L.c. call., bs + S.
Deficit: Right homonymous hemianopia, alexia without agraphia, visual anomia.
Intact: Graphia, memory.
Note: REM awakenings, surgical removal of an angioma in the left major forceps of corpus callosum.
35 Muller 1892. F, 50, -, 6m, V?, O.BL.R.Pred., Sympt.
Deficit: Left homonymous hemianopia, partial right superior hemianopia, object anomia, color anomia (associative agnosia), prosopagnosia, topographical memory loss, numbers alexia.
Intact: Language, sight, calculia, praxia, color matching, singing, melodies recognition, object matching.
Note: Illiterate, able to read street numbers, count up to 100 and to make simple computations before the stroke.
36 Nielsen 55. M, -, -, 7m, S, L.O., S.
Deficit: Right homonymous hemianopia, alexia without agraphia, finger agnosia, spatial disorientation.
Intact: Ancient personal memories.
Note: Left occipital lobectomy.

37 Nielsen 55. -, -, -, -, Tu, L.O., -.
Deficit: Right homonymous hemianopia, revisualization
38 Nielsen 55. -, -, -, -, Tu, L.O., -.
Deficit: Upper right quadrantanopia, revisualization.
39 Nielsen 55. F, -, -, -, Tr, O.BL., -.
Deficit: Vision.
40 PenaCasanova ea 85. M, 47, R, 2m, V, O-T.L. Inf. -Med., ct.
Deficit: Right homonymous hemianopia, semantic paraphasia, alexia without agraphia, object and picture visual anomia, optic apraxia, semantic errors in pointing out named objects, color anomia, total drawing from memory, picture completion, object assembly, visual imagery, letters and words, grouping objects in categories, prosopanomia, explaining the meaning of concrete words, logical memory, associative learning, mild visual memory.
Intact: Language prosody–articulation–grammar, sentence length, spontaneous writing, writing the name of a visual-object, performance on verbal commands, picture copying, hand posture imitation, praxia on verbal command (ideative–ideomotor).
Note: 7 months after illness onset, together with improvement in naming, the patient had one dream "but no more since".
41 Schanfald ea85. -, -, -, 6m, -, F-P.R. + BL. Thal.
Deficit: Visuospatial, associative agnosia, memory.
Note: 16 REM and NREM awakenings.
42 Wapner ea78. M, 73, L, 1m, V, O-T.BL. Med.L.Pred., ct.
Deficit: Right homonymous hemianopia, restriction visualfields, mild anterograde memory, total Wais pf, spatial and visual imagery, stm visual, strong simultanagnosia for objects-wordspictures, mild ocular pursuit, mild color to form, mild color misnaming, visual underspecification, matching faces from different perspectives, geographical memory, visual disorientation in copy drawing, contour perception difficulties, visual object and picture agnosia, memory drawing, mild auditory recognition.
Intact: Wais V: 123, place and time orientation, right–left orientation, body parts, verbal reasoning, color discrimination, private memory, language and comprehension, ocular accommodation, stereopsis, writing, tactile recognition.
Note Painter.
43 Wilbrand 1892. F, 62, -, 4y, V, O.BL. Inf-O.R.Pred., a.
Deficit: Left homonymous hemianopia, prosopagnosia, visual disorientation, topographical disorientation, symultanagnosia, mild object recognition (apperceptive type).
Intact: Language, verbal memory, reading, depth and color perception, topographical imagery, tactile and olphactive recognition, comprehension of pantomimes.

Note: Almost no dreams 4–5 years later, Superior occipital and parietal lobes completely normal on autopsy.

Section 2

Cases with persistence of the dreaming experience

No. Ref. S, A, Hd, Id, E, Loc, Dm.

1 Botez ea. 64. M, 49, R, 2y, V, T.L., eeg.

Deficit: Bilateral narrowing of nasal visual fields, motor disturbances, mild dyscalculia, alexia, visual construction, fixation of gaze, object-picture-letters visuospatial agnosia, prosopagnosia, spatial disorientation, visuo-attentional inspective disorders, general intellectual impairment.

Intact: Verbal comprehension, language, mild writing, color recognition, stereognosis.

Note: Diffuse eeg anomalies.

2 Botez ea. 64. F, 33, R, -, Tu, O.L., S.

Deficit: Right homonymous hemianopia, slight motor disturbances of right limbs, mild verbal inattention, recall of proper nouns, alexia, words writing, acalculia, mild visual underspecification, topographical disorientation, general intellectual impairment.

Intact: Visual acuity, eye movements, writing of of letters and numbers, copy, praxia, face recognition, spatial judgment, right–left orientation, oculomotor functions.

Note: Left occipital lobectomy.

3 Brain 41.M,15,R,8y, infective,/,r.

Deficit: Right visual inattention, total alexia and agraphia (previously normal for his age: 7y), visual object agnosia, prosopagnosia, mild color recognition and naming, mild drawing from memory, right–left valuation, topographical orientation in unknown sites, copy drawing, visual construction.

Intact: Visual acuity, ocular movements, sensory–motor coordination, visual imagery, speech articulation-vocabulary-comprehension, simple calculations, shape visual matching, body parts recognition, object praxia.

Note: Streptococcal septicaemia, no skull abnormality on radiograms.

4 Ettlinger ea 57.F,43,R,18m, Tu,P-O.R.,S.

Deficit: Left homonymous hemianopia, left visual-tactile heminattention piecemeal approach in drawing and copying, left hemineglect in describing from memory, slight deformation of spatial coordinates.

Intact: Tactual maze, manual performance, abstract orientation, paper cutting, Weigl's test, arithmetics, visualization, right–left body orientation, topographical memory.

5 Gloning & Sternbach 53. M, 33, -, -, infective, T.R., eeg.

Deficit: Left homonymous hemianopia, left nystagmus, slight left hemiparesis.

6 Gloning & Sternbach 53. F, 31, -, 1y, cyst, T.R., S.

Deficit: Left homonymous hemianopia, left hemihypoesthesia, left hemiparesis.

7 Gloning & Sternbach 53. M, 48, -, 7m, Tu, F-T.R., S.

Deficit: Slight frontal ataxia.

8 Gloning & Sternbach 53. M, 56, -, 1m, V, O-T.L., sympt.

Deficit: Right homonymous hemianopia, right nystagmus, slight right leg paresis, alexia, color agnosia, associative agnosia, visualization.

Note: Recovery of dreaming experience 3 months after illness onset together with recovery from agnosic-associative defects and from visualization deficit.

9 Gloning & Sternbach 53. F, 45, -, 3y, V, Thal.R., sympt.

Deficit: Trigeminal left hypoesthesia, left extremities weakness, left hypoesthesia, left astereognosia.

10 Gloning & Sternbach 53. F, 64, -, 19m, V, Thal.R., sympt.

Deficit: Slight left central facial paresis, left extremities tendon reflex, left hemibody weakness and hypoesthesia, left hypersensitivity for cold and pain.

11 Gloning & Sternbach 53. M, 54, -, 5y, Tu, 3 ^{ite} Ventr.Medial, r.

Deficit: Slight left hemiparesis, medial left sensory, hemiballismus of the left hand.

12 Gloning & Sternbach 53. M, 54, -, -, V, Thal.R. O.R., sympt.+ vascular exam.

Deficit: Left homonymous hemianopia, left nystagmus, slight left hemiparesis, left sensory, slight spatial orientation.

Intact: Time orientation, music perception.

13 Gloning & Sternbach 53. M, 51, -, 4m, V, Thal.L., sympt.+ eeg.

Deficit: Mild right hemiparesis, right hypoesthesia, jerks of the right arm, slight bilateral labyrinthic excitability, time disorientation, right visual perceptive distortion.

Intact: Sight, visual fields, eeg.

Note: Dream interruption for 5m. Recovery of dreaming concomitant to recovery from vertigo and of time perception.

14 Gloning & Sternbach 53. M, 9, -, 2m, Tu, Left Cerebellum, a.

Deficit: Left facial paresis, right rotatory nystagmus, left trigeminal hypoesthesia, ataxia, cerebellar symptoms in left extremities, left vestibular hyperactivity.

Note: Rare dreams. Exitus letalis 4m after illness onset.

15 Gloning & Sternbach 53. F, 27, -, 1y, Tu, F.L.+ Callosum F., S.

Deficit: Right central facial paresis, right spastic paresis, hemihypoesthesia, motor aphasia, apathy.

Intact: Praxia, no cerebellar ataxia.
Note: Rare dreams.
16 Gloning & Sternbach 53. M, 24, -, 3m, V, Thal. + T-P.R., S.
Deficit: Left hemiplegia, left hemianesthesia, left arm anosognosia.
Note: Rare dreams.
17 Michel ea.81. M, 56, R, -, V?, O-T.L.
Deficit: Right homonymous hemianopia, alexia without agraphia, visual imagery, mnesic disturbances.
18 Schanfald ea.85. M, 50-65, R, 45m, V, F-P.L., ct.
Deficit: Dysarthric, Broca's aphasia, oral and written paraphasias.
Note: 1 dream recalled on 3 REM awakenings.
19 Schanfald ea.85. M, 50-65, R, 1.5m, V, F.L., ct.
Deficit: Mild Broca, paraphasias, anomia, neologism, word blends.
Note: 2 dreams recalled on 6 REM awakenings.
20 Schanfald ea.85. M, 50-65, R, 30m, V, F-T-P.L., ct.
Deficit: Severe Broca, paraphasia, neologism, perseveration, anomia, paragraphia, color misnaming, mild visual impairment.
Note: 1 dream recalled on 11 REM awakenings.
21 Schanfald ea.85. M, 50-65, R, 1m, V, T-P.L., ct.
Deficit: Wernicke aphasia, naming, repetition, paraphasia, neologism, anomia, melodic rhythm.
Note: 3 dreams recalled on 11 REM awakenings.
22 Schanfald ea.85. M, 50-65, R, 16 days, V, F-P.R., ct.
Deficit: Drawing distortion, left–right inattention, visual perception, memory, dressing apraxia.
23 Schanfald ea.85. M, 50-65, R, 5y, V, T-P.R., ct.
Deficit: Prosopagnosia, simultanagnosia, drawing from memory, left inattention, mathemathics, dressing apraxia.
Note: 1 dream recalled on 9 REM awakenings.
24 Schanfald ea.85. M, 50-65, R, -, cg, R, ct.
Deficit: Slight copy drawing, drawing from memory, object assembly, sequence arrangement of picture stories.
Note: Right arteriovenous malformation, 1 dream recalled on 4 REM awakenings.
25 Shuttleworth ea. 82. F, 49, -, 16y, S + Tr, T-P-O.BL., S.
Deficit: Right superior hemianopia, severe prosopagnosia, visually distinguishing object of the same class (clothes, animals, cars), mild spatial disorientation, minimal achromatopsia, mild visual identification of line drawings, animal recognition, gollin incomplete figures, slow ghent overlapping figures, drawing from memory, revisualization for faces, severe nonvisualizable immediate memory, mild difficulty in spelling.
Intact: Visual acuity, depth perception, color naming, color–object matching, object identification, copy, visual verbalizable-tactile-kinetic-

olfactive-gustative memory, revisualization of places, matching noniden-
tical views of the same person, intelligence.

Note: Trauma on operative site 1y later.

Section 3

Cases with cessation of the visual component of dreaming.

No. Ref., S, A, Hd, ld, E, Loc, Dm.

1 Adler 44, 50. F, 22, -, 1y, Tx, P-O.BL., eeg.

Deficit: Strong visual underspecification for objects-letters-faces, prosopagnosia, spatial relationship, ghent overlapping figures, topographical
disorientation, topographical memory, mild writing due to distorted visual
feedback, paper folding, visual imagery, calculia, finger agnosia, reading
handwritings, copying of geometrical figures, mild block design, mild
object recognition.

Intact: Visual fields, sight, color perception, language, comprehension,
temporal and spatial orientation.

Note: Carbon monoxide poisoning.

2 Bernard 1883. M, -, -, 18m, V?, Post.?, sympt.

Deficit: Form and color visual memory, topographical amnesia, topographical imagery, drawing from memory, imagery for faces, mild prosopagnosia, mild alexia for foreign languages, mild color perception.

Intact: Visual fields, sight, language, comprehension, mild calculia.

Note: Strong familial visual memory, polyglot.

3 Botez ea 85. M, L +, 38y, Cg, Post.Bl.R. Pred., ct.

Deficit: Total visual imagery, topographical disorientation, right–left
disorientation, anterograde prosopagnosia, drawing from memory, hypnagogic imagery, tv movies comprehension, map orientation.

Intact: Writing, mirror writing, copy drawing (excellent), naming of
famous faces, color recognition and denomination, color–object matching,
Ottawa Wechsler: Verb.132- Pf.139-Total: 154, tactile left–right transfer,
tactile matching, visual evoked potentials.

Note: Congenital strechted splenium, right ventricule dilatation.

4 Brain 54. M, 36, R, 5y, Tr, P-O.BL. L.pred., eeg.

Deficit: General visual imagery, topographical memory, slight verbal
aphasia, mild verbal learning.

Intact: Topographical orientation, describing from memory, praxia,
spatial perception, visual recognition, visual fields.

Note: Frontal *"contre coup,"* no changes over 15 years.

5 Gloning & Sternbach 53. M, 53, R + L, 17y, V, Thal.L., sympt.

Deficit: Slight right extremities sensory–motor, slight right hemibody sensory, transitory associative agnosia, visual object anomia, word finding, time orientation.

Intact: Visualization, object function, tachistoscopic recognition, letter recognition, visual fields.

6 Grunstein 24. F, 23, -, 1m, V?, Post., sympt.

Deficit: Transitory right homonymous hemianopia (1 day), prosopagnosia, topographical memory, visual underspecification for faces.

Intact: Language, reading, reading of musical notes, writing, calculation, object identification, drawing, ocular convergence, ocular movements, visual fields, color perception, motricity.

Note: Persistent dream deficit.

7 Kerr ea.78. F, 21, -, 21y, -, -, -.

Deficit: Mathematics, object assembly, block design, total kinemathic imagery.

Intact: Wais Vb. 101, Pf.93, recall of static visual displays, verbal comprehension.

Note: Normally sighted TurnerXO, 11 Rem awakenings.

8 Kerr ea.81. M, 44, -, 28y, S, T.R., S.

Deficit: Mild embedded figure test, mild block design, perceptual speed, visual scanning, visualization (vz 2 kit test), spatial orientation, (S-2 kit test), total Thurstone space test.

Intact: Verbal l.Q. WAIS.

Note: Lack of kinemathical visual component, 6 Rem awakenings.

9 Tzavaras 67. M, 54, R, 4m-15y, S, T-O.L., eeg.

Deficit: Superior bilateral hemianopia, prosopagnosia, mild color perception, mild spatial orientation.

Intact: Language, reading, calculia, body schema, praxia, recognition of physionomical expressions, object recognition, map orientation.

Note: Lack of the physiognomical visual component.

II VISUAL IMAGERY AND COGNITIVE PROCESSES ACROSS WAKING AND SLEEP STATES

7 The Visual Appearance of Dreams

Allan Rechtschaffen and Cheryl Buchignani
University of Chicago

Whereas enormous attention has been devoted to the emotional characteristics, cognitive mechanisms, and physiological correlates of dreams, little research has been done on the sensory phenomenology of dreams. For example, during a recent 8-year period, *Sleep Research* (Chase 1980–1987) listed 110 publications on the neurophysiology of the visual system during sleep and only six publications which were substantially concerned with visual characteristics of dreams. The meaningfulness of the neurophysiological data is necessarily limited by the paucity of data about the corresponding visual experience.

It is appropriate that inquiry on sensory experience in dreams begin with vision, since it is normally the most frequently reported modality in dreams. Snyder's (1970) review of seven studies of sensory experience in dreams revealed the following median percentages (across studies) of reported dreams with these sensory elements: visual 100%; auditory 69%; kinesthetic 11.5%; touch 10%; taste 1%; smell <1%. Snyder wisely noted that, had reports of waking experience been similarly examined, they might have yielded similar results. Furthermore, the uniqueness of dreams is not to be found in their "visuality." Kerr, Foulkes, and Schmidt (1982) showed that, in spite of the absence of visual imagery, the dreams of blind subjects were cognitively similar to those of sighted subjects. These caveats notwithstanding, there is reason to suspect that when dreams do contain visual experiences, as they most usually do, the sensory qualities of these experiences might contain distinctive features. At least Hollywood acknowledges this possibility when it uses special visual effects to portray dream sequences. However, there is little systematic data on the visual character-

143

istics of dreams. Most of it has been limited to assessing the percentage of reported dreams with color: Kahn, Dement, Fisher, & Barmack, (1962) 83%; Herman, Roffwarg, and Tauber (1968) 68%; Snyder (1970) 61 to 77%, depending on length of report; Padgham (1975) 50% (from dreams recalled in the morning); Jankowski, Dee, and Cartwright (1977) 62%. One study progressed beyond the dimension of color; Herman, Roffwarg, and Tauber reported "ability to discern form" in 83% of REM reports and depth perception in 78%. Such studies are a start, but several additional dimensions of visual experience must be assessed to answer the question tackled by the present study: What do dreams look like?

Researchers ordinarily rely on verbal reports from the subject to convey the dream experience. In modern dream research, subjects are typically awakened from REM sleep and, if it is also of interest, from NREM sleep as well, and give verbal reports of their pre-awakening experiences. Verbal reports, however, can be poor conveyors of visual information. A report that a dream image is "unclear" could mean that it is either out of focus, diffused, poorly illuminated, perceptually disorganized, or simply of unfamiliar, unrecognizable content.

We approached this problem by a variant on classical psychophysiology methodology whereby subjects convey personal experience by matching it to physical objects. In this study, the objects were 129 5 × 7 inch photographs that were all variations, made mostly by darkroom techniques, of a single, simple photograph of a young woman sitting on a couch (Fig. 7.1). Upon being awakened from REM periods, subjects were presented with a notebook of the photographs and instructed to select those that best captured the visual qualities of the dream they had just experienced. The photographs were varied along the major visual dimensions of Color Saturation, Brightness (illumination), Figure Clarity, Background Clarity, and overall Hue. In some photographs, a single dimension departed from "normal" appearance. In others, variations in two or more dimensions were accented simultaneously. Ideally, each dimension would have been varied systematically along a formal scale in all combinations with the other dimensions. In practice, it was difficult to regulate photographic variations so precisely, and the size of the photograph collection would have been unmanageable in the test situation. Instead, we tried to achieve representation of each major dimension across the range between extremes and to include all major combinations with intuitive appeal as possibly dream-like. The final set of 129 photographs was selected after extensive pilot testing of a larger set, during which some of the photos that were never selected by subjects were discarded, and some photos were added to capture visual qualities that pilot subjects reported, but which we had not yet captured in the original photo series.

SUBJECTS AND PROCEDURE

The subjects were 24 young adults (11 males and 13 females) who were recruited by an advertisement in the University of Chicago undergraduate newspaper. Most subjects were students at the university; some subjects were employed at the university or in the surrounding community. Potential subjects were excluded only if their applications indicated that they had poor dream recall or sleep problems.

All subjects slept in the laboratory for one practice night during which they were briefed on procedures and given several practice awakenings. Written instructions emphasized that the purpose of the study was not to evaluate the subjects or their dream content, but to learn about the visual qualities of dreams, and that selection of photographs to match dreams should be based on visual quality, not content. Subjects were further instructed that when no photograph captured all the visual qualities of the dream, they should choose the one that minimized the largest differences, for example, "you should make a match which tolerates small differences in brightness and color rather than a match in which dream and photo are perfectly matched for brightness but very different in color." Eighteen subjects then spent 2 experimental nights each in the laboratory. Six subjects were asked to return for a third experimental night because one or both of the first two experimental nights produced relatively little data.

At the start of each REM period, a coin was tossed to determine whether the awakening would be phasic, that is, after 5 of vigorous eye movements and periorbital phasic potentials, or tonic, that is, after 10 s with little or no phasic activity. Subjects were awakened approximately 5 min after the start of the first REM period of the night. Thereafter, a coin was tossed to determine whether the awakening would be made approximately 5 min or 15 min after the start of the REM period.

After being awakened, the subject was asked to describe briefly the last scene in the dream, and, if different, the best remembered scene in the dream. Then the subject was presented with the book of photographs. The photos were arranged in groups according to prominent visual characteristics (e.g., achromatic, chromatic-realistic, bright illumination, dim illumination, diffused, varying hues, etc.) so that he or she could zero in quickly on the group from which the final choice was made. The subjects were asked to select the photo that best captured the visual characteristics of the very last scene of the dream and the photo that best captured the visual characteristics of the best remembered scene of the dream. Thus, for each awakening, there could be no matches (if there was no recall); one match — if there was recall for either a best remembered or very last scene, or if the best remembered and very last scene were the same; or two matches — if

FIG. 7.1. Examples of variations among achromatic photographs. *top:* "Normal" black-and-white photograph. *bottom:* Differential loss of background clarity due to "bleaching" effect.

FIG. 7.1. cont. *top:* Moderate overall loss of clarity due to overall diffusion. *bottom:* Differential loss of background clarity due to low illumination.

there was recall for both a last-and best-remembered scene. Altogether, 312 matches were made: 40% were from best-remembered scenes; 40% were from very last scenes; and 20% were from scenes that were both best remembered and very last. Since the results were very similar for best-remembered and very last scenes, these distinctions will not be considered further.

After making their matches, the subjects made a series of ratings on simple 4-point scales for each of the following questions.

1. How well do you remember the scene?
2. How well does the photo you selected match the dream scene?
3. How strange or bizarre was the dream scene?
4. How much emotion was there in the dream scene?

The ratings were done with an absolute minimum of conversation between the subject and the experimenter. As an internal check on whether the subjects understood the nature of the matching task, they were also asked to state briefly how the visual quality of the dream scene differed from that of everyday life. By comparing the response with the photo selected, the experimenter could quickly determine whether there were any gross disparities between the photos selected and the features of the dream image as verbally described. Only in the very few cases in which such disparities arose did the experimenter intervene with further questions.

Apparently, subjects had little difficulty in matching dream scenes and pictures for visual qualities, in spite of their different contents. Matches were usually made in less than 1 min. After making their matches, subjects were asked to rate how well the picture matched the dream scene in visual quality on a scale of 1 (very well) to 4 (very poor). The mean rating was 1.57 with a standard deviation of .31, indicating that on the average, dream scenes and photographs were matched between "very well" and "moderately well," with relatively little variation around this average.

RESULTS

Two major strategies were used to describe the results. In the first strategy, we assigned the photographs selected by subjects to groups according to their overall appearance and noted the relative sizes of the groups. This approach had the merit of providing composite descriptions that could include more than one visual dimension, but it had the weakness that the assignment was in some cases somewhat arbitrary. We tend to minimize this weakness, because, in practice, we did not find the assignment task very difficult. Since subjects did not differ greatly in the number of dream-photo matches made (mean = 13.0, SD = 2.1), the data were not corrected to give equal weight to the responses of each subject.

The major categories of photo quality and the percentages of times they were selected were as follows:

Normal (40.1%). By far, the single most frequently selected category was of photographs that were either normal, that is, like external reality, in most respects, or deviating only slightly from normal in one or two dimensions. Most subjects had several choices in this category.

Achromatic (20.2%). This category consisted of entirely achromatic pictures. Within the achromatic category, there was a wide range of variation in contrast, illumination, and so on, but this breakdown is not presented here. The value of 20.2% is in good agreement with the results of other studies on the incidence of achromatic dreams. Most of the achromatic matches came from 29% of the subjects; 33% of the subjects chose only color photos; 7 of the 24 subjects chose only achromatic photos. 7.1 shows some of the variations among achromatic photos.

*Moderate Desaturation (11.2%).*These photos were characterized by a moderate desaturation of color, relatively high illumination, and some loss of detail in the background. In general, the photographs in this category were characterized by a moderate "bleaching" effect.

Differential Bleaching or Diffusion of Background (7.7%). In this category, the figure, that is, the young lady, was very clear with normal color and illumination, but the background detail was severely diminished or completely lost due to a bleaching effect or very heavy diffusion.

Soft Haze (6.1%). Photographs in this category were characterized by mild desaturation, slightly elevated illumination, and a soft haze that pervaded the entire scene. This is the kind of image that moviemakers frequently use to depict dream scenes.

Low Background Illumination (3.5%). This category was characterized by a moderate to severe loss of background detail due to differentially low illumination of the background. Combining this category, the photographs with moderately desaturated backgrounds, and the photographs with bleached out or heavily diffused backgrounds (22.4% combined), it is clear that there was a substantial tendency to select photographs with a differential loss of background detail.

Magenta Color Balance (1.6%). Photographs in this category were characterized by a magenta color balance, or a relative absence of yellows and greens.

Overall Low Illumination (1.6%). Photographs in this category were characterized by an overall low illumination.

Yellow Hue (1.6%). Photographs in this category were characterized by overall yellow hue, sometimes combined with a mild diffusion.

These results indicate that the single most frequently reported category of dream image was one that visually resembles external reality. Nevertheless, dream images were frequently reported to be visually different from reality. The most frequent departures from a realistic appearance were a loss of color saturation and a loss of background detail. There were no verbal reports of visually disorganized dream scenes, for example, kaleidoscopic, multiple-image, double-exposure, solarization, or optical distortion effects. The few photographs with such effects that were included in the photo book were never matched to dream scenes.

DIMENSIONS OF VISUAL IMAGERY

A second strategy for describing the results was to use judges to determine a specific value for each photo on specific visual dimensions. Then, the photo choices of the subjects could be described quantitatively by noting the dimension values of the photos they selected. The quantitative descriptions facilitated comparisons with other variables. The results of the previously described analysis guided the selection of the visual dimensions.

Each of the 129 photographs was rated on each of the following six dimensions by either 9 or 10 judges: Color Saturation; Brightness; Figure Clarity; Background Clarity; Figure–Ground relationship; Hue. For all dimensions, the judges were instructed to assign a scale value of 5 whenever the photograph resembled external reality. The median of the judges' ratings defined the value of each dimension for each photograph. Whenever judges showed poor agreement in rating a particular photograph on a particular dimension, that photograph was not included in subsequent analyses of that dimension.

On Color Saturation, the ratings could range from 0 for completely achromatic photographs to 10 for photographs with very heavy color saturation. On Brightness, the ratings could range from 0 for photographs with very low illumination to 10 for very high illumination.

On Figure Clarity, judges were carefully instructed to rate on the basis of the clarity of the central figure alone, that is the young lady, independent of the clarity of the background. Normal was arbitrarily defined as maximal clarity, that is, a rating of 5. From there, ratings could range down to 0 for photographs in which the figure was almost completely obscured. As noted earlier, clarity is a confounded dimension, since low clarity can result from a variety of reasons, including diffusion, poor illumination, poor contrast, or poor focus. A formal analysis of the separate sources of loss of clarity was not made, but inspection of the photos selected by subjects to match their dream imagery indicated that, most frequently, Figure Clarity was lost because of diffusion, followed by low Brightness. Only very rarely was Figure Clarity lost because the figure seemed out of focus. Background Clarity was rated in much the same way as Figure Clarity. In photos selected by subjects, Background Clarity was most frequently lost as a result of a bleaching, low background illumination, or heavy diffusion.

Figure-ground was rated for each photograph based on the relative prominence of the figure and the background. Where figure and background were essentially the same in visual quality, a rating of 5 was assigned. When prominence of one or the other differentially suffered as a result of diminished clarity, saturation, illumination, and so on, a lower rating was assigned. In almost all cases where subjects selected a photo with a rating lower than 5 on Figure-ground, the photo showed a relative loss of background prominence.

The dimension of Hue refers to the presence of an overall cast of any one particular color, as if the entire scene were bathed by a light of that color. A rating of 5 was defined as normal. Progressively higher ratings were assigned as overall hues became more intense.

Table 7.1 shows for each dimension the mean values (averaged across subjects) of all the selected photos; their standard deviations (SDs); the mean of the within-subjects SDs; the subject reliabilities (across the first two experimental nights) and the respective p-values of the reliability coefficients; and the means and SDs for photos selected to match very well-recalled dream images.

As indicated in the previous analysis by photo categories, the photos selected to match dream scenes deviated most from "normal" appearance (a scale value of 5) by a loss of Color Saturation and a loss of Background Clarity. Although Color Saturation showed considerable within-subject variability, there were, in addition, large individual differences in the tendency to desaturation, as indicated by the large SD across subjects and the very substantial 2-night reliability. These results mirror the analysis by photo characteristics, that is, although there was a tendency in most subjects toward some color desaturation, it was especially and consistently pronounced in specific subjects.

Although there were sizable and reliable individual differences in Background Clarity, they were considerably less than for Color Saturation. The

TABLE 7.1
Results of Dimensional Analyses of Photograph Choices

Dimension	Scale range	Photo Choice for all Dream Scenes					Very Good Recall	
		Mean across Ss	SD across Ss	Mean within S SD	Night 2 vs 3 reliability		Mean across Ss	SD across Ss
					r	p<		
Color saturation	0–10	3.63	1.41	1.52	.81	.001	3.87	1.36
Brightness	0–10	5.99	.67	1.62	.41	.05	5.98	.87
Figure clairity	0–5	4.27	.34	.78	.24	ns	4.38	.38
Ground clarity	0–5	3.78	.71	1.16	.61	.01	3.99	.66
Figure-ground	0–5	4.19	.67	1.05	.53	.01	4.34	.65
Hue	5–10	5.41	.37	.68	.32	ns	5.38	.51

relatively low mean value and the subject reliability for Figure-ground probably reflect the loss of Background Clarity. Figure Clarity was not markedly reduced from "normal," nor were there marked individual differences in this dimension.

There was some tendency for matched photos to be somewhat brighter than "normal" and for some individual differences in this respect. Apparently, dream images are not characteristically dark. However, as indicated in the earlier analyses, there were some definitely dark dream images, although they were in the minority. The relatively large variation within subjects would seem to reflect variability in illumination from scene to scene, which is not unlike changes in illumination in real life. There was no substantial evidence that dream images are characteristically pervaded by dominant hues.

Suspicions must be immediately raised as to whether the loss of saturation and background clarity might not have been epiphenomena of poor recall. Colors might fade with the fading of memory. Loss of memory for background detail might become manifest in recalled imagery as a blur, an area of darkness, or an area of undifferentiated high illumination. To evaluate this possibility, we recomputed the mean scale values using only those images the subjects rated 1 ("very good recall") on the 1–4 scale. Table 7.1 shows that the mean scores for Color Saturation and Background Clarity were raised for the very well recalled images, but the increase was quite small. The mean values remained substantially lower than the "normal" value of 5 and also remained the lowest values of all the dimensions. Thus, it would appear that poor recall was not the overriding factor in the loss of saturation and background clarity.

Nevertheless, the issue is not completely settled. When a subject reports that recall for the image was excellent, he or she may be conveying his recall for the figure, the object of greatest attention, not recall for the background. The issue then becomes whether the subjects had good recall for a murky, darkened, or diffused background, or whether the background was poorly recalled. In cases where the subject chose photographs with a complete loss of background detail and yet reported that he or she had excellent recall of the image, we are inclined to believe that indeed the background did originally appear murky in the dream. The murkiness in such cases could represent a loss from some primeval earlier memory which never achieved representation in the dream imagery. Alternatively, it could be argued that dream images are formed through active cognitive processes (Kerr et al., 1982), and that in some dreams, it might not be cognitively important to form an image of the background at all.

Table 7.2 shows the relationships between the visual dimensions and other variables. There were no significant sex differences on any dimension. Neither were there any significant differences between the two experimental nights. The first REM period of the night showed a significant loss of Saturation, Figure Clarity, and Background Clarity, compared with the remaining REM periods. These significant relationships held even for reports with good recall (data not presented). This finding echoes the familiar "weakness" of the first dream of the night. There were no significant differences between images 5 min into the REM period and images 15 min into the REM period. Figure Clarity was significantly higher for phasic than for tonic awakenings. One could speculate that the increased neural activity in the visual cortex during phasic events enhances dream images. However, the absence of a phasic–tonic relationship to Background Clarity or Saturation attenuates this speculation. Furthermore, a single significant relationship like this in a large matrix of mostly nonsignificant relationships must be treated with caution prior to replication. There was no evidence that the emotionality or the bizarreness of the

TABLE 7.2
P-values for T-tests of Differences in Visual Dimensions for Dichotomized Variables

Variables*	Saturation	Bright	Figure clarity	Ground clarity	Figure–ground	Hue
Men vs. women	ns	ns	ns	ns	ns	ns
Night 3 vs. night 2	.10	ns	ns	ns	ns	ns
First REM P vs. others	.001	ns	.01	.001	ns	ns
Short vs. long REM	.10	ns	ns	ns	ns	ns
Tonic vs. phasic	ns	ns	.02	ns	ns	ns
Low vs. high emotion	ns	ns	ns	ns	ns	ns
Low vs. high bizarre	ns	ns	ns	ns	ns	ns
Poor vs. good recall	.10	ns	.05	.01	ns	ns

*Variable with lower value in significant relationships is given first.
Note: p values are for 2-tailed paired t tests.

dream image relates to the visual quality of the image. Finally, both Figure and Background Clarity were significantly reduced for more poorly recalled images, and there was a nonsignificant tendency for poor recall to be related to lower Saturation. There is no way to determine from these data alone whether poor recall was a cause or an effect of the visual qualities, or whether a third factor produced both poor recall and reduced image salience.

In considering all the results, it must be remembered that, although the subject reported on subjective dream experience by selecting a physical object, that is, one of the photographs, the physical object remained, like the verbal dream report, a derivative of personal subjective experience that we cannot know directly. The use of the physical object served *only* to enhance communication about imagery. If all subjects were wonderful poets, little might be gained by the psychophysical method. In fact, something might be lost because of the different contents of the photographs and the personal dream images. But most subjects cannot describe imagery like Coleridge, Blake, or Wordsworth. Therefore, for most subjects, there probably is something to be gained by substituting the physical choice for verbal description.

Nevertheless, since the physical choice remains a derivative of the personal experience, we cannot guarantee its accuracy. We can only make judgments, based upon the circumstances of the experiment and the demeanor of our subjects, on how good the correspondence between the personal experience and the physical object might be.

In this particular experiment, our own personal judgment is that the results do convey some truths about dream imagery. One is that most dreams do not depart very radically from normal waking imagery. One most frequent departure is a tendency toward color desaturation, which is manifest in the extreme in the completely achromatic dream image. Such images are indeed mysterious. The layperson frequently asks why we dream in color. Of course, the question should be, "Why should we ever dream in black and white?", considering that normal waking experience is always in color. We do not have an answer.

The other major departure from waking imagery is the loss of background clarity. The loss in background clarity could reflect some yet unspecified characteristic of visual mechanisms during sleep. At the psychological level, it may be suspected that background clarity is relatively low because all of the dynamic energies and cognitive work that go into the formation of the dream story focus on the figure. The psyche may simply not pay much attention to constructing a background if it is not germine to the message of the dream.

These departures from reality notwithstanding, it must be recognized that dreams only very rarely have the dark, murky, confused qualities that are frequently attributed to them in myths and movies. From what subjects have conveyed to us by their matches of photographs to dream images, the dream is most frequently a highly organized, coherent, perceptual production that is usually not drastically different from the way we see the outside world while we are awake.

Even the departures from "normal" that have been described may be, in a sense, somewhat exaggerated. Normal in this study was defined by what the judges considered the appearance of external reality. We had no reason to question their judgments. However, the dream is an "imagined" mental experience, not an original direct experience. If judges had been asked to define normal by images of prior waking experiences or by daydream images, these images might have suffered from the same loss of color saturation and background clarity as the recalled dream images. Therefore, the descriptions of the visual characteristics of dream images reported here have some validity in comparison with direct, original waking experience. However, we have hardly begun to understand how they might resemble or differ from the visual characteristics of *imagined* visual experiences during wakefulness.

REFERENCES

Chase, M.H. (Ed.). (1980–1987). *Sleep research* (Vols. 9–16). Los Angeles: Brain Information Service.

Herman, J., Roffwarg, H., & Tauber, E. (1968). Color and other perceptual qualities of REM and NREM sleep. *Psychophysiology, 5,* 223.

Jankowski, W.L., Dee, S.C., & Cartwright, R.D. (1977). A distribution of colorimetric imagery in REM sleep. *Sleep Research, 6,* 123.

Kahn, E., Dement, W., Fisher, C., & Barmack, J.E. (1962). Incidence of color in immediately recalled dreams. *Science, 137,* 1054–1055.

Kerr, N.H., Foulkes, D., & Schmidt, M. (1982). The structure of laboratory dream reports in blind and sighted subjects. *Journal of Nervous and Mental Disease, 170,* 286–294.

Padgham, C.A. (1975). Colors experienced in dreams. *British Journal of Psychology, 66,* 25–28.

Snyder, F. (1970). The phenomenology of dreaming. In L. Madow & L.H. Snow (Eds.), *The psychodynamic implications of the physiological studies on dreams* (pp. 124–151), Springfield; IL: C. C. Thomas.

8 Bizarreness in Dreams and Waking Fantasy

Ruth Reinsel, John Antrobus, and Miriam Wollman
City College of the City University of New York

This chapter is divided into five sections. The first part introduces the concepts of cortical activation and auditory thresholds as determinants of bizarre thought. The second section tests the predictions of two competing models of bizarreness on four sets of mentation reports drawn from laboratory subjects in sleep and waking states. Part three continues the content analysis of bizarre features of dreams and waking thought, while part four introduces concepts from cognitive psychology that are helpful in understanding the origins of bizarreness. The chapter concludes with a brief description of how a neural network (PDP) model could successfully account for bizarre features of thought in various states of consciousness.

INTRODUCTION: ACTIVATION AND THRESHOLDS

Dreams have fascinated people for centuries, due to their apparent distinctiveness from ordinary waking thought. The vivid hallucinatory experience coupled with illogical, bizarre, and sometimes highly emotional aspects were thought to be the special characteristics of the dream state. With the advent of experimental dream research, physiological correlates (such as sleep stage) have been sought for these cognitive characteristics. Early laboratory studies found dreaming to be almost exclusively confined to REM sleep. Later studies, however, with more precise definitions of "dreaming" and better sampling of other sleep stages, found a substantial proportion of "dreaming" occurring in Stage 2, as well as varying amounts in Stages 3 and 4, depending on the definition of dream employed (Herman,

Ellman, & Roffwarg, 1978). Some of these non-REM "dreams" were found to be equally vivid, visual, dream-like, and bizarre as REM dreams. In general, laboratory dreams were similar to home-recorded dreams on these qualities (Weisz & Foulkes, 1970).

Extending these techniques to the waking state, Foulkes and Scott (1973), Foulkes and Fleisher (1975), and Singer (1978) found that ordinary waking thought, far from being exclusively goal-directed, rational, and formally structured, was sometimes just as visual and even as bizarre as dreams could be. Subjects reclining in a dimly lit room were instructed to relax but remain awake. These subjects gave reports of dramatic, bizarre, visual, and hallucinatory experiences that were accompanied by unambiguous EEG signs of wakefulness.

The potential for waking fantasy to be equally as bizarre as dreaming was fully recognized by Klinger (1971). In his detailed review of studies that compared waking fantasy (TAT stories, thinking aloud, problem solving, mentation sampling, etc.) with dreams, he concluded that they are basically one process observed under different conditions of the internal (physiological) and external stimulus environments.

[f]antasy and dreams are part of a single continuing fantasy process which is subject to certain transformations imposed by physiological and stimulus events. It is unnecessary to sleep in order to generate dream-like ideation, and, apparently, it is unnecessary to be awake in order to produce relatively coherent, undream-like ideation; but the regular mutations of ideational structure and content observed in dreams are apparently the effects of physiological variations on a continuous fantasy process that normally occurs during sleep. (Klinger, 1971, pp. 57–58)

Klinger anticipates several key ideas that are at the heart of current theoretical approaches to bizarreness. First is the concept of dreams and fantasy being the product of a single mentation process that is influenced by variations in physiological arousal. Second is the recognition that the thought process is responsive to demands of the external stimulus environment. Third is the suggestion that activity in the visual system may cause hallucinatory intrusions into the more ordinary thought process. In Klinger's own words,

[i]t seems reasonable to posit the existence of a single waking and sleeping baseline stream of ideation whose properties are modulated by fluctuation in the states of arousal and whose flow is interrupted only by certain incompatible activities. In the waking state, perceptual scanning and directed, operant activity must perforce be considered to interrupt the flow of fantasy. . . . It is unclear what may interrupt the baseline state during sleep. It is possible, for example, that the most vividly hallucinatory phenomena usually regarded as

dreams are sufficiently unlike other sleeping mentation to constitute interruptions, playing a functional role more like that of perceptual scanning than like fantasy. (Klinger, 1971, pp. 63–64)

Klinger's formulation anticipates the role of cortical arousal, external stimulation and perceptual thresholds in Antrobus's (1986) model of dreaming, and at the same time includes the role postulated for phasic neural firing in the visual system in the Activation–synthesis model of dreaming (Hobson & McCarley, 1977). Both of these models will be examined in more detail later in this chapter.

The importance of activation and sensory thresholds for dreaming has been further elaborated by Zimmerman (1970), who took as his starting point the assumption that auditory arousal thresholds can be taken as an inverse index of general cerebral arousal. Thresholds are highest in slow-wave sleep, where the cortex is least activated, and lowest in waking, followed by REM sleep, where cortical activation is at high levels (Bonnet & Johnson, 1978; Rechtschaffen, Hauri, & Zeitlin, 1966). Whether thresholds are found to differ significantly between REM and Stage 2 sleep appears to depend on the sensitivity of the response measure; averaged evoked potentials yield lower estimates of threshold than do EEG signs of arousal, or behavioral responses (Wills & Trinder, 1978).

Zimmerman (1970) selected subjects on the basis of their auditory arousal thresholds (AATs) during sleep. He formed a group of light sleepers ($n = 16$), who awoke from sleep at less than 60–65 db, and a group of deep sleepers ($n = 16$), whose AATs were greater than 65–70 db over 1 night of sleep. On a second night in the laboratory, these subjects were awakened from REM and Stage 2 sleep and asked for mentation reports. The light sleepers and deep sleepers did not differ on the amount or the characteristics of dreaming reported from REM awakenings. On the other hand, light sleepers reported dreaming after 71% of NREM awakenings, compared with 21% of awakenings for deep sleepers. The light sleepers tended to experience their NREM mentation as "dreaming," while the deep sleepers categorized it as "thinking." This difference in NREM mentation between the groups selected on the basis of AATs was interpreted as a surface indication of underlying stage and individual differences in cerebral arousal. Zimmerman (1970) proposed that

[d]reaming is a function of cerebral arousal in the absence of reality contact. Given the loss of reality contact during sleep, dreaming mentation would occur when the level of cerebral arousal exceeds a certain critical point. Levels of cerebral arousal below this point might be sufficient only to sustain thinking. During REM sleep a particular organization of cerebral functioning would usually increase cerebral arousal above the threshold for dreaming for

all Ss. During NREM sleep, certain Ss at certain times may exceed the threshold for dreaming. According to this proposal, AAT light sleepers usually have sufficient cerebral arousal during NREM sleep for dreaming, while cerebral arousal in AAT deep sleepers usually remains below the dreaming threshold. (pp. 547–548)

Zimmerman's thesis is provocative, but is weakened by his use of auditory thresholds to infer cerebral arousal. An independent measure of cerebral arousal (such as EEG spectral power) would be necessary to show arousal is indeed the intervening variable between peripheral sensory thresholds and the experience of dreaming, independent of sleep stage.

COMPARISON OF MODELS: EMPIRICAL ANALYSES

The next part of this chapter will empirically evaluate two models of bizarre mentation that are based on the factors delineated herein. Specifically, the General Cortical Activation/Thresholds model proposed by Antrobus (1986) and the Activation/Synthesis model formulated by Hobson and McCarley (1977) and other phasic REM events models, will be assessed with reference to measurements of bizarreness in mentation reports from Waking, REM, and Stage 2 sleep. Each of these two approaches will be discussed in more detail. But first a brief digression is necessary to consider the data sets and the methods used in assessment of bizarreness in mentation reports.

Measurement of Bizarreness

To evaluate the relative success of these contrasting explanations of bizarreness in accounting for the presence of bizarre elements in sleeping and waking thought, several groups of mentation reports were examined and scored for Bizarreness and the more undifferentiated, global variable of "Dream-like Quality." The present analyses combine several sets of data, totaling 625 individual mentation reports, in order to compare mentation elicited after awakenings from REM and Stage 2 sleep with fantasies from various conditions of the Waking State. The waking reports were solicited under exactly the same conditions as those of sleep: the subject was lying quietly in a darkened room, wearing electrodes, and was asked to "tell everything that was going through your mind before I called you." The individual report sets will be described in more detail as the appropriate statistical analyses are introduced.

Judges' Ratings. We then gave these report sets to several groups of 3 or 4 judges, and asked them to evaluate the reports for nonredundant information-bearing content (Total Report Count or TRC), and for counts of words expressing visual and verbal imagery. Bizarreness event counts were also obtained on three scales: Discontinuities, a measure of thematic disruption; Improbable Combinations, and Improbable Identities, which are counts of improbable or unusual events in the dreams. These three scales were summed to yield a single Bizarreness score. The directions for these scales are found in the Appendix. All event count scales were taken from the Psycholinguistic Coding Manual (Antrobus, Schnee, Lynn, Silverman, & Offer, 1976) and judges were trained to a reliability of .8 or above on the criterion scale, Total Report Count, from which all the others are ultimately derived. Judges were blind to the condition from which the reports were obtained.

Forced Normal Sorts. A different technique of judging was also used on some of the reports. Judges were asked to sort the reports into eight categories, varying from most to least "bizarre," or from most to least "dream-like." It was left up to the judges to define these qualities for themselves. By forcing the judges to put a specified number of reports in each of the eight categories, it was possible to achieve a normal distribution for Bizarreness and Dream-like Quality ratings. The number of the category to which a report was assigned was taken as a numerical score for that report. These scores were averaged across judges and used in the data analyses.

Having considered the methods and report samples for evaluating bizarreness in the report samples described herein, we can turn now to an examination of the results we received in these analyses. First, let us address the model of cortical activation/perceptual thresholds advanced by Antrobus (1986). For simplicity, this model will be referred to as the General Cortical Activation and Thresholds (GCAT) model for the rest of this discussion. Secondly, the Phasic Events model of bizarreness in dreaming will be evaluated.

GCAT Model: Activation, Thresholds, and Bizarreness

We will first consider the explanation of bizarreness given by the GCAT model (Antrobus, 1986; Wollman & Antrobus, 1986). This theoretical approach explains dream-like quality of mentation as the product of two factors: (1) Activation level of the cortex, where higher levels of neurophysiological activation are associated with higher levels of cognitive activation, in the production and retrieval of associative trains of thought, and (2)

The level of environmental stimulation (or sensory thresholds) that determines whether the associative sequence is interrupted and fragmented into separate topics by intrusive stimuli. The GCAT model predicts that dream-like quality/bizarreness will be greatest with intermediate levels of both cortical activation and external stimulation, since the fragmented quality of thought is a major component of bizarreness. These conditions are met both by REM sleep and by relaxed wakefulness.

Cortical activation is often measured by spectral power in the higher frequency bandwidths of the EEG (beta and alpha). By these measures, waking is the state of highest activation, followed closely by REM sleep. Stage 2 sleep has been shown to contain significantly less power in the high-frequency bands than does Stage 1–REM.

The first parameter of the GCAT model, cortical activation, was examined using the reports of Data Set A. Data Set A ($N = 146$) consists of 73 pairs of REM and Stage 2 reports, each pair being contributed by a single subject, and both reports being drawn from about the same time of night. Detailed analyses of the cognitive characteristics of these reports have been published by Antrobus (1983).

Since physiological arousal is presumed to correlate with activation of cognitive and information-processing systems, the report length (TRC) variable indexes this parameter. As previously reported by Antrobus (1983), the higher activation levels of REM sleep are reflected in the higher TRC counts of REM mentation reports in Data Set A (55.8 words in REM, compared with an average of 19.0 words in Stage 2). The number of discrete topic units (TU) is basically equal in the two states (REM = 2.0, Stage 2 = 1.3), reflecting their similar levels of auditory thresholds.

For the present purpose, these same reports of Data Set A were also submitted to bizarreness counts and forced normal sorts. The results are presented in Table 8.1. As shown in the table, on the sum of the three bizarreness subscales (BIZ), REM and Stage 2 do not differ.

The forced normal sort technique, on the other hand, places REM higher

TABLE 8.1
Data Set A ($N = 146$): Means and Standard Deviations and paired t-tests for Bizarreness and Dream-like Quality, by Stage of Sleep

Variable		Stage 1–REM (n = 73)	Stage 2 (n = 73)	t(72 df)	p
BIZ	$\overline{X}$	0.21	0.22	−0.158	ns
	s.d.	0.60	0.51		
BIZ SORT	$\overline{X}$	5.19	3.81	7.168	0.0001
	s.d.	1.12	1.42		
DQ SORT	$\overline{X}$	5.34	3.66	9.846	0.0001
	s.d.	1.20	1.34		

TABLE 8.2
Data Set B (*N* = 84): Means and Standard Deviations for Bizarreness and
Dream-like Quality, by Stage

Variable		Waking (n = 28)	Stage 1–REM (n = 28)	Stage 2 (n = 28)
BIZ	X̄	1.74*	0.70†	0.42
	s.d.	1.52	1.06	1.01
DQ SORT	X̄	5.07*	4.80	3.57@
	s.d.	0.78	0.90	1.34

† W vs. REM: $p < .01$.
*W vs. Stage 2: $p < .001$.
@REM vs. Stage 2 (paired t-test): $p < 0.001$.

than Stage 2 in level of bizarreness (BIZSORT) and in the global concept of "dream-like quality" (DQSORT). The similarity in the scores of BIZSORT and DQSORT in the two states suggests that these qualities are highly intercorrelated and most probably are tapping into the same underlying construct. In this case, the forced normal sort technique appears to be a more sensitive measure of bizarreness than the event count scales of BIZ.

To find how the waking state compares with bizarreness in REM and Stage 2 mentation, we solicited mentation reports from 14 additional subjects, who were reclining in a darkened room and interrupted at varying intervals for a report of their thoughts and imagery. The reports comprising Data Set B (*N* = 84) are 28 samples of waking thought from these 14 subjects, compared with an equal number of paired REM and Stage 2 reports drawn at random from Set A. The reports in Set B have been previously described by Reinsel, Wollman, and Antrobus (1986).

As shown in Table 8.2, bizarreness appears to present a graded continuum across states of consciousness. The BIZ variable shows highest levels in Waking, somewhat less in REM sleep and least in Stage 2 mentation. Similar results are obtained with the forced normal sort for Dream-like Quality; Waking is again found to be the most dream-like state, followed by REM and Stage 2 in that order.* The most significant finding would appear to be the greater quantity of bizarreness in Waking, by both the event count and forced normal sort techniques. Since the waking state does have a higher cortical activation level than REM sleep, this result is consistent with the GCAT model.

A second parameter of the Antrobus (1986) model is the influence of

---

* For statistical analysis the Waking reports were averaged within subject (*n* = 14) and independent *t* tests were computed between Waking and both sleep stages. BIZ discriminated Waking from Stage 1-REM ($p < .01$) and Waking from Stage 2 ($p < .001$). DQ Sort also discriminated Waking from Stage 2 ($p < .001$) but Waking and REM did not differ on this variable.

external stimulation (primarily in the auditory modality), which is affected by the levels of sensory thresholds. Auditory thresholds are lower in waking than in sleep and become elevated immediately upon sleep onset (Bonnet & Johnson, 1978). The activated cortex is presumed to be continually generating thoughts and imagery that will proceed along the chains of association established by prior learning (see Anderson, 1983) until interrupted by some novel external stimulus, which sets off a new train of associations. These interruptions are more frequent in waking, due to the low level of sensory thresholds; therefore, waking thought is characterized by frequent shifts in topic, and short sequences of elaboration of each topic.

In REM sleep, however, sensory thresholds are elevated above waking levels so that interruptions of the mentation process are less frequent, allowing each topic to be developed and elaborated to a much higher degree. This greater topic length in REM as compared with waking is responsible for the narrative quality of REM dreams, or as Rechtschaffen (1978) has called it, the "single-mindedness" of dreams. In Stage 2 sleep, average thresholds are similar to those in REM (Rechtschaffen et al., 1966), but cortical activation is much less, so the generation of mentation proceeds at a lower level, and recall is correspondingly brief or absent.

Wollman (1984; Wollman & Antrobus, 1986) conducted a doctoral dissertation to test this model. The reports comprising Data Set C ($N = 257$) are drawn from this study. The set consists of waking and REM reports contributed by 30 subjects in a within–subject design involving two conditions of waking reports as well as REM sleep awakenings. In brief, waking conditions were used as comparison/control conditions for REM reports. The waking/REM state difference samples different points on the cortical activation continuum, while the two conditions of waking manipulate the level of auditory stimulation. The Waking with Stimulation (WS) condition is intended to model the normal responsiveness of the cognitive system to intrusive stimulation in the waking state. The Waking without Stimulation (WO) condition is an attempt to use masking white noise to duplicate, in the waking state, the elevated sensory thresholds of REM sleep.

As reported by Wollman and Antrobus (1986), both Waking conditions were indeed higher than REM in report length (TRC), which is presumed to be an index of cortical activation. Discrete Topic Units (TU), reflecting the fragmenting influence of external stimulation, were most numerous in the WS condition and at lower levels when stimulation was absent (WO and REM). Here, the presence of masking white noise in the WO condition successfully mimicked the elevated sensory thresholds of REM sleep. In both WO and REM, fewer changes of topic were noted, and each thematic unit was elaborated to a greater degree than in the WS condition. These results were interpreted as providing support for the predictions of the GCAT model.

To evaluate bizarreness under these conditions, these reports of Data Set C were submitted to the bizarreness coding and forced normal sorts. For analysis, reports were averaged within condition by subject. The P values reported are from the one degree of freedom contrasts from the repeated measures ANOVA ($N = 30$). The results are shown in Table 8.3. As we saw previously in Data Set B, bizarreness and dream-like quality are both found to be greater in Waking than in REM sleep. There is no apparent difference in the two waking conditions, except in the number of discontinuities, as expected from the manipulation of white noise stimulation.

We interpret these data as reflecting the role of cortical activation in producing bizarreness and dream-likeness in thought. EEG measures gathered just prior to the mentation reports show more alpha and beta in the waking reports, while REM sleep shows more power in the lower frequency bands, theta and delta (Wollman & Antrobus, 1987). The reports that are judged more bizarre thus come from the most activated EEG states. In addition, waking consciousness is more responsive to external stimulation, and the frequent changes in topic predispose to the identification of bizarre elements (i.e., those that do not follow from the surrounding context).

In summary, the data so far considered appear to provide good support

TABLE 8.3

Data Set C: ($N = 257$). Comparison of Waking with Stimulation (WS) and Waking without Stimulation (WO) to REM Reports on the Summary Bizarreness Score (BIZ) and its Component Scales: Discontinuities (DISC), Improbable Combinations (IC), and Improbable Identities (II) and the Forced Normal Sort on Dreamlike Quality (DQ SORT)

Variable		WS ($n = 87$)	WO ($n = 87$)	REM ($n = 83$)
BIZ	$\overline{X}$	1.34*	1.26†	0.89
	s.d.	0.85	0.80	0.65
DISC	$\overline{X}$	1.15**@	0.92††	0.57
	s.d.	0.76	0.57	0.40
IC	$\overline{X}$	0.16	0.31	0.26
	s.d.	0.28	0.36	0.25
II	$\overline{X}$	0.02	0.02	0.07
	s.d.	0.04	0.05	0.14
DQ SORT	$\overline{X}$	4.66*	4.59	4.21
	s.d.	0.80	0.92	1.10

WS vs REM: *$p < .05$, **$p < .01$.
WO vs REM: †$p < .05$, ††$p < .01$.
WS vs WO: @$p < .05$.

for the predictions of the GCAT model. Bizarreness is found to be maximal in conditions of high to moderate cortical activation, when external stimulation is reduced (or alternatively, sensory thresholds are increased). These conditions are met both in relaxed wakefulness and in REM sleep. For contrast, let us turn now to another influential model of bizarre mentation, which focuses especially on REM sleep.

The Phasic Events Model

In attempting to account for the characteristics of dream mentation, several theorists have focused on the transient neural "phasic events" that intrude into REM (and NREM) sleep, and are tempting candidates for psychophysiological isomorphism in dream theory (Rechtschaffen, 1973). These approaches may be collectively termed the Phasic Events model, for simplicity.

Phasic events (see Pivik, 1978) are transient physiological responses that intrude into, or are superimposed on, the more steady-state or "tonic" background of the state. In Stage 2 sleep, K-complexes and spindles are phasic events, while the low-frequency, high-amplitude EEG is the tonic or background state. Of the phasic events associated with REM sleep, particular attention has been given to rapid eye movements (REMs), the associated periorbital integrated potentials (PIPs) and the subcortical ponto–geniculo–occipital (PGO) spikes generated by neural firing in the visual system. Also present is transient peripheral activation of the auditory system, as seen in middle ear muscle activity (MEMAs). The occurrence of phasic muscle activity in the middle ear has been found to be more frequent in REM than in NREM sleep (Benson & Zarcone, 1979). Within REM periods, MEMAs are associated with phasic eye movement activity.

The most completely developed of these phasic REM sleep proposals has been presented by Hobson and McCarley (1977) and Hobson (1988) their neurophysiological rebuttal of Freud's theory of dreaming. Hobson and McCarley's Activation–synthesis model consists largely of a detailed description of centers of neural firing in the pons and elsewhere during REM sleep. Phasic REM phenomena are produced by the intermittent activation of these subcortical centers. These intrusive neural events are presumed to disrupt the ongoing mentation process by introducing random images. The model postulates a rather ill-defined "cognitive synthesis" process, which tries to incorporate these random elements into a somewhat plausible cognitive experience. The inevitable distortion that results from the attempt to combine mismatched elements gives the dream its quality of bizarreness. The Activation–synthesis model has been formulated largely in terms of the neurophysiology of the cat and few direct tests of human neurophysiological processes and dreaming have been carried out.

In a later version (Nelson, McCarley, & Hobson, 1983), the model says that in REM sleep, "the forebrain receives information from the relatively autonomous brain stem REM sleep-generating areas; that information is then combined with memory traces and emotional responses in order to elaborate the complete dream phenomena" (p. 795). The ponto–genicu-lo–occipital (PGO) waves that activate the forebrain include input from PGO burst neurons that correspond in their laterality to the direction of rapid eye movements. It is therefore inferred that the PGO pathways convey visual information to the forebrain, where the information is synthesized with other input to form a visual dream. Hobson and McCarley proposed that the high-amplitude PGO activity might be sufficiently disruptive of the ongoing mentation sequence to account for the bizarre character of REM dreams. In other words, they conclude that the bizarre quality of dreams may be attributed to the difficulty of making sense of such random input from subcortical, and therefore noncognitive, genera-tors.

Support for this prediction comes from a study of the cognitive correlates of MEMAs conducted by Ogilvie, Hunt, Sawicki, and Samahalskyi (1982). Their nine subjects were awakened four times on each of 3 experimental nights, twice from REM and twice from Stage 2 sleep, with one awakening in each stage marked by phasic MEMAs. Mentation reports were judged for auditory involvement, affect, bizarreness, hallucinatory quality, and "clouding." (The latter scale refers to confusion in memory, reasoning or action, as well as to narrative discontinuities, i.e., unexplained sudden changes in dream action or setting.) Overall findings were that REM reports showed more of all these qualities than did Stage 2, but the presence of absence of phasic ear activity was not related to auditory imagery or affect. Instead, they found MEMAs to be correlated with bizarre visual imagery and discontinuities in the mentation reports, regardless of which stage of sleep the reports were drawn from.

Periorbital integrated potentials (PIPs) are correlated in time with PGO spikes (the latter have not yet been observed in human subjects). Evidence in support of the PIP-bizarreness relationship was advanced by Rechtschaf-fen, Watson, Wincor, Molinari, and Barta (1972). This initial research found an association between the quantity of PIPs and bizarreness in the mentation reports. However, when new data were collected and analyzed with more carefully controlled procedures (e.g., interrogators blind to the awakening condition), the PIP–bizarreness relationship was present for only one out of four subjects (Watson, Bliwise, Friedman, Wax, & Rechtschaffen, 1978).

In an attempt to evaluate independently the Activation–synthesis model, we employed a data set previously reported on by Arkin, Antrobus, Ellman, and Farber (1978, Experiment 3). In this study, REM reports were obtained from either phasic or tonic awakenings (defined by the presence or absence of eye movements). The 138 reports of Data Set D were obtained from 19 subjects over the course of 4 nonconsecutive nights of normal sleep, with subjects being awakened twice a night, early and late in the sleep period. Following the prediction of the Activation–synthesis model, our expectation was that phasic reports would be the most bizarre. As we have previously reported (Reinsel, Antrobus, & Wollman, 1985) this expectation was not borne out by the data. Table 8.4 presents the means for log word count variables for the phasic and tonic REM reports, averaged within subject over early and late awakenings. Paired t-tests between these variables were not significant. Notably, no measure of imagery discriminated between the phasic and tonic REM conditions. (In their previous report on this data set, Arkin et al. [1978] also found no difference in Dream-like Quality — by forced normal sort — for the phasic/tonic comparisons in either REM or NREM sleep.)

To evaluate bizarreness as a function of phasic or tonic REM awakenings, a repeated-measures analysis of variance was performed on the reports of Data Set D. This analysis found the time-of-night variable to be uniformly nonsignificant as a main effect, while the Phasic/Tonic Condition difference failed to reach the .05 level for word count, imagery, or bizarreness. However, the Condition by Time of Night interaction came quite close to reaching significance for visual imagery variables ($p < .08$), as well as for Total Report Count ($p < .08$). One might speculate that these trends suggest that the intensity of phasic stimulation increases, and is accompanied by more pronounced cognitive effects, as the night progresses. This trend did not however hold true for bizarreness.

The Phasic/Tonic family of models, and the Activation–synthesis model in particular, suffer from their narrow focus on patterns of neural activation that appear to be specific to REM sleep. The phasic events of REM sleep have few, if any, equivalents in waking. As such, the Activa-

TABLE 8.4
Data Set D: ($N = 138$). REM Phasic and REM Tonic Reports. Means and Paired t tests for Log Word Count Variables for Total Report Count (TRC), Visual Imagery (VIS), Speech Imagery (SPCH), and Bizarreness counts (BIZ). (Each score represents the average of up to 8 reports for each of 19 subjects.)

Variable	Stage 1–REM Tonic (n = 71)	Stage 1–REM Phasic (n = 67)	t(18 df)	p
TRC	1.329	1.485	1.469	ns
VIS	1.019	1.144	1.015	ns
SPCH	0.263	0.367	1.368	ns
BIZ	0.289	0.251	−0.419	ns

tion–synthesis model is limited to REM sleep and cannot account for the persistent finding of bizarre mentation in the waking state. The cognitive correlates of these REM phasic phenomena are obscure even in REM, and have not been established at all in waking.

In sum, these data, and that of the other studies cited, do not strongly support the position of Hobson and McCarley (1977) that phasic activation of brainstem centers resulting in PGO spikes, PIPs, and eye movements may play a role in production of bizarre mentation or other cognitive characteristics of dream reports. While it may be premature to conclude that no relationship exists between phasic brainstem events and bizarre mentation, it would appear that the formulations of the GCAT model provide a better fit to the data reported in the first section of this chapter.

BIZARRENESS: ONE DIMENSION, OR MANY?

Component Structure of Bizarreness

Most previous discussions of dream qualities appear to have considered bizarreness as a one-dimensional variable. As we have seen, the forced normal sort technique gives essentially the same results when done for bizarreness as when instructions are given for dream-like quality. These qualities would appear to overlap substantially. Indeed, in these global sorts, as in most nonspecific global ratings, the criteria for the judges' ratings are not well defined. The cues on which judges rely in making their ratings have not been specified by the experimeter, and may remain largely unknown.

That bizarreness does have more than one dimension becomes apparent upon further inspection of Table 8.3. An interesting dissociation is present between the component scales of the BIZ variable. Discontinuities (DISC), Improbable Combinations (IC) and Improbable Identities (II) respond differently to the Waking/REM state shift in activation and to the manipulation of environmental stimulation levels in the two Waking conditions. Consistent with the GCAT model, which predicts that external stimuli disrupt ongoing mentation and send it off on new tangents, DISC is highest when external stimulation is high (WS condition) and shows a declining gradient across the other conditions. IC is lowest in Waking with Stimulation, which keeps attention focused on the environment and task-related processing demands, but increases when stimulation is removed, such that WO and REM have similar levels of IC. The II variable follows a slightly different course from IC. The II variable also increases in REM, but is low in both waking conditions. One could interpret these results as being consistent with the concept of spreading activation in the semantic memory network, which will be discussed in the next section.

The fact that the three component subscales of BIZ do not respond identically to change in state or in stimulation levels implies that they are tapping into relatively independent aspects of the bizarreness construct. Table 8.5 shows the proportion of unique variance contributed by each of the three subscales. DISC accounts for most of the variance in bizarreness in all three conditions, with IC adding from 12% to 22% of additional variance not accounted for by DISC. Although the IC scores are similar in WO and REM, this scale makes its greatest contribution to total variance in the WO condition. Variable II makes the smallest contribution, about 1%-2% in the two waking conditions, but it jumps to nearly 8 per cent in REM sleep. Thus, the combination of high activation in the cortex and a reduction in external stimulation can lead to waking fantasy that is even more improbable than REM dreaming. The particular attributes of the bizarre mentation will depend on variations in these two parameters.

This dissociation between the three component scales of BIZ implies that bizarreness in waking and bizarreness in REM do not really reflect the same quality. Waking bizarreness comes from the discontinuous nature of the reports, where intrusive external stimuli trigger associations that may seem unrelated to the preceding thought. Bizarreness in REM, though, is more due to the genuinely "strange" nature of the images, and the mutable, chameleon-like nature of the characters. The possibility remains that these two types of bizarreness may be associated with different neurophysiological events, which have yet to be identified; although MEMAs and sawtooth waves in the EEG have been suggested (Foulkes & Pope, 1973; Ogilvie et al., 1982). The influence of subcortical structures on mentation has been highlighted by the Activation–synthesis model, though little hard evidence can be found to support it. This area is wide open for future investigation, and would benefit from a clearer conceptualization of the cognitive processes involved in the generation of thought sequences. More precision is also required in the measurement of transient subcortical neurophysiological events. In human subjects, such opportunities are scarce

TABLE 8.5
Data Set C: (*N* = 257). Proportion of Variance in Bizarreness scores (BIZ) Contributed by the Individual Subscales of Discontinuities (DISC), Improbable Combinations (IC), and Improbable Identities (II)

Scale	WS	WO	REM
DISC	86.6%	75.6%	78.6%
IC	12.8%	22.4%	14.9%
II	2.0%	1.4%	7.8%

(but see Cooper, Winter, Crow, & Walter, 1965; Brazier, 1968; Moiseeva, 1979), and have rarely been used to explore cognitive issues.

The Report Length Factor

In contrast to the foregoing indications that bizarreness may be a multidimensional construct is the finding by Antrobus that bizarreness, as well as dream-like quality, may be totally covariant with report length. Antrobus (1983, 1986) has posited that differences between states in cortical activation are reflected by the amount of mentation produced. When a waking subject is asked to report on his or her thoughts, more mentation is available for recall than if the subject is awakened from sleep. While this position does not discriminate between production, storage, and retrieval of spontaneous thought, the assumption is that the word count or length of the verbal report is an index of underlying cognitive activation.

It is well known that mentation reports tend to be considerably longer after REM awakenings than after NREM interruptions. Thus, report length represents a confounding variable in judgments of other dream characteristics such as emotionality, vividness, and bizarreness. In order to control statistically for the report length variable, Antrobus (1983) partialed out Total Report Count (TRC) from the 73 paired REM/NREM reports of Data Set A. Subsequently, he found that other variables such as visual and verbal imagery, dreamer participation, and rated dream-like quality, no longer showed significant differences between REM and Stage 2. In other words, these variables were confounded with report length, and did not significantly add to the variance accounted for by report length alone.

To identify the amount of unique variance contained in the bizarreness variables, Data Set A was submitted to a trichotomous classification. For each of the BIZ scales, J. Antrobus and N. Antrobus (unpublished data) instructed a computer to sort each of the REM/NREM report pairs by whether the REM report was greater than, equal to or less than the NREM report score for each of the three component scales of Bizarreness (Discontinuities, Improbable Combinations, and Improbable Identities). Table 8.6 shows the results of ANOVAs for each of these scales and the Bizarreness forced normal sort. Each individual Bizarreness subscale was able to classify correctly the REM and NREM reports. However, when the variance associated with report length (TRC) is subtracted from the total variance of the BIZ scores, the remaining variance is no longer sufficient to reach significance at the .05 level. This result indicates that differences between states in report length account for nearly all the perceived bizarreness as well as the perceived dream-like quality in mentation reports from different sleep stages.

TABLE 8.6
Data Set A: (N = 146). Results of Analysis of Variance for Each of the
Component Scales of the Bizarreness Event Count Measure (BIZ) and the
MANOVA Incremental F-test to Remove TRC Variance

Variable	F	p
Discontinuities	6.84	.01
Improbable Combinations	8.56	.05
Improbable Identities	2.99	.09
Bizarreness FN Sort	72.53	.0001
MANOVA	206.46	
(all Bizarreness variables)		
minus TRC variance	− 196.01	
Difference	$F < 1$	n.s.

The same result has also been found when applying a different technique of measurement. Porte and Hobson (1986) and Hobson (1988) present a two-stage classification system for categorizing bizarre elements in dreams (see also Hobson, Hoffman, Helfand, & Kostner, this volume). By this scale, a bizarre item may consist of a discontinuity, an incongruity, or an uncertainty; and may be located either in the manifest dream action, or in the dreamer's thoughts and feelings. This rating technique was applied to the REM/NREM pairs of Data Set A. In contrast to the BIZ event count scores, Hobson et al.'s classification system found REM dreams to have many more bizarre elements than Stage 2 reports. The higher levels of bizarreness identified by this method may be largely due to more liberal instructions to the judges, which allow an item to be scored simultaneously in more than one category, thus inflating the scores. However, when report length (TRC) was partialed out of Porte and Hobson's bizarreness scores, differences between REM and Non-REM reports were no longer significant (Antrobus, unpublished data).

The effect of controlling for report length is further shown by a direct comparison of semantic predictability levels of dreams and fantasies. Using the mentation reports of Data Set B, a set of 28 reports from each of three states of consciousness (Waking, REM, and Stage 2 sleep), Wollman, Reinsel, and Antrobus (1983) compared judges' ability to supply missing words from the surrounding verbal context. Known as the Cloze technique, this method is a way of assessing the difficulty level of text samples; it is also a measure of the predictability of speech, its internal logic and connectedness. As such, the lower the predictability of words from context, the greater the unpredictability, or bizarreness, of the thought process reflected. It was expected that REM reports would provide more evidence of bizarreness on these Cloze scores; but instead, there were no significant differences between Waking, REM, and Stage 2 mentation segments of equal length. This finding does not support the idea that REM mentation is inherently more bizarre than any other form of thought, when length is controlled.

Summary of Content Analyses of Bizarreness

We have identified a variety of factors contributing to judgments of bizarreness in dreams and waking thought. There is good evidence that (a) state differences in cortical activation levels, and (b) environmental stimulation levels and/or perceptual thresholds play a role in the production of bizarre mentation. While the possibility remains that phasic neural intrusions during REM sleep may provide one source of bizarre images, support for the GCAT model (Antrobus, 1986) seems more convincing than the evidence for the Activation–synthesis model (Hobson & McCarley, 1977).

From the results of the content analyses described previously, there are several points which bear repeating:

First, we can no longer assume that REM "dreams" are automatically more bizarre than any other mental activity, given the same environmental conditions. When released from direct stimulus–response ties to the environment, waking thought can be quite bizarre in its own right.

Second, there is good evidence that bizarreness bears a positive (though not necessarily linear) relationship to cortical activation. To the extent that stage 1–REM is a state of higher cortical activation, REM reports will be more bizarre than Stage 2. In individuals with high activation levels in NREM sleep, there is a greater amount of "dreaming" reported (Zimmerman, 1970). With the even higher cortical activation levels of relaxed wakefulness, mind-wandering may under some conditions be even more bizarre than dreaming.

Third, our data argue against a unidimensional approach to sleep (or waking) mentation. We have shown that the three component scales of the BIZ measure do not vary uniformly across states. Discontinuities seem to be the major factor in predicting bizarreness scores, in both waking and sleep. Improbable Combinations rank second, and are equally prevalent in relaxed wakefulness as in dreams. The mutable identities and transformations indexed by the Improbable Identities subscale are much rarer in waking, but increase in frequency in REM. (This latter finding agrees with earlier normative data; and it must be cautioned that these genuinely bizarre events in laboratory REM reports are not as frequent as one might assume. Even in home dream diaries, Hall and Van de Castle (1966) report that less than 1% of a sample of 1,000 dreams contained any transformation of characters' identities.)

Fourth, the various measurement techniques employed appear to give quite consistent results when compared with each other. The forced normal sort method generally shows the same pattern of findings as do the event counts, though the normalized sorts appear to be more sensitive in discriminating between REM and Stage 2. Event counts are, however, to be preferred over Likert rating scales for the psychometric reasons of low validity and low interjudge reliability in the latter.

And, last but not least: Given the confounding of bizarreness measures with length in most studies, it would seem imperative to control somehow for the variable of report length in studies of this type, either by partialing word count out of the regression equation, or by truncating the selections to a standard length. Bizarreness scores that are confounded with report length, as in the traditional comparisons of REM and Stage 2 mentation, may give a misleading impression of the prevalence of bizarre mentation in any particular state of consciousness.

THE COGNITIVE PERSPECTIVE

Further elucidation of bizarreness in mentation, whether waking or dreaming, may come from the perspective of cognitive psychology. Among the conceptual tools of that field that may be useful are the concepts of context effects, spreading activation in semantic memory, top–down and bottom-up processing, and the new wave in cognitive psychology: parallel distributed processing, or the PDP model. Each of these topics will be briefly considered.

We do not have to go far to find a valuable insight into the nature of bizarreness. In *Webster's New Collegiate Dictionary* (2nd ed., 1972) "bizarre" is defined as "strikingly out of the ordinary, as (a) odd, extravagant or eccentric in style or mode (b) involving sensational contrasts or incongruities (c) atypical" (p. 83). The leading synonym for "bizarre" is given as "fantastic," and in commenting further on the distinction between these two terms, bizarre is seen to apply to "the sensationally queer or strange and implies violence of contrast or incongruity of combination" (p. 302).

Context. Cognitive psychologists have used a similar approach in defining bizarreness. Antrobus (1977, 1978, 1986) and Foulkes (1985) have viewed bizarreness as caused by incongruous elements within a larger context of narrative mentation. These incongruous elements become apparent only when there is sufficient surrounding context to establish expectations for the most probable next element in the sequence, and consequently to evaluate a discrepancy as a non sequitur. Thus, longer narrative sequences are inherently more likely to be judged bizarre. Bizarre sequences are seldom seen in Stage 2 reports because the recalled information is too brief to establish both a context and an improbable item within that context. REM reports, however, do possess just such an extended sequence of thought and imagery, leading to greater perceived bizarreness.

In the theoretical approach presented by Antrobus (1977, 1978) and by Foulkes (1985), bizarreness is taken to be an incongruity of imagery or occurrence with surrounding contextual elements. For example, consider the following mentation report:

> I was sort of dreaming about Janis Joplin . . . of all people apparently somehow or other she was appearing in a dream with Abbott and Costello (laugh) ahm . . . who were all in a subway station and ah . . . I wasn't there . . . but . . . the conversation that they were engaged in had to do with apple pie . . . there also appeared a kid from my high school ahm at one point he joined the conversation . . .

To have a dream about Janis Joplin or Abbott and Costello separately would not necessarily be considered bizarre, but a dream where the three have a conversation together is definitely incongruent. The subway station environment is inappropriate for the Abbott and Costello characters, and the conversation about apple pie in that context is not logically connected. The sudden appearance of a high school friend does not follow from the previous elements.

Spreading Activation. An explanation of the disjointed, disconnected nature of many dreams may be found in the spreading activation approach of cognitive psychology. Antrobus (1986) has presented a psychophysiological adaptation of Anderson's (1983) model of spreading activation in semantic memory processing. Again, waking and sleep states are presumed to differ in the degree of cortical (and by implication, cognitive) activation. Mentation from the various points along the activation continuum will vary in depth of associative processing (see Craik & Lockhart, 1972; Collins & Loftus, 1975). That is, spreading activation in the cognitive network will proceed from a starting concept or "node" to related or associated features or concepts. In fully activated waking thought, many associated features will be activated, giving rise to well-elaborated concepts, complete with their appropriate defining features. However, in REM sleep, less cortical activation is present, so that activation of a given node is not accompanied by activation of as many associated features as would be reached by spreading activation in the waking state. Thus, in REM, activation of subsequent nodes may not be appropriately constrained by waking knowledge of relationships between events in memory.

For instance, in the following dream, one might surmise that knowledge of which persons belonged to one or the other summer camp memory was not fully activated, and the different memory experiences are fused into one general summer camp scene.

> I was dreaming of some days when I was back in boys camp in Massachusetts and New York. I was talking with some of my counselors telling them what it was like from my end to go camp with those counselors uh I was wrestling when you woke me up I was wrestling with a big guy named John I think uh I was on the waterfront launching some sort of a water shell at the time that this wrestling match took place. It was a queer mixture because I've been to two camps and people from both camps were at the same place.

In this example, activation might have spread through the memory network, beginning with the node "summer camp," and reaching the nodes for "counselors," "waterfront," "watershell," "wrestling match," and "John." The spread of activation through the network ceased before it reached the associated nodes for "Massachusetts" and "New York," which would have discriminated the two sets of memories from one another. The higher activation level of the waking state allows activation of these identificatory features and generally prevents confusion of separate events.

In Stage 2 sleep, the overall level of activation is so low that images are often vague, lacking in details, and the cognitive system is much less capable of sustaining the generation of a narrative sequence required for the experience of a "dream" or, alternatively, of preserving the memory trace in short-term memory long enough for the report of the mentation after awakening. The following postawakening report can be taken as typical of Stage 2 mentation:

> I think I was in the sleep lab um I remember the white walls and stuff it's sort of similar to the second time you woke me up tonight although I think this time I was dreaming more certainly uh the dream wasn't as vivid I can't recall it as clearly as the last time but it was here.

Bottom-up Vs. Top-down Processing. These terms are in use in cognitive psychology to indicate the source of activation in semantic memory (see Lindsay & Norman, 1973). Bottom-up processing is stimulus-generated, beginning with the early steps in encoding and processing the external sensory input, and identifying it with reference to templates stored in memory. This sensory input provides the source for spreading activation in the neural nets that relate these templates to one another. On the other hand, top-down processing begins without benefit of sensory activation. The cognitive system is already biased to encode or process stimuli in accordance with its internally generated context of already activated nodes, features, or nets. This internal source for entry into neural net circuits is an example of top–down processing. The brain generates its own context, and interprets external stimuli in the light of the already activated features in memory. Mental set, expectation, and priming effects in cognitive psychology, and expectations and attitudinal effects in social psychology reflect the influence of top–down processing.

When external stimulation is attenuated, as by merely closing the eyes, or under mild sensory deprivation conditions (ganzfeld, shielded chamber) this internal source of mentation comes to the forefront of consciousness, and is experienced as mind-wandering or daydreaming thought. This thought can be highly visual and may lack the highly focused and logical quality we assume to be the hallmark of waking thought. Indeed, the bizarreness associated with dreams can be found even more markedly in waking thought under the right environmental conditions (Foulkes & Fleisher, 1975; Foulkes & Scott, 1973; Reinsel et al., 1985).

PARALLEL DISTRIBUTED PROCESSING MODELS

Recent developments within artificial intelligence and cognitive science have culminated in a new approach to human information processing. This new approach is based on parallel distributed processing (PDP). A consideration of PDP models may afford some new insights into the problem of bizarreness in sleep and waking mentation.

As described in recent volumes by Hinton and Anderson (1981) and Rumelhart et al. (1986), the family of models which share in common their reliance on the concept of "parallel distributed processing" reject the serial model of memory processing as inefficient in terms of time and energy. It is also generally conceded that the brain is more likely to be a parallel processor than a serial one (Reeke & Edelman, 1988; Schwartz, 1988).

The PDP models propose that memory search does not proceed serially to exhaustion before beginning another search path, but instead proceeds in parallel along many different pathways. The probability of a given pathway being searched depends on the association strength to the current node and on the frequency with which that node has been activated in the past (see also Antrobus, 1977, 1978, 1991; and Anderson's ACT* model, 1983). These models also abandon the idea of fixed memory locations for individual concepts or events. Instead, memories are seen as complex patterns of neural signals stored in a distributed fashion throughout the brain. The brief description of PDP models given by McClelland and Rumelhart (1986) is clear and succinct:

> In a distributed memory system, a mental state is a pattern of activation over the units in some subset of the modules. The patterns in the different modules

capture different aspects of the content of the mental states in a kind of partially overlapping fashion. Alternative mental states are simply alternative patterns of activation over the modules. Information processing is the process of evolution in time of mental states. (McClelland and Rumelhart, 1986, p. 176).

Insofar as a given stimulus is similar on various occasions, the resulting neural signals will have similar patternings. Recall becomes a matter of recreating the pattern of activation over the units in the network.

Retrieval amounts to partial reinstatement of a mental state, using a cue which is a fragment of the original state. For any given module, we can see the cues as originating from outside of it. Some cues could arise ultimately from sensory input. Others would arise from the results of previous retrieval operations, fed back to the memory system under the control of a search or retrieval plan. (McClelland and Rumelhart, 1986, p. 176)

Failure of recall would occur only if the cue was not strong enough to reinstate the entire pattern over the set of units in the network. More often, the partially activated network would be similar enough to another stored pattern to cause that one to be activated instead. The result would be the kind of superimposition of one set of features on another that is characteristic of bizarre dreaming—as in "It was my brother but he was a girl."

An important assumption of the PDP models is that the brain has its own internal sources of activation, which continually support cognitive processing operations in the neural nets. The brain can generate its own activation (probably via self-maintaining links of the ascending and descending reticular formations to mediate cortical arousal via thalamic cortical relay fibers). Energy in the neural nets gives rise to thoughts, imagery, and planning sequences. These operations continue in parallel with external, task-related attention (Antrobus, 1968; Antrobus, Singer, & Greenberg, 1966); and are not stopped even in sleep, as shown by the high prevalence of mentation reports from both REM and NREM sleep (Herman et al., 1978).

The self-generating activation feature of the neural nets model is one of its most powerful characteristics. It is this property that allows the PDP model to produce autonomous sequences of thought and imagery. These sequences are constructed as a succession of states of many interrelated nets. The number of combinations of separate elements is virtually infinite, constrained only by the connection strengths between elements determined by prior experience or learning. In contrast to conventional schema models that store a limited number of sets of schemata in memory, PDP models store only the sets of connection strengths among the nets. Consequently the nets may be assembled in any configuration as a function of the pattern of inputs and the weights of the connections between the neurons in each net. This freedom to activate internally and rearrange cognitive elements stored in memory makes the PDP models very attractive for explaining the process of dream production.

Activation Level and Thought

The ability of PDP neural nets to respond equally well to top–down and bottom–up input (Hinton & Anderson, 1981) is an essential characteristic of any cognitive model, and particularly for a model of sleep mentation, which must produce output in the absence of sensory input. To the extent that sleep mentation, and even waking fantasy, is generally independent of concurrent external stimulation, the production of such mentation must necessarily be produced by something other than the conventionally defined bottom–up process that originates in sensory receptors or the projection areas of the cortex.

In a PDP model, different parts of the distributed networks might activate nets dedicated to visual imagery, and, depending on the overall level or pattern of activation, might simultaneously activate neural nets concerned with the meanings and attributes of the images. Alternatively, in less activated neural states, the meanings might be activated, but the associated visual images activated only weakly or not at all. If general cortical activation were high, the pattern of neural net activation that represents one's person, one's values, wishes, and capabilities, might also be activated. In the first case, the awakened subject might report simply the visual properties of the dream; in the second case, the subject might report the names and meanings of the objects and events without having had a clear visual experience; in the last case, the subject might recall the experience of being aware of watching and even participating in the sleep experience.

PDP Models and Sleep Mentation

The cognitive characteristics of REM sleep mentation can be mapped onto a PDP model that is either fully activated, or more likely activated at some level intermediate to that of waking and NREM sleep. It is further assumed that the model is unresponsive to all but high intensity sensory input, including feedback from its own motor commands and the autonomic system. Such a PDP system should produce an uninterrupted flow of story-like thought and imagery, be able to save or reproduce this material as memory and, isolated from external sensory input, process this input as though it were veridical perceptual productions. Such thought and imagery, if recalled subsequent to awakening, may be identified as false perceptions and labeled as hallucinatory or a dream. Because most of these characteristics are similar to those already proposed for top-down processes by PDP models, the mapping of PDP models onto the REM sleep neurophysiology requires little comment. The bizarre and metaphorical qualities of sleep mentation, however, require additional consideration.

Bizarre, Anomalous, and Metaphoric Imagery and Thought

Two possible antecedents of bizarre mentation are proposed. The first makes use of PDP neural nets' ability to produce output in response to both top-down and bottom-up input. It is proposed that the absence of external sensory input during REM sleep deprives the system of the contextual constraints that normally coordinate top-down and bottom-up processes in the waking state. In the absence of external sensory input, self-generated local activity in any of the modules that normally send input up to the associative part of the system may be processed as though it were bottom-up input from an external source. Random neural firing in pontine centers (e.g., PGO spikes) may also be an internal source of activation, and be processed in bottom-up fashion, as proposed by Hobson and McCarley (1977) in the Activation-synthesis model. The perceptual output of this bottom-up process may then appear "bizarre" in that it is "out of context" with respect to the output of associative nets that are controlled by top-down processes, independently and in parallel.

The second antecedent of bizarre mentation production in REM sleep relates to the GCAT model presented earlier. Compared with the waking state, REM sleep may show an overall drop in the level of associative processing. An intermediate level of diffuse activation of the associative system, posited for REM sleep, may be insufficient to support the ability of local nets to fully activate the same patterns of associated networks that they typically activate in the waking state. The resulting atypical patterns of neural net activation may correspond to the production of images with improbable or bizarre features.

The special features of a PDP model, as summarized above, offer a fruitful approach to the study of bizarre mentation, both in waking and in sleep states. Further elaboration and a preliminary implementation of the PDP approach to dreaming and bizarre mentation can be found in Antrobus (1991). The perspective offered by a PDP model of mentation is able to explain the effects of context and report length on bizarreness through top-down processing and the spreading activation concept, and incorporates phasic brain stem events, such as PGO spikes, as internally generated sources of cognitive activation through bottom-up processing.

With its focus on concepts and their features not as single items stored in a specific location, but as variants of energy patterns in entire neural networks, a PDP model can explain bizarreness as slight deviations in the overall energy pattern of a network that do not exactly duplicate the pattern as it would normally be experienced perceptually. The PDP approach may be the most powerful conceptual tool yet brought to bear on the question of bizarreness.

REFERENCES

Anderson, J. (1983). *The architecture of cognition.* Cambridge, MA: Harvard University Press.

Antrobus, J. S. (1968). Information theory and stimulus-independent thought. *British Journal of Psychology, 59,* 423–430.

Antrobus, J. S. (1977). The dream as metaphor: An information processing and learning model. *Journal of Mental Imagery, 2,* 327–338.

Antrobus, J. S. (1978). Dreaming for cognition. In A. M. Arkin, J. S. Antrobus, & S. J. Ellman (Eds.), *The mind in sleep* (pp. 569–581). Hillsdale, NJ: Lawrence Erlbaum Associates.

Antrobus, J. S. (1983). REM & NREM sleep reports: Comparison of word frequencies by cognitive classes. *Psychophysiology, 20,* 562–568.

Antrobus, J. S. (1986). Dreaming: Cortical activation and perceptual thresholds. *Journal of Mind and Behavior, 7,* 193–212.

Antrobus, J. (1991). Dreaming: Cognitive processes during cortical activation and high afferent thresholds. *Psychological Review, 98,* 96–121.

Antrobus, J. S., Schnee, R., Lynn, A., Silverman, S. & Offer, V. (1976). *A psycholinguistic coding manual for reports of sleep experience.* Educational Testing Service Test Collection, Set D, No. 008737, 1977 revision.

Antrobus, J. S., Singer, J. L. & Greenberg, S. (1966). Studies in the stream of consciousness: Experimental enhancement and suppression of spontaneous cognitive processes. *Perceptual and Motor Skills, 23,* 399–417.

Arkin, A. M., Antrobus, J. S., Ellman, S. J., & Farber, J. (1978). Sleep mentation as affected by REMP Deprivation. In A. M. Arkin, J. S. Antrobus, & S. J. Ellman (Eds.), *The Mind in Sleep* (pp. 459–484). Hillsdale, NJ: Lawrence Erlbaum Associates.

Benson, K., & Zarcone, V. P., Jr. (1979) Phasic events of REM sleep: Phenomenology of middle ear muscle activity and periorbital integrated potentials in the same normal population. *Sleep, 2,* 199–213.

Bonnet, M. H., & Johnson, L. C. (1978) Relationship of arousal threshold to sleep stage distribution and subjective estimates of depth and quality of sleep. *Sleep, 1,* 161–168.

Brazier, M. A. B. (1968). Electrical activity recorded simultaneously from the scalp and deep structures of the human brain. *Journal of Nervous and Mental Disease, 147,* 31–39.

Collins, A. M., & Loftus, E. F. (1975) A spreading-activation theory of semantic processing. *Psychological Review, 82,* 407–425.

Cooper, R., Winter, A. L., Crow, H. J., & Walter, W. G. (1965). Comparison of subcortical, cortical and scalp activity using chronically indwelling electrodes in man. *Electroencephalography and Clinical Neurophysiology, 18,* 217–228.

Craik, F. I. M., & Lockhart, R. S. (1972). Levels of processing: A framework for memory research. *Journal of Verbal Learning and Verbal Behavior, 11,* 671–684.

Foulkes, D. (1985). *Dreaming: A cognitive-psychological analysis.* Hillsdale, NJ: Lawrence Erlbaum Associates.

Foulkes, D., & Fleisher, S. (1975). Mental activity in relaxed wakefulness. *Journal of Abnormal Psychology, 84,* 66–75.

Foulkes, D., & Pope, R. (1973). Primary visual experience and secondary cognitive elaboration in Stage REM: A modest confirmation and extension. *Perceptual and Motor Skills, 37,* 107–118.

Foulkes, D., & Scott, E. (1973). An above-zero waking baseline for the incidence of momentarily hallucinatory mentation. *Sleep Research, 2,* 108.

Hall, C. S., & Van de Castle, R. L. (1966). *The content analysis of dreams.* New York: Appleton–Century–Crofts.

Herman, J. H., Ellman, S. J., & Roffwarg, H. P. (1978). The problem of NREM dream recall re-examined. In A. M. Arkin, J. S. Antrobus, & S. J. Ellman (Eds.), *The mind in sleep* (pp. 59–92). Hillsdale, NJ: Lawrence Erlbaum Associates.

Hinton, G. E., & Anderson, J. A. (Eds.) (1981). *Parallel models of associative memory.* Hillsdale, NJ: Lawrence Erlbaum Associates.

Hobson, J. A. (1988). *The dreaming brain.* New York: Basic Books.

Hobson, R. A., & McCarley, R. W. (1977). The brain as a dream state generator: An activation-synthesis hypothesis of the dream process. *American Journal of Psychiatry, 134,* 1335–1348.

Klinger, E. (1971) *Structure and functions of fantasy.* New York: Wiley.

Lindsay, P. H., & Norman, D. A. (1973). *Human information processing* (2nd ed.). New York: Academic Press.

McClelland, J. L., & Rumelhart, D. E. (1986). A distributed model of human learning and memory. In J. L. McClelland, D. E. Rumelhart, & the PDP Research Group (Eds), *Parallel distributed processing: Explorations in the microstructure of cognition. Volume 2: Psychological and biological models* (pp. 170–215). Cambridge, MA: The MIT Press.

Moiseeva, N. I. (1979). The significance of different sleep stages for the regulation of electrical brain activity in man. *Electroencephalography and Clinical Neurophysiology 46,* 371–381.

Nelson, J. P., McCarley, R. W., & Hobson, J. A. (1983). REM sleep burst neurons, PGO waves, and eye movement information. *Journal of Neurophysiology, 50,* 784–797.

Ogilvie, R. D., Hunt, H. T., Sawicki, C., & Samahalskyi, J. (1982). Psychological correlates of spontaneous middle-ear muscle activity during sleep. *Sleep, 5,* 11–27.

Pivik, R. T. (1978). Tonic states and phasic events in relation to sleep mentation. In A. M. Arkin, J. S. Antrobus, & S. J. Ellman (Eds.), *The mind in sleep: Psychology and psychophysiology* (pp. 245–271). Hillsdale, NJ: Lawrence Erlbaum Associates.

Porte, H. S., & Hobson, J. A. (1986). Bizarreness in REM and NREM reports. *Sleep Research, 15,* 81.

Rechtschaffen, A. (1973). The psychophysiology of mental activity during sleep. In F. J. McGuigan & R. A. Schoonover (Eds.), *The psychophysiology of thinking* (pp. 153–205). New York: Academic Press.

Rechtschaffen, A. (1978). The single-mindedness and isolation of dreams. *Sleep, 1,* 97–109.

Rechtschaffen, A., Hauri, P., & Zeitlin, M. (1966). Auditory awakening thresholds in REM and NREM sleep stages. *Perceptual and Motor Skills, 22,* 927–942.

Rechtschaffen, A., Watson, R., Wincor, M. Z., Molinari, S., & Barta, S. G. (1972). The relationship of phasic and tonic periorbital EMG activity to NREM mentation. *Sleep Research, 1,* 114.

Reeke, G. N., Jr., & Edelman, G. M. (1988). Real brains and artificial intelligence. *Daedalus, 117* (Winter), 143–173.

Reinsel, R., Antrobus, J., & Wollman, M. (1985). The phasic-tonic difference and the time-of-night effect. *Sleep Research, 14,* 115.

Reinsel, R., Wollman, M., & Antrobus, J. S. (1986). Effects of environmental context and cortical activation on thought. *Journal of Mind and Behavior, 7,* 259–275.

Rumelhart, D. E., McClelland, J. L., and the PDP Research Group. (1986). *Parallel distributed processing: Explorations in the microstructure of cognition. Vol. 1: Foundations.* Cambridge, MA.: MIT Press.

Schwartz, J. T. (1988). The new connectionism: Developing relationships between neuroscience and artificial intelligence. *Daedalus, 117* (Winter), 123–142.

Singer, J. L. (1978). Experimental studies of daydreaming and the stream of thought. In K. S. Pope & J. L. Singer (Eds.), *The stream of consciousness* (pp. 187–223). New York: Plenum Press.

Watson, R. K., Bliwise, D. L., Friedman, L., Wax, D., & Rechtschaffen, A. (1978). Phasic EMG in human sleep: periorbital potential and REM mentation. *Sleep Research, 7,* 57.

Weisz, R., & Foulkes, D. (1970). Home and laboratory dreams collected under uniform sampling conditions. *Psychophysiology, 6,* 588–596.

Wills, N., & Trinder, J. (1978). Influence of response criterion on the awakening thresholds of sleep stages. *Waking and Sleeping, 2,* 57–62.

Wollman, M. (1984). *Sleeping and waking thought: The effects of cortical arousal and external stimulation.* Unpublished doctoral dissertation, City University of New York.

Wollman, M. C., & Antrobus, J. (1986). Sleeping and waking thought: Effects of external stimulation. *Sleep, 9,* 438–448.

Wollman, M. C., & Antrobus, J. S. (1987). Cortical arousal and mentation in sleeping and waking subjects. *Brain and Cognition, 6,* 334–346.

Wollman, M. C., Reinsel, R. A., & Antrobus, J. S. (1983). Predictability of speech generated from wakefulness and after awakenings from REM and Stage 2 sleep. In W. P. Koella (Ed.), *Sleep 1982* (pp. 378–382). Basel: Karger.

Zimmerman, W. B. (1970). Sleep mentation and auditory awakening thresholds. *Psychophysiology, 6,* 540–549.

APPENDIX: INSTRUCTIONS TO JUDGES FOR THE 3
COMPONENT SCALES OF BIZARRENESS

Discontinuities

A discontinuity occurs when a part of a mentation report is inconsistent with other parts of the mentation report, according to your waking experience. For example in a mentation report the subject says that he was talking with his brother in an apartment and then, with no transition reported, says he was speaking with a woman in the hall.

A discontinuity should also be counted if the subject indicates that the mentation report content is inconsistent with his own waking experience by comments such as "and somehow, and suddenly, it was very strange." So if the subject comments that a change in scene, action, speech, etc., took place without sense of transition this is also a discontinuity.

The subject may recall (and report) parts of his experience out of the order in which he or she experienced them. For example, the subject may at the end of his report say "oh yes, my brother was there at the beginning." We do not want to count this sort of disjointed reporting as a discontinuity. You should reassemble the report in your mind in the sequence in which things occurred. If a discontinuity exists after this, rather than as a result of poor reporting, it should be counted.

On your answer sheet, mark the total number of discontinuities in each report.

Improbable Combinations

This scale measures the incidence of improbable or bizarre elements in mentation reports. Objects such as winged men, or talking trees, or actions such as men flying or changing into stone are counted, since they are improbable or impossible according to your waking experience.

This scale differs from the Discontinuity scale in that the Discontinuity scale measures internal consistency in the plot or sequence of events while this scale is for counting bizarre elements of mentation reports regardless of context.

For each report, you should count the total number of improbable combinations and mark this on your answer sheet.

Improbable Identities

In some mentation reports the subject reports that a person "was my Uncle Jack but was really my father," or "she was my sister but it was a man." This scale counts the number of such multiple, or impossible, or changing identities of characters or objects.

For each report, you should count the total number of such entities in the mentation report and mark this on your answer sheet.

9 Associative Mechanisms In Dream Production

C. Cipolli
Institute of Human Physiology, University of Modena, Italy

D. Battaglia, C. Cavallero, P. Cicogna, and M. Bosinelli
University of Bologna, Italy

In the last 10 years, following widespread rejection of the approach provided by psychophysiological models (which assume direct correspondence between psychological and physiological indicators), research into the cognitive aspects of dreaming has generally focused on the specific components and strategies operating in dream production. While the overall perspective of such studies is clearly cognitive, it is often unclear which of the various models of cognitive processes in waking has been transposed to the context of sleep mentation. Therefore, even if there have been many more investigations of the cognitive components of dreams (or, in more general terms, mental sleep experiences: MSEs) than of the emotional–affective ones, any attempt to elaborate a general model of the cognitive aspects of MSE seems as yet too ambitious, given the difficulty of combining the evidence provided by different studies into a theoretically coherent framework (Cavallero & Cicogna, 1984).

What seems well supported by experimental findings is the fact that certain cognitive models are particularly fruitful in assessing the processes operating in MSE production and recall (Antrobus, 1978, 1983; Foulkes, 1982). One cognitive paradigm from which useful strategies for investigating MSE production can be derived is that of Information Processing. We see the application of such strategies as a continuation of previous research on the characteristics of sleep mentation, which has led to insight into such processes as storage of MSE content during sleep, recall after night awakening (Salzarulo & Cipolli, 1979) and further recall in the morning (Cicogna, Cavallero, & Bosinelli, 1982; Cipolli, Calasso, Maccolini, Pani, & Salzarulo, 1984; Cipolli, Salzarulo, & Calabrese, 1981).

The basic assumption in an information-processing approach to MSE production is that information to be converted into MSE content (such as presleep stimuli, memories of recent or remote events, etc.) is elaborated at various levels, that is, sensorial, linguistic, and abstract. Explicit hypotheses as to the modifications taking place on particular levels of elaboration can thus be formulated, and their experimental testing can cast light on the nature of the mechanisms at work. However, the use of research strategies derived from the field of waking cognition requires caution. Even if we assume a basic analogy between the information-processing system(s) in the two conditions, in sleep research it is usually impossible to carry out the direct comparisons of input and output typical of the information-processing paradigm, since the input materials of MSE (such as day residues, episodic experiences, general frames, or abstract knowledge) are neither directly controllable nor indeed fully knowable (Cipolli & Fagioli, 1988). Notwithstanding these constraints, the studies we have carried out in recent years show that an information-processing approach may be useful both in identifying the characteristics of materials recruited in memory as sources of MSE content and in establishing how those materials are processed. While dreams appear to derive from mnemonic sources (such as presleep stimuli), they do not usually reproduce these memories directly in their content. To account for this fact, all psychological models of MSE production have explicitly or implicitly posited the presence of associative mechanisms. In particular, their function has been hypothesized by Foulkes (1982) in terms of insertion of individual content into MSE frames.

In designing experiments to provide evidence on the functioning of these mechanisms and the nature of the materials they process, we have assumed that: (a) The functioning of the associative mechanisms is reflected in the relationships observable between presleep stimuli and the content of MSE reports; (b) The characteristics of mnemonic sources (such as their informational value) of MSE content can be identified by using the same criteria as are employed in analyzing responses to waking association tasks.

There appear to be 4 main experimental contexts where relevant data can be collected.

1. *Presleep free associations,* where the subject is invited to associate aloud without stimulus presentation. By comparing these associations with MSE reports, the manner and extent to which materials of the associative chain before sleep are incorporated into MSE contents can be assessed. This technique has been used, among others, by Baekeland, Resch, and Katz (1968).

2. *Presleep stimuli,* where the subject is presented with stimuli in comprehension or memorization tasks. Incorporation of these stimuli into MSE can then be directly assessed. The advantage over

the previous technique is that the input material can be controlled by the researcher, so that the processing of stimuli with different characteristics and/or during various sleep stages can be analyzed.

3. *Within-sleep stimuli.* Examining the incorporation of such stimuli into MSE content allows study not only of the workings of associative mechanisms during sleep, but also of the memory processing of the stimulus during sleep.

4. *Postsleep free associations* with MSE content. The characteristics of associations provided after the MSE report can be analyzed to draw inferences as to the characteristics of the source materials activated and the associative mechanisms involved.

In our work we have applied the second and fourth of these techniques, analyzing the relationships between experimentally delivered stimuli and the content of MSE reports, and between MSE reports and materials obtained via free associations. The two strategies are complementary, since the first allows inferences as to associative mechanisms that operate on controlled external stimuli, while the second one provides access (albeit limited) to the natural sources of MSE content.

THE INCORPORATION OF PRESLEEP STIMULI

By examining the associative relationships between presleep verbal stimuli and MSE reports, we aimed to ascertain whether the characteristics of these stimuli influence the operations of associative mechanisms in MSE production. The use of sentences as stimuli offers the advantage of direct comparability of stimulus and report and facilitates the identification of associative relationships. The criteria applied in identifying these relationships were derived from Clark's (1970) feature-matching model of linguistic associations (Table 9.1).

These criteria allow us to distinguish two main types of associative relationships between stimulus and response material, paradigmatic and syntagmatic. These types reproduce the two ways through which information is usually supposed to be interconnected in semantic memory (that is, abstract and general: Anderson, 1976; Collins & Loftus, 1975). Information is represented as connected as in a network, whose properties have been partly studied in waking conditions (Anderson, 1980). One of the best attested properties of such networks concerns their organization: by analogy (that is, partial or complete substitutability of items in compatible contexts) and by combination, whereby further items add information to a node in the network. As usual in studying associations to dream content, we

TABLE 9.1
Clark's System of Associative Rules

Rules		Examples
Paradigmatic		
Minimal Contrast	(a) identity	car–car
	(b) antonymy	northern–southern
	(c) synonymy	my dog–Spot
Marking		leave–abandon
Feature addition/deletion		fruit–apple
		grandfather–old man
		mountain–fountain
Category maintenance		take for granted–preume
Syntagmatic		
Selectional feature–realization		academic context–seminar
Idiom–completion		Christmas–merry

assume that there are two main modalities of association, operating in MSE production, corresponding to this organizational typology.

In the two experiments where a sentence was presented to subjects before sleep, stimuli were constructed to ascertain whether characteristics such as semantic acceptability influenced:

1. The frequency of incorporation of the stimulus into reports in different sleep stages or at different times of the night. Given the well-known differences in the characteristics of MSE reports from NREM and REM sleep (REM reports being usually longer and more organized; Foulkes, 1962), higher rates of incorporation may be expected in REM than in NREM reports. Moreover, if memory retention of presleep stimuli decreases over time, and in particular in the second half of the night (Fowler, Sullivan, & Ekstrand, 1973), the longer the interval between stimulus presentation and its activation during sleep, the lower should be the rate of incorporation into current MSE.

2. The type of associative relationships between stimulus and reported MSE content. Since the type of relationship indicates the level of linguistic analysis that is involved in transforming the stimulus and long-stored information into MSE content, different frequencies of particular types of relationships for semantically acceptable and unacceptable stimuli would provide evidence of the way in which associative mechanisms are activated by stimulus characteristics.

In the first experiment (Cipolli, Fagioli, Maccolini, & Salzarulo, 1983) 16 subjects, for 4 nights, heard in alternate sessions either a semantically acceptable (SEM +) or unacceptable (SEM –) Italian sentence before sleep. They were awakened once each night either in descending stage 2-NREM (sleep onset: SO) or REM of the first cycle of sleep. These stages were chosen because normative data predicted high probability of content reports and, thus, balancing the number of reports across stages. After awakening, a test of recall of the presleep stimulus was given as a masking task and a report of dream experience requested.

The associative relationships between presleep verbal stimuli and MSE content were distinguished into *paradigmatic* associations (substitution with elements of the same grammatical category) and *syntagmatic* associations (combination of elements from different grammatical categories) (Table 9.2). When the content of a report was related to the stimulus heard before sleep, it was classified as a current (i.e., valid) stimulus incorporation; when content was related to a stimulus not used in that session, it was classified as a noncurrent (i.e., chance) incorporation.

Current incorporations were more frequent than noncurrent ones both in SO (47% vs. 6%) and REM (62% vs. 12%). SEM + stimuli led to frequent paradigmatic incorporations both for SO (44% vs. 6%) and REM (56% vs. 0%); SEM – stimuli led to both paradigmatic and syntagmatic incorporations in both sleep types. The incorporations directly reproducing part of the stimulus (classified under identity; see 9.1) in MSE content were rare (7% of the total of current incorporations).

These results led us to two main inferences. First, the semantic acceptability of the stimulus significantly affects the characteristics of the associative relationships involved, but not the frequency of incorporation. It may therefore be argued that the processing that leads to incorporation can operate on different linguistic levels (clausal, phrasal, lexical, phonetic) of the stimulus. The choice of the level of representation of the stimulus to

TABLE 9.2
Examples of Incorporations of Presleep Verbal Stimuli

SEM + Stimulus: "The sord is pulled forth from the stone and a rock breaks loose from the mountain peak."
"I was trying to pull the cork out of a bottle. ..."
(*Cork–sword:* paradigmatic association)
"God, you are my cliff of defense. ..."
(*Cliff–rock:* paradigmatic association)

SEM- Stimulus: "Green ideas gallop sleeping furiously and after appointment read hysterical stamps."
"I was at the hippodrome. ..."
(*Hippodrome–gallop:* syntagmatic association)
"I was reading some Sumerian sentences onf a blackboard. ..."
(*Blackboard–stamps:* paradigmatic association)

---

be elaborated, however, does not depend only on its linguistic characteristics. In fact, when a stimulus produced current incorporations in both the sessions in which it was presented, the associative relationships between stimulus and reported contents were nearly always different. The semantic characteristics of the stimulus influence, therefore, the output of the associative mechanisms, not their success in producing content as output.

Secondly, the high frequencies of incorporation in both SO and REM sleep of the first cycle suggest that associative mechanisms operate successfully in both sleep types, and that the stimulus is repeatedly accessed and processed, being matched with other information in memory not just once, but many times during the same night, that is, with iterative processing across sleep stages.

The second experiment (Cipolli, Salzarulo, Baroncini, Fagioli, Fumai, Maccolini, & Tuozzi, 1983) was set up to ascertain whether the same information (in this case, a presleep stimulus) is differently incorporated in various reports of the same night, being differently processed by the associative mechanisms. This experiment followed the same procedure as the previous one, with 12 subjects who were instead awakened twice each night, once in the first half (in SO or in REM sleep of the first cycle) and once in the second half (in REM sleep and at least 6 hours after the first sleep onset). Current stimulus incorporations were significantly more frequent than noncurrent ones in the first-half reports, for both SEM + (50% vs. 8%) and SEM − (67% vs. 4%). Current stimulus incorporations were more frequent in the reports in the second half for SEM − (62% vs. 8%), but not for SEM + (29% vs. 37%). Where SEM + was presented, associative relationships were prevalently paradigmatic in both reports (first half, 42% vs. 8%; second half, 29% vs. 0%); where SEM − was presented, they were both paradigmatic and syntagmatic (first half, 33% vs. 33%; second half, 42% vs. 22%). Where both reports of the same night showed current stimulus incorporations, the specific relationships involved were nearly always different (23% vs. 2%), and no specific relationship was significantly more frequent than others in any condition. These facts support the hypothesis that information processing in sleep is iterative.

Associative mechanisms, therefore, operate in the same way not only in different stages of sleep, but also in different moments of the night (the proportions of paradigmatic relationships being very similar in first- and in second-half reports). Moreover, current matching is not directly dependent on earlier matching operations. This means that matching can be activated by any feature of the stimulus and operate with respect to various features of the material to be matched. The fact that the iteration of the matching process gives rise to different outputs in the same night suggests that this process is not simply dependent on the strength of the relationships between features of the stimulus and features of other information in memory, but that it may be guided by some higher-order processes, such as those of MSE planning (Foulkes, 1982). Further evidence in favor of a hypothesis that planning processes actively guide the recruitment of information in memory is provided by the second series of experiments, described in the next section.

FREE ASSOCIATIONS AND MNEMONIC SOURCES OF MSE

The second group of experiments aimed to ascertain the characteristics of mnemonic sources of MSEs, examining the type of information recruited in different stages of sleep.

These experiments relied on the assumption that free associations, that is, genuine, as distinct from reflections, interpretations or simple additions of other contents to those previously reported, to MSE content, made the day after the dream, can provide reliable information about its mnemonic sources, in that some characteristics of the information from which contents were generated will still be accessible. This assumption obviously does not imply that the subject's associative processing follows the steps of MSE production in reverse. This would be a much stronger assumption as to the reliability of free associations as a tool of accessing mnemonic sources than that we made. Even if we are aware that it is impossible to establish the eventual correspondence as a reverse process of free associations with the associative mechanisms involved in MSE production, the study of the "natural" sources of MSE content appears a useful complement to that of the mechanisms activated by presleep stimuli. That is to say, the study of mnemonic sources of MSE through a controlled form of the free-association technique allows us access to (some) sources of MSE, while the study of presleep stimulus incorporation allows us access to their processing.

The association technique we employed was slightly modified with respect to that used in psychoanalytic sessions. Each report was subdivided into thematic units, with each of which the subject was requested to associate freely. A new thematic unit was scored whenever there was a change in characters, activity, or setting (Table 9.3). The segmentation of the MSE into thematic units was carried out by a pretrained judge before the replay of the verbal report to the subject. The judge had previously achieved an interscorer reliability of $R > .90$ with the segmentation made by one of the authors using reports collected in a preceding experiment. To reduce the likelihood of episodic associations being enhanced by segments directly referred to waking episodes (that is, episodic segments, such as "I saw a friend of mine, who came yesterday afternoon to get an anatomy book"), each element explicitly referring to or directly reproducing a recent

TABLE 9.3
Examples of Single- and Multi-unit Reports

Single-unit report
"There was a can of coca-cola which had so many unlight canles on top of it."

Mutli-unit report
(With division into thematic units)

"/ I was walking along a corridor, like a school corridor, with doors./ I went in through one/ and there was my little sister, sitting at the table making a fuss/."

---

or remote event was removed from the text of the report before presentation to the subject for association task.

In a first experiment (Cicogna, Cavallero, & Bosinelli, 1986), 10 subjects who had been previously trained to provide free associations in a non clinical context were awakened once in each of 4 nights in the laboratory, alternately in SO and REM sleep. Twenty REM and 20 SO reports were thus obtained. These reports were then divided into thematic units with which subjects were asked to provide associations. Adapting Tulving's model (1972), the associative materials were classified as: (1) Episodic, for example: "I remember that I was going to the theater a week ago"; (2) Abstract self-references, subdivided into general self-knowledge, for example: "I remember that I once had a long beard," and habits, for example: "I remember that I used to go for long walks in the evening"; (3) Semantic memories, for example: "I remember that there was an island, which was a bit like the island of Saint Helen, in the Atlantic."

Associations between content and episodic information were more frequent in SO (64%) than in REM reports (40%), while abstract self-references and habits associations were more frequent in REM (37%) than in SO reports (21%). Semantic associations were not significantly more frequent in REM (23%) than in SO reports (15%). Moreover, the interaction between type of associations and sleep stage failed to reach statistical significance.

The data of this experiment support Foulkes and Schmidt's hypothesis (1983) that the availability of memory traces differs in various sleep conditions, with more information of an episodic type (i.e., relative to the subject's personal experience) being processed in SO than in REM sleep.

In a second experiment, Cicogna, Cavallero, Bosinelli, Battaglia, and Natale (1987) considered whether the characteristics of mnemonic sources of MSE content varied with respect to the length of the report. The possible interaction between report length, sleep stage, and kind of mnemonic traces activated during dream production was assessed by analyzing free associations on 60 reports (30 REM and 30 SO) provided by 20 subjects. Immediately after dream reporting, each subject was asked to provide free associations with the thematic units of his or her verbal report, and the associative materials thus obtained were classified as in the first experiment. The reports were classified according to length: 19 single-unit reports (a single scene or action) and 11 multi-unit reports (an organized narrative sequence) in the SO condition, and 14 single-unit and 16 multi-unit reports in the REM condition.

The results showed a significant interaction between sleep stage and report length only for episodic sources, whose proportion was higher in single-unit SO reports, while REM reports showed no significant difference. Activation of mnemonic sources does not vary significantly in REM mentation, whereas in SO mentation it varies, perhaps according to the functioning of higher-level processes operating in MSE production (such as those related to the planning of the entire MSE; see Foulkes, 1982). This would imply both that episodic information is more easily accessed and, thus, recruited for insertion into ongoing MSE, and that processes operating on larger units of MSE, such as story episodes, which are the framework of multi-unit reports, may be varyingly successful in different sleep stages. Therefore, the selection of the materials activated in memory for insertion into MSE may be influenced by the planning which guides MSE development.

Support for the hypothesis that the activation of mnemonic sources is not simply a function of memory organization of events and information was obtained in a further experiment (Cavallero, 1987).

Twenty SO reports and 20 REM reports were collected from 10 subjects awakened once in REM sleep in each of 4 nonconsecutive nights and associations provided immediately after reports were compared with those provided 2 months later. The rationale was that while temporal proximity should allow access to many of the mnemonic sources of MSE, after a prolonged interval access should only be possible to those sources that are stably organized in memory, being independent of the context of MSE report.

Comparison of free associations obtained in the two sessions, classified using the same procedure as in the first experiment, showed that while relatively few of the associations of the first session were also present, even fewer episodic associations (Tulving, 1972) were retained in second sessions than the other two types, there being no difference between SO and REM reports in this respect.

These findings, showing that temporal distance from MSE strongly influences the possibility of accessing its mnemonic sources, suggest that the recruitment of materials to be transformed into MSE content does not merely depend on the strength of the (relatively stable) memory links between materials. They are, however, compatible with the hypothesis that higher-level processes, such as planning operations, may guide recruitment.

CONCLUSIONS

The main findings of the experiments described were as follows:

1. MSE production involves associative mechanisms in NREM and REM sleep. Presleep stimuli were almost always incorporated into reports by substitution or combination of their features with ones from long-stored information, in both sleep types. As stimuli are not directly reproduced in MSE content, but are to some degree re-elaborated independently of their semantic characteristics, it may be argued that re-elaboration on an associative basis of information activated in memory is a general characteristic of MSE production.
2. The semantic characteristics of the information activated in memory influence the output (and, therefore, the associative relationships between content and stimuli) of these mechanisms and this influence is independent of the type of sleep in which MSE production takes place. Stimulus incorporations were paradigmatic for semantically acceptable stimuli, while both paradigmatic and syntagmatic for semantically unacceptable stimuli, in both REM and NREM sleep.
3. The same information (such as a presleep stimulus) may be repeatedly accessed during subsequent sleep periods, being incorporated into the content of different MSEs of the same night. Each matching of features of the stimulus with those of other memories is independent of the outcome of previous matching operations.
4. The proportions of various kinds of information accessed as mnemonic sources are not the same in all sleep stages, but may differ in SO and REM sleep. The number of episodic memories activated in the former varies with the length of the report.
5. The mnemonic sources of each MSE, in particular episodic ones, are not permanently accessible through free associations. Access to certain elements of these sources varies over time.

Even if our discussion has considered only cognitive aspects of MSE production, this last finding is one where consideration of emotive–affective aspects appears relevant. The dream may be seen as a result of the processing of the mnemonic sources made available at a given moment. The organization of memory is dynamic. New connections can be continually established between long-stored information and life events or cognitive contexts and lead to new memory states. Our finding that the accessibility of mnemonic sources of an MSE varies over time may be accounted for in terms of this changing memory organization, with events occurring between the moment of MSE production and the session in which the subject is asked to associate tending to reorganize the frame of the mnemonic elements underlying a particular MSE.

The role of emotive–affective components in the dynamics of memory organization is currently unclear. There is widespread agreement that dreams have cognitive and emotive–affective components, which interact in both production and recall (Foulkes, 1978, 1982; Koulack, Prevost, & De Koninck, 1985), and recent experiments have demonstrated the possibility of interaction (Cipolli, Baroncini, Cavallero, Cicogna, & Fagioli, 1988) and of interference (Koulack et al., 1985) between cognitive and emotional components of presleep stimuli in determining MSE content. Nevertheless, evidence in this area remains scarce, in the absence of a research paradigm of similar productivity to that developed for cognitive aspects of dreaming. Consequently it seems premature to attempt to integrate emotive–affective aspects into the general model developed using those cognitive approaches that have been shown adequate to describe specific processes (such as associative ones) in MSE production.

ACKNOWLEDGMENT

This work was supported in part by the C. N. R. Grant No. 87.01613.04.

REFERENCES

Anderson, J. R. (1976). *Language, memory, and thought.* Hillsdale, NJ.: Lawrence Erlbaum Associates.

Anderson, J. R. (1980). *Cognitive psychology and its implications.* San Francisco: Freeman.

Antrobus, J. (1978). Dreaming for cognition. In A. Arkin, J. Antrobus, & S. Ellman (Eds.), *The mind in sleep: Psychology and psychophysiology* (pp. 569–581). Hillsdale, NJ.: Lawrence Erlbaum Associates.

Antrobus, J. (1983). REM and NREM sleep reports: Comparison of word counts by cognitive class. *Psychophysiology, 20,* 562–568.

Baekeland, F., Resch, R., & Katz, D. (1968). Presleep mentation and dream reports. *Archives of General Psychiatry, 19,* 300–311.

Cavallero, C. (1987). Dream sources, associative mechanisms, and temporal dimension. *Sleep 10,* 78–83.

Cavallero, C., & Cicogna, P. (1984). Models and strategies of sleep mentation research. In M. Bosinelli & P. Cicogna (Eds.), *Psychology of dreaming* (pp. 65–78). Bologna, Italy: Cooperativa Libraria Universitaria Editrice.

Cicogna, P., Cavallero, C., & Bosinelli, M. (1982). Analyzing modifications across dream reports. *Perceptual and Motor Skills, 55,* 27–44.

Cicogna, P., Cavallero, C., & Bosinelli, M. (1986). Differential access to memory traces in the production of mental experience. *International Journal of Psychophysiology, 4,* 209–216.

Cicogna, P., Cavallero, C., Bosinelli, M., Battaglia, D., & Natale, V. (1987). A comparison between single and multi-unit dream reports. *Sleep Research, 16,* 228.

Cipolli, C., Baroncini, P., Cavallero, C., Cicogna, P., & Fagioli, I. (1988). Incorporation of cognitive stimuli into mental sleep experience and contextual emotive stress. In W.P. Koella, F. Obal, H. Schulz, & P. Visser (Eds.), *Sleep '86* (pp. 388–390). Stuttgart, Germany: Fischer.

Cipolli, C., Calasso, E., Maccolini, S., Pani, R., & Salzarulo, P. (1984). Memory processes in morning recall after multiple night awakenings. *Perceptual and Motor Skills, 59,* 435–446.

Cipolli, C., & Fagioli, I. (1988). Approaching the study of mental sleep experience from an information processing perspective. In W.P. Koella, F. Obal, H. Schulz, & P. Visser (Eds.), *Sleep '86* (pp. 95–98). Stuttgart, Germany: Fischer.

Cipolli, C., Fagioli, I., Maccolini, S., & Salzarulo, P. (1983). Associative relationships between pre-sleep sentence stimuli and reports of mental sleep experience. *Perceptual and Motor Skills, 56,* 223–234.

Cipolli, C., Salzarulo, P., Baroncini, P., Fagioli, I., Fumai, A., Maccolini, S., & Tuozzi, G. (1983). Incorporation of pre-sleep sentence stimuli in different halves of the night. In W.P. Koella (Ed.). *Sleep 1982* (pp. 375–377). Basel, Switzerland: Karger.

Cipolli, C., Salzarulo, P., & Calabrese, A. (1981). Memory processes involved in morning recall of mental REM-sleep experience: a psycholinguistic study. *Perceptual and Motor Skills, 52,* 391–406.

Clark, H. H. (1970). Word associations and linguistic theory. In J. Lyons (Ed.), *New horizons in linguistics* (pp. 271–286). Harmondsworth, England: Penguin Books.

Collins, A. M., & Loftus, E.F. (1975). A spreading-activation theory of semantic processing. *Psychological Review, 82,* 407–428.

Foulkes, D. (1962). Dream reports from different stages of sleep. *Journal of Abnormal and Social Psychology, 65,* 14–25.

Foulkes, D. (1978). *A grammar of dreams.* New York: Basic Books.

Foulkes, D. (1982). A cognitive-psychological model of REM dream production. *Sleep, 5,* 169–187.

Foulkes, D., & Schmidt, M. (1983). Temporal sequence and unit composition in dream reports from different stages of sleep. *Sleep, 6,* 265–280.

Fowler, M. J., Sullivan, M. J., & Ekstrand, B.R. (1973). Sleep and memory. *Science, 179,* 302–304.

Koulack, D., Prevost, F., & De Koninck, J. (1985). Sleep, dreaming and adaptation to an ego-threatening intellectual activity. *Sleep, 8,* 244–253.

Salzarulo, P., & Cipolli, C. (1979). Linguistic organization and cognitive implications in REM and NREM sleep related reports. *Perceptual and Motor Skills, 49,* 767–777.

Tulving, E. (1972). Episodic and semantic memory. In E. Tulving & W. Donaldson (Eds.), *Organization of memory* (pp. 381–403). Englewood Cliffs, NJ: Prentice-Hall.

10 A Connectionist Model of Bizarre Thought and Imagery

Jeffrey Fookson
New York University

John Antrobus
City College of New York

1. INTRODUCTION

Recent models of brain function have been successful in showing that the emergent properties to higher-level mental processes such as learning and memory can be obtained from the collective behavior of an enormous number of simple processing units. These models, in general called parallel distributed (PDP), or "connectionist" models, are appealing because they seem to capture certain basic features of what kinds of computations brains are good at and these features are obtained by architectures that are at least somewhat consistent with biological reality. This chapter will summarize the appealing aspects of PDP models and will then describe a complex application: the modeling of the characteristics of dream and waking fantasy mentation.

As demonstrated by Reinsel, Antrobus, and Wollman (this volume), the bizarre qualities of REM sleep dreaming and waking while lying in a dark, sound-attenuated room, are remarkably similar, or at least difficult to discriminate with existing psychometric instruments. The model described here is, therefore, designed to simulate three of the four possible classes of bizarre mentation described in that paper, without regard to whether the mentation is generated in REM sleep or waking. The classes are: (1) discontinuities in temporal sequence, (2) improbable spatial combinations, and (3) improbable combinations of visual and meaning characteristics.

2. PARALLEL-DISTRIBUTED PROCESSING MODELS

Parallel distributed-processing models are based on the simple underlying assumption that higher-order mental functions result from the interactions of a large number of interconnected simple processing units that operate simultaneously and communicate with each other via simple signals transmitted over the interconnections (called links). Each processing unit typically receives inputs from many other units and these inputs are processed in a relatively simple way (for example, by summing them) to determine the unit's output (called its activation). This activation is communicated to all units to which the unit is connected. However, its effect on different units varies, because each interconnection has an associated "strength" and the actual input to a unit from another is the product of the sending unit's activation and the strength (called the weight) of the link. In general, some inputs act to decrease the activation of a unit (inhibitory input) while others increase the activation (excitatory input). The "intelligence" of such a network is embedded in the pattern of connections and their strengths. The connection geometry is usually fixed for a particular model, but the model can vary its own connection strengths as it operates and thus can "learn." Last, some units are designated as *input* units, receiving activation from the external world (e.g., being set to given activation values by the experimenter). Other units may be designated as *output* units and their activations examined by the experimenter to evaluate the model's performance. Other units are *internal* to the model.

PDP models accurately reflect that the brain must function through the massively parallel cooperation of many neurons, each of which is slow, noisy, and prone to failure. (Given the known speeds of neural transmission and psychological response times, any realistic model must produce useful output in about 100 operations, and it is extremely difficult to imagine any kind of serial processing that can satisfy this limitation.) A PDP network comes to a "solution" more by a process of settling or relaxing into a pattern of activations that is consistent with imposed constraints (represented by the connections and weights) than by a process of computation. Because "intelligence" often involves just this type of constraint satisfaction (for example, choosing the appropriate meaning of an ambiguous word based on context) this feature of PDP models is extremely powerful in application to modeling cognitive phenomena.

It is important to note that units in a PDP model do not likely represent individual neurons but rather assemblies of neurons (called "netlets" by Paul Smolensky). This provides one form of robustness because the degradation in performance due to loss of neurons is gradual. In addition, the distributed representation implies that the system is not seriously damaged by even the loss of units.

It is realized that the problem studied here will ultimately require the solution of fundamental problems at every level of modeling. In particular, the generation of sequential thought from a starting point of either the static schema (Rumelhart, Smolensky, McClelland, & Hinton, 1986) or the back propagation (McClelland, Rumelhart, & Hinton, 1986) network structures on which this work is based has not yet been worked out in detail. This, in turn, depends on a successful model of short-term memory. Since the power of modeling lies in its ability to predict results or features that have not been explicately built into it, each stage of modeling a complex process should be motivated by an effort to obtain results that are testable by experiment in a decisive fashion. For example, It seems possible that the temporal sequencing of states of the network can be obtained by dynamic weight modification, perhaps by means of sigma-pi sites on the cognitive units but this hypothesis must be evaluated by building such a PDP network and then exploring its emergent properties so that those properties can be searched for in human behavior.

A further point that should be emphasized here is that the simulation of bizarre thought and imagery in a parallel distributed-processing (PDP) model, constitutes a rather fundamental dilemma for PDP systems. Consider as a starting point a large network of units such as that described by Rumelhart, Smolensky et al., (1986) in their introduction to PDP models of schemata and sequential thought. Each units may be linked to each other by a set of positive and negative weights. If activation is initially provided to one or more units, activation and inhibition will spread throughout the network in a pattern dictated by the positive and negative weights among the units. Within several cycles of this process, some clusters of units will win out over others to create and overall pattern, a simulation of a schema, that represents a solution of maximum harmony among all the units in the entire network. In the process of computing this solution, individual units, and small set of units, that are incompatible with the overall pattern of the emerging solution are subdued or inhibited. Thus improbable, or bizarre, subpatterns do not tend to be produced in a PDP model.

One solution to this apparent dilemma is that the schema-like episodes of dreaming sleep are, indeed, harmonious solutions of the networks that are active within states such as REM sleep, but these networks differ in some way from those of the fully awake person. Thus, with rare exceptions, the bizarre qualities of dreams do not seem to be recognized until recollection upon waking.

A second solution is that some bizarre elements are the result of new and novel input from independent modules within the larger cognitive system, and this new input is quickly "absorbed" by the larger network so that overall harmony is sustained, - within the limits suggested in the preceding paragraph. This latter solution might account for discontinuities in temporal sequence; the paragraph might explain more sustained discontinuities within a given time frame, discontinuities that are unique to REM sleep.

Yet a third possibility is that the "bizarre" states represent local extrema in the state space of the network; that is, solutions that satisfy a subset of the constraints represented by the network weights and ignore others. This possibility is attractive because it seems to yield solutions that contain some aspects of "rational" relatedness and yet ignore others. Furthermore, the symbolic content of dreams may be related to these local extrema, as is discussed in Sec. 4.4.

Despite the difficulties outlined herein, the successes of PDP models in such areas as sentence comprehension (McClelland & Kawamoto, 1986) and schema production (Rumelhart et al. 1986) point to the need to push the work into the more complex areas of cognitive science. In particular, the authors believe that once the modeling of sequential thought processes has been obtained, that the production of models for other mental states will follow rather directly since it will likely involve perturbations to modules of the "rational waking consciousness" system that are suggested clearly by the known neurophysiology of these other metal states.

3. DREAMING AND IMAGERY MODEL

3.1 Background

The dramatic shifts in cognitive processes that occur between wake and sleep states make the study of sleep mentation an important route to understanding the organization and function of the brain. The crucial initial observation came from the findings of Aserensky and Kleitman (1953) that subjects are much more likely to report dream-like mentation when awakened from EEG-defined Stage 1 (rapid eye movement:-REM) sleep than when from other sleep stages (non-REM). For example, Antrobus (1983) found that when the same subject was awakened at approximately the same time of night in pairs of REM and non-REM sleep, that 93.5% of the awakenings could be separated into the sleep states from which they were obtained by noting which member of the pair resulted in a more dream-like mentation report. Although the 30-odd years since the initial REM report have not seen as much progress as might have been expected, three models of sleep mentation have been recently formulated. The first of these, proposing that the right hemisphere specifically generates dream imagery, suggested by Ornstein (1972), Van Valen (1973) and Galin (1974) does not seem to have much empirical support, as shown by a review by Antrobus (1987).

The second model, due to Hobson and McCarley (1977), assumes that shifts in sensory and perceptual thresholds that occur in the different states produce dream imagery. The effect of increased sensory thresholds on the quality of waking fantasy has been recently simulated by Reinsel, Antrobus, and Wollman (1987). This model, called the Activation–Synthesis model, is crucial for several reasons: (1) It highlights a central assumption of all neurocognitive models that dreaming is the output of an activated brain (and therefore, presumably, an activated cognitive production system); (2) It provides a detailed model of the subcortical control of the REM–non-REM cycle. While these physiological mechanisms are described in detail, the model does not specify in detail how the cognitive system operates to produce sleep mentation, subsuming this description under a single metaphor —synthesis.

A third class of models, those proposed here, attempt to develop the Activation–Synthesis description further and in particular to provide a description of the connections between the activated neural processes described by that model and the cognitive processes observed in dream-report studies. Our models, which we denote by the general acronym DREAMIT (Distributed Recurrent Activation Model of Imagery and Thought) employ both data from the last decade of neurophysiological research (for example, Hobson, Lydic, & Baghydoyan, 1986) and the recent development of parallel distributed-processing models of cognitive processes (McClelland, et al., 1986).

It is crucial to note before continuing that a neurocognitive model of sleep mentation requires much more than relating sets of corresponding neurophysiological and cognitive measures. Between the neurophysiological side, comprising the microscopic level of synaptic transmission, the level of neural nets and maps, and the macroscopic level of global brain organization and the cognitive side, corresponding to the limited range of (mostly waking report) cognitive data obtainable from intact humans is a vast middle ground of phenomena that cannot be measured. With this caveat, we proceed with the description of the sleep-stage control processes and the model.

3.2 REM–non-REM Control

The sleep of all mammals alternates between REM and non-REM stages. During REM sleep, there is Cortical desynchronization, eye movements, skeletal atonia, and high sensory thresholds. During non-REM, the cortical EEG is synchronized. Using data from rats, cats, and primates, Hobson and McCarley (1977), Hobson and Steriade (1986), Massaquoi and McCarley (1982), and McCarley and Massaquoi (1986) postulate that the alternation of REM and non-REM sleep is controlled by two sets of brain stem generators distributed across several nuclei. At sleep onset, a noradrenergic network controlled by the locus coeruleus and dorsal raphe nucleus inhibits a second center, mostly found in the mesencephalic reticular formation (mRF). The mRF controls a cholenergic network activating several thalamic nuclei (the medial and intralaminar thalamic nuclei, primarily) that desynchronize the cortex, activating both excitatory and inhibitory cortical neurons in both waking and in REM sleep. In fact, it seems that as measured by extracellular recording, there is no visible difference in the mechanisms of cortical activation between waking and stage REM sleep. During non-REM sleep, on the other hand, the medial thalamic nuclei are underactivated, due to the inhibition of the mRF-controlled cholenergic network. This state is characterized by the low-frequency, high-amplitude, periodic EEG seen in non-REM sleep. But the control center itself is thus deprived of its source of activation and its inhibitory influence therefore decays, and the mRF-based center begins to activate the thalamus and cortex to produce REM sleep. Although both association and motor cortical areas are activated, postsynaptic inhibition of the brain stem and final-common-path motor neurons tonically paralyze all skeletal muscle movement except eye movements and respiration. Thus any motor commands originating in the motor cortex during REM sleep cannot be expressed.

The work of Foote, Bloom, and Aston-Jones (1983) and Tucker and Williamson (1984) suggest that the locus ceuruleus-controlled network in the waking state is important in the early stages of selective perception. These stages, which correspond roughly to the processing that occurs between the initial cortical response to sensory input and the associative operations of naming, categorizing, and interpreting. We also here assume that mRF-activated cortical processes extend from this early recognition stage(s) through the production of motor commands. We call these processes the association stage. Our fundamental hypothesis is that during REM sleep, the association system is activated but receives no input from the recognition module which in the waking state, seems to be controlled by the changes in external stimuli. This detachment results in the general characteristics of dream mentation. In general, during non-REM sleep, the locus ceuruleus activation in the absence of an activated association cortex results in at most a vague awareness of auditory stimuli and possibly a slight sense of not being quite asleep. There is usually little higher-level thought connected with these perceptions. On the other hand, during REM sleep, the associative processes are active in the production of thoughts and imagery, but without current sensory input.

3.3 Description of Network Layer

Our initial model, which we call DREAMIT-S, is based on the single-layer, flat associative network as described by Rumelhart et al. (1986) Although this model was able to simulate the sequential flow of thought to some extent, it was deficient in several crucial ways and we are therefore currently exploring a second architecture, DREAMIT-BP, derived from the back propagation network of Rumelhart, Hinton, and Williams (1986). The topology and behavior of each of these networks is detailed herein.

3.3.1 Single Layer Associative Networks. A single-layer associative network consists of a set of units, each of which has both inhibitory and excitatory links to all other units. Each of the units represents some feature of the associative domain that the network has been designed to represent, with the weight of each link being proportional to the conditional probability of the presence of the feature represented by the *receiving* unit, given the occurrence of the feature represented by the *sending* unit. The behavior of such a network, when some set of units is initially activated and the network allowed to cycle, is to come to a steady state with some subset of units active and all others inhibited. The subset of units remaining on consists of the pattern of units that best satisfies the constraints implied by the conditional probabilities that govern the co-occurrence of features. Such a network has been very successfully employed to represent schemata for categorizing different types of rooms, for example (Rumelhart et al. 1986). In that model, 40 features were used as room descriptors and the probabilities used as weights obtained by asking a set of subjects whether each of the features would be expected to be present, given each of five types of room. When a set of units were initially activated, the network settled into one of five final states (out of a possible 2^{40}) that represented a particular type of room.

Note that one can imagine such networks at many different scales. In a network that is designed to recognize a class of objects, for example, the features coded by the individual units would be the microfeatures that distinguish members of that class of objects. At a higher level, in a network that modeled action scripts, units could represent persons, places, roles of the individual, and actions. In general we envision the cognitive system as a hierarchy of such networks. The lower levels correspond to feature extraction based on the even lower level of microfeature detection by sensory areas; the highest levels correspond to abstract generalization. In a sense, this hierarchy spans the neural–cognitive gap and reduces the need to create metaphoric explanations for intermediate processing.

3.3.2 Back-propagation Network. Back propagation is a general algorithm that can be employed by networks to modify their weights to minimize the difference between the output pattern produced by a given input, and a teaching pattern that represents the output *desired* for that input. It is, therefore, a method that networks can use to learn to classify patterns. A back-propagation network typically consists of an input layer, an output layer, and some number of intermediate or "hidden" layers. If the number of hidden units is sufficient, the network can learn to classify arbitrary patterns. The network first operates in a "teaching" phase in which inputs are presented, the output compared to the desired output (usually expressed as activations in a set of teaching units) and the errors between the two used to modify the weights on the links between the output and last hidden layer. By an iterative process, the corrections are propagated backwards through the layers in the network until finally, corrections are developed to weights between the input and first intermediate layers. After some number of cycles of this teaching process, the weights in general stabilize to values that represent the best solution (in the least-squares sense) to minimizing the differences between the entire set of teaching patterns and the network output. An important question, however, as demonstrated, for example, by Pavel, Gluck, and Henkle (1988), is the extent to which such algorithms can learn to generalize; this question is clearly crucial to the use of back propagation to model the more complex aspects of intelligence. An example of back propagation used to model the automatization of a visual motor task is given by Fookson and Antrobus (1988). Back propagation represents a potential algorithm for "learning" weights in associative networks or for encoding a sequence of states.

3.4 Sequential Thought

As described in the introduction, a fundamental difficulty exists in converting the two network architectures that we have detailed so that they can produce a sequence of outputs. The schemata, for example, in the room classification example (Rumelhart et al. 1986) are static; with a given input, the network settles into a stable state and remains in that state. In this stable state, the network is not particularly sensitive to perturbations in its input values (this is exactly the reason such associative networks are well behaved even with noisy or incomplete input). Furthermore, such a network has no procedure for developing weights appropriate to a given situation: In the room classification simulation, weights were assigned by interviewing a number of people as to their impressions that a particular room feature be present in each of the five room types in the model and tabulating the results as conditional probabilities of *feature*$_i$ given *roomtype*$_j$). Last, the single layer network is linear which implies that it can only differentiate points in its state space that are linearly separable (i.e., it must be possible to pass a collection of planes through the space that divide the space into a set of regions, each containing one of the desired points). This further implies that no interactive or second-order probabilistic information exists in the network. A can send activation to B but cannot have the strength of this activation depend on the activity of a third unit C. for example, activating a unit representing *I'm hungry* should activate *kitchen* and *cook* only if *I'm at home* is also active.

On the other hand, a back-propagation network can associate an arbitrary output to a given input. As a simple example, note that the nonlinear "exclusive or" problem is trivial for a back-propagation network (Rumelhart, Hinton, & Williams, 1986) but cannot be solved by a single-layer net. This arbitrary associativity suggests a procedure by which a network could be taught to encode a sequence of patterns. Imagine, for example a network having the same number of units in its input and output layers, and assume that during the teaching phase the first pattern in the sequence is used as input and mapped into the second pattern in the sequence, the second used as input mapped into the third, and so on. Once the network has learned the required associations each output unit can be connected to its corresponding input unit; if the input is then initialized to the first pattern in the sequence, the entire sequence should be produced as the network cycles. This design, however, lacks the rich associative behavior of the flat, densely connected schema network. This is primarily because there are no links between units in the same layer, nor are there links from the output layer to the hidden or input layers.

Another way for producing a sequence of outputs from a flat network is to assume that some network parameters can vary dynamically. For example, units can be inhibited after they are activated, analogous to the neuronal "negative after-potential" (see Sec. 3.5), which would then allow another subpattern to become active. Another possibility is that the weights can be modified by the use of sites with variable gain ($\sigma\pi$ sites).

Our models have thus far explored the flat network (DREAMIT-S), which models a fairly rich cognitive space but does poorly in sequence production or imagery, and the back-propagation network (DREAMIT-BP), which models a much smaller domain but produces stable sequences and imagery. We have yet to experiment with dynamic parameters in a successful way. We note again that robust simulation of of sequential thought production is central to any attempt to simulate a stream of consciousness.

3.5 Simulation Software

The PDP layer of DREAMIT is implemented using the Rochester Connectionist Simulator (Goddard, 1987). The simulator is a software tool usable to construct a wide class of network simulations. It consists of data structures for representing units, different functional sites on those units, and links between units and an interactive command interface for running and examining simulations. A library of functions is provided for constructing units and links, for setting and displaying input, output, and unit activation values, and for the back-propagation algorithm. In addition, user functions for accessing and modifying network data structures or providing activation functions not in the standard library can be written in C and called from the command interface. Although considerable programming is required for complex applications, the Simulator is a powerful aid to development of PDP models.

3.6 DREAMIT-S Schema Network

Each unit of the DREAMIT-S associative network consists of five basic simulator units, as shown in Fig. 10.1. Inhibitory and excitatory links enter

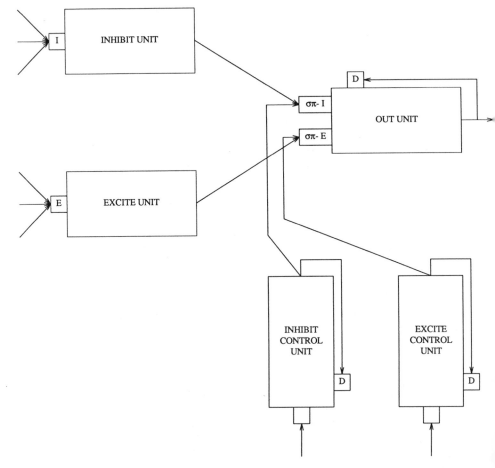

FIG. 10.1. Diagram of set of units that represents each feature in the DREAMIT-S schema network.

on separate units. The sites "I" and "E" on these units simply form the sum of the product of the activation on each incoming link (i.e., the activation of the unit at which the link originates) times the weight of that link. The outputs of the inhibitory and excitatory units are combined at a common output unit, but each enters the output unit at its own site, at which it is multiplied by a control signal from a corresponding inhibitory or excitatory control site (-I or -E, respectively). These control signals represent activation or inhibition coming from brain stem nuclei and permit overall modulation of activity of desired parts of the network, as is postulated to occur between different sleep states, and between sleep and waking. Note that the site has the same effect as changing the weights on all links that enter the site. The output and control units also have links to themselves, to the site labeled "D," to provide for self-decay at a rate that can be varied by changing the weight on that link.

The activation function for the output units (the function that maps the input of a unit into its output) is a sigmoid. The bias point of this sigmoid (the output activation produced for an input of zero) can be set by the user for each unit. This bias corresponds to a "resting potential" and allows some units to be set to be more easily turned on than others (corresponding, for example, to more stable or older concepts). It is also possible to bias the activation function strongly for a particular unit in the "off" direction for some number of network cycles immediately after that unit has turned on to provide an analogue to the well-known neural afterpotential. This bias can prevent the same units from being repeatedly activated. In the future, we intend to explore the resting and after potentials as a way of producing sequences rather that the stationary states that are characteristic of the behavior of the flat network.

3.6.1 Preliminary Results of Simulations.   The network configuration described here in has been used in a simulation of mind wandering in the context of visual–motor task automatization. In this simulation (Fookson & Antrobus, 1988) the schema domain represented was a student environment: Units represented examinations, studying, persons in the students family, friends, and the particulars of the visual–motor task (which itself was modeled using a back-propagation network). Although the point of that work was not directly related to the present model, the simulations showed that the control sites allowed subtle modulation of the overall level of network activation. At intermediate levels of activation, the schema network displayed sensitivity to noise (which was added to a random subset of units on each network cycle). Both of these behaviors are needed for the models described in the present chapter. Note that the schema-generating part of this these simulations was not intended to display sequencing.

In a related experiment, a schema network was developed to simulate a scenario of two persons playing a game of catch. This was done to explore the idea that simple asymmetry in the weights could represent temporal sequencing (the original theory for the flat networks described in Sec. 3.3.1 assumes that weights between units are symmetric). These studies are still under way, and will be reported elsewhere.

3.7 DREAMIT-BP

The weights in the flat DREAMIT-S network were determined in a heuristic fashion by making initial guesses as to "reasonable" values and fine-tuning these values by running the simulation for a small number of cycles. When these networks were then seeded with an initial state (a particular subset of units activated) and cycled for longer intervals (corresponding to an "imaginal" sequence), it was impossible to determine whether a "bizarre" final state was due to anything other than small errors in the initial weight assignment. In addition, the constraints imposed by the linearity of the flat network, seemed severely limiting. We thus began to experiment with a network structure that could learn sequences as suggested in Sec. 3.3.2. Although this network has only 10 or 12 units, lacks the - control elements and does not model an explicit, real-life situation (as does the DREAMIT-S net) simulations with this architecture have yielded insights into how the learning of perceptual sequences in the waking state may account for some of the features of dreaming that we call "bizarre."

3.7.1 Perceptual Sequence Learning. DREAMIT-BP is a three-layer back-propagation network with the same number of units (10) in the input, output, and hidden layers. Initially the network is "taught" a sequence $S_1, S_2, \ldots S_N$, where each S_i labels a particular binary pattern of *on* (maximum output) and *off* (minimum output) input units. For reasons detailed later, each pattern actually consists of a string of paired binary digits, for example, 1100001100. Weights are adjusted by back propagation so that the input S_i produces the output S_{i+1} (with S_N yielding S_1). Note that while the inputs are binary patterns, the output of each unit is continuous and must be thresholded to obtain a patterned output. It is characteristic of the network that the outputs of a well-learned pattern are close (within 5.0%) to the minimum and maximum possible outputs. We term such responses "strong responses." On the other hand, the network output may contain intermediate values and we label such responses "noisy."

3.8 Imaginal Mode. After teaching, the output of every unit in the output layer is linked back to the input of the corresponding unit in the input layer so that the response of the network at t_i is the input at t_{i+1}. Note that in this case the outputs are not passed through thresholding units so the inputs may not be clean binary patterns from the teaching set. Of interest, then, is the behavior of this network when the input is initialized to some pattern from the teaching sequence. When this was done, the network continued to produce the appropriate response (the next number in the sequence) even after 5,000 iterations. In comparison, DREAMIT-S output became noisy after approximately 50 cycles.

3.8.1 Temporal Discontinuity. In order to determine behavior of the network when presented with an input not in the teaching set, the net was first taught four seven-event sequences, but with no feedback from the last to first pattern in each sequence. The first four digits of each pattern in a particular sequence were kept constant, and the other digits were variable. These initial digits, because they were the same within a given sequence symbolize a "context" for the events in that sequence, that is, an aspect that remains constant. If the network output was then linked to the input as described and the input initialized to an early member of one of the sequences, the elements of that sequence were produced in order until the last member. The response to that stimulus (to which the net had not been trained) was noisy. However, after a few noisy responses, the net restabilized and produced a strong response that was another pattern from the original sequence. The net then produced the members of the sequence set in order, starting from the new initial point. This behavior was repeated for many iterations, without degeneration in the quality of the responses. Thus the context (constant part) of the patterns was preserved, and the sequencing maintained, but with discontinuities in the time-course at those points when the network had no training.

During these initial simulations, the network never produced a strong response that was not in the training set. We postulated that the absence of "novel" responses (strong responses not in the training set) might be that most (28 of 32) of the possible available patterns (2^5) were in the teaching set. In comparison, in the real world, only a small fraction of the total number of possible combinations of patterns occur. In order to test this hypothesis, the network was retrained on a smaller subset (8 out of 32) of the available patterns. In this case, simulations in the imaginal mode did produce some patterns that were not in the teaching set after the noisy responses that occurred at the end of a learned sequence. These responses typically only differed in one digit pair.[1] from a sequence in the training set, and were followed by a return to patterns from within that set. This behavior simulates the appearance of bizarre combinations of elements in a dream or fantasy. In summary, the DREAMIT-BP network was able to

---

[1] The output patterns always consisted of digit pairs (the outputs of units in the pair were at most 0.05 from each other), which was presumably the result of the paired aspect of all the inputs.

simulate the mixture of characteristics of waking consciousness (context, sequencing) and disorder (time discontinuities and improbable combinations of features) typical of dream mentation.

4. GENERAL ASPECTS OF PRODUCTION OF BIZARRE THOUGHT AND IMAGERY

Because PDP networks are not constrained by fixed templates of the entities they represent, they are theoretically capable of generating combinations of features that are not typical combinations that occur in the waking state and are hence "bizarre." As mentioned previously, the bizarre states of the network are not those that are the stable states of the whole network, and thus some additional assumptions are required. We have already suggested one such possibility: The network in REM sleep receives little sensory input and that motor output is blocked at the spinal level. Thus the coordination of top–down and bottom–up processing that is likely controlled by sensory input and motor response is absent. In its absence, spontaneous noise in sensory channels may be processed as though it originated externally. The second assumption is that the level of activation of associative cortex is diffusely lower in REM sleep, compared with waking consciousness (this hypothesis is supported by dream mentation reports) and therefore that the activation of the network is less broadly distributed ("on" units have less effect on the units to which they are linked). Lower overall activation also implies that the associate networks are more sensitive to internal noise.

4.1 External Sources of Discontinuity

Reinsel, Wollman, and Antrobus (1986) and Wollman and Antrobus (1986) have demonstrated that ambient noise in the waking environment accounts, at least partly, for discontinuities in waking mentation. Although the awake person may often "notice" an abrupt discontinuity in thought, judges regard these events as the major subclass of bizarre waking thought and imagery. Fookson and Antrobus (1988) have recently created a PDP simulation of mind wandering while performing a visual motor task. While in the process of learning the task, each new stimulus tends to disrupt the spontaneous process of creating thought and imagery. As the task becomes better learned, the disruptive process diminishes until task performance and mind wandering are carried on in parallel. Since this disruption by external stimuli is described elsewhere and does not bear directly on sleep, it will not be described further here.

4.2 Internal Sources of Discontinuity in Time

Antrobus (1988) has proposed that cortical visual modules may produce visual imagery during REM sleep that is occasionally independent of higher cortical top–down control. Such images may reach high cortical centers but be out of context with respect to the ongoing stream of thought and imagery being created. He suggests that these images may disrupt the associative stream of thought and create bizarre discontinuities in both time and space. Neurophysiological evidence for possible independent visual inputs to associative cortical centers within REM sleep is suggested by the occipital evoked potentials that accompany rapid eye movements within REM sleep (McCarley, Winkelman, & Duffy, 1983).

There are many ways in which an independent visual module might provide input to a more central network that computes solutions based on input from bottom–up visual and top–down goal and associative meaning modules. It is well known that visual information moves rostrally from the line detectors of the striate cortex through successive cortical layer and regions until the visual input is recognized as an object or person with known properties. Since only a few of the boundaries between these layers and region are well defined, the present simulation is based on a somewhat arbitrary boundary, that between visual features of parts of persons or objects, and the recognitions of the persons or objects constituted by the features. The choice of this boundary point is based in part on dream reports in which subjects describe an object or person with specific visual features that the dreamer cannot identify. Much of the dream may, in fact, be devoted to trying to recognize or make sense of the unfamiliar person or object. Upon awakening, the event seems bizarre. Yet while asleep, the dreamer seems to do just what he or she would in waking life, namely, make every reasonable effort to identify or come to terms with the unfamiliar object or person. In this regard, the harmony principles of PDP models appear to hold within the constraints of input from an independent source.

4.3 Bizarre or Improbable Combinations within a Given Point in Time

Although the major class of bizarre mentation in both waking and sleep is temporal discontinuities, Reinsel et al. (this volume) have shown that improbable combinations of features and improbable identities of imagined persons are also characteristic of bizarre thought and imagery. The former is equally likely in quiet wakefulness and REM sleep in laboratory conditions, whereas the latter, although infrequent is almost unique to REM sleep.

As has been pointed out, the computation of a harmonious solution to any initial pattern of network activation generally precludes the activation of low-frequency, or improbable subsets becoming activated. Antrobus (1988) has proposed, therefore, that improbable combinations and identities may be constructed from information that is initially compiled in different subnetworks. Consider, for example, a visual image of "my brother," but "he was a woman in my physics class." The visual image may have been created in a visual module, but the identity as "brother" in another more concerned with a more abstract recognition process. Well coordinated during waking perception, the transfer of information between these modules may be reduced in an imaginal state, particularly REM sleep. An example of an improbable combination, nuns driving a red car all over the lawn, may be similarly explained by a lack of communication between the visual module and a module that stores more abstract information about such things as the characteristic behavior of nuns. Other improbable combinations are less plausibly accounted for. One dream report describes a man holding a set of enormous false teeth that he couldn't possibly put in his mouth, another reports that an elevator door opens up onto the living room wall. They don't report that the visual features are distorted, only their relation to other visual features. Thus some more abstract visual information may be stored in separate modules that, in REM sleep, do not readily communicate to the module that constructs the visual image.

4.4 Symbolic and Metaphoric Content of Dream Mentation

We conclude with some general remarks on the widespread belief that objects and events in dreams has symbolic meaning to the dreamer. It seems to us that this property is consistent with the postulate that the level of activation during REM sleep is diffusely lower than during waking. Typically the symbolic objects in the dream share features with the objects that they symbolize. Furthermore, the units that represent those symbolic features may be readily activated because they correspond to deepseated psychological reality or to objects or events that have a long history to the dreamer. Thus in a state of lowered overall activation, the symbolic content replaces the actual persons, places, or events. A good example is a dream cited by Breger, Hunter, and Lane (1971), in which a railroad worker about to have surgery for a leg aneurism dreamed of cleaning out the rust and sand out of a line switch, allowing the switch to function so that the train could move down the correct track. If one assumes that the concepts relating to surgery: fix, clean out, allow to flow, are highly activated prior to the operation, but that their specific connection to hospitals and surgery is not strongly developed (because they are recent concepts), it is plausible that the activation of the surgical images is translated metaphorically to the images of the dreamer's lifetime occupation. A logger, in a similar medical situation dreamed of cleaning water out of trap for a logging engine.

5. FINAL REMARKS

The ideas outlined in this chapter are in their initial stages of development, and their full expression should require many years of collaborative effort on the part of neurophysiologists, cognitive psychologists, computer scientists, physicists, and many experiments to test the predictive features of the evolving models. But it is clear to the authors that with development of microscopic theory and technique by the neurophysiologists and powerful models of parallel distributed processing, and computer systems on which to implement those models by psychologists, computer scientists, and physicists, that the tools are at hand to create a credible description of waking and sleep states that spans the gamut from the neuron to the person.

REFERENCES

Antrobus, J.S. (1983). REM and NREM sleep reports: Comparison of word frequencies by cognitive classes. *Psychophysiology, 20,* 562–568.

Antrobus, J. (1987). Cortical asymmetry and sleep mentation. *Psychological Review, 94,* 359–368.

Antrobus, J. (1988). *Cortical and cognitive activation, perceptual thresholds and sleep mentation.* Submitted for publication.

Aserensky, E., & Kleitman, N. (1953). Regularly occurring periods of ocular motility and concomitant phenomena during sleep. *Science, 118,* 361–375.

Breger, L., Hunter, I., & Lane, R. (1971). The effect of stress on dreams. *Psychological Issues, 7,* (3, Monograph 27).

Fookson, J. E., & Antrobus, J. (1988). Executive control in a PDP. *Neural Networks, 1,* (Supp. 7), 174.

Foote, S. L., Bloom, F. E., & Aston–Jones, G. (1983). The nucleus locus coeruleus: New evidence of anatomical and physiological specificity. *Physiological Reviews, 63,* 844–914.

Galin, D. (1974). Implications for psychiatry of left and right cerebral specialization: A neurophysiological context for unconscious processes. *Archives of General Psychiatry, 31,* 572–585.

Goddard, N. (1987). *Rochester connectionist simulator: Advanced programming manual.* Department of Computer Science, University of Rochester, NY.

Hobson, J. A., Lydic, R., & Baghydoyan, H. A. (1986). Evolving concepts of sleep cycle generation: From brain centers to neuronal populations. *Behavioral and Brain Sciences, 9,* 371–448.

Hobson, J. A., & McCarley, R. W. (1977). The brain as a dream state generator: an activation–synthesis hypothesis of the dream process. *American Journal of Psychiatry, 134,* 1335–1348.

Hobson, J. A., & Steriade, M. (1986). Neuronal basis of behavioral state control in V. B.

Mouncastle, F. E. Bloom, & S. R. Geiger (Eds.). *The handbook of physiology* (pp. 701-828). Bethesda; MD: American Physiological Society.

Massaquoi, S. G., & McCarley, R. W. (1982). Extension of the reciprocal interaction sleep stage control model: A "Karma" control model. *Sleep Research, 11,* 216.

McCarley, R. W., & Massaquoi, S. G. (1986). A limit cycle mathematical model of REM sleep oscillator system. *American Journal of Physiology, 251,* R1011-R1019.

McCarley, R. W., Winkelman, & Duffy (1983). Human cerebral potentials associated with REM sleep and rapid eye movements: Links to PGO waves and waking potentials. *Brain Research, 274,* 359-364.

McClelland, J. L., & Kawamoto, A. H. (1986). Mechanisms of sentence processing: Assigning roles to constituents of sentences. In J. L. McClelland, & D. E. Rumelhart (Eds.), *Parallel distributed processing: Explorations in the microstructure of cognition* (Vol. 2, pp. 272-325). Cambridge, MA: MIT Press.

McClelland, J. L., Rumelhart, D. E., & Hinton, G. E. (1986). The appeal of parallel distributed processing. In J. L. McClelland & D. E. Rumelhart (Eds.), *Parallel distributed processing: Explorations in the microstructure of cognition* (Vol. 2, pp. 122-169). Cambridge, MA: MIT Press.

Ornstein, R.E. (1972). *The psychology of consciousness.* San Franscico: Freeman.

Pavel, M., Gluck, M. A., & Henkle, V. (1988). Comparing generalization by humans and adaptive networks. *Neural Networks,* (Supp. I), 208.

Reinsel, R., Wollman, M., & Antrobus, J. (1986). Effects of environmental context and cortical activation. *Journal of Mind and Behavior, 7,* 259-276.

Reinsel, R., Antrobus, J., & Wollman, M. (1987). *Bizarreness in waking and sleep mentation: Waking, REM-NREM and phasic-tonic differences in bizarreness.* Manuscript submitted for publication.

Rumelhart, D. E., Hinton, G. E., & Williams, J.R. (1986). Learning internal representations by error propagation. In J. L. McClelland, & D. E. Rumelhart (Eds.), *Parallel distributed processing: Explorations in the microstructure of cognition* (Vol. 1, pp. 318-362). Cambridge, MA: MIT Press.

Rumelhart, D. E., Smolensky, P., McClelland, J. L., & Hinton, G. E. (1986). Schemata and sequential thought processes in PDP models. In J. L. McClelland & D. E. Rumelhart (Eds.), *Parallel distributed processing: Explorations in the microstructure of cognition* (Vol. 2, pp. 7-57). Cambridge, MA: MIT Press.

Tucker, D. M., & Williamson, P. A. (1984). Asymmetric neural control systems in human self-regulation. *Psychological Review, 91* 185-215.

Van Valen, L. (1973). A note on dreams. *Journal of Biological Psychology, 15,* 19.

Wollman, M., & Antrobus, J. (1986). Sleep and waking thought: Effects of external stimulation. *Sleep, 9,* 438-448.

The Effect of Postawakening Differences in Activation on the REM–NREM Report Effect and Recall of Information From Films

11

Stuart I. Rosenblatt
Teachers College, Columbia University

John S. Antrobus
City College of New York

Jerome P. Zimler
Hillside Hospital/Long Island Jewish Center

REM/NREM differences in the word length of dream reports have been known for some time (Foulkes, 1962); however, it has never been clearly determined whether the greater output in REM verbal reports is due solely to the fact that REM dreams are intrinsically more informative or to memory and attention processes operating during and/or upon awakening from REM sleep. As Cohen (1981) pointed out, it is conceivable that better memory, rather than better dreams, is associated with REM sleep.

Within this chapter, these authors describe a study that examined the notion that dream recall depends on activation, memory, and attention processes, which serve to impede or enhance recollection, particularly during the postawakening phase. This study was based on the well-documented findings (see Chapters 1, 10, & 12) that REM sleep is a state of heightened cortical activation. Since dreaming and dream reporting are closely linked to cortical activation, the authors reasoned that REM's heightened activation must persist into wakefulness and facilitate dream retrieval ability. It may be that subjects wake up more quickly from REM, attain a higher degree of activation before giving a report, and are thus better able to remember their dreams. Because NREM sleep, in contrast to REM, is assumed to be a less activated neurophysiological state, it follows that dream reports proceeding from this state should be less informative than those elicited after REM awakenings.

If differences in activation during the postawakening interval are responsible for REM/NREM differences in dream recall, then the recall of information from other-than-sleep events should also reveal a REM/NREM difference. By introducing a new technique—having subjects recall films upon REM and NREM awakening—this study provides a test of this hypothesis.

THE MNEMONICS OF DREAMING

The arousal-retrieval model of dream recall, as espoused by Koulack and Goodenough (1976), emphasizes the role of arousal from sleep (especially REM) in determining the accessibility (or retrievability) of the prior sleep experience. In their view, dreams are best remembered when the sleeper is awakened during or shortly after the dream itself, because consolidation of the dream memory is thought to take place during this period of wakefulness. Without this interval of arousal, the dream may be forgotten because of the lack of opportunity for consolidation. The arousal-retrieval theory is a variant of the more traditional consolidation model of memory.

In traditional consolidation theory, the short-term trace is said to last for minutes or hours, and consolidation or transfer to long-term memory occurs gradually. In Koulack and Goodenough's (1976) arousal-retrieval model, the life of the short-term memory trace lasts only for a period of seconds, and consolidation occurs more quickly. For this reason, the arousal-retrieval theory is referred to as a "rapid" consolidation model of memory. Koulack et al. based their belief in a short-term memory trace, which lasts for seconds (rather than for longer periods), on evidence from waking studies carried out by such researchers on memory as Peterson and Peterson (1959) and Waugh and Norman (1965).

With respect to the problem of dream recall, consolidation of the dream experience is believed to be impaired during sleep, primarily because the dream content is not effectively rehearsed in the short-term store. Although the dream information may be transferred to long-term memory during sleep, it is thought to be in a form that is difficult for the dreamer to retrieve. With an awakening arousal, however, the dream can be consolidated and thereby successfully retrieved. Goodenough (1979) describes this process in a clearer fashion.

> Dream recall failures should occur unless the sleeper awakens within a matter of seconds after the dream experience occurs. If arousal takes place during the life of the short-term trace then the content of the dream experience which immediately preceded the awakening may be retrievable from the short-term store directly. Given this retrieval as an entry into the long-term store, the dreamer may then be able to recall some of the preceding content of that dream experience. If the awakening is delayed until the short-term trace has expired, then retrieval may no longer be possible, or it may be much more difficult. (p. 138)

With the presentation of the Activator–Synthesis model (Hobson & McCarley, 1977) it became clear that the concepts of cortical and cognitive activation should be distinguished from that of arousal. Unlike cortical and cognitive activation, the term includes the concepts of behavioral and emotional or autonomic activity. But it is the cortical and cognitive activation that are the most likely vehicles for dream production in REM sleep and the consolidation of the dream memory upon awakening.

This activation-retrieval model suggests that the REM/NREM differences in dream recall derive from differences in activation during the life of the short-term trace of the dream. The higher degree of activation in REM suggests that there will be less decay from short-term memory and less transfer to long-term memory after a REM awakening, leading to a longer report when compared with NREM. If decay is rapid enough, no mentation report may be available as is usually the case from slow wave sleep and sometimes the case from Stage 2 NREM awakenings.

In considering the role that activation following awakening from sleep serves in the consolidation and retrieval of the recent dream material, it is important to recognize that the role of activation in affecting dream recall has been largely inferred from examining dream report data. In fact, it has never even been demonstrated that REM's high level of activation persists into the waking state.

With the exception of a few studies that documented that heart rate, blood pressure, muscle tonus, and body temperature increase during the period of awakening (Kleitman, 1963) and the performance laterality studies (see Chapters 2, 3, & 4), there has been to date no systematic laboratory study on activation levels during the waking-up process. However, given the evidence that REM sleep is itself a heightened state of activation, it is entirely logical to hypothesize that this activation may endure into wakefulness and enhance dream recall ability.

This experiment was prompted by the findings that the major difference between REM and NREM dream reports has been in the length of the verbal report (Antrobus, 1983; Antrobus, Fein, Jordan, Ellman, & Arkin, 1979). Antrobus proposed that these REM/NREM differences in word output may be due to differences in cortical activation within these two stages and to the influence of this cortical activation on memory and attention during the postawakening period of reporting. Whether this REM activation factor actually persists into the waking state and improves retrieval of the dream, or whether more information to recall is readily available in REM sleep cannot, however, be decided solely by examining dream reports. For this reason, we decided to compare REM and NREM for retrieval of information previously stored in some other state, such as wakefulness.

By introducing a film segment as the object of recall, this research tested the influence of activation on the postawakening recall of information for an experience other than a dream. The presence of a postawakening effect was assessed by determining whether REM/NREM dream-reporting differences also held for reports of nonsleep events: specifically, for film clips presented before sleep onset each night and reported on following REM/NREM awakenings. The study assumes that the act of reporting sleep imagery and thought and reporting the perceptual responses to a film are relatively comparable mental events.

The primary difference is that the dream is generated and attended to by the subject during sleep, while the film is viewed in the waking state. If it is true that the postawakening activation state of the subject accounts for REM/NREM differences in dream recall, the differences in the subject's ability to recall the films ought to show the same differences as in dream recall. Specifically, subjects should recall more information about films following REM awakenings than following NREM awakenings.

DESIGN AND PROCEDURE

Data were collected from 31 paid subjects (16 men and 15 women), ranging in age from 18 to 35. Subjects were native English speakers, with good eyesight and color vision. The rationale for these criteria was that it was important for subjects to be able to view clearly, comprehend, and report on films that were in color and contained English-spoken dialogue. All subjects slept in the City College of New York Sleep Laboratory.

EEG was recorded on a Beckman Type R Dynograph. Recordings were taken from sites C3 and C4 (left and right central) and 04 (right occipital) as defined by the Ten Twenty Electrode System of the International Federation for Electroencephalography and Clinical Neurophysiology. The EOG was recorded from both eyes with electrodes applied to a site slightly lateral to and above the outer canthi. In both EEG and EOG reference electrodes were attached to the contralateral and homolateral ear lobe (mastoid) respectively. The EMG was recorded bilaterally from the submental muscle located beneath the chin. Six channels of the dynograph were used for recording biopotentials from the left eye, right eye, bipolar eye, central EEG, occipital EEG, and EMG.

Film Segments

Eight different super 8 ten-minute color cartoons were carefully selected and edited so that each cartoon consisted of one episode and lasted 60 s. Each film depicted cartoon characters (animals and people) involved in carrying out a relatively simple plot from beginning to end. Cartoons rather than real-life movies were used to avoid the confounding of a film report with a report of a prior sleep experience. Had real-life movies been shown prior to sleep and recalled following REM and NREM awakenings, it might have been difficult to differentiate those characters, actions, and conversations from those belonging to the dream experience. The eight cartoons were viewed and recalled by three reviewers.

These reports were then rated by two judges, who scored them on the Total Recall Count (TRC) scale of the Psycholinguistic Coding Manual (PCM) to ascertain their equality with respect to content, visual and auditory imagery, and visual action. Interjudge reliability was calculated at .90. Using the average of the judges' scores, a chi-square analysis was performed to determine whether any significant differences existed among the eight films on the Total Recall Count measure. No significant differences between the films were found.

A 5-s excerpt in the eight films served as a postawakening cue so that subjects knew which film they were to recall upon awakening. A Ewing projector placed inside the bedroom was used for showing the cartoons. Tape cassette recorders to record subjects' responses were also part of the laboratory equipment.

Subjects were informed that, prior to going to sleep, they would view four short films to which they should pay close attention because they would be asked to recall them later in the night, and that upon certain awakenings, they would be shown a brief excerpt from one of the films viewed earlier, and that they would be asked to identify and recall as much of the entire film as they could remember.

There were four types of awakenings made in this study: (1) a REM awakening for film recall; (2) a Stage 2–NREM awakening for film recall; (3) a REM awakening for dream recall; and (4) a Stage 2–NREM awakening for dream recall. When it was possible, all four types of awakenings were made on each of the 2 nights for all subjects.

In order to prevent the idiosyncratic characteristics of a particular film becoming associated with a particular sleep-state-awakening condition, the order of the film cues was counterbalanced as follows. One-half of the subjects viewed films numbered one through four on night 1 and films five through eight on night 2. This order was reversed for the other half of the subjects. In order to reduce the effects of primacy and recency on recall, cues from films one, four, five, and eight were not used in the study.

During the course of this experiment, it was decided to conduct a pilot substudy to test the hypothesis that REM and NREM film reports would not differ significantly following a 30-s pause between the time of the awakening and the time of recall. It was assumed that a 30-s postawakening delay should permit subjects to achieve equal levels of cortical activation following REM and NREM sleep. Since part of this study assumes that film reports will be better immediately following REM sleep, due to the subject's heightened level of arousal, this 30-s pause should lead to film reports that are more similar in quantity and quality of information recalled. For the purpose of this substudy, four subjects underwent a somewhat different procedure from those in the main experiment. In addition to recalling two of the films immediately following REM and NREM awakenings, these four subjects were instructed to delay reporting on two of the other films for a 30-s period of time. The four cartoons previously not reported on by subjects in the main study were therefore employed.

These four subjects were thus required to report on all eight films over the 2 nights. As with the main experiment, counterbalancing was accomplished by having two of the subjects view and report on films numbered one, two, three, and four on night 1, and films five, six, seven, and eight on night 2, and then reversing the order for the other two subjects. Once again, the type and order of awakenings as well as the time of night was held constant for each subject from night 1 to night 2.

Scoring Film and Dream Reports

All transcribed dream and film reports were independently rated by two judges on 7 scales of the PCM (Antrobus, Schnee, Offer, & Silverman, 1977). This manual was developed for reliably counting the words in several cognitive classes. The scales include total amount of information reported or Total Recall Count (TRC), 4 scales for scoring visual imagery, 2 for aural verbal experiences, and 10 additional scales not employed here. Interjudge reliability for all of the scales was in the high .90s with the exception of the Implicit Speech scale which was .83.

Total Visual and Total Speech scales were created by summing three visual imagery scales (not Spatial Relations) and the two auditory scales respectively.

As there were large differences in the length of reports, the word count scores were positively skewed. They were therefore normalized by the log X + 1 transformation (Kirk, 1976) prior to being submitted for data analysis. For the purpose of further reducing skewness and increasing the homogeneity of variance, reports that fell beyond three standard deviations from the mean on Total Recall Count were removed from the analysis. This procedure eliminated a total of seven reports, which were each in excess of 400 words.

Data Analysis

The data analysis was performed using the SAS General Linear Model (GLM) statistical method. The GLM was the preferred statistical method because of its efficiency in processing data in unbalanced situations, that is, where there are unequal numbers of observations for the different variables. All hypotheses were tested at two-tailed levels of significance.

RESULTS

REM/NREM Differences in Film Recall

The Activation hypothesis predicted that subjects would demonstrate a greater ability to recall the information from film segments following REM, relative to NREM awakenings. Table 11.1 presents the results of the GLM analysis.

In direct support of the Activation–Recall hypothesis, a significant REM/NREM difference in film recall was found on TRC, the strongest scale of the PCM. The mean scores revealed that subjects recalled more information about the films when awakened from REM sleep than from NREM sleep. On the Visual Noun word variable, the GLM results were similar; again, significantly more visualized objects from the films were remembered upon REM awakenings than following NREM awakenings. Subjects also recalled significantly more Total Visual information about the films upon REM awakenings (see Tables 11.1 and 11.2). When analyzed independently, the Visual Action and Visual Modifier word variables did not significantly account for differences between REM and NREM film

TABLE 11.1

Means and Standard Deviations of Word Variables for Film Reports and Tests of Differences between REM and NREM Awakenings (N = 27). (averaged over nights)

| Word Variable | Sleep State | | | | F |
| | REM | | NREM | | |
	MEAN	SD	MEAN	SD	(DF = 1, 60)
Total recall	1.95	.28	1.83	.51	5.17*
Visual noun	.98	.20	.90	.27	5.96*
Visual modifier	.65	.33	.58	.36	3.80
Visual action	.83	.26	.78	.33	1.69
Spatial relations	.52	.26	.48	.28	.80
Implicit speech	.45	.57	.52	.55	.66
Explicit speech	.35	.54	.39	.54	.11
Total speech	.63	.66	.72	.62	.95
Total visual	1.28	.25	1.19	.35	5.41*

Note: All scores are log transformed.
*$p \leq$ .05.

TABLE 11.2
Means and Standard Deviations of Word Variables for Delayed Film Reports
and Tests of Differences between REM and NREM Awakenings (N = 4).
(averaged over nights)

Word Variable	REM		NREM		F
	MEAN	SD	MEAN	SD	(DF = 1, 15)
Total recall	1.89	.37	1.93	.40	.58
Visual noun	.89	.19	.89	.19	.06
Visual modifier	.64	.32	.62	.35	.06
Visual action	.81	.29	.83	.25	.17
Spatial relations	.61	.21	.55	.35	.53
Implicit speech	.34	.48	.57	.62	4.14
Explicit speech	.45	.64	.52	.72	.04
Total speech	.70	.61	.97	.64	2.15
Total visual	1.23	.26	1.22	.27	.10

Note: All scores are log transformed.
*$p \leq .05$.

reports. No significant effects were found on the three auditory word variables — Implicit Speech, Explicit Speech, and Total Speech — indicating that dialogue from the films was equally remembered following REM and NREM awakenings. REM/NREM differences in the recall of spatial information (Spatial Relations) were also not significant.

REM/NREM Differences in Film Recall (Delay Condition)

A pilot substudy was conducted to determine whether REM/NREM film reports would be attenuated or disappear if subjects delayed reporting on them for a 30-s interval following awakening.

The GLM analyses are summarized in Table 11.2. As can be seen, significant F-values were not found for any of the word variables. The low statistical power of the test, however, does not permit any conclusion about the attenuating effect of the 30-s delay.

DISCUSSION

This research was undertaken to explore the influence of activation and memory on dream recall ability following REM and NREM awakenings. It identified a cortical and cognitive postawakening activation effect that enhances REM more than NREM dream recall. To the extent that activation has been shown to play a role in postawakened film report REM/NREM differences, then the REM/NREM difference in dream recall cannot be attributed solely to cognitive processes that occur *within* the sleep states. To the extent that the REM/NREM dream recall effect is much larger than the REM/NREM film recall effect, then we may conclude that a substantial part of the dream recall effect is the result of *pre*-awakening processes. That is, only a small part of the REM/NREM dream recall effect can be attributed to postawakening differences in cortical and cognitive activation.

This study's most important finding was that subjects' REM film reports were more informative than NREM film reports on the Total Recall Count word variable. This finding is interpreted as evidence of a cortical–cognitive activation effect that is strongest during REM awakenings. This activation effect, which serves to facilitate attention and memory retrieval, is thought to represent the carry-over of REM sleep's heightened activation into the waking state. Additional support for the activation hypothesis is provided in the analysis of visual content where significantly more visual information from the films was recalled following REM than NREM awakenings.

This interpretation is supported by the study of Fiss, Klein, and Bokert (1966), in which subjects were asked to make up a story about a TAT card presented to them immediately upon awakening from both REM and NREM sleep. Their results demonstrated that TAT stories produced following REM awakenings were significantly longer and more elaborate than stories following NREM sleep. Fiss and his colleagues postulated that the distinguishing characteristics of REM sleep are not switched off upon awakening, but continue briefly into the waking state. In a replication of the Fiss et al. (1966) study, Starker and Goodenough (1970) found that REM and NREM sleep differentially influenced TAT stories produced immediately upon awakening. These TAT findings, along with the present film report findings, lend support to the proposition that the psychophysiological state of persons at the time they give their dream reports differs following REM and NREM awakenings and differentially affects the ability to report pre-awakening experiences.

When subjects were required to delay reporting on films for a 30-s period following awakening, their REM and NREM film reports were not significantly different. The delayed film report findings thus suggest that the REM arousal factors that initially facilitate recall ability, dissipate quickly. The low statistical power of these tests prohibits any firm conclusions, however. It may be helpful to explore the postawakening retrieval process further. By examining the fundamental parameters of the postawakening retrieval process, perhaps insight may be gained into the earlier stages of generating and storing sleep mentation.

ACKNOWLEDGMENT

Stuart I. Rosenblatt is presently Assistant Vice-President of the Office of Mental Hygiene Services for the New York City Health and Hospitals Corporation. Jerome P. Zimler is deceased.

REFERENCES

Antrobus, J. S. (1983). REM and NREM sleep reports: Comparison of word frequencies by cognitive classes. *Psychophysiology, 20,* 562-568.

Antrobus, J. S., Fein, G., Jordan, L., Ellman, S. J., & Arkin, A. M. (1979). Measurement and design in research on sleep reports. In A. M. Arkin, J. S. Antrobus, & S. J. Ellman (Eds.), *The mind in sleep* (pp. 19-55). Hillsdale, NJ: Lawrence Erlbaum Associates.

Antrobus, J. S., Schnee, R. K., Offer, V., & Silverman, L. (1977). *A psycholinguistic scoring manual for mentation reports.* Unpublished text. Princeton, NJ: Educational Testing Service, ETS Test Collection, Set D, No. C008737.

Cohen, D. B. (1981). *Sleep and dreaming: Origins, nature and functions.* New York: Pergamon.

Fiss, H., Klein, G. S., & Bokert, E. (1966). Waking fantasies following interruption of two types of sleep. *Archives of General Psychiatry, 14,* 543-551.

Foulkes, D. (1962). Dream reports from different stages of sleep. *Journal of Abnormal and Social Psychology, 65,* 14-25.

Goodenough, D. R. (1979). Dream recall: History and current status. In A. M. Arkin, J. S. Antrobus, & S. J. Ellman (Eds.), *The mind in sleep* (pp. 113-140). Hillsdale, NJ: Lawrence Erlbaum Associates.

Hobson, J. A., & McCarley, R. W. (1977). The brain as a dream-state generator: Activator-synthesis hypotheses of the dream process. *American Journal of Psychiatry, 134,* 1335-1368.

Kirk, R. E. (1976). *Experimental design procedures for the behavioral sciences.* Belmont, CA: Wadsworth.

Kleitman, N. (1963). *Sleep and wakefulness* (2nd ed.). Chicago: University of Chicago Press.

Koulack, D., & Goodenough, D. R. (1976). Dream recall and dream recall failure: An arousal-retrieval model. *Psychological Bulletin, 83,* 975-984.

Peterson, K. R., & Peterson, M. J. (1959). Short-term retention on individual items. *Journal of Experimental Psychology, 58,* 193-198.

Starker, S., & Goodenough, D. R. (1970). Effect of sleep state and method of awakening upon TAT productions at arousal. *Journal of Nervous and Mental Disease, 150,* 188-194.

Waugh, N. C., & Norman, D. A. (1965). Primary memory. *Psychological Review, 72,* 89-104.

III TONIC AND PHASIC ACTIVATION MODELS

12

A New Model of Brain–Mind State: Activation Level, Input Source, and Mode of Processing (AIM)

J. Allan Hobson
Laboratory of Neurophysiology, Department of Psychiatry,
Harvard Medical School

TOWARD A 3-STATE MODEL OF BRAIN-MIND

The activation–synthesis hypothesis (ASH; Hobson & McCarley, 1977) of dreaming was designed to provide an account of the psychophysiology of the most typical form of REM-sleep mentation. Because the physiological model of reciprocal interaction (1975), upon which this particular psychophysiological account was based, is relevant to all states of the brain, it seems reasonable to begin to extend the theory to an account of mentation in other states, especially that associated with NREM sleep and waking.

Complementing the intrinsic rationale of such an extension is extrinsic pressure arising in such criticism of the activation–synthesis hypothesis (ASH) and the reciprocal-interaction model (RIM) as that offered by Vogel (1978) and the emergence of the first serious competitive model in the cognitive psychology–artificial intelligence (AI) domain, the ACT-star hypothesis of Anderson (1985), as discussed by Antrobus (1991) in relation to mentation reports from states other than REM sleep.

It is the purpose of this chapter to develop a preliminary sketch of a new, more general theory of state psychophysiology, called AIM, which is based upon the data of modern sleep research and theoretical considerations that have emerged in elaborating the physiological basis of the reciprocal interaction model and its application to the activation–synthesis hypothesis of dreaming.

WHAT IS AIM?

Three basic factors will be defined and developed: Activation Level (A), Input Source (I), and Information-processing Mode (M). The three factors will be shown to vary across the states in such a way as possibly to account for typical mentation features. Furthermore, each of the three factors will be shown to be a function of the physiological condition of the reciprocally interacting brain stem neuronal populations that constitute the sleep-cycle control oscillator.

We caution the reader that this formulation is schematic and tentative, rather than systematic and final. The attempt to be precise—and even mathematical—is enjoined for heuristic purposes and has, as its goal, only an approximate quantitative estimation of the adequacy of the factors and of their interactions, not a measurement of their minute accuracy.

A brief comment is in order to explain the assumptions behind the use of the hybrid term, "brain–mind." This term assumes a formal isomorphism between all mind- states and all brain states, and views the two levels, the subjective and the objective, as parts of a unified system. This view has monistic overtones but specifically denies the "nothing-but" eliminative implications of the current materialist position. It rather suggests that when we ultimately achieve an adequate account of brain, we will have an adequate account of mind; likewise, an adequate account of mind depends on an adequate account of brain.

THE RECIPROCAL-INTERACTION HYPOTHESIS: A 3-STATE PHYSIOLOGICAL MODEL

Designed with reference to REM sleep, the model of reciprocal interaction has strong implications for the states of waking and slow-wave (or NREM) sleep. This is because, as shown in Fig. 12.1, the oscillator operates continuously and thus has values that vary continuously during waking, NREM, and REM sleep.

Based upon the data shown in Fig. 12.1, Table 12.1 quantifies the relative activity levels of the cholinergic (Ch) and aminergic (Am) neuronal populations that constitute the putative oscillator in the three states. Fig. 12.2 then illustrates the effect on mode (M) of the oppositely directed changes in Ch and Am in REM sleep.

Cholinergic neurons are, on average, about twice as active in waking and REM sleep as they are in NREM sleep. This assumption is supported by the work of Jasper and Tessier (1971), who showed that the release of

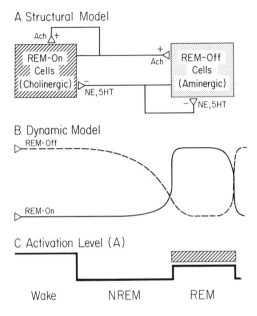

A. Structural Model

B. Dynamic Model

C. Activation Level (A)

Wake   NREM   REM

FIG. 12.1   Physiological mechanisms determining alterations in activation level (A). (A) Structural Model of Reciprocal Interaction. REM-on cells of the pontine reticular formation are cholinoceptively excited and/or cholinergically excitatory (ACh+) at their synaptic endings (open boxes). Pontine REM-off cells are noradrenergically (NE) or serotonergically (5HT) inhibitory (−) at their synapses (filled boxes). (B) Dynamic Model. During waking the pontine aminergic (filled box) system is tonically activated and inhibits the pontine cholinergic (open box) system. During NREM sleep aminergic inhibition gradually wanes and cholinergic excitation reciprocally waxes. At REM sleep onset aminergic inhibition is shut off and cholinergic excitation reaches its high point. (C) Activation Level (A). As a consequence of the interplay of the neuronal systems shown in A and B, the net activation level of the brain (A) is at equally high levels in waking and REM sleep and at about half this peak level in NREM sleep. See Table 12.2 for quantitative estimates of these functions.

TABLE 12.1
Physiological Features of RIM Neurons

	State		
Chemical subtype	Wake	NREM	REM
Cholinergic (Ch)	+ +	+	+ +
	(2)	(1)	(2)
Aminergic (Am)	+ +	+	0
	(2)	(1)	(0)
Ch/Am Ratio	1	1	∞

acetylcholine from the cerebral cortex of the cat was equally high in the two electrically activated brain states (waking and REM sleep) but fell to half that level in NREM sleep when the brain was electrically deactivated. I have therefore entered the relative values 2:1:2 into Table 2.1. This 2:1:2 proportion is also true of many central sensorimotor neuronal assemblies:

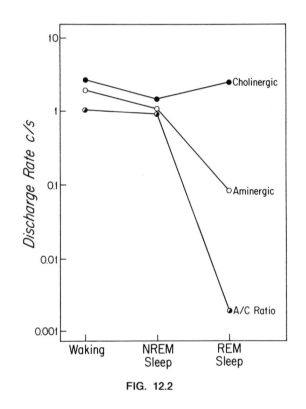

	Waking	NREM Sleep	REM Sleep
Aminergic	LC, DRN		
Cholinergic	Ch 1-4 Ch 5		

FIG. 12.2

pyramidal tract cells of the motor system, visual cortical and geniculate neurons, oculomotor neurons, and midbrain reticular neurons (see Hobson & Steriade, 1986, for details).

Aminergic neurons share with cholinergic cells the 2:1 reduction in activity that occurs when waking gives way to NREM sleep (see, again, Hobson & Steriade, 1986). But they depart markedly from cholinergic neurons in showing a virtual arrest — to near-zero level — of activity in REM sleep. The assumption that the values 2:1:.01, which are entered in Table 12.1, actually reflect changes in release is partly supported by the findings of Cespuglio et al. (1980) showing that serotonin release is reduced to half its waking level in NREM sleep. Unfortunately, it has not yet been possible to measure norepinephrine or serotonin release in REM sleep. *In vivo* microdialysis is a new method, which may help to solve this problem (Ungerstedt et al. 1982; Zetterström, Sharp, Marsden, & Ungerstedt, 1983). It should be emphasized, however, that the low value of aminergic output in REM sleep in Table 12.1 is an unproved assumption based on the unit recording data.

As a consequence of the differential changes in the values of Ch and Am in REM sleep versus waking, the ratio of the two chemical estimators,

---

FIG. 12.2 Biochemical mechanisms determining alternations in modulatory influences (M). (A) State dependent changes in aminergic and cholinergic neuronal function. Schematic representation of the progressive decrease of aminergic neurotransmitter release in the cerebral cortex as animal passes from wake, through non-REM to REM sleep. As a consequence, the cortical concentrations of norepinephrine and serotonin are highest in waking, lowest in REM sleep, and intermediate in non-REM sleep. On these sagittal sections of the brain the aminergic neurons of the nucleus locus ceruleus (noradrenergic and dorsal raphe nucleus [serotonergic] are represented by cell A. The cholinergic neurons of Ch 1–4 (in the basal forebrain) and of Ch 5 of the peribrachial pontine tegmentum are represented by neurons C. Cholinergic neurons (C) release levels of acetylcholine that are as high in REM sleep as they are in waking; non-REM sleep release is lower. (B) State-dependent changes in aminergic/ cholinergic ratio. A quantitative estimate of the aminergic and cholinergic neurotransmitter concentrations may be derived from single-unit recording studies and by direct and indirect measurements of neurotransmitter release. Because the values are similar and parallel in making and non-REM sleep, but diverge in REM sleep, the ratio of the two values amplifies the difference between REM and the other two states.

The values of A are computed by averaging the mean rate of putatively noradrenergic and serotonergic neurons recorded by microelectrodes in the brain stem of cats. The inferred decrease in release has been confirmed voltametrically, for serotonin, in waking and in REM sleep. The values of C are computed by averaging the mean rate of unidentified cortical neurons. These estimates are compatible with direct measure of acetylcholine release from the cerebral cortex (modified from Hobson 1988).

Ch/Am, goes from about 1 in waking (when both values are high) and NREM sleep (when both values are low) to near infinity in REM sleep. Put another way, cholinergic and aminergic systems run in parallel (and can hence be said to be in balance) during waking and NREM sleep but go in opposite directions in REM sleep, such that cholinergic systems greatly predominate in that state, as shown in Fig. 12.2A.

This Ch/Am ratio value, which estimates the modulatory state of the brain, is called factor M in the new model, as shown in Figure 12.2B. It is an important conceptual innovation because it enables us to envisage — and to quantify — those differences in brain biochemistry and metabolism that must underlie the changes in the mode (M) of information processing that differentiate dreaming and waking. For example, such large changes in Ch/Am could be related to the loss of self-reflective awareness and insight, the instability of orientation, the breakdown of linear logic, and the poor memory of REM sleep-dreaming.

One reason for believing that a modulatory factor such as M could explain these information-processing differences is the known role of the aminergic neurotransmitters in behavioral and cell biological models of learning and memory. For detailed discussion of this topic, see Flicker, McCarley, and Hobson (1981) and Schmajuk and Hobson (1988). Another reason for exploring this factor M concept is that the it provides a link to molecular biology via the second messenger function. For example, it is known that in addition to altering membrane electrical properties, NE and 5HT release the second messenger cAMP while ACh releases cGMP. These two cyclic nucleotides differentially regulate intracellular metabolism via their interaction with DNA. Hence a radical change in Ch/Am, measured in the new model as factor M, could be translated via a corresponding change in cGMP/cAMP to a change in genetically controlled enzyme production. Further details of this concept are given in Hobson (1988).

INPUT–OUTPUT TRANSACTIONS AND THEIR CENTRAL REPRESENTATIONS AS COROLLARY DISCHARGE

In addition to the differences in the way the activated (A) brain processes information (M) is a state-dependent change in the input–output (I–O) functions of the system from which the AIM model's factor I is derived. To understand the physiology and the reasoning used in defining and measuring I, consider the schematic illustration in Fig. 12.3.

Three classes of neuron (two of which are possibly cholinergic and one which is almost certainly aminergic) have distinctive state-dependent firing characteristics that are quite different from those of the RIM oscillator in the pontine brain stem. All three of the neuronal subtypes may be

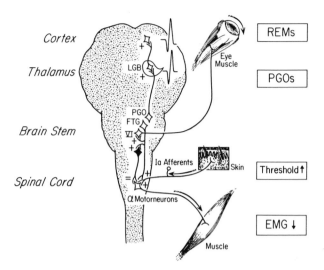

FIG. 12.3 Three mechanisms underlying state-dependent changes in AIM model factor *I* are shown: *Efferent Copy.* During REM sleep, neurons of the pontine reticular formation (FTG) are activated. When they fire in bursts, ipsiversive REMs are generated and ipsilateral PGO waves are triggered in the LGB and posterolateral cortex. *Presynaptic Inhibition.* Via axons descending from the FTG, the primary afferent terminals of the group Ia cutaneous afferents are depolarized, making them *less* responsive to incoming volleys from the skin. In this way sensory thresholds are raised. *Postsynaptic Inhibition.* Cells of the medullary reticular formation are also excited by volleys from the pons, but they convey inhibitory signals to the anterior horn motoneurons and muscle tone is suppressed (EMG). In this way the threshold to motor activation is raised. This circuitry and dynamics of this figure should be compared with the data in Table 12.2.

considered *sensorimotor* in that they participate either in input–output (reflex) transactions or in their internal representation as corollary discharges (efferent copy signals). The concept of efferent copy and its possible contribution to state-dependent changes in cognition are discussed in Hobson and Steriade (1986) and Callaway, Lydic, Baghdoyan, and Hobson (1987).

As shown in Table 12.2, the primary sensory group I and group II afferent neurons, and the final common path alpha motoneurons both share the 2:1 reduction in level that is characteristic of the wake-to-NREM-sleep state transitions of other central neurons but differ from them in being *actively inhibited* in REM sleep. (See Hobson & Steriade [1986] for details as to absolute values and mechanism). This input–output (or I–O) function appears in Table 12.2 as the external signal factor, *SE*. It is shown first to decrease in NREM sleep, and then to undergo active blockade in REM sleep.

By apparently unique contrast, the neurons of at least one "efferent copy"

TABLE 12.2
Physiological Features: Input-Output Neurons

Function	Neuronal subtype	W	NREM	REM
			States	
Input	Group Ia afferents	+ +	+	−
		(2)	(1)	(~0)
Output	Brain stem and Spinal	+ +	+	−
	motoneurons	(2)	(1)	(~0)
Efferent	PGO burst cells	+	+ +	+ + +
Copy		(1)	(2)	(3)

system show a marked and progressive (= 1:2:3) *enhancement* of activity across the three states (see Table 12.2). These neurons are involved in the generation of PGO waves and convey information about the lateral direction of eye movement to the central sensorimotor systems. (This function is carried into Table 12.3 as the value of the internal signal factor, *SI*.)

A QUANTITATIVE ESTIMATION OF MENTAL STATE PROBABILITY

We have now identified three physiological factors that contribute to mental state determination.

Activation Level, factor A, determines the energetic "power" of the system to process information of whatever source, quantity or kind. This factor can be estimated most simply from the firing level of reticular activating neurons in the midbrain. Actually, the 2:1:2 ratio found in the MRF also applies to many sensorimotor neurons in the visual, association, and motor areas of the cortex. Activation level thus discriminates NREM sleep from waking and REM sleep but cannot discriminate between the latter two states. In other words, if only activation level were involved in generating mental state, then waking and REM sleep would be identical. The values 2:1:2 are entered in Table 12.3 as estimates of Activation Level.

Stimulus Source (factor I) determines the *kind* of information that will be processed by the activated brain–mind. In the case of external stimuli, the stimulus channel and strength will be determined by the interaction of extrinsic stimulus properties and the excitability of the intrinsic sensory systems. In the case of internal stimuli, the excitability and phasic firing properties of the system channel alone determine sensory modality and strength. Consider the visual system: A change in stimulus source, from external to internal will shift the information processed by the system from

TABLE 12.3
Brain-Mind State "Function" Features

	States		
	Wake	**NREM**	**REM**
Activation level (A)	+ +	+	+ +
	(2)	(1)	(2)
Stimulus source (I)			
External stimulus	+ +	+	0
strength (SE)	(2)	(1)	(1)
Internal stimulus	+	+ +	+ + +
strength (SI)	(1)	(2)	(3)
Output (O)	+ + +	+	≅ 0
	(3)	(1)	(0)
Processing mode (M)	+ +	+	≅ 0
	(2)	(1)	(0.1)

external to internal. Hence the mental state will shift, visually, from reproductive to innovative.

In the case of external stimuli the form of the external world is represented, while in the case of internal stimuli only information already stored in memory can provide the form of imagery. The simplest way to represent this shift is by the relative strength of the ratio of response to external stimuli (R:SE) to internal stimuli (R:SI). Thus $I = SE/SI$

We may estimate *External Stimulus Strength* as the product of the energy of the proximal stimulus and the excitability of primary afferents. Proximal visual stimulus energy differentiates waking from both states of sleep simply by virtue of eye closure. In other words, this input factor falls to zero very quickly and thus plays a major role (with activation level) in differentiating waking mentation from sleeping mentation. In all sleep states, external stimuli therefore will be considered to play a negligible formative role. We note, however, that although threshold varies, it is never absolutely exclusive, and external stimuli can always gain access to the system if sufficiently strong.

We may estimate *Internal Stimulus Strength* as the frequency of PGO waves since these waves appear to represent all-or-none, internally generated signals for the visual system. Observed values (waves per second) of about 0.1 for waking, 0.2 for NREM, and 10.0 for REM sleep, strongly differentiate REM sleep from the other two states, giving 1:2:100 ratios. It should also be pointed out, however, that the NREM sleep value increases sharply as REM sleep approaches, so that internally generated sensation can be expected in the later, lighter stages of NREM sleep. Thus, for purposes of preliminary exploration, we enter the conservative ratios 1:2:3 in Table 12.3.

Factor *I* also assesses *Input-output Transactions*. Motor output, (*O*), is markedly reduced (3:1) at sleep onset and then virtually extinguished in REM sleep (1:0). For the purposes of this preliminary sketch of the theory we ignore this factor in subsequent analysis but note that it is not entirely negligible and so enter the values 3:1:0 in Table 12.3.

Information-processing Mode (*M*), is the third major determinant of brain–mind state. The simplest way of conceptualizing this processing factor is as the relative strength of linear, serial, or analytical processing, assuming such a mode to be the converse, or at least the competitor, of a parallel, multichannel symbolic mode of processing. In simpler terms, the contrast may be expressed as the analytical tendency to feature extraction versus the synthetic tendency to form recognition. Assuming that what the sensorimotor (including cortical) neurons do with information provided to them is determined in large part by the modulatory influences arising from the aminergic interneurons of the brain stem, we may estimate this factor simply as the strength of modulatory neuronal systems and take the values of firing level of aminergic neurons as first approximations of *M*. The ratios are 2:1:0.1 (the latter value being generously high). This factor strongly discriminates all three states but most impressively distinguishes REM sleep from the other two.

PREDICTING MENTAL STATE BY COMBINING THE PHYSIOLOGICAL FUNCTION FACTORS

Table 12.3 lists the five function features contributing to *A, I,* and *M,* as estimated from physiological variables. This *S* (for State) function is later referred to as *S* (for the physiological state). In predicting mental states we use the subterm *S* to indicate the psychological state that is most profoundly associated with it.

Having defined five variables, I now wish to explore their interaction. It is clear that the state of the brain and its correlated state of mind is a function of activation level (*A*), stimulus source and strength (*I*), and modulatory set (*M*). The three factors may thus be used to predict the state (*S*) of the brain–mind.

State (*S*) = f [*A, I, M,*]

In particular the probabilities, *p*, of the three states is as follows:

$$p\ W = A,\ I,\ M$$

$$p\ NREM = \frac{1}{A},\frac{1}{I},\frac{1}{M}$$

$$p\,REM = \frac{A,\,1,\,1}{I,\,M}$$

To elaborate a bit, the probability that an organism will evince waking behavior and, if human, report mentation characterized by such features as external orientation, linear logical thought, and self-reflective awareness (see Fig. 12.4) is a conjoint function of the activation level of the brain (that is mediated by the reticular formation), the input source (that is mediated by the relative strengths of external and internal sensory stimulation), and

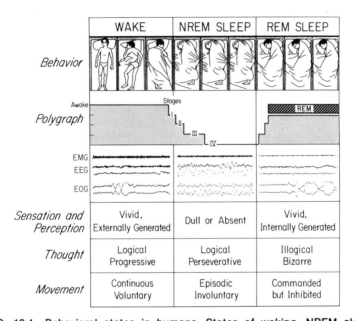

FIG. 12.4 Behavioral states in humans. States of waking, NREM sleep, and REM sleep have behavioral, polygraphic, and psychological manifestations. In behavior channel, posture shifts (detectable by time-lapse photography or video) can occur during waking and in concert with phase changes of sleep cycle. Two different mechanisms account for sleep immobility: disfacilitation (during Stages I–IV of NREM sleep) and inhibition (during REM sleep). In dreams we imagine that we move but we do not. Sequence of these stages represented in polygraph channel. Sample tracings of three variables used to distinguish state are also shown: electromyogram (EMG), which is highest in waking, intermediate in NREM sleep, and lowest in REM sleep; and electroencephalogram (EEG) and electrooculogram (EOG), which are both activated in waking and REM sleep and inactivated in NREM sleep. Each sample record is 20 s. Three lower channels describe other subjective and objective state variables. (J. A. Hobson & M. Steriade, "Neuronal basis of behavioral state control." In *Handbook of physiology: The nervous system,* vol. 4 Edited by V. Mountcastle & F. E. Bloom, pp. 701–823, 1986.)

strength and the mode of information processing (that is set by the biochemistry of modulatory systems in the hippocampus and cerebral cortex). Thus the values of all three factors A, I, M, are high in waking. And conversely, as the values of each and/or all three decline, NREM sleep becomes more and more likely. In this case, mentation becomes less sensitive to immediate external stimulus conditions, self-reflective awareness is lost, and the speed and logic of thought is retarded. Judging from the relative strength of the three factors shown in the NREM sleep column of Table 12.3, it is clear that the differences from waking are mainly determined by declines in A and I, and it would appear that these two factors interact powerfully so that even small changes in A (and/or M) may determine very large changes in I. This fits well with our subjective experience of first failing to process external information effectively when drowsy and then, suddenly, failing altogether at sleep onset.

REM sleep is quite a different case. Although it is on the same continuum as NREM with respect to factors I and M, the changes in factors I and M are much larger than those that distinguish waking and NREM sleep, as we will see. And as a result, external world orientation is even more thoroughly abandoned at the same time that internal stimuli are very powerfully enhanced. Simultaneously, the mode of processing shifts radically. In REM sleep the activation level (A) is high, but both the source (I) and the fate (M) of the signals are quite different from waking. Thus we experience vivid percepts but are disoriented and without self-reflective awareness, have bizarre and illogical thoughts, and later cannot easily remember these dream experiences.

A UNDIMENSIONAL VIEW OF AIM

We would now like to combine the values in such a way as to create a single variable that would estimate the probability of a given mental state as a continuous function of the interaction of the factors. Because of the very large effect of A upon I (especially at sleep onset) and of M upon A and I (especially in REM sleep) we model the interaction of the factors as interacting in a multiplicative rather than a simply additive fashion. This gives the factors added strength in that relatively small changes in two or more factors — especially if of opposite sign — are more heavily weighted. Put another way, the model has considerable *gain* in keeping with what we know of both the physiology of the state control oscillator (which has an exponential gain component) and with our subjective experience (which shows sharp and dramatic state transitions with very small changes in activation level and stimulus conditions). Thus, to quantify S, we solve the formula:

$$S \quad = \quad (A \quad \times \quad I \quad \times \quad M)$$

(state) (Activation Level) (Input Source) (Processing Mode)

The formula says that the probability of a brain–mind state favoring the linear processing of external information (W) is given by the product of A, I, and M. If the values of the functions during quiet waking are, as indicated in Table 12.3, approximately,

$$A = 2, \quad I = 2, \quad M = 2$$

Then $A \times I \times M = 2\,(2)\,2 = 8$

During intense arousal, the values of these functions might increase as follows:

$$A = 3 \quad I = 3 \quad M = 3$$

$$\therefore A \times I \times M = 3\,(3)\,3 = 27$$

In transition to NREM sleep all three values would fall as follows:

$$A = 1 \quad I = 1 \quad M = 1$$

$$\therefore A \times I \times M = 1\,(1)\,1 = 1$$

In REM sleep, despite the return of A to 2, the more radical fall in I and M bring all the values of S down by an order of magnitude as follows:

$$A = 2 \quad I = .3 \quad M = .1$$

$$A \times I \times M = 2\,(0.1)\,0.1 = .06$$

Thus whether or not the formula for S is minutely accurate, it is highly sensitive to known changes in physiological state factors, since it provides more than a 100-fold range of values.

A 3-DIMENSIONAL VIEW OF AIM

Because this undimensional state variable is both arbitrary and rather difficult to visualize, an alternative, three-dimensional vectorial approach may be heuristically useful. On this view, the values would tend to cluster in one or another part of a state space as shown in Fig. 12.5.

As values of A, I, and M increase during waking, points move to the right upper back corner of the state space; this movement would be maximal during arousal in the presence of novel stimuli that commanded attention and more likely to be memorable.

As values of A, I, and M decrease, points move back toward the left lower front of the state space; drowsiness, sleepiness, and NREM accom-

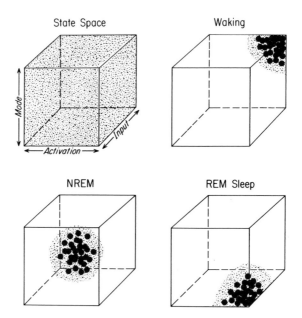

FIG. 12.5   Three-dimensional state space defined by the values for brain activation (A), input source and strength (I), and mode of processing (M). It is theoretically possible for the system to be at any point in the state space and an infinite number of state conditions is conceivable. In practice the system is normally constrained to a boomerang-like path from the back upper right in Waking (high A, I, and M), through the center in NREM (intermediate A, I, and M) to the front lower right in REM sleep (high A, low I, and M).

pany this movement, which normally stops at about the center because of the increasing values of A; in the second half of each sleep cycle the points pull to the right again.

But despite the increases in A, the simultaneously falling values of I and M pull the points down and forward so that the REM sleep points are clustered at the lower, right front corner of the state space.

The constant fluctuations of the values of A, I, and M have the effect of keeping the instantaneous state points in continuous motion. For example, the trajectory of AIM movement through one sleep cycle is shown in Fig. 12.6A. The points would be expected to move slowly along an arc from right, upper rear to left, lower front as waking gave way to NREM and REM sleep. At cycle end, the point would zoom back along a diagonal in the right-hand wall of the state space as the system reset. These considerations immediately suggest three-dimensional computer graphic displays of the data.

To illustrate further the heuristic value of the AIM model, we consider

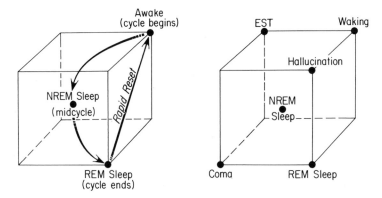

FIG. 12.6 (A) Movement through the state space during the sleep cycle. (B) Segments of the state space associated with some normal, pathological, and artificial conditions of the brain.

some other realistic possibilities (in Fig. 12.6B). Were the values of A, I, and M to continue to fall along the diagonal from the right upper rear corner to the left lower front, we would be modeling coma (due to CNS trauma) or anesthesia (due to CNS depression by drugs). If A were high and I decreased (as in REM), but M remained high (as in arousal, or anxiety), the points would move toward the front upper right corner and the system would process internally generated data as if they came from the outside world. This is hallucinosis. If A were low and I very high, as with the modified seizures of electroshock therapy (EST) the position of AIM would be shifted to the front upper left of the state space.

Thus certain sectors of the state space might be associated with specific mental states as follows:

1. Right upper rear — arousal
2. Center — sleep
3. Right lower front — dreams
4. Right upper front — hallucinations
5. left lower front — coma
6. Left upper front — EST

CAVEAT LECTOR: ALL STATE FACTORS ARE DYNAMIC, NOT STATIC

It is important to point out that the values that have been given in Tables 12.1, 12.2, and 12.3 are presented as if they were steady-state values. This implies sharp discontinuities at state boundaries. However, in its use of Volterra–Lotka mathematics, RIM clearly responds to the robust physiological evidence of a dynamic and constantly changing set of values, and we have already considered one aspect of the dynamic movement of points in the foregoing discussion of the three-dimensional state space. In addition to constant dynamism, there is an absence of sharp, step-like state boundaries. This boundary-blurring is critical to understanding many mental state phenomena that may vary within and between states and is a source of variability that is particularly important to recognize in dealing with the many departures from typicality in mentation reports which have been taken by critics of ASH-RIM to invalidate that theory.

As will be shown below, much of the NREM sleep is characterized by a continuous shift away from waking toward the dominance of REM sleep phenomena. As a consequence, NREM sleep mentation may be thought-like early but increasingly dream-like during late REM sleep. At sleep onset, the brain–mind is characterized by a sudden shift away from the exteroceptive processing mode. Consequently, low-level internal stimuli may give rise to REM-like information-processing operation since the higher-order neurons are still in an activated state.

ARE THE ESTIMATES REALISTIC?

We now turn our attention to the ways in which known (or reasonably inferred) changes in the numerical value of S could account for known changes in mental state. Here we revert to the unidimensional version of the model.

Over time, the several determinants of S might change as follows in Fig. 12.7.

Considered as a function of time it therefore seems likely that S might vary *discontinuously*. How might the function S change so as to account for the exceptional cases of dream-like mentation occurring outside of REM sleep?

At sleep onset a sudden and precipitous drop in the value of S could be caused by the sudden drop in the value SE (with eye closure) after a slow decline in A. This might have the paradoxical effect of enhancing the relative value of SI, which would suddenly act unopposed by SE while the persistence of A might be significant. Thus, despite the still high value of M, the still-activated system would be suddenly shifted from externally to internally driven. We might expect low bizarreness scores in these reports which would be dream-like mainly on the basis of imagery. As activation then fell rapidly, the low SI would no longer be capable of sustaining imagery in the system and the nonperceptual plodding thought of NREM sleep would ensue.

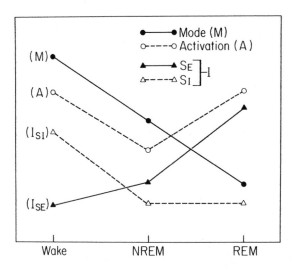

FIG. 12.7   How Factors A, I & M change over the Sleep Cycle. The values for mode (M) decline progressively from wake to REM while the level of internal stimulation (I_{SE}) reciprocally increases. External stimulus strength (I_{SI}) declines at sleep onset as does the general activation level A. But while external stimulus strength remains low in REM, the activation strength rises again to waking level. The AIM model explains the major differences in cognitive states in terms of these changes in brain physiology.

The transition from NREM to REM sleep may begin as early as midway through the first NREM period. The factors $SI(\uparrow)$ and $M(\downarrow)$ would all be tending to lower the value of S at a time when the increase in A could again be high enough to support dream-like mentation. These reports would be expected to be increasingly both bizarre and visual with pulsatile increases in the factor SI responsible for phasic increases in D-like content, although the EEG signs of NREM sleep would still be present.

Considerations such as these tell us that our psychophysiology is both incomplete and erroneous because we are still using superficial methods to assess brain physiology (especially the EEG). But even if we were able to record neuronal activity in humans, we might need not only instantaneous discharge rate values (as in this preliminary consideration) but the first or even the second differential of those neuronal discharge rates. By introducing exponential components to measure the change in rate or the rate of change in rate, we might better assess the inertia of the system. But that is for a future elaboration of the theory.

SUMMARY AND CONCLUSIONS

It has been the purpose of this chapter to outline a new model of brain state with special reference to the states of mind that are likely to be its subjective concomitants. Based upon the observations of neurophysiologists studying the brain of experimental animals as it spontaneously changes state from waking through NREM sleep to REM, three factors are defined: activation (*A*), input source (*I*), and mode of processing (*M*).

Activation (*A*) is defined as the discharge rate of neurons in the reticular activating system on the assumption that such rates are, at a first approximation, measures of the energy level of the system or its capacity to do the work of information processing. This activation factor brings the model into register with state-of-the-art cognitive neuroscience. When *A* is high (in waking and REM sleep) information processing is equally rapid, though it may differ qualitatively.

Input source (*I*) is defined as the ratio of external (*SE*) to internal (*SI*) sensory stimulus strength. When *I* is high (in waking), cognition tends to be related to external stimulus properties. When it is low (in dreaming), internal stimulus properties dominate and external world reference is lost. Aspects of dream cognition attributable to this factor include visual hallucinosis, stereotypy, and automaticity with sense of total perceptual involvement with a scenario beyond one's control being the hallmark.

Mode of processing (*M*) is defined as the rate of brain stem aminergic neuronal discharge on the assumption that critical aspects of cognition are determined by the shift from a level of high noradrenergic and serotonergic modulation of the cortex (in waking) to a negligibly low level in REM sleep. Since levels of cholinergic–neuronal discharge are as high in REM as in waking (and hence can be modeled as *A*), then REM sleep is not only hypo-aminergic but, relatively, hypercholinergic. Cognitive features possibly attributable to this factor include attention, self-reference, orientation, and memory.

In an effort to combine the three factors so as to obtain a unidimensional estimate of brain state *S,* a multiplicative combination of realistic values of A, I, and M may be made. The resulting solution has a wide range of values. A three-dimensional conception is also useful to explore the effect of realistic values of *A, I,* and *M* upon the position of *S* as a point in a state space. Finally, an extension of the model to other conditions such as coma, hallucinosis, and EST is suggested.

ACKNOWLEDGMENT

This work was supported by USPHS Grant MH13923. I am grateful to John Antrobus and Adam Mamelak for helpful suggestions.

REFERENCES

Anderson, J. (1985). *Cognitive psychology and its implications.* New York: W. H. Freeman (2d ed.).

Antrobus, J. (1991). Dreaming: Cognitive processes during cortical activation and high afferent thresholds. *Psychological Review, 98,* 96–121.

Callaway, C. W., Lydic, R., Baghdoyan, H. A., & Hobson, J. A. (1987). Pontogeniculooccipital waves: spontaneous visual system activation occurring in REM sleep. *Cellular and Molecular Neurobiology, 7,* 105–149.

Cespuglio, R., Rion, F., Buda, M., Faradji. H., Gonon, F., Jouvet, M., & Pujol, J. F. (1980). Mesure in vivo, par voltametrie impulsionelle differentielle, du 5-HIAA dans le striatum du rat [The effect of 5-HIAA on differential spike voltage in the rat, measured in vivo]. *C.R. Academy of Science, 290,* 901–906.

Flicker, C., McCarley, R. W., & Hobson, J. A. (1981). Aminergic neurons: State control and plasticity in three model systems. *Cellular and Molecular Neurobiology, 1,* 123–166.

Hobson, J. A. (1988). Homeostasis and heteroplasticity: A new theory of the functional significance of behavioral state consequences in clinical physiology of sleep. *American Physiological Society,* 1988, 199–220.

Hobson, J. A., & McCarley, R. W. (1977). The brain as a dream-state generator: An activation-synthesis hypothesis of the dream process. *American Journal of Psychiatry, 134,* 1335–1368.

Hobson, J. A., & Steriade, M. (1986). Neuronal basis of behavioral state control. In V. Mountcastle & F. E. Bloom (Eds.), *Handbook of physiology: The nervous system* (Vol 4, pp. 701–823). Bethesda, MD: American Physiological Association.

Jasper, H. H., & Tessier, J. (1971) Acetylcholine liberation from cerebral cortex during paradoxical (REM) sleep. *Science, 172,* 601–602.

McCarley R. W., & Hobson, J. A. (1975). Neuronal excitability modulation over the sleep cycle: A structural and mathematical model. *Science, 189,* 58–60.

McCarley, R. W., & Massaquoi, S. G. (1986). A limit cycle mathematical model of the REM sleep oscillator system. *American Journal of Physiology, 251,* (Regulatory Integrative Comp. Physiology 20) R1011–R1029.

Ungerstedt, U., Forster, C., Herrera-Marschitz, M., Hoffman, I., Jungnelius, U., Tossman, U., & Zetterström, T. (1982). Brain dialysis – a new in vivo technique for studying neurotransmitter release and metabolism. *Neuroscience Letters, Supplement 10,* 493.

Vogel, G. W. (1978). An alternative view of the neurobiology of dreaming. *American Journal of Psychiatry, 135* 1531–1535.

Zetterström, T., Sharp, T., Marsden, C. A., & Ungerstedt, U. (1983). In vivo measurement of dopamine and its metabolites by intracerebral dialysis: Changes after d-amphetamine. *Journal of Neurochemistry, 41,* 1769–1773.

13 Phasic Integrated Potentials and Ego Boundary Deficits

Robert Watson
*Yale University School of Medicine, and New Haven Sleep
Disorders Center*

Ponto–geniculo–occipital (PGO) spikes may be the most critical phasic physiological event associated with REM sleep. PGO spikes have been studied extensively in animals with depth electrodes, but cannot be recorded directly in humans. Phasic integrated potentials (PIPs) recorded from the eye muscles may be one correlate of PGO activity in humans (Rechtschaffen, Molinari, Watson, & Wincor, 1970). Like PGO spikes, most PIPs are concentrated within REM sleep, although some are scattered in NREM sleep. PIPs, and PGO spikes, always accompany rapid eye movements during REM, but may also occur without rapid eye movements. The amount of NREM PIP activity is an individual characteristic; that is, someone who has many NREM PIPS on one night will have many on the next, whereas someone who has relatively few NREM PIPs on one night will have few on the next. A number of studies have been carried out on the relationship between PIPs and mental activity during sleep, PIPs and psychosis, and PIPs and individual differences in personality.

PIPs are associated with more bizarre and disorganized dream reports elicited from REM sleep (Watson 1972; Watson, Bliwise, Friedman, Wax, & Rechtschaffen, 1978). Middle-ear muscle activity (MEMA), which may be another indicator of PGO activity in humans, has also been reported to be associated with more bizarre reports from REM sleep (Ogilvie, Hunt, Sawicki, & Samanhalskyi, 1982). PIPs have been found to be associated with more bizarre reports of NREM mentation (Bliwise & Rechtschaffen, 1978; Rechtschaffen, Watson, Wincor, Molinari, & Barta, 1972).

Watson, Liebmann, and Watson (1976a) found that the NREM PIP frequencies of five acute psychotic patients were much elevated during the first 2 weeks of their hospital admission, but were significantly reduced in frequency during the final weeks of their hospitalization during partial remission. The night-to-night amount of NREM PIP activity was significantly correlated with repeated independent ratings on the New Haven Schizophrenia Index. Rechtschaffen, Litchman, Pivik, and Bliwise (1978), however, did not find a significant increase in NREM PIP activity in groups of psychotic patients recorded just at the beginning of their hospitalization, compared with a normal control group.

Rechtschaffen et al. (1978) did find that in a group of normal college women a greater amount of NREM PIP activity was significantly associated with higher scores on the schizophrenia scale and the manifest anxiety scale of the MMPI. One interpretation may be that NREM PIPs are related to individual differences in control over anxiety and openness to strange experience. Watson, Liebmann, and Watson (1976b), studying 26 hospitalized psychiatric patients, found that the amount of NREM PIP activity was significantly related to the number of human movement responses on the Rorschach elicited from the patients the next morning. That study was replicated with a group of normal men (Watson, Butler, & Liebmann, 1983). The study of PIPs and Rorschach suggests that individuals with more NREM PIPs show signs of greater imagination and richer inner life than those with relatively few NREM PIPs.

All these studies taken together suggest that PIPs, and PGO activity, may be associated with a loose organization of both waking and sleep cognition. Whatever neurophysiological mechanisms underlie the distribution of PIPs during sleep may be related to cognitive variables that have to do with imagination, control of anxiety, openness to strange experience, vulnerability to psychosis, and to relative strength or weakness of ego boundaries.

In the present study, we looked at the amount of PIP activity in relationship to ego boundary deficits. Subjects were 15 men ranging in age from 19 to 48, with a mean age of 28.8, who were recruited by a newspaper advertisement. None was taking medication. None was in psychiatric treatment, although later the psychological test results of some of the patients would suggest underlying thought disorders. The patients slept 1 night in the laboratory, where in addition to standard EEG, EOG, and submental EMG, two channels of PIPs were continuously recorded, using standard electrodes placed lateral to and just below the eyes. The records were scored using the Rechtschaffen–Kales system. In addition, PIPs were scored as the frequency of one or more PIPs occurring within 2.5-s intervals both in NREM sleep and in REM sleep. The scoring was done by a technician who was blind to the results of the Rorschach testing.

The morning after their night in the sleep laboratory, the subjects were administered a Rorschach by a psychologist who was unaware of the results of the PIP recordings. The PIP protocols were later scored by two psychologists who were also blind to the results of the PIP recordings, using an ego boundary deficit scoring system developed by Ernest Hartmann with Ilana Sivan in his study of lifelong nightmare sufferers (Hartmann, 1984). In this scoring system, points are given to Rorschach responses that are suggestive of ego boundary deficits by revealing amorphousness, incongruous combinations of images, merging of separate ideas, and a sense of vulnerability and of penetration. A few examples may help illustrate the scoring system. Ego boundary deficit points would be given to the following responses: "This looks like one of those battered paintings where people just throw colors on a screen and it is all disconnected," "Two squirrels standing on a gigantic acorn," "This is a transparent person; you can see his lungs," "A man and woman in the same person." "This is a figure falling upside-down into a void." Much of the ego boundary deficit scoring system developed by Hartmann and Sivan follows the classical Rorschach scoring for pathological thinking devised by Rapaport, Gill, and Schafer (1946), Holt and Havel (1960), and Blatt and Ritzler (1974). However, the system scores responses on the basis of content as well as the formal quality of the responses. For example, the Rorschach response "snails outside of their shells" does not necessarily show formal thought pathology, but is scored in the present system based on the theme of being exposed and vulnerable. The scores attained by the two psychologists were highly correlated ($r = +.93$), and the two sets of scores were averaged.

The relative frequency of NREM PIPs was significantly related to higher scores on the ego boundary deficit scale ($r = +.516$, $p < .05$). That is, those in the sample of "normal" men who had relatively more NREM PIP activity showed greater signs of ego boundary deficits on the Rorschach; those men with relatively few NREM PIPs revealed stronger ego boundaries.

The results of the present study are consistent with the findings of other studies of PIPs. That is, PIPs, and probably PGO activity, are associated with the looser organization of both waking and sleeping cognition. The amount or distribution of PIPs during sleep may be associated with underlying neurophysiological events that generate individual differences in personality and cognition. A person with relatively few NREM PIPs, whose PIPs are well organized and confined almost entirely to REM sleep, would tend to show better control over his or her anxiety, to have relatively rigid and firm ego boundaries, to be less imaginative, to be less vulnerable to strange and odd experiences and generally to be more predictable and in a sense better organized. A "normal" person with a relative abundance of NREM PIP activity might tend to have less control over one's anxiety, to have more fluid ego boundaries, to be more imaginative and creative, and to have perhaps a more flexible and loosely organized cognitive style. One could speculate further that, carried to an extreme, someone with these traits might be vulnerable to psychosis.

REFERENCES

Blatt, S. J., & Ritzler, B. A. (1974). Thought disorder and the boundary disturbances in psychosis. *Journal of Consulting and Clinical Psychology, 42,* 370–381.

Bliwise, D., & Rechtschaffen, A. (1978). Phasic EMG in human sleep: III. Periorbital potentials and NREM mentation. *Sleep Research, 27,* 58.

Hartmann, E. (1984). *The nightmare.* New York: Basic Books.

Holt, R. R., & Havel, J. (1960). A method for assessing primary and secondary process in the Rorschach. In M. A. Rickers–Ovsinkina (Ed.), *Rorschach psychology,* (pp. 263–315). New York: Wiley.

Ogilvie, R., Hunt, H., Sawicki, C., & Samanhalskyi, J. (1982). Ogilvie Psychological correlates of spontaneous middle ear muscle activity during sleep. *Sleep, 5,* 11–27.

Rapaport, D., Gill, M. M., & Schafer, R. (1946). *Diagnostic physological testing* (Vol. 2). Chicago: Year Book.

Rechtschaffen, A., Bliwise, D., & Litchman, J. (1978). Phasic EMG in human sleep: V. PIPs and MMPI scores in normals. *Sleep Research, 7,* 60.

Rechtschaffen, A., & Chernick, D. (1972). The effect of REM deprivation on periorbital spike activity in NREM sleep. *Psychophysiology, 9,* 128.

Rechtschaffen, A., & Kales, A. (Eds.). (1968). *A manual of standardized terminology, and scoring system for sleep stages of human subjects.* Washington, DC: U. S. Government Printing Office.

Rechtschaffen, A., Litchman, J., Pivik, T., & Bliwise, D. (1978). Phasic EMG in human sleep: VI. PIPs in acute psychotics. *Sleep Research, 7,* 61.

Rechtschaffen, A., Molinari, S., Watson, R., Wincor, M. (1970). Extraocular potentials: A possible indicator of PGO activity in the human. *Psychophysiology, 7,* 336.

Rechtschaffen, A., Watson, R., Wincor, R., Molinari, S., & Barta, S. (1972). The relationship of phasic and tonic periorbital EMG activity to NREM mentation. *Sleep Research, 1,* 123.

Watson, R., (1972). Mental correlates of periorbital PIPs during REM sleep. *Sleep Research, 1,* 75.

Watson, R. Bliwise, D., Friedman, L., Wax, D., & Rechtschaffen, A. (1978). Phasic EMG in human sleep: II. Periorbital potentials and REM mentation. *Sleep Research, 7,* 57.

Watson, R., Butler, S., & Liebmann, K. (1983). Individual differences in the Rorschach M response and the distribution of phasic integrated potentials (PIPs) during sleep. *Perceptual and Motor Skills, 57,* 507–514.

Watson, R., Liebmann, K., & Watson, S. (1976a). Comparison of NREM PIP frequency in schizophrenic and non-schizophrenic patients. *Sleep Research, 5,* 154.

Watson, R., Liebmann, K., & Watson, S. (1976b). Individual differences in frequency in NREM PIPs and Rorschach scores. *Sleep Research, 5,* 153.

14

Transmutative and Reproductive Properties of Dreams: Evidence for Cortical Modulation of Brain-stem Generators

John H. Herman
Department of Psychiatry, University of Texas
Southwestern Medical Center at Dallas

INTRODUCTION

Sufficient data have been accumulated through sleep and dream research to permit a re-examination of the recollected dream and the concurrently occurring phasic activity of the REM state. This chapter contends that the REM sleep dream, strictly from the standpoint of manifest content, may be examined from both a narrative and a sensory–motor level. Equally exhaustive information can be elicited with respect to the dreamer's recollection of the sensory–motor activity in the dream or the more traditional description of the dreamed narrative. The manifest content contains both a narrative story line, or plot, and a plethora of detail that is equivalent to the dreamer's waking experience of the sensory world and its proprioceptive feedback. These details are readily elicited with careful questioning. Furthermore, it is hypothesized that the dream re-creates the waking perceptual experiences of the dreamer with a degree of verisimilitude not usually appreciated. Far from bizarre, waking perceptual experience reappears in the dream in remarkably lifelike detail.

In humans, phasic activity may be assessed in REM sleep by monitoring neuromuscular contractions. The relationship of this muscle activity to dream content may be assessed in laboratory studies in which the subject is awakened from REM sleep. It is argued *that motor activity during REM sleep is the neuromuscular equivalent of the hallucinated images and actions of the dreamer.* In summary, this chapter will present evidence that the nocturnal world of oneiric hallucinations re-creates the waking world, transmogrified though it may be, at cognitive, perceptual, and sensory–motor levels.

It is postulated that in the intact nervous system, cortical influences modulate certain aspects of the timing and patterning of brain stem activation during the REM state, not completely vice versa. This chapter hypothesizes the existence of descending systems providing corticofugal modulation of the pontine and midbrain generators of the ascending ponto-geniculo-occipital (PGO) neurons underlying phasic activity in REM sleep. Of course, such pathways have not yet been elucidated.

SENSORY DETAIL IN DREAMS

We intuitively "tell" others about our dreams much like we tell stories, typically describing the action and the participants. We recall only important visual details upon which events hinge (Foulkes, 1978). In general, sensory details in the dream content are mostly irrelevant to the description of the dream. The fact that the dreamer remembers turning to the right, lifting a hand, or noticing the color of wallpaper is seldom included in the dream as it is told. Nevertheless, the impression is quite common that more detail was present than available to waking memory. The dream is a multisensorial recreation of everyday perceptual and motor experiences within which a narrative is built, characters interact, and a plot unfolds. While others stress the "bizarreness" of the dream narrative (Hoffman, Kostner, Helfand, & Hobson, 1984), they ignore the consistently concrete collusiveness of sensory motor detail.

Similar to reports following REM sleep awakenings in our laboratory in which questioning reveals sensory detail, Freud's "specimen dream," the first that he interpreted rigorously in *The Interpretation of Dreams* (Freud, 1900-1955), could also be approached from a sensory in addition to a narrative manner. He reports dreaming of "a large hall — numerous guests, whom we were receiving — among them was Irma. I at once took her to one side. . . ." (Freud, 1900-1955. Thus the dream report begins. Although irrelevant to Freud's focus upon the ensuing interaction among himself, Irma, and Dr. M., one could ignore the story of the injection that follows and focus instead upon sensory detail. What did the hall look like? What was Freud wearing? Was he standing or seated? Who does "we" refer to? Just as in recollecting events in the awake state, in dream reporting, seemingly irrelevant details are typically ignored.

When a technician awakens a sleeping laboratory subject from REM sleep and initiates an inquiry to ascertain certain aspects of dream recall, a process is begun in which *the nature of the questioning determines greatly what material will be reported.* For instance, one typical approach involves asking the subject to report everything. The experimenter's misconception would be to confuse the supposedly exhaustive report of the subject for the totality of material consciously available. That is, in all probability, sensory detail would still be excluded. A second approach, equally fraught with the potential for omitting recollected material, is the use of a questionnaire to inquire along predetermined routes relevant to the particular experimental hypothesis.

Following the approach of encouraging spontaneous dream description, the subject's report is typically limited to a narrative entwining actions, sequences, and locations. The narrative follows a temporal progression characteristically ending with the subject's recollection of the awakening. The interviewer, in this type of experimental design, usually asks certain questions at this point: "Was there anything else?," "Do you recall any other scenes or events?," "Do you have anything more to add?".

Studies of dream reports from our laboratory suggest that this approach totally neglects a nonnarrative substratum of recollected material consciously available. Following, by way of an example, is the thematic content voluntarily provided by a subject immediately subsequent to an awakening followed by additional sensory detail elicited through specific questions.

This subject had been trained to focus upon and report the last 10 s of dreamed narrative prior to and ending with the experimental awakening. The subject was in a study investigating the relationship between eye movements and dream imagery in which he was awakened and questioned by an experimenter in a double-blind protocol. Each awakening followed a burst of eye movements (Herman, Erman, Boys, Peiser, Taylor, & Roffwarg, 1984).

About 8 to 10 s prior to the awakening, the subject dreamed that he was driving his car at night toward the Houston Astrodome, about a mile away. His father was seated to his right and a group of joggers ran along the side of the car to his left. He didn't remember what preceded this scene, nor did he recollect talking to his father. As the runners approached the car threateningly, the subject recounted becoming apprehensive and at that moment being awakened. This chapter asserts that accepting the spontaneous portrayal described here as the complete dream narrative fails to fathom an equally impressive category of available material that may be referred to as the sensory and motor infrastructure of the dream.

In support of this assertion, the following material from the same awakenings is presented. Through further questioning, the subject demonstrated that he was as capable of reporting the sequence of shifts of gaze prior to the awakening as he was capable of describing the progres,ion of dreamed events: he looked from the Astrodome to the joggers whom he watched for 2 s as they ran in the same direction as his car. Next, he turned his head to look at his father in the passenger's seat for 2 s. He then glanced back to the joggers for less than a second, and finally stared in the direction of the Astrodome for the 2 s immediately prior to the awakening.

The subject was able to describe the Astrodome in some detail as well as the tall grass on either side of the road. His left arm rested on the open window frame, his right hand gripped the top of the steering wheel. He felt his foot push on the gas pedal when he experienced apprehension because of the menace of the joggers. He remembered that his head as well as his eyes moved with glances from left to right and back. Potholes in the road could be seen in front of the car. He could hear the car's engine. He felt the warm night air.

In order to obtain the additional details described, exhaustive examination of a brief segment of the dream was required. These details provide evidence of a substratum of sensory and motor detail that is available, *but not voluntarily reported* in the so-called "complete" dream narrative. Admittedly, most subjects are not capable of recalling dreams in this type of detail. Similarly, research has shown that most individuals cannot describe their waking surround or their previous direction of eye movements in *any more detail* than they are able to describe dreams (Bussel, Dement, & Pivik, 1972). The subject in our experiment was specifically selected for several reasons. One was his ability to recall pre-awakening dream experience copiously and with certainty. Another was his capability to state with equal certainty when he did *not* recollect an aspect of dream activity.

Nevertheless, the suspicion could still exist in the critical reader that such precise recall from REM awakenings contains embellishments to please the experimenter or could be affected by experimental bias. In double-blind experiments, including the foregoing one, any biased responses would *decrease* the probability of detecting a significant psychophysiological relationship such as between eye movements and shifts of gaze in the dream. Therefore, the experimenter's bias was to minimize possible embellishments. As part of another experiment, we conducted a study of four subjects with whom a deliberate attempt was made to induce bias (Roffwarg, Herman, Bowe–Anders, & Tauber, 1978). Without describing the study, the results may be summarized by stating that each of the bias-control subjects manifested direct evidence of resisting attempts by the experimenter to suggest what was "expected" to be contained in dream recall. A third line of evidence that the reporting of sensory detail in response to experimental inquiry is not artifactual is the manner in which subjects report it: They do so with a certainty equal to their description of the dream narrative. Why then, should the sensory detail be suspect any more than the dream narrative?

To summarize our arguments against sensory detail being the result of fabrication: (1) Because of the subject's ability to state both that he or she does or does not recollect asked for details (such as direction of gaze); (2) Because of the demonstration of reasonable resistance to experimenter bias, and (3) Because of the general level of subject's certainty with regard to sensory and motor detail, we are reasonably confident that much of the material provided by subjects in response to detailed inquiry is as free of confabulation as any aspect of dream recall.

MODIFICATION OF DREAM IMAGERY BY RECENT EXPERIENCE

The dream described (Herman, et al., 1984) is an example of the near-complete manner in which sensory modalities are present in detail far beyond that necessary to weave a narrative or plot. What then, would be the functional significance of a hallucinatory experience re-creating virtually every afferent system as well as incorporating neuromuscular sensations? That is, simultaneous with the dream narrative, a plethora of detail exists that for all appearances is totally superfluous to conveying plot, story, or narrative.

Let us begin to approach the foregoing question by examining three properties of the Astrodome dream and all REM dreaming relevant to sensory–motor activity in REM sleep. First, experimental evidence from our laboratory indicates that the visual properties of the dream are re-creations of sensory impressions from the awake state in the recent past (Roffwarg, et al., 1978). That is, the colors, forms, and perceptual qualities of dreams are, in some part, the direct product of recent sensory impressions. This is in contrast to the more notable level of dream recall that employs significant thematic material, including characters, actions, and plot. What is being referred to as the perceptual substratum of dreaming includes the colors, forms, sense of perspective, and the physical sense of self, including limb, trunk, and head position. The various sensory elements of dreaming are derived from recent sensory and sensory–motor experience in the awake state.

We describe an experiment in which continuous modification of chromatic properties of waking visual perception resulted in the alteration of colors in dreams (Roffwarg, et al., 1978). In this experiment, the subjects wore goggles throughout the day containing Wratten No. 29 red filters that excluded *all* light of wavelengths less than 600 millimicrons. These goggles were worn every waking minute with the exception of brief rest periods when the subjects' eyes were closed (covered with black patches). No light of normal chromatic properties was seen by the subject throughout this entire phase of the experiment. A fundamental but unappreciated constancy of dream construction was made evident by *changing* visual experience in waking. The visual experience created by looking through colored filters was replicated in the construction of the visual surround of dream settings (e.g., rooms, furniture, clothing, lawns, trees, lights, and sky) as each became transformed into colors similar to those observed through the filters during the preceding few days (Roffwarg, et al., 1978).

First REM periods were found to be most affected by the preceding day's visual experience, requiring only 1 day for penetrance of the goggle effect in half of dreamt "scenes". Within a week, penetrance was evident in latter REM periods as well. Although the experiment was limited to demonstrating that visual characteristics of dreams may be rapidly modified by altering waking visual experience, we postulate that modification of *any* sensory or motor system in the awake state would result in a corresponding alteration of the representation of that system in dream content.

This demonstration of the relevance of recent perceptual input indicates that a continuous "refreshing" process is operative with regard to the visual–perceptual aspects of the dream. What could be the significance of hallucinated representation of sensory and motor systems during the REM state that shows evidence of rapid modification as well as the ability to incorporate recent perceptual motor experiences?

THE RELATIONSHIP OF DREAMING TO CONCURRENT MOTOR ACTIVITY

The third property of REM sleep dreaming that is of relevance involves the near-total authenticity with which the oculomotor system in the REM state re-creates patterns of waking eye movement activity. For example, the characteristics of saccadic eye movements in REM sleep are similar to those of waking eye movements with the eye lids closed (Herman, Barker, Rampy, & Roffwarg, 1987; Herman, Barker, & Roffwarg, 1983; Jeannerod & Mouret, 1962). In contrast to what would be expected, REM saccades are most similar, in velocity and pattern, to waking eye movements when the head and eyes move in synchrony, and not similar to eye movements in the awake state when the head is still (Herman, Barker, Rampy, & Roffwarg, 1987; Herman, Barker, & Roffwarg, 1983). This finding is somewhat enigmatic because the head does not move with the eyes during REM sleep.

In the awake state, the eyes rotate to align the object of regard so that its image strikes the fovea to maximize visual acuity. Linked by the vestibulo-ocular reflex, reflexive head movements in addition to eye movements combine to determine gaze direction. The pattern of eye movements accompanied by head movements is readily distinguishable from the pattern of eye movements alone. With the head restrained, eye movements mostly occur singly, usually separated by at least 150 ms (Carpenter, 1977). In contrast, when accompanied by head movements, ocular activity most frequently occurs in a burst pattern formed by sequences of eye and head movements (Meiry, 1971). The vestibulo-ocular reflex initiates compensatory saccades in a burst-like pattern to compensate for the continual motion of the head (Meiry, 1971).

In waking, head movements influence the velocity of eye movements, their duration, and amplitude (Morasso, Bizzi, & Dichgns, 1973). In the awake state, only with the head in motion may a rotatory component be observed in saccadic eye movements. With the head stationary, rotatory components are absent from saccadic trajectories (Nakayama, 1975). These characteristics of head–movement–type eye movements are provided to indicate how distinguishable they are from eye movements without head movements.

Contrary to the immobility of head and neck during the REM dream, we demonstrated that the eye movements of REM sleep are most similar to those of the awake state when the head is free to move. This was observed with regard to each of the parameters that have been described: velocity, intersaccadic interval, burst pattern, and the presence of rotatory components (Herman, et al., 1987; Herman, et al., 1983).

The demonstration of head-movement-type eye movements in REM sleep implies yet another level of "memory" or "encoding" that is manifest in neuromuscular systems during the REM state: REM sensory (dream memory) and motor (phasic) events replicate many details of awake-state sensory and motor experience. *The characteristics of REM sleep eye movements are more congruent with the hallucinated locomotion within the dream than with the postural immobility of the dreamer.*

THE REM DREAM AS A RE-CREATION OF AWAKE-STATE ACTIVE BEHAVIOR

Another property of sensory–motor systems during REM dreams relevant to this chapter is the demonstrated relationship between shifts of gaze in the dream and the direction of the EOG-recorded eye movements (Dement & Kleitman, 1957; Dement & Wolpert, 1958; Herman et al., 1984; Roffwarg, Dement, Muzio, & Fisher, 1962). A degree of concordance exists among the number, direction, and amplitude of REM-sleep eye movements and the shifts of gaze described in postawakening interrogations (Herman, et al., 1984). In the Houston Astrodome dream, the direction of EOG activity was consistent with the subject's description of looking back and forth between joggers and father (Herman, et al., 1984). This study demonstrated that dreamed gaze and REM-sleep eye movements are directionally linked. Various authors have employed logical arguments, based on the presence of REM eye movements in the decerebrate cat or the continuation of eye movements in REM sleep in blind individuals, to argue against a relationship to dream imagery (Oswald, 1962). A major premise of this chapter is that with respect to dreaming, *the functional organization of the REM state may only be examined in the intact human.*

The relationship of eye movements to dream imagery is but one of a number of psychophysiological correspondences in the REM sleep of humans (Cohen, 1979). Nevertheless, the oculomotor system represents a special case of the concordance between mentation and neuromuscular activity. The extra-ocular muscles, similar to the middle ear muscles, are innervated by cranial nerves and are spared the skeletal muscle atonia of the REM state. Thus, eye movements are a case of a relatively uninhibited expression of motor activity in REM sleep. Only with eye movements may we attain a level of specificity (i.e., direction) sufficient to demonstrate the nature of the concordance between the REM dream and concurrent phasic events.

To summarize our contentions to this point: First, dreaming involves both a narrative and a sensory–motor level, the latter demonstrating none of the "bizareness" that others claim characterizes dream content (Hoffman et al., 1984; Mamelak & Hobson, 1989). Secondly, the REM sleep sensory–motor material is a re-creation of recent perceptual–motor experience from the awake state and may be readily modified by altering perceptual experience. Thirdly, in some systems, the phasic muscular contractions of the REM state are more similar to the properties of those same muscles in an active, moving individual than to that of an immobile sleeper. Fourthly, a concordance may be demonstrated between discrete events in the dream and specific systems (e.g., eye movements) that are spared neuromuscular atonia during the REM state. Therefore, it may be argued that the thematic narrative of the dream, the sensory–motor aspects of dream content, and the neuromuscular discharges that occur during dreaming (REM sleep only) are isomorphic. If this be the case, there is the clear implication that cortical centers related to dreaming must modulate and perhaps "gate" brain stem and midbrain regions responsible for the propagation of PGO spikes.

NEUROPHYSIOLOGICAL EVIDENCE OF CORTICOFUGAL PATHWAYS ACTIVE IN THE REM STATE

In a landmark publication, Jeannerod (Jeannerod, 1966) described the effects of decerebration upon REM sleep oculomotor activity in the cat. Of significance was the observation of the continuation of periods of eye movements accompanied by postural atonia, or clear indications of REM sleep subsequent to decerebration. This finding was taken by many to indicate that the necessary and sufficient structures for the occurrence of REM sleep under *normal* conditions were restricted to brain stem and midbrain locations.

Reviewing Jeannerod's publication, in comparison with baseline values, the postoperative decerebrate cat evidenced qualitative and quantitative alterations in the properties of "REM state" eye movement activity accompanying skeletal atonia. First, there was a reduction in the total number of eye movements by approximately 80%. Secondly, the propensity for eye movements to occur in bursts was eliminated. Thirdly, what remained of ocular activity during atonia, both from the authors' description and clear in their illustrations (p. 34), were repetitive and stereotypical eye movements, that is, in the same direction and separated by regular intervals (Jeannerod, 1966).

The occurrence of stereotypical eye movement patterns subsequent to decerebration in the cat during atonia was also reportedly by Mergner and Pompeiano (1981). During atonic episodes, the animals exhibited uniform bursts of three to six horizontal saccades separated by extremely regular intervals of ocular quiescence. Their report provides no statistical evidence or illustrations of the pre-operative animals to allow critical comparison. The disparity between the stereotypical and unchanging eye movement pattern during atonia in both of these reports (Jeannerod, 1966; Mergner & Pompeiano, 1981) is in sharp contrast to the variable and irregular pattern normally observed.

Gadea–Ciria (1976) reported that bilateral frontal lobectomy caused more regular intervals between both eye movements and PGO waves in the cat. Frontal combined with occipital lobectomy lead to a further reduction in the frequency of and variability in intervals between eye movements. The author concludes that *specific cortical areas modulate the sequential pattern of brain stem discharges and associated eye movements.*

This finding demonstrates (1) that the cerebral cortex is not necessary for the expression of periodic episodes neurophysologically similar to the REM state and (2) that there are differences in oculomotor discharge patterns between the normal and decerebrate cat. Therefore, Jeannerod (Jeannerod, 1966), Mergner and Pompeiano, and Gadea–Ciria's (1976) decerebrate preparations indicate *a cortical contribution to the properties to REM phasic events.* Each of these investigators describes stereotypical, repetitive saccades in the decorticate expression of REM sleep, totally different from normal oculomotor patterns. The variegated and irregular properties of REM-sleep phasic discharge in the intact brain is, in some manner, under cortical control.

Thus, there is evidence that patterns and quantities of brain stem phasic discharge during the REM state are modulated by extrapontine mechanisms in the intact organism. The descending pathways from cortical centers active during dreaming remain to be elucidated. Various authors (Parmeggiani, Morrison, Drucker–Colin, & McGinty, 1985) have argued against the use of reductionist experiments (e.g., decorticate preparation) in which component elements are studied under abnormal conditions and then used to formulate a model for normal sleep. These authors argue for a diffuse or global view of sleep and arousal "modulated by virtually every brain site (p. 19)." The "aggregate" quality of sleep, they maintain, is of critical importance and defies the search for putative sleep centers. McCarley and Ito (1985), while reiterating the unambiguous evidence for the existence of REM pontine generators, recognize the possible role of suprapontine input in the intact organism. The evidence for modulatory influence of an extrapontine locus that the authors site is the "less complex" nature of eye movements and PGO waves in the pontine cat (McCarley & Ito, 1985). Morrison and Reiner (1985) do not believe that the evidence for a pontine initiation of REM sleep is compelling, and suggest that episodes of REM sleep in the decerebrate cat could be triggered abnormally by the absence of normal modulatory inputs (Morrison & Reiner, 1985).

Earlier in this chapter, evidence was presented for an isomorphism between the narrative content of dreams, the multisensorial perceptual aspects of dream recall, and the various systems exhibiting phasic discharge during the REM state. Furthermore, evidence was forwarded indicating that a multilevel correspondence exists between dream experience and waking sensory–motor perception. It is argued that cortical involvement integrates the multiple levels of brain processes activated during the REM state. Pontine generating mechanisms may be necessary and sufficient for the physiological expression of atonia and phasic activity in the cat. In the intact, adult human, comprehending the multiple levels and multiple facets of dream/REM activity is most parsimonious only with a model including descending influences from forebrain structures.

Perhaps the most striking aspect of the dream/REM process is the near-total re-creation of the waking world. This chapter demonstrates that the extent of correspondence and verisimilitude is even greater than previously appreciated. The REM-state dream creates an environment that, for all intensive purposes, *is* the waking experience of the dreamer (Foulkes, 1983). Morrison and Reiner (1985) state that the CNS during REM sleep is in a state of continual orientation, and that the similarity of this state to alert wakefulness is profound. These authors claim that the task of sleep researchers is to discover how REM sleep and waking *differ,* "for there probably lies the secret of PS (REM sleep)." There is little doubt that the decerebrate human would suffer uniformly in the awake state and REM sleep, despite the continued presence of physiological evidence of the continuation of both.

Clearly, the process that we describe involves all levels of the central nervous system: forebrain, midbrain, and brain stem. The data in this chapter strongly argue for a REM-state executive role carried out by forebrain structures. In answer to questions raised earlier in this chapter concerning the function of dreams, the activation of the central nervous system in a manner similar to awake state experience emerges as a central feature. The brain does not know it is dreaming. Our studies do not support a model in which a passive cortex merely submits docilely to incoming volleys from subcortical structures. Instead, these data suggest a forebrain with as much of an executive and control function in REM sleep as is present in waking.

REFERENCES

Bussel, J., Dement, W. & Pivik, T. (1972). The eye movement–imagery relationship in REM sleep and waking. In M. H. Chase, W. C. Stern, & P. L. Walter (Eds.), *Sleep research, 1,* (p. 100). Los Angeles: Brain Information Service/Brain Research Institute.

Carpenter, R. S. (1977). *Movements of the eyes* (pp. 60–64). London: Pion.

Cohen, D. B. (1979). *Sleep and dreaming: Origins, nature and functions* (pp. 183–206). Oxford; England: Pergamon.

Dement, W., & Kleitman, N. (1957). The relation of eye movements during sleep to dream activity: An objective method for studying dreaming. *Journal of Experimental Psychology, 53,* 339–346.

Dement, W., & Wolpert, E. A. (1958). The relation of eye movements, body motility, and external stimuli to dream content. *Journal of Experimental Psychology, 55,* 543–553.

Foulkes, D. (1978). *A grammar of dreams* (pp. 3–12). New York: Basic Books.

Foulkes, D. (1983). Cognitive processes during sleep. In A. Mayes (Ed.), *Sleep mechanisms and functions in humans and animals: An evolutionary perspective* (pp. 313–337). Cambridge, MA: Van Nostrand Reinhold.

Freud, S. (1900-1955). *The interpretation of dreams* (pp. 138–139). New York: Basic Books.

Gadea–Ciria, M. (1976). Sequential discharges of phasic activities (PGO waves) during paradoxical sleep after selective cortical lesions in the cat. *Archives Italiennes de Biologie, 114,* 399–408.

Herman, J., Barker, D., Rampy, P., & Roffwarg, H. (1987). Further evidence confirming the similarity of eye movements in REM sleep and the awake state. In M. H. Chase, D. J. McGinty, & C. O'Connor (Eds.), *Sleep research, 16* (p. 38). Los Angeles: Brain Information Service/Brain Research Institute.

Herman, J. H., Barker, D. R., & Roffwarg, H. P. (1983). Similarity of eye movement characteristics in REM sleep and the awake state. *Psychophysiology, 20,* 537–543.

Herman, J. H., Erman, M., Boys, R., Peiser, L., Taylor, M. E., & Roffwarg, H. P. (1984). Evidence for a directional correspondence between eye movements and dream imagery in REM sleep. *Sleep, 7,* 52–63.

Hoffman S., Kostner, D., Helfand R., & Hobson A. (1984). In M. H. Chase, W. B. Webb, & R. Wilder-Jones (Eds.), *Sleep Research, 13:* 120.

Jeannerod, M. (1966). Les phenomenes phasiques du sommeil paradoxal [phasic events in paradoxical sleep]. *Revue Lyonnaise de Medecine, 15,* 27–44.

Jeannerod, M., & Mouret, J. (1962). Etude des mouvements oculaires observeś chez l'homme au cours de la veille et du sommeil [Eye movements in humans during sleep and waking].

Societé de Biologie de Lyon, 25, 1407–1410.

Mamelak, A. N., & Hobson J. A. (1989). Dream bizarreness as the cognitive correlate of altered neuronal behavior in REM sleep. *Journal of Cognitive Neuroscience, 1,* 201–222.

McCarley, R. W., & Ito, R. (1985). Desynchronized sleep-specific changes in membrane potential and excitability in medial pontine reticular formation neurons: Implications for concepts and mechanisms of behavioral state control. In D. L. McGinty, R. Drucker-Colin, A. Morrison, & P. L. Parmeggiani (Eds.), *Brain mechanisms of sleep* (pp. 63–80). New York: Raven.

Meiry, J. L. (1971). Vestibular and proprioceptive stabilization of eye movements. In P. Bach-Y-Rita & C. C. Collins (Eds.), *The control of eye movements* (pp. 483–496). New York: Academic.

Mergner, T., & Pompeiano, O. (1981). Basic mechanisms for saccadic eye movements as revealed by sleep experiments. In A. Fuchs & W. Becker (Eds.), *Progress in oculomotor research* (pp. 107–114). Amsterdam: Elsevier.

Morasso, P., Bizzi, E., & Dichgns, J. (1973). Adjustment of saccade characteristics during head movements. *Experimental Brain Research, 16,* 492–500.

Morrison, A. R., & Reiner, P. B. (1985). A dissection of paradoxical sleep. In D. L. McGinty, R. Drucker-Colin, A. Morrison, & P. L. Parmeggiani (Eds.), *Brain mechanisms of sleep* (pp. 97–110). New York: Raven.

Nakayama, K. (1975). Coordination of extraocular muscles. In P. Bach-Y-Rita & C. C. Collins (Eds.), *The control of eye movements* (pp. 193–207). New York: Academic.

Oswald, I. (1962). *Sleeping and waking: Physiology and psychology.* Amsterdam: Elsevier.

Parmeggiani, P. L., Morrison, A., Drucker-Colin, R. R., & McGinty, D. (1985). Brain mechanisms of sleep: An overview of methodological issues. In D. J. McGinty, R. Drucker-Colin, A. Morrison, & P. L. Parmeggiani (Eds.), *Brain mechanisms of sleep* (pp. 1–34). New York: Raven.

Roffwarg, H. P., Dement, W. C., Muzio, J. N., & Fisher, C. (1962). Dream imagery: Relationship to rapid eye movements of sleep. *Archives of General Psychiatry, 7,* 235–258.

Roffwarg, H. P., Herman, J. H., Bowe-Anders, C., & Tauber, E. S. (1978). The effects of sustained alterations of waking visual input on dream content. In A. M. Arkin, J. S. Antrobus, & S. J. Ellman (Eds.), *The mind in sleep: Psychology and psychophysiology* (pp. 295–350). Hillsdale, NJ: Lawrence Erlbaum Associates.

IV LUCID DREAMING

15 Interhemispheric EEG Coherence in REM Sleep and Meditation: The Lucid Dreaming Connection

Jayne Gackenbach
University of Alberta/Athabasca University

The experience of dreaming lucidly, that is, awareness of dreaming while dreaming, has been suggested by Hunt (1989) to be a form of meditation in sleep. He identifies this dream state as "involving the attainment and maintenance of an attitude identical to that sought within the insight or mindfulness meditative traditions" (Hunt & McLeod, 1984, p. 3). Although empirical evidence in support of this view is briefly reviewed here, the focus of this chapter is a potential neurocognitive model for dream lucidity. The degree of interhemispheric balance (EEG coherence) reflecting an efficient transfer of information between the hemispheres will be examined. This construct has been associated in the meditation research literature (Orme–Johnson, Wallace, Dillbeck, Alexander, & Ball, in press) with a state of mind thought to be developmentally related to dream lucidity (Alexander, 1987; Alexander, Boyer, & Orme–Johnson, 1985). Three major hypotheses will be considered:

1. REM sleep shows a close coordination of the electrical manifestations of activity of the two hemispheres, higher EEG coherence, for selected frequencies.
2. As a result of increases in alpha/theta interhemispheric EEG coherence during the practice of meditation, which is not the same as Stage 1 sleep, there is less need to experience as much REM sleep.
3. The emergence of consciousness in sleep (lucidity) is enhanced by the practice of meditation and is most likely to occur during the stage of sleep that shows interhemispheric balance in the alpha/

theta range, REM. Further, lucidity is likely to be accompanied by additional increases in interhemispheric coherence over normal REM levels similar to those reported during key points in meditation.

Previous models of exclusive hemispheric specialization of the brain have given way more recently to models of its interactiveness. Levy (1985) points out that "the two-brain myth was founded on an erroneous premise: that since each hemisphere was specialized each must function as an independent brain. But in fact, just the opposite is true" (p. 43). She goes on to point out that although each hemisphere may be specialized for function, all activities require input from both hemispheres. For instance, when a person reads a story using the language-based left hemisphere, "the right hemisphere may play a special role in decoding visual information, maintaining an integrated story structure, appreciating humor and emotional content, deriving meaning from past associations and understanding metaphor" (p. 43). Further Levy notes, "there is no evidence that either creativity or intuition is an exclusive property of the right hemisphere" (p. 44).

Sleep and dream researchers paralleled other behavioral scientists in focusing on an asymmetrical model of hemispheric specialization as a function of stage of sleep (Broughton, 1975; Ornstein, 1972). Also paralleling research in the waking states, these models, which enjoyed early support (Goldstein, Staltzfus, & Gardocki, 1972), failed to stand up to rigorous scientific examination (Antrobus, 1987). More recent work on the relative role of each hemisphere in sleep continues to parallel that in waking. Relative hemispheric synchronization is seen as changing as a function of stage of sleep (Armitage, Hoffmann & Moffitt, in press).

Several EEG measures potentially reflect this integrative view of brain functioning. Of concern here are: EEG Coherence (COH), which is broadly defined as "a statistical estimate of the correlation between pairs of signals as a function of frequency . . . and is mathematically independent of signal amplitude" (French & Beaumont, 1984, p. 241), and interhemispheric EEG differences (DIFF), which is the "absolute difference in period-analyzed EEG between homologous electrode sites" (Armitage, Hoffman, Loewy, & Moffitt, 1988). Although these measures are methodologically different in their derivation, they are conceptually similar in that they have both been said to reflect interhemispheric synchronization. It should be noted, however, that COH is more commonly used as an indication of the degree to which the hemispheres are working in concert. COH validity was recently determined by Boivin, Cote, Lapiene, and Montplaisir (1987), who examined interhemispheric COH in sleep before and after an anterior callostomy. Although there are differences in computational methods for COH, in a review of the literature, French and Beaumont (1984) point out that they could not discern any pattern relating differences in findings to mathematical derivation differences. This is not to say that there are not methodological concerns in the COH literature. Banquet (1972) points to the importance of separating frequency from phase synchronization, while French and Beaumont (1984) and Koles and Flor–Henry (1987) argue that the major problems in the literature are because of the use of an active common reference for the recording of the EEG. In sum, although no one has directly looked at the relationship of COH to DIFF, both have been used in sleep research to determine relative hemispheric specialization as a function of stage of sleep. Both measures, but especially COH, can be conceptualized as measuring the degree to which selected components of the brain are working in unison, or as indications of neural connectivity.

WAKING CORRELATES

The bulk of the work on waking correlates of interhemispheric balance is with COH and may be viewed as associated with arousal and subsequent attention. Grindel (1985) found that "during coma . . . the values of coherence function were sharply decreased. With recovering consciousness and speech, a gradual appearance of alpha-activity was observed as well as an increase of coherence values at the frequency of the alpha-rhythm" (p. 750). Relatedly, Ford, Goethe, and Dekker (1986) found that interhemispheric COH in alpha range (temporal and occipital) increased across psychiatric groups differing in arousal. That is, it was highest in paranoid schizophrenics and lowest in a geriatric group.

The most frequent use of COH has been in differentiating psychiatric populations (Flor–Henry, Koles, & Lind, 1987; Ford, et al., 1986; Prichep, 1987; Takigawa, 1987). In a review of the COH literature French and Beaumont (1984) conclude that for psychological abnormality lower interhemispheric coherence is found in individuals with learning disorders than in normals during rest. Prichep (1987) found that interhemispheric anterior incoherence was a powerful indicator differentiating primary depressed patients from normals. In general, nonmental patient populations show higher interhemispheric coherence during rest than mental patient populations (Flor–Henry, et al., 1987). Other individual-difference variations in interhemispheric COH include, higher COH in females than males (Flor–Henry & Koles, 1982; Flor–Henry, Koles, & Reddon, 1987, Koles & Flor–Henry, 1981), decreasing COH with age (Flor–Henry et al., 1987), and higher COH in field-independent individuals (O'Connor & Shaw, 1982)

Relative interhemispheric COH in normals varies most as a function of cognitive activity. As Armitage, Hoffmann, and Moffitt (in press) point out, "a central nervous system which has access to the specialization of both sides of the brain at the same time would be expected to excel at a variety of tasks." Most (Armitage, et al., 1987, Beaumont, Mayes, & Rugg, 1978; Busk & Galbraith, 1975; Ford et al., 1986; Livanov, Gavrilova, & Aslanov, 1974;), but not all (Thatcher, Krause, & Hrybyk, 1986; Koles & Flor--Henry, 1986), researchers have found that hemispheric balance (DIFF or COH) is associated with increased task performance. Specifically, high interhemispheric coherence has been found to be positively associated with performance on a concept-learning task (Dillbeck, Orme–Johnson, & Wallace, 1981); with creativity (Orme-Johnson & Haynes, 1981; Orme-Johnson et al., in press); with high grade-point averages (Orme–Johnson et al., in press); with good performance in two verbal tasks rather than in a block design task (Flor-Henry, Koles, & Reddon, 1987), and with increased psychomotor speed and flexibility (Bersford Jedrczak, Toomey, & Clements, Dillbeck, et al.,1981; in press). DIFF has been noted as lower (implicating higher COH) for better visuospatial performance in females (reported in Armitage, et al., in press).

A complete review of the COH in waking literature is beyond the scope of this chapter, but a brief summary of Orme–Johnson et al.'s (in press) model of the role of EEG coherence in information processing is germane. They propose three principles of neurophysiological organization:

1. An anterior–posterior axis represents an abstract–concrete dimension.
2. High EEG coherence in the alpha and theta frequencies represents the neurophysiological correlate of the more generalized, abstract, synthetic, holistic, integrative functions of the brain, while low coherence, desynchronization, and high frequencies are correlates of more concrete, specialized functions of particular cortical areas, such as perceptual and motor functions.
3. Any cortical area can perform general or specialized functions; cortical tissue can perform its regional, specialized function, associated with a desyncronized, low coherence state, or can join other tissues via high coherence to perform a general, integrative function. (pp. 27–28)

Orme–Johnson and associates note that the respective roles of the two hemispheres can be viewed as figure ("active hemisphere") to ground ("inactive hemisphere"). They further argue that during activity the relevant hemisphere is desynchronized, indicating more efficient differentiation while during inactivity intrahemispheric synchronization reflects increased efficiency of integration. In other words, while one hemisphere is engaged in a task specific for its specialization and hence requires attention, its intrahemispheric coherence is low. At the same time the contralateral hemisphere shows high intrahemispheric coherence that provides an integrating context of interpretations for the activities of the hemisphere in use. It is also noted that the same process occurs with reference to the anterior–posterior axis. They argue that the frontal lobes (anterior) are involved with selection and storage of information implicated in attention. In contrast, they point to the occipital lobes (posterior) as involved in concrete processes such as various stages of feature analysis, "which build up the perceptual boundaries giving visual forms their concrete definition" (p. 27). Later in this chapter we will return to this model in relating lucid dreaming mentation to COH.

MEDITATION AND EEG COHERENCE

Another waking experience that has received considerable attention in the COH literature is meditation. The relationship of high alpha and theta interhemispheric COH from all cortical placements to experiences of "transcending" during the practice of Transcendental Meditation (TM) has been reported in a number of studies (c .f. Orme–Johnson & Haynes, 1981; Farrow & Herbert, 1982). Clear experiences of "transcending" to a state of pure consciousness are discussed by Orme–Johnson and Haynes (1981), who note that it is "an experience describable as unbounded awareness or . . . one's deepest inner nature" (pp. 212–213). They offer several case reports such as from this Canadian subject:

> The predominant experience in meditation was a deep, expansive silence, stable and immovable in its character, with thoughts proceeding on the surface . . . meditations became more and more effortless, blissful, and comfortable. . . . I began to notice thoughts being experienced as waves or ripples of consciousness . . . it seemed as if there was no coming or going, only absolute pure consciousness moving within and for itself. . . . Quite literally, when I had a thought or desire, immediately it would take a form that could be seen, and usually it had a very clear sound associated with it.

French and Beaumont (1984) concluded that TM has been shown to increase COH especially in the alpha and theta bands relative to eyes-closed, resting conditions. Further, these COH measures correlate with the maintenance of pure consciousness outside TM practice (Alexander, et al., 1990; Orme–Johnson, Clements, Haynes, & Badaovi, 1977) as well as with moral reasoning, verbal and figural creativity, fluid intelligence, and grade-point average (cited in Alexander, Boyer, & Alexander, 1987).[1]

---

[1] It should be noted that work on COH and the quality of experiences during meditation has in recent years also examined homolateral as well as bilateral COH (Orme–Johnson et al., in press).

Ornstein (1972) was first to suggest that the practice of meditation may produce greater integration of interhemispheric functioning. Wescott (1977) found that EEG was more correlated from hemisphere to hemisphere in the alpha frequency in a group of meditating meditors than in two control groups of nonmeditators, one relaxing and the other not. This enhanced interhemispheric EEG COH finding was confirmed by Dillbeck and Bronson (1981) in a longitudinal within-subject design; Taneli and Krahne (1987) with meditators before and during meditation, and Levine (1976) and Levine, Herbert, Haynes, and Strobel (1977) during meditation.

This work has been carried further to examine the relationship of COH to specific meditation experiences. Farrow and Herbert (1982) reported that experiences of "transcending" during TM were associated with alpha, theta, and beta global COH, while Orme–Johnson et al. (1977) and Orme-Johnson and Haynes (1981) found total alpha EEG coherence related to experiences of transcending during meditation.

In two recent reviews of the COH and TM literature Orme–Johnson et al. (in press) and Alexander, et al. (1987) point out that, although global COH measures show increases in meditation, the bulk of the variance is from frontal placements and in the alpha/theta ranges.

A possible methodological concern should be pointed out. Armitage, Hoffmann, and Moffitt (in press) note that the relative balance of the hemispheres is characteristic of a rhythmic hemispheric process that regularly appears. This is supported by Manseau and Broughton (1984), who found 90-min synchronous interhemispheric EEG rhythms in theta activity while awake. Systematic control for such ultradian influences has not been done with the TM studies, although they are typically run at random points in time. However, since subjects in research at the Maharishi International University, where much of this research has been done, are drawn from a pool of meditators who regularly meditate together twice a day, might not their ultradian rhythms be synchronized?

REM/NREM CYCLES AND EEG COHERENCE

Dumermuth and Lehmann (1981) point out that it is difficult to compare the results of examined interhemispheric EEG COH in sleep because of varying recording criteria and the studies seem to show partly contradictory results. The authors argue that although there is agreement for COH increases paralleling power in slow-wave sleep there is no agreement for REM sleep. However, in more recent work, interhemispheric coherence for each sleep stage has been examined separately for each frequency and a clearer picture emerges. Three groups of sleep researchers (Armitage, et al., in press; Barcaro, Denoth, Murri, Navona, & Stefanini, 1986; Dumermuth,

TABLE 15.1
Summary of Studies Examining Coherence-type Measures as a Function of
Stage of Sleep and EEG Frequency

	Study		
	Armitage et al. (in press)	Dumermuth et al. (1983)	Barcaro et al. (1986)
Measurement	DIFF	global COH	interhemispheric correlations from homolateral COH
Sites	F3-F4/P3-P4	F3, F4, P3, P4, O1, O2, T3, T4, CZ	F4-C4/F3-Cs
Frequency			
Delta	REM > NREM	REM > NREM	NREM > REM
Theta	REM > NREM	REM > NREM	REM > NREM
Alpha	—	NREM(4) > REM	REM > NREM
Sigma	—	NREM(4) > REM	NREM > REM
Beta	—	REM > NREM	—
Notes:	A greater difference in NREM than REM implies more coherence in REM than NREM.	Frontal sites for alpha REM > NREM.	One subject's data for alpha and theta.

et al., 1983; Dumermuth & Lehmann, 1981; in press) found with different measures, all of which conceptually measure interhemispheric coherence, that REM evidences more interhemispheric balance in a specific frequency than slow-wave NREM. These studies are summarized in Table 15.1.

Focusing on bilateral differences defined earlier, and abbreviated DIFF, Armitage, Hoffmann, et al. (1988) found for delta and theta smaller interhemispheric differences in REM than in Stage 2, or Slow-wave NREM, using F3-F4 and P3-P4 sites. A slightly different approach is that of the Bacaro et al. data, where homolateral (F4-C4 and F3-C3) COHs within each frequency was sampled and then interhemispheric correlations as a function of stage of sleep were computed. Barcaro et al. found higher interhemispheric correlations in REM than in NREM for alpha and theta on the one subject for whom this data was reported but the opposite for delta and sigma.[2] In the best studies of this work, Dumermuth and Lehmann (1981) and Dumermuth et al. (1983) found global coherence higher in REM than in NREM for both slow (delta, theta) and fast (beta) frequencies, but

---

[2] Armitage, Stelmack, Miles, Robertson, and Campbell (1988) have also found that "REM sleep appears to be better described as a period of hemispheric balance" using auditory evoked potentials.

for midrange frequencies (alpha/sigma) they found Stage 4 NREM was more coherent for grand averages across nine sites (F3, F4, P3, P4, O1, O2, T3, T4, and CZ). Particularly relevant to this thesis in the Dumermuth et al. (1983) study, bifrontal coherence in the alpha band was maximum in REM. Although there is some disagreement among the three groups, they all agree that within the theta frequency interhemispheric balance is evident during REM and in the best of the three studies, bifrontally for alpha (Dumermuth et al., 1983).[3]

Because one can get high COH values (correlations) for a wide range of microvolt signals it is advantageous to consider power in interpreting COH. A full report of both power and COH as a function of frequency, stage of sleep and electrode placements is offered by Dumermuth et al. (1983). They found for averages across six subjects that maxima power never occurred for REM in any of their eight sites or 10 frequency bands for which they analyzed their data. REM was characterized consistently as a low-power state. Despite the low power they found again for grand averages across six subjects, as noted, maxima COH over all NREM stages and waking at low and high frequencies both inter- and intrahemispherically.

One might further ask what is the relative magnitude of interhemispheric coherence, especially for alpha/theta in eyes-open waking rest, eyes-closed waking rest, meditation, and sleep (REM and NREM)? Bacaro et al. and Dumermuth and Lehmann note less coherence during eyes-open waking than during NREM sleep. In a detailed breakdown of percentage COH values by EEG sites by frequencies by stage of sleep, including waking, Dumermuth et al. (1983) show over all frequencies a lower percentage coherence in eyes-open waking than in REM, excepting the 8–10-Hz band, which showed no REM–waking difference over all leads with a decrease bifrontally. Within waking, excepting variations in cognitive activity and individual differences reviewed earlier, eyes-closed rest shows more inter-hemispheric COH than eyes-open rest (Flor–Henry, et al. 1987). Interhemispheric COH and alpha power is higher during the practice of Transcendental Meditation than during eyes-closed rest (Banquet, 1972; West, 1980). To our knowledge, no one has looked at the relative magnitude of COH in meditation versus REM sleep. Nonetheless these studies imply a curvalinear relationship between depth of rest and COH intensity. COH increases as we move towards lower states of somatic arousal (i.e., eyes-open rest to eyes-closed rest to meditation and REM) peaking for alpha/theta in meditation and REM and then lessen again in NREM and is very low in coma (Grindel, 1985).

---

[3] Bacaro et al. did not compute statistical tests on alpha and theta but did for delta and sigma.

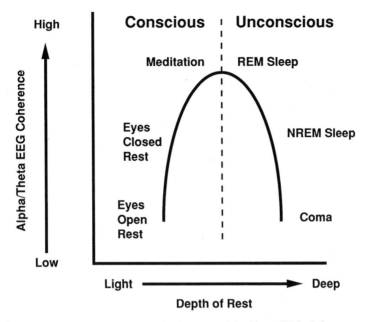

FIG. 15.1 Hypothesized relationship between alpha/theta EEG Coherence as a function of depth of rest. It should be noted that the conscious-unconscious split is as traditionally understood whereas consciousness in sleep is a central point to this discussion.

SLEEP AND MEDITATION

If one assumes, as in the Orme–Johnson et al. model, that COH serves an integrating function and, as Manseau and Broughton (1984) point out, that for theta it cycles while awake every 90 min, it appears that during sleep this theta cycling is maximal in rapid eye-movement sleep. The practice of meditation with its corresponding increase in EEG alpha/theta COH may compensate for the COH needs of the system filled typically by REM sleep. There are some data supporting this hypothesis.

In two classic papers on the sleep of meditating subjects, Banquet and colleagues (Banquet, Sailhan, Cavette, Hazout, & Lucien, 1976; Banquet & Sailhan, 1976) compared 15 long-term meditators to 5 controls. They examined "sleep" during meditation as well as nighttime sleep in TM subjects and controls. Banquet and Sailhan (1976) found that the total duration of sleep in long-term meditators is shorter than average, with dream phases becoming shorter or less frequent. Becker and Herter (1973) found less REM time and percentage in subjects during weeks with meditation than during weeks with no meditation. Relatedly, Miskiman

(1972) found that meditators show less REM rebound after sleep deprivation than controls, while Becker and Herter found less REM rebound
during weeks with meditation than during weeks with no meditation.
One might argue that meditation is simply light sleep; however, in a
review of the meditation and EEG research, West (1980) concluded that
"the work on meditation and the EEG has produced results which suggest
that meditation might be differentiated from other altered states (including
Stage 1 sleep) and is therefore of some importance" (p. 374). This was the
same conclusion of Pagano and Weanenberg (1983) in a well-controlled
study looking at sleep during meditation.[4]

Banquet et al. (1976) propose a neurophysiological theoretical explanation for meditation based on their EEG work. They suggest that meditation
may enhance the link between the "transmission of information and
computation and integration of this information" in the cortex. Related to
COH, they note in their model that "the hypersynchronous bursts recorded
on the scalp could be one of the effects of easier propagation of activation
from one point of the nervous system to the other" (p. 171). The end result
of more flexible neuronal relationships would be "better integration at all
levels of neural functioning" (p. 171).

On the psychophysiological level, Banquet et al. argue that transcendental Meditation transfers the open loop of ascending, information
gathering, and descending, information output neuronal systems into a
closed loop. By open they mean open to either the external world or to the
body. Of the closed loop they say that "the subjective experience is a
decrease in the awareness of the environment and body with a simultaneous
increase in the degree of vigilance" (p. 172). They further argue that this
closed loop is essential to the maturation and evolution of the brain.

Such closed-loop functioning also obviously occurs during sleep and is
especially manifest during the aroused and attentional state of REM with
peaks in attention resulting in self-awareness of state or lucid sleep (Snyder
& Gackenbach, 1988; 1991). To extend further the analogy between REM
sleep and meditation, we can consider the beneficial cognitive effects of the
practice of TM and the association of such effects to EEG coherence
(Alexander et al., 1987). Such cognitive enhancement, especially information processing and memory retrieval, has been pivotal in recent REM
function models, which all point in some form to a cognitive-processing
function for this stage of the sleep cycle (Foulkes, 1985).

---

[4]It is also important to point out here that despite a recent review of the rest-
versus-meditation literature, concluding that they are the same (Holmes, 1984), an extensive
meta-analysis has concluded that rest does not produce the same physiological responses as
meditation (Dillbeck & Orme–Johnson, 1987).

THE LUCID DREAMING CONNECTION

We will now turn to a consideration of the third hypothesis: The emergence of consciousness in sleep (lucidity) is enhanced by the practice of meditation and is most likely to occur during the stage of sleep, which shows interhemispheric balance in the alpha/theta range, REM. Further, lucidity is likely to be accompanied by additional increases in interhemispheric coherence over normal REM levels similar to those reported during key points in meditation.

Hunt has proposed that dream lucidity is essentially a spontaneously realized meditative state (Hunt, 1989; 1991). Several lines of evidence from historical, phenomenological, cognitive, individual-difference, and physiological domains support this conceptualization (for a full review see Hunt & Olgivie, 1988; Gackenbach & Bosveld, 1989; Gackenbach, 1991). Historically, lucid dreams are specifically spoken of in classic Tibetan Buddhist texts (for a review, see Gillespie, 1988a; 1991) where lucidity is presented as form of meditation available during dreaming. For a critical phenomenological discussion of this dream relative to the states desired to be achieved through meditation, see especially the papers of Gillespie (1985a; 1985b; 1985c; 1985d; 1985e; 1985f; 1985g; 1986; 1987a; 1987b; 1988b), as well as books by Sparrow (1976a), Kelzer (1987), Garfield (1979), and LaBerge (1985).

Hunt has addressed the cognitive parallels between mental states experienced in waking meditation and sleeping lucid dreaming (Hunt, 1989; 1991; Hunt & McLeod, 1984; Hunt & Ogilvie, 1988). Gackenbach (1991; Gackenbach & Bosveld, 1989) has recently contextualized her extensive work on the lucid dreams (including content analysis, Gackenbach, 1988) in terms of lucidity as a form of meditation. Many of the individual-difference variables associated with the practice of meditation have also been found to be true of individuals who frequently dream lucidly controlling for dream recall (for reviews, see Snyder & Gackenbach, 1988, and Alexander, Boyer, & Alexander, 1987).

Most noteworthy of the individual-difference variables is that the waking practice of meditation increases dramatically the frequency of experiencing lucidity in dreams (Hunt & McLeod, 1984; Reed, 1977; 1978; Sparrow, 1976b) even when dream recall differences are controlled (Gackenbach & Bosveld, 1989; Gackenbach, Cranson, & Alexander, 1986; 1991). Further, reports of consciousness during deep sleep are correlated to clear experiences of transcending during meditation (reported in Alexander et al., 1987). Alexander et al. also report data on a group of meditators who showed breath suspension during meditation, which is thought to be a key indicator of transcending (Kesterson, 1985). They reported more experiences of consciousness during sleep than a group of meditators who showed no breath suspensions. The physiological parallels between dream lucidity and waking meditation will be taken up in detail.

Except that the individual is awake, depth of somatic arousal during meditation is equivilant to that of light sleep (Kesterson, 1985) but, as was noted earlier, it is not the same as light sleep (Pagano & Weanenberg, 1983; West, 1980). However, REM sleep shows increases in oxygen consumption and heart rate over Stages 1 and 2 NREM and lucid REM is significantly higher on these dimensions than nonlucid REM (LaBerge, Levitan, & Dement, 1986; LaBerge, 1985; 1988). This lucid somatic arousal associated with consciousness in REM would seem to argue against our parallel. LaBerge (personal communication, June, 1987) pointed out that the continued somatic arousal after the eye-movement signal that he has found could be an artifact of the demand characteristics of the experiment. That is, his subjects are typically told to signal when they know they are dreaming and then to do a predesigned task; active engagement in a dream task while conscious in sleep could keep the system relatively somatically aroused.

A study by Gackenbach, Moorecroft, Alexander, and LaBerge (1987) sheds light on this apparent discrepancy. They had a long-term meditator, who during meditation showed physiological signs of transcending that, correlated with his self-reports. This individual claimed that he was conscious of his true state throughout his sleep cycle. That is, he knew he was sleeping and sometimes dreaming through the entire night. This ability, which in the TM literature is called "witnessing" sleep, is thought to be a result of the regular practice of meditation (Alexander et al., 1985). Further, the association of consciousness in sleep to the practice of meditation was pointed out by the early meditation researchers. For instance, Banquet and Sailhan (1976) commented on the qualitative nature of the sleep of meditators, "a certain level of awareness can be observed in normal subjects during hypnagogic phases or morning dreams. In long-term meditators awareness apparently can extend to the entire period of sleep including phases of deep sleep" (p. 183).

In the sleep laboratory this meditator was able to signal with prearranged eye movements that he knew he was dreaming/sleeping during REM, Stage 1 and Stage 2 sleep. Interestingly, and in line with this hypothesis, he showed physiological arousal around the eye-movement signal but, contrary to the data of LaBerge et al. (1986), he rapidly returned to quiet somatic levels shortly thereafter. With at least this one subject, signaling was somatically arousing but his continued consciousness in sleep was not.

Further supporting the meditation–lucidity link is a finding with the Hoffman or H-reflex, an electrically evoked monosynaptic spinal reflex that has been viewed as an indication of the flexibility of central nervous system response. Brylowski found greater H-reflex *suppression* associated with lucid REM sleep than with nonlucid REM sleep. This is in line with studies by Dillbeck et al. (1981) and Haynes, Hebert, Reber, and Orme–Johnson (1977). Dillbeck et al. found greater H-reflex *recovery* indirectly associated with an advanced form of meditation practice while Haynes et al. note positive correlations between H-reflex recovery, clarity of experience of transcendental state and high EEG coherence. Enhanced H-reflex suppression in REM and recovery in waking both indicate a system that is maximizing its functioning appropriate for the state.

Further, based on their work with lucid-dreamer-type differences in vestibular sensitivity as measured by caloric stimulation (Gackenbach, Snyder, Rokes & Sachau, 1986) and gross motor balance (Snyder & Gackenbach, 1991), Snyder and Gackenbach conclude that semicircular vestibular subsystems (feedback from ocular systems) rather than otolithic functioning (feedback from muscles and gravity) accounted for the vestibular superiority of lucid dreamers. From this they hypothesized that REM sleep might involve internalization of attention.

> This proposal is conceptually attractive because it can incorporate the intense activation of the vestibular nuclei which precedes REM bursts, the increase in cortical arousal which occurs during dreaming the high sensory thresholds which enable redirection of attention from exogenous stimulation, and rapid eye movements which may be related to the overt eye movements and mechanisms of covert attention described by Posner and Friedrich (1986). Lucid dreaming in this context, can be conceived as a state of increased internalized attention in which the consciousness of wakefulness commingles with the mentation of Stage 1 REM sleep. The self-awareness of lucidity and the resultant imposition of cognitive control over sleep mentation would then be viewed as a neurocognitive process mediated by the heteromodal prefrontal cortex, an example of what Stuss and Benson (1986) have termed the highest level of cognitive functioning (p. 12).

It is worth noting that meditation has most often been conceptualized as a process of internalizing attention (Goleman, 1988) and recall that the bulk of the variance for COH surges associated with transcending comes from the frontal lobes (Orme–Johnson et al., in press).

EEG AND DREAM LUCIDITY

EEG work with dream lucidity is unfortunately fairly limited at this point with the bulk having been done by Ogilvie, Hunt, and associates (Hunt & Ogilvie, 1988; Ogilvie, Hunt, Sawicki & McGowan, 1978; Ogilvie, Hunt, Tyson, Lucescu, & Jeakins, 1982; Ogilvie, Vieira, & Small, 1988; Tyson, Ogilvie, & Hunt, 1984). In this series of studies they sought to demonstrate the lucidity–meditation connection by examining the power of alpha waves in lucid and nonlucid REM. Reviews of the EEG and meditation literature have fairly consistently pointed to the association of alpha power with meditation (Taneli & Krahne, 1987; West, 1980). The Ogilvie and Hunt group found, consistent with the meditation literature, variations in alpha as a function of stage of lucidity. Specifically, they found increased alpha in prelucid (i.e., such as dreaming you wake up or suspecting you are dreaming but concluding you are awake when in fact you are asleep) REM periods and have likened this to the access phases of waking meditation. West (1980) and Taneli and Krahne (1987) have summarized the EEG and meditation literature for power measures and note changes as a function of stage of meditation. Both reviewers agree that at the beginning and at the end of meditation increases in alpha are observed. Later theta occurs, often mixed with alpha, and at the "transcending" or "samadhi" phase bursts of beta occur. In their most recent study Ogilvie et al. (1988) suggest a three-step process in the lucidity/alpha relationship. It may begin "with relatively low levels of alpha (typical REM dreaming), move to higher alpha levels (prelucid dreaming), and end with moderate alpha levels (lucid dreaming), while still in the REM state. (p.5).

West (1980) has pointed out that a more sophisticated examination of EEG changes in meditation would include the investigation of EEG coherence. As reviewed earlier, this is being pursued in the Transendental Meditation research literature and thus offers the potential for identifying EEG associations to consciousness during sleep. Further, as noted, REM has already been identified as interhemispherically coherent in the theta range relative to NREM, thus making it the state in which meditation-like experiences (lucidity) would be most likely to occur. Several investigators have shown that lucidity primarily emerges out of REM (see LaBerge, 1988, for a review).

In the current TM model of COH, it is thought to peak in times of state transition (Orme–Johnson et al. in press). Armitage et al. (1987) found that high dream recallers, especially females, show a greater continuity of rhythmic EEG in transition from sleep to waking a finding consistent with the TM view. Further, from this we can say that individuals who frequently remember their dreams are responding verbally to information from a coherent state of brain functioning while remaining in some sense in that state. One of the most robust findings in both the individual difference (for a review, see Snyder & Gackenbach, 1988) and content analysis (for a review, see Gackenbach, 1988) literature on dream lucidity is the association of high dream recall to lucidity. Lucid dreamers in general are high dream recallers so they should show more COH at the state transition to waking.

But will lucid dreams themselves be higher in COH? In self-evaluations of the recallability of lucid versus nonlucid dreams, the former are continually perceived as significantly easier to remember (Gackenbach, 1988). Although one might argue that the phasic nature (LaBerge, 1988; LaBerge et al. 1986) of lucid dreams might be responsible for their increased recallability, Pivik (1978) points out that dreams recalled from phasic versus tonic REM do not differ in recall. Indeed the "tonic" witnessing of the dreams reported in Gackenbach et al. (1987) were rated as highly recallable by the subject (Gackenbach, 1988) if phenomenologically quiet (Gackenbach & Moorecroft, 1987). Despite the REM decrease in meditators (Banquet & Sailhan, 1976; Becker & Herter, 1973) it does not follow that they recall fewer dreams. In fact, just the opposite seems to be the case. For virtually all (excepting Fuson, 1976) of the few studies looking at dream recall in meditators versus nonmeditators, meditators show more dream recall than nonmeditators for questionnaire (Gackenbach, Cranson, & Alexander, 1986; 1991) home diary (Reed, 1978) and sleep laboratory (Busby & DeKoninck, 1980; Faber, Saayman, & Touyz 1978) samples. Considering that normal for dream recall is dream forgetting (Belicki, 1987), it may be that even though there is less quantity of material to recall (less REM) there is an increase in inner orientation with meditation (West, 1982), which has also been associated with enhanced dream recall (Belicki, 1987). On a physiological level, the increases in COH due to the practice of meditation would also occur, it would seem, at state transition from REM to waking, thus increasing the likelihood of the material to be recalled. However, the picture is not that clear.

Gackenbach, Cranson, and Alexander (1986) found that for *nonmeditators* dream recall and interest in keeping a dream journal were highly predictive of lucidity frequency whereas among *meditators neither predicted lucidity frequency,* although they reported significantly more lucid dreams than the nonmeditators controlling for dream recall differences.[5] A high predictor of lucid frequency in their meditation group was field independence. Field independence (FI) is a construct that has been implicated in both the meditation (Orme–Johnson & Granieri, 1977) and lucid dreaming (Gackenbach, Heilman, Boyt, & LaBerge, 1985; Snyder & Gackenbach, 1988) literatures. Both frequently lucid dreamers, controlling for dream recall, and meditators are more field-independent than field-dependent. These findings are on right-handers and are consistent across sex although they are more strongly associated with the practice of meditation than with the spontaneous occurrence of lucidity in nonmeditators (Gackenbach, Cranson, & Alexander, 1986). Field independence associated with lucidity and meditation is also associated with interhemispheric parietal COH during rest with eyes closed for alpha in right-handers

---

[5] It should be noted that this may vary as a function of length of practice.

(O'Connor & Shaw, 1982).[6] Clearly some physiological mechanism under-
lies the emergence of lucidity in these two groups. It is suggested here that
it is COH.

In pilot data, LaBerge looked at EEG coherence twice. In his dissertation
(1980) he had only central EEG leads and found no COH differences as a
function of lucidity. More recently (LaBerge, personal communication,
Feb. 20, 1988), he compared a 5-min lucid dream during REM to the 15 min
of REM prior to the onset of dream consciousness in one subject. Looking
at interhemispheric EEG coherence at the parietal lobes, he found an
increase in COH during the lucid phase of REM for the alpha frequency.
Although these findings are highly preliminary, they are in the direction we
would expect. That he found increased COH in the parietal lobes is
interesting as the central role of visual–spatial functioning, associated with
this area of the brain, has been strongly implicated in lucid dreamers
(Snyder & Gackenbach, 1988; 1991) and in lucid dreams (Gackenbach,
1988) and was the location of interhemispheric alpha COH reported by
O'Connor and Shaw (1982) for field-independent individuals.

STAGES OF CONSCIOUSNESS IN SLEEP

There may be a psychophysiological justification to conceptualize dream
lucidity as a sleeping form of, but not the same as, meditation as theorized
by Hunt by building on the findings of research in REM sleep and
meditation with interhemispheric COH. Further, lucidity is not the end
state of self-reflectiveness, as indicated in Moffitt, Purcell, Hoffman,
Pigeau, and Wells (1986) Self-Reflectiveness Scale but rather it is towards
the beginning.

Alexander and colleagues (1987; Alexander et al. 1985) have postulated
at least two states of self-awareness during sleep: lucidity and witnessing.
The former has been found to be a physiologically and phenomenologically
active consciousness, while the latter is quiet on both accounts (Gackenbach
et al., 1987; Gackenbach & Moorecroft, 1987). Alexander (1987; Alexander
et al., 1985; Gackenbach, Cranson, & Alexander, 1986) suggests a developmental relationship between these two forms of sleep consciousness with

---

[6] Zoccolotti (1982) criticized O'Connor and Shaw's (1978) reliance on a relatively new
method of calculating relative FI/FD, but he, too, drew the same general conclusion.
However—, in a rebuttal to Zoccolotti—O'Connor and Shaw (1982) admit errors in the
reporting of their original data but in reanalysis with the new calculation approach, which they
argue, "gives a more standardized assessment of FD and is therefore likely to reflect the more
enduring cognitive correlates of FD rather than the transient sensory factors" (p. 211), they
found the opposite of their original conclusion. O'Connor and Shaw (1982) finally concluded
that for right-handers high coherence is associated with FI.

lucidity emerging prior to witnessing which is further detailed in Gackenbach (1991). Further, Alexander, as have others, argues that witnessing can occur during deep sleep and actually represents a fourth major state of consciousness beyond waking, sleeping, and dreaming (Alexander, Cranson, Boyer, & Orme–Johnson, 1987; Maharishi Mahesh Yogi, 1969). By way of validating Alexander's proposed lucid–witnessing developmental relationship Gackenbach (unpublished data reported in Gackenbach & Bosveld, 1989) found in a group of 80 TM meditators that prelucidity and lucidity occurred most frequently followed by witnessing dreams and that in those who had received instruction in the TM–Sidhi program there was an increase in witnessing of dreams and deep sleep over those who had not been so instructed (parts of this data are reported in Gackenbach, Cranson, & Alexander, 1986; 1991).

The cognitive dimension that appears to be similar in meditation and consciousness during sleep is enhanced attention resulting in a form of self-awareness with an inherent duality. (i.e., you know that you are in your own dream and the dream is being manufactured by you). This duality, or silent witness, has been conceptualized in the Orme–Johnson et al. (in press) model of the role of EEG coherence in information processing, which was briefly outlined earlier in this chapter. Maharishi Mahesh Yoga (1969) has described as characteristic of the first stage of enlightenment the dual process of maintaining pure consciousness together with focused waking activity (Orme–Johnson et la., in press). Alexander et al. (1990) have noted that one of the first signs of the emergence of this duality is consciousness during dreaming and that dream lucidity represents the first stage of a range of conscious experiences available in dreaming and nondream sleep (Alexander, 1987; Alexander et al., 1985).

It will be recalled that in the Orme–Johnson et al. information-processing model the active area of the brain (anterior–posterior or left–right or a specific area) serves as figure to ground of the inactive area and that the active area would show low COH suggesting differentiation while the inactive area would show high COH suggesting integration. In this context they maintain that the silent partner in dual consciousness, or the witness, is the inactive–coherent area in relation to the engaged active–incoherent brain area. To apply this to the aware self in a lucid dream and LaBerge's finding of increased COH parietally would suggest that the self-awareness was located parietally to the active areas of the brain engaged in the dream details. As noted, Gackenbach's (1988) findings of the role of spatial parameter's in lucid dreams and lucid dreamers supports this conceptualization. It is hypothesized that with the push from lucidity to full witnessing we would see COH frontally with an increase in the nonintrusive nature of self-awareness in the dream.

Support for this comes from a recent content analysis of lucid dreams versus witnessing dreams from 67 long-term, highly trained TM meditators who have devoted their lives to the practice. Gackenbach, Cranson, and Alexander (1991) found that they are distinct experiences of consciousness in sleep. Witnessing dreams is primarily characterized by a sense of separateness from the dream, whereas lucid dreams are characterized primarily by the use of a trigger in the dream to gain consciousness and a sense of control over the dream events.

Ultimately though mentation fades in sleep and we would be left with global COH without a focus of attention other than attention itself or what is called the "point" of consciousness (Orme–Johnson et al., in press). Clearly we are moving into considerations of the development of higher states of consciousness[7] that are beyond the scope of this chapter, but these speculations point out that full awareness that one is dreaming while one is dreaming is just the beginning.

ACKNOWLEDGMENT

The Author thanks the Department of Psychology at the University of Alberta, where she spent her sabbatical year as a visiting scholar and during which this chapter was written. Thanks also to Rosanne Armitage of the Univeristy of Ottawa and Fred Travis of Maharishi International University for their comments on earlier drafts.

REFERENCES

Alexander, C. (1987). Dream lucidity and dream witnessing: A developmental model based on the practice of Transcendental Meditation. *Lucidity Letter, 6*(2), 213–124.

Alexander, C., Boyer, R., & Alexander, V. (1987). Higher states of consciousness in the Vedic psychology of Maharishi Mahesh Yogi: A theoretical introduction and research review. *Modern Science and Vedic Science, 1*(1), 89–126.

Alexander, C., Boyer, R., & Orme–Johnson, D. (1985). Distinguishing between transcendnental consciousness and lucidity. *Lucidity Letter, 4*(2), 68–85.

Alexander, C.N., Davies, J.L., Dixon, C.A., Dillbeck, M.C., Oetzel, R.M., Muehlman, J.M., & Orme–Johnson, D.W. (1990). Higher stages of consciousness beyond formal operations: The Vedic psychology of human development. In C.N. Alexander & E.J. Langer (Eds.), *Higher stages of human development: Adult growth beyond formal operations.* New York: Oxford University Press.

Antrobus, J. (1987). Cortical hemisphere asymmetry and sleep mentation. *Psychological Review, 94*(3), 359–368.

Armitage, R., Hoffmann, R., Loewy, D., & Moffitt, A. (1988). Interhemispheric EEG during REM and NREM sleep. *Sleep Research, 17.*

Armitage, R., Hoffman, R., & Moffitt, (1987). The continuity of rhythmic EEG synchronicity

---

[7] For a more detailed discussion of higher states of consciousness beyond formal operations the reader is directed to Alexander et al. (1990), or Wilber (1987).

across sleep and wakefulness. *Sleep Research, 16,* 5.

Armitage, R., Hoffmann, R., & Moffitt, A. (in press). Interhemispheric EEG activity in sleep and wakefulness: Individual differences in the basic rest–activity cycle (BRAC). In J. Antrobus (Ed.), *The mind in sleep* (Vol. 2).

Armitage, R., Stelmack, R., Miles, J., Robertson, A., & Campbell, K. (1988). Asymmetrical auditory evoked potentials during sleep. *Sleep Research, 17,*.

Banquet, J. P. (1972). EEG and meditation. *Electroencephalography and Clinical Neurophysiology 33,* 454.

Banquet, J. P., & Sailhan, M. (1976). Quantified EEG spectral analysis of sleep and Transcendental Meditation. In D.W. Orme–Johnson & J.T. Farrow (Eds.), *Scientific research on the Transcendental Meditation progrram: Collected papers* Vol. 1 (pp. 182–186). West Germany: MERU Press.

Banquet, J. P., Sailhan, M., Carette, F., Hazout, S., & Lucien, M. (1976). EEG analysis of spontaneous and induced states of consciousness. In D.W. Orme–Johnson & J.T. Farrow (Eds.), *Scientific research on the Transcendental Meditation program: Collected papers* Vol. 1, (pp. 165–172). West Germany: MERU Press.

Barcaro, U., Denoth, F, Murri, L, Navona, & Stefanini, A. (1986). Changes in the interhemispheric correlation during sleep in normal subjects. *Electroencephalography and Clinical Neurophysiology, 63,* 112–118.

Beaumont, J.G., Mayes, A.R., & Rugg, M.D. (1978). Asymmetry in EEG alpha coherence and power: Effects of task and sex. *Electroenephalography and Clinical Neurophysiology, 45,* 393–401.

Becker, M. & Herter, G. (1973). Effect of meditation upon SREM. *Sleep Research, 2,* 90.

Belicki, K. (1987). Recalling dreams: An examination of daily variation and individual differences. In J.I. Gackenbach (Ed.), *Sleep and dreams: A sourcebook* (pp. 187–206). New York: Garland.

Bersford, M., Jedrczak, A., Toomey, M. &Clements, G. (in press). EEG coherence, age-related psychological variables, and the Transcendental Meditation and TM–Sidhi program. In R.A. Chalmers, G. Glements, H. Schenkluhn, & M. Weinless (Eds.), *Scientific research on the Transcendental Meditation and TM–Sidihi programme: Collected papers* (Vol. 3). Vlodrop, the Netherlands: MIU Press.

Boivin, D., Cote, J., Lapiene, G. & Montplaisir, J. (1987). Interhemispheric coherence during sleep before and after anterior callosotomy in human. *Sleep Research, 16,* 6.

Broughton, R. (1975). Biorhythmic variations in consciousness and psychological function. *Canadian Psychological Review, 16,* 217–239.

Brylowski, A. (1986). H-reflex in lucid dreams. *Lucidity Letter, 5*(1), 116–118. (also in 1987 *Sleep Research*)

Busby, K., & DeKoninck, J. (1980). Short-term effects of strategies for self-regulation on personality dimensions and dream content. *Perceptual and Motor Skills, 50,* 751–765.

Busk, J., & Galbraith, G.C. (1975). EEG correlates of visual–motor practice in man. *Electroencephalography and Clinical Neurophysiology, 38,* 415–422.

Dillbeck, M.C., & Bronson, E.C. (1981). Short-term longitudinal effects of the Transcendental Meditation technique on EEG power and coherence. *International Journal of Neuroscience, 14,* 147–151.

Dillbeck, M. & Orme–Johnson, D. (1987). Physiological differences between Transcendental Meditation and rest. *American Psychologist,* 879–881.

Dillbeck, M.C., Orme–Johnson, D.W., & Wallace, R.K. (1981). Frontal EEG coherence, H-reflex recovery, concept learning, and the TM–Sidhi program. *International Journal of Neuroscience, 15,* 151–157.

Dumermuth, G., Lange, B., Lehmann, D., Meier, C. A., Dinkelmann, R., & Molinari, L. (1983). Spectral analysis of all-night sleep EEG in healthy adults. *European Neurology, 22,* 322–339.

Dumermuth, G., & Lehmann, D. (1981). EEG power and coherence during Non-REM and REM phases in humans in all-night sleep analyses. *European Neurology, 20,* 429–434.

Faber, P.A., Saaayman, G.S., & Touyz, S.W. (1978). Meditation and archetypal content of nocturnal dreams. *Journal of Analytical Psychology, 23,* 1–21.

Farrow, J.T., & Herbert, J.R. (1982). Breath suspension during the Transcendental Meditation technique. *Psychosomatic Medicine, 44,*(2), 133–153.

Flor-Henry, P., & Koles, Z.J. (1982). EEG characteristics in normal subjects: A comparison of men and women and of dextrals and sinistrals. *Research Communications in Psychology, Psychiatry, and Behavior, 7,* 21–38.

Flor-Henry, P., Koles, Z.J., & Lind, J. (1987). Statistical EEG investigation of the endogenous psychoses: Power and coherence. In R. Takanhashi, P. Flor-Henry, J. Gruzelier, & S. Niwa (Eds.), *Cerebral dynamics, laterality and psychopathology.* New York: Elsevier Science Publishers.

Flor-Henry, P., Koles, Z.J., & Reddon, J.R. (1987). Age and sex related EEG configurations in normal subjects. In A. Glass (Ed.), *Individual differences in hemispheric specialization.* New York Plenum Press.

Ford, M.R., Goethe, J.W., & Dekker, D.K. (1986). EEG coherence and power in the discrimination of psychiatric disorders and medication effects. *Biological Psychiatry, 21,* 1175–1188.

Foulkes, D. (1985). *Dreaming: A cognitive-psychological analysis.* Hillsdale, NJ: Lawrence Erlbaum Associates.

French, C. C., & Beaumont, J.G. (1984) A critical review of EEG coherence studies of hemisphere function. *International Journal of Psychophysiology, 1,* 241–254.

Fuson, J.W. (1976). *The effect of the Transcendental Meditation program on sleeping and dreaming patterns.* Unpublished doctoral thesis, Yale Medical School, New Haven, CT.

Gackenbach, J.I., & Bosveid, J. (1989). Control your dreams. New York: Harper & Row.

Gackenbach, J.I. (1988). The psychological content of lucid dreams. In J.I. Gackenbach & S.L. LaBerge (Eds.), *Conscious mind, sleeping brain: Perspectives on lucid dreaming.* New York: Plenum Press.

Gackenbach, J. I. (1991). A developmental model of consciousness in sleep: From sleep consciousness to pure consciousness. In J. I. Gackenbach & A. Sheikh (Eds.), *Dream images: A call to mental arms.* Amityville, NY: Baywood.

Gackenbach, J.I., Cranson, R., & Alexander, C. (1986). Lucid dreaming, witnessing dreaming, and the Transcendental Meditation technique: A developmental relationship. *Lucidity Letter, 5,*(2), 34–40.

Gackenbach, J. I., Cranson, R., & Alexander, C. (1991, June). *The relationship between lucid dreaming and witnessing dreaming.* Paper presented at the annual meeting of the Association for the Study of Dreams, Charlottesville, VA.

Gackenbach, J. I., Heilman, N., Boyt, S., & LaBerge, S. (1985). The relationship between field independence and lucid dreaming ability. *Journal of Mental Imagery, 9*(1), 9–20.

Gackenbach, J. I., Moorecroft, W., Alexander, C., & LaBerge, S. (1987). Physiological correlates of "consciousness" during sleep in a single TM practitioner. *Sleep Research, 16,*230.

Gackenbach, J.I., & Moorecroft, W. (1987). Psychological content of "consciousness" during sleep in a TM subject. *Lucidity Letter, 6*(1), 29–36.

Gackenbach, J.I., Snyder, T.J., Rokes, L., & Sachau, D. (1986). Lucid dreaming frequency in relationship to vestibular sensitivity as measured by caloric stimulation. In R. Haskel (Ed.)., *Cognition and Dream Research: The Journal of Mind and Behavior (special issue), 7,*(2 & 3), 277–298.

Garfield, P. (1979). *Pathway to ecstasy* New York: Holt, Rinehart, & Winston.

Gillespie, G. (1985a). Lucid dreaming and mysticism: A personal observation. *Lucidity Letter, 2*(3), 64.

Gillespie, G. (1985b). Memory and reason in lucid dreams: A personal observation. *Luvidity Letter, 3*(4), 76–78.

Gillespie, G. (1985c). Problems related to experimentation while dreaming lucidly. *Lucidity Letter, 3*(2 & 3), 87–88.

Gillespie, G. (1985d). Can we distinguish between lucid dreams and dreaming-awareness dreams? *Lucidity Letter, 3*(2 & 3), 95–96.

Gillespie, G. (1985e). The phenomenon of light in lucid dreams: Personal observations. *Lucidity Letter, 3*(4), 99–100.

Gillespie, G. (1985f). Statistical description of my lucid dreams: *Lucidity Letter, 3*(4), 104–111.

Gillespie, G. (1985g). Comments on "Dreams lucidity and near-death experience — A Personal report." *Lucidity Letter, 4*(2), 21–23.

Gillespie, G. (1986). Ordinary dreams, lucid dreams and mystical experiences. *Lucidity Letter, 5*(1), 27–30.

Gillespie, G. (1987a). Dream light: Categories of visual experience during lucid dreaming. *Lucidity Letter, 6*(1), 73–79.

Gillespie, G. (1987b). Distinguishing between phenomenon and interpretation: When does lucid dreaming become transpersonal experience? *Lucidity Letter, 6*(2), 125–130.

Gillespie, G. (1988a). Lucid dreams in Tibetan Buddhism. In J.I. Gackenbach & S.L. LaBerge (Eds.), *Conscious mind, sleeping brain: Perspectives on lucid dreaming.* New York: Plenum Press.

Gillespie, G. (1988b). Without a Guru: An account of my lucid dreaming. In J.I. Gackenbach & S.L. LaBerge (Eds.), *Conscious mind, sleeping brain: Perspectives on lucid dreaming.* New York: Plenum Press.

Gillespie, G. (1991). Early Hindu speculation about dreams: Implictions for dream Yoga. In J. I. Gackenbach & A. Sheikh (Eds.), *Dreams images: A call to mental arms.* Amityville, New York: Baywood.

Goldstein, L., Staltzfus, N., & Gardocki, J. (1972). Changes in interhemispheric amplitude relations in EEG during sleep. *Physiological Behavior, 8,* 811–815.

Goleman, D. (1988). *The meditative mind.* Los Angeles: Tarcher.

Grindel, O.M. (1985). Intercentral relations in the cerebral cortex revealed by EEG coherence during recovery of consciousness and speech after protracted coma. *Zhurnal Vysshei Nervnoi Deyatel'nosti, 35*(1), 60–67. (references in Psychological Abstracts)

Haynes, C.T., Hebert, J.R., Reber, W., & Orme-Johnson, D.W. (1977). The psychophysiology of advanced participants in the Transcendental Meditation program: Correlations of EEG coherence, crativity, H-reflex recovery, and experience of transcendental consciousness. *Collected Papers 1,* 208–212.

Holmes, D. (1984). Meditation and somatic arousal reduction: A review of experimental evidence. *American Psychologist 39,*(1), 1–10.

Hunt, H. (1987). Lucidity as a meditative state. *Lucidity Letter, 6*(2), 105–112.

Hunt, H. (1989). *The multiplicity of dreams: A cognitive psychological perspective.* New Haven, CN: Yale University Press.

Hunt, H. (1991). Lucid dreaming as a meditative state: Some evidence from long-term meditators in relation to the cognitive-psychological bases of transpersonal phenomena. In J. I. Gackenbach & A. Sheikh (Eds.), *Dream images: A call to mental arms.* Amityville, New York: Baywood.

Hunt, H. T., & McLeod, B. (1984, April). *Lucid dreaming as a meditative state: Some evidence from long term meditators in relation to the cognitive-psychological bases of transpersonal phenomena.* Paper presented at the annual meeting of the Eastern Psychological Association, Baltimore.

Hunt, H., & Ogilvie, R. (1988). Lucid dreams in their natural series: Phenomenological and psychophysiological findings in relation to meditative states. In J.I. Gackenbach & S.L.

LaBerge (Eds.), *Conscious mind, sleeping brain: Perspectives on lucid dreaming.* New York: Plenum Press.

Kelzer, K. (1987). *The sun and the shadow: My experiment with lucid dreaming.* Virginia Beach, VA: A.R.E. Press.

Kesterson, J. (1985). *Respiratory control during Transcendental Meditation.* Doctoral dissertation, Department of Neuroscience of Human Consciousness, Maharishi International University, Fairfield, IA.

Koles, Z.J., & Flor-Henry, P. (1981). Mental activity and the EEG: Task and workload related effects. *Medical and Biological Engineering and Computing, 19,* 185–194.

Koles, Z.J., & Flor-Henry, P. (1986). EEG correlates of male–female differences in verbally and spatially-based cognitive tasks. *Abstracts for the 12th C.M.B.E.C./1st Pan. Pacific Symposium,* Vancouver, Canada.

Koles, Z.J., & Flor-Henry, P. (1987). The effect of brain fucntion on coherence patterns in the bipolar EEG. *Internationmal Journal of Psychophysiology 5,* 63–71.

LaBerge, S. (1980). *Lucid dreaming: An exploratory study of consciousness during sleep.* Unpublished doctoral dissertation, Stanford University, Stanford, CA.

LaBerge, S. (1985). *Luciid dreaming.* New York: Ballantine.

LaBerge, S. (1988). The psychophysiology of lucid dreaming. In J.I. Gackenbach & S.L. LaBerge (Eds.), *Conscious mind, sleeping brain: Perspectives on lucid dreaming.* New York: Plenum Press.

LaBerge, S., Levitan, L. & Dement, W. C. (1986). Lucid dreaming: Physiological correlates of consciousness during REM sleep. *Journal of Mind and Behavior, 7,* 251–258.

Levine, P.H. (1976). The coherence spectral array (COSPAR) and its application to the study of spatial ordering in the EEG. In J.I. Martin (Ed.), *Proceedings of the San Diego Biomedical Symposium* (Vol. 15). New York: Academic Press.

Levine, P.H., Herbert, R., Haynes, C.T., & Strobel, U. (1977). EEG coherence during the Transcendental Meditation technique. In D.W. Orme–Johnson & J.T. Farrow (Eds.), *Scientific research on the Transcendental Meditation program: Collected papers* (Vol. 1). Rheinweiler, West Germany: MERU Press.

Levy, J. (1985). Right brain, left brain: Fact and fiction. *Psychology Today,* 38–44.

Livanov, M.N., Gavrilova, N.A., & Aslanov, A.S. (1974). Intercorrelations between different cortical regions of human brain during mental activity. *Neuropsychologica, 2,* 281–289.

Maharishi Mahesh Yogi. (1969). *Maharishi Mahesh Yogi on the Bhagavad–Gita: A new translation and commentary* (Chaps 1–6). Baltimore: Penguin.

Manseau, C., & Broughton, R. (1984). Bilaterally synchronous ultradian EEG rhytms in awake adult humans. *Psychophysiology, 21,* 265–273.

Miskiman, D.E. (1972). The effect of the Transcendental Meditation program on compensatory paradoxical sleep. In D.W. Orme–Johnson & J.T. Farrow (Eds.), *Scientific research on the Transcendental Meditation program: Collected papers* (Vol. 1). Rheinweiler, West Germany: MERU Press.

Moffitt, A., Purcell, S., Hoffman, R., Pigeau, R., & Wells, (1986). Dream psychology: Operating in the dark. *Lucidity Letter, 5*(1), 180–196. (also appears in *Conscious mind, sleeping brain,* 1988).

O'Connor, K. P. & Shaw, J.C. (1978). Field dependence, laterality and EEG. *Biological Psychology, 6,* 93–109.

O'Connor, K. P., & Shaw, J.C. (1982). Comment on Zoccolotti's field dependence, laterality, and the EEG: A reanalysis of O'Connor and Shaw. *Biological Psychology, 15,* 209–213.

Ogilvie, R.D., Hunt, H.T., Sawicki, C. & McGowan, K. (1978). Searching for lucid dreams. *Sleep Research, 7,* 165.

Ogilvie, R.D., Hunt, H.T., Tyson, P.D., Lucescu, M.L. & Jenkins, D.B. (1982). *Motor Skills, 55,* 795–808.

Ogilvie, R. D., Vieira, K.P., & R.J. Small (1988, June). *EEG activity during signaled lucid dreams.* Paper presented at the annual meeting of the Association for the Study of Dreams, Santa Cruz, CA.

Orme-Johnson, D., Clements, G., Haynes, C.t., & Badaoui, K. (1977). Higher states of consciousness: EEG coherence, creativity and experience of the Sidhis. In D.W. Orme-Johnson & Farrow (Eds.), *Scientific research on the Transcendental Meditation program: Collected papers* (Vol. 1). Rheinweiler, West Germany: MERU Press.

Orme-Johnson, D., & Granieri, B. (1977). The effects of the Age of Enlightenment Governor Training Courses on field independence, creativity, intelligence, and behavioral flexibility. In D.W. Orme-Johnson & J.T. Farrow (Eds.), *Scientific research on the Transcendental Meditation program: Collected papers* (Vol. 1). Rheinweiler, West Germany: MERU Press.

Orme-Johnson, D.W., & Haynes, C.T. (1981). EEG phase coherence, pure consciousness, creativity, and TM-Sidhi experiences. *Neuroscience, 13,* 211-217.

Orme-Johnson, D., Wallace, R. K., Dillbeck, M., Alexander, C., & Ball, O. E. (in press). The functional organization of the brain and the Maharishi technology of the unifield field as indicated by changes in EEG coherence and its cognitive correlates: A proposed model of higher states of consciousness. In R. Chalmers, G. Clements, H. Schenkluhn, & M. Weinless (Eds.), *Scientific research on the Transcendental Meditation and TM-Sidhi programme: Collected papers* (Vol. 4). Vlodrop, the Netherlands: MIV Press.

Ornstein, R (1972). *The psychology of consciousness.* San Franscisco: W.H. Freeman.

Pagano & Weanenberg (1983). Meditation in search of a unique effect. In S. Davidson, T. Scheat, & P. Shapiro (Eds.), *Consciousness and self regulation: Advances.*

Pivik, R.T. (1978). Tonic states and phasis events in relation to sleep mentation. In A.M. Arkin, J.S. Antrobus, & S.J. Ellman (Eds.), *The mind in sleep: Psychology and psychophysiology.* Hillsdale, NJ: Lawrence Erlbaum Associates.

Posner, M.I., & Friedrich, F.J. (1986). Attention and the control of cognition. In S.L Friedman, K.L. Klivington & R.W. Peterson (EDs.), *The brain, cognition, and education.* New York: Academic Press.

Prichep, L.S. (1987). Neurometric quantitative EEG features of depressive disorders. In R. Takahashi, P. Flor-Henry, J. Gruzelier, & S. Niwa (Eds.), *Cerebral dynamics, laterality and psychopathology* (pp. 55-69). New York: Elsevier.

Reed, H. (1977). Meditation and lucid dreaming: A statistical relationship. *Sundance Community Dream Journal, 2,* 237-238.

Reed, H. (1978) Improved dream recall associated with meditation. *Journal of Clinical Psychology, 34,* 150-156.

Snyder, T. J., & Gackenbach, J.I. (1991). *Vestibular involvement in the neurocognition of lucid dreaming.* In J. I. Gackenbach & A. Sheikh (Eds.), Dream images: A call to mental arms. Amityville, NY: Baywood.

Snyder, T. J., & Gackenbach, J.I. (1988). Individual differences associated with lucid dreaming. In J.I. Gackenbach & S. LaBerge (Eds.), *Conscious mind, sleeping brain: Perspectives on lucid dreaming,* New York: Plenum Press.

Sparrow, G. S. (1976a). *Lucid dreaming: Drawning of the clear light.* Virginia Beach, VA: A.R.E. Press.

Sparrow, G.S. (1976b) Effects of meditation on dreams. *Sundance Community Dream Journal, 1,* 48-49.

Stuss, D.T., & Benson, D.F. (1986). *The frontal lobes.* New York: Raven Press.

Sun, F., et al. (1984). An analysis of EEG power spectrum and coherence during quiet state in Qigong. *Acta Psychologica Sinica, 16*(4), 422-427.

Takigawa, M. (1987). Directed coherence and EEG prints in schizophrenia. In R. Takahashi, P. Flor-Henry, J. Gruzelier, & S. Niwa (Eds.), *Cerebral dynamics, laterality and psychopathology,* New York: Elsevier.

Taneli, B., & Krahne, W. (1987). EEG changes of Transcendental Meditation practitioners. *Advances in Biological Psychiatry, 16,* 41-71.

Thatcher, R.W., Krause, P.J., & Hrybyk, M. (1986). Cortico–cortical associations and EEG coherence: A two-compartmental model. *Electroencephalograpy and Clincial Neurophysiology, 64,* 123–143.

Tyson, P., Ogilvie, R., & Hunt, H. (1984). Lucid, prelucid, and nonlucid dreams related to the amount of EEG activity during REM sleep. *Psychophysiology, 21,* 442–451.

Wescott, M. (1977). Hemispheric symmetry of the EEG during the Transcendental meditation technique. In D.W. Orme–Johnson & J.T. Farrow (Eds.), *Scientific research on the Transcendental Meditation program: Collected papers* (Vol. 1). Rheinweiller, Germany: MERU Press.

West, M.A. (1980). Meditation and the EEG. *Psychological Medicine, 10,* 369–375.

West, M.A. (1982). Meditation and self-awareness: Physiological and phenomenological approaches. In G. Underwood (Ed.), *Aspects of consciousness. Vol. 3: Awareness and self-awareness.* New York: Academic Press.

Wilber, K. (1987). The spectrum model. In D. Anthony, B. Ecker, & K. Wilber (Eds.), *Spiritual choices.* New York: Paragon.

Zoccolotti, P. (1982). Field dependence, laterality and the EEG: A reanalysis of O'Connor and Shaw (1978). *Biological Psychology, 15,* 203–207.

16 Physiological Studies of Lucid Dreaming

Stephen LaBerge
Stanford University

A century ago, Frederic W.H. Myers wrote

> I have long thought that we are too indolent in regard to our dreams; that we
> neglect precious occasions of experiment for want of a little resolute direction
> of the will. . . . We should constantly represent to ourselves what points we
> should like to notice and test in dreams; and then when going to sleep we
> should impress upon our minds that we are going to try an experiment; — that
> we are going to carry into our dreams enough of our waking self to tell us that
> they *are* dreams, and to prompt us to psychological inquiry. (1887, p. 241).

Myers then quoted a "curious dream" of his own, hoping that "its paltry
commonplaceness may perhaps avert the suspicion that it has been touched
up for recital":

> I was, I thought, standing in my study; but I observed that the furniture had
> not its usual distinctness — that everything was blurred and somehow evaded a
> direct gaze. It struck me that this must be because I was *dreaming*. This was
> a great delight to me, as giving the opportunity of experimentation. I made a
> strong effort to keep calm, knowing the risk of waking. I wanted most of all
> to see and speak to somebody, to see whether they were like the real persons,
> and how they behaved. I remembered that my wife and children were away at
> the time (which was true), and I did not reason to the effect that they might
> be present in a dream, though absent from home in reality. I therefore wished
> to see one of the servants; but I was afraid to ring the bell, lest the shock
> would wake me. I very cautiously walked downstairs — after calculating that I
> should be more sure to find someone in the pantry or kitchen than in a

289

workroom, where I first thought of going. As I walked downstairs I looked carefully at the stair-carpet, to see whether I could visualise better in dream than in waking life. I found that this was *not* so; the dream-carpet was not like what I knew it in truth to be; rather, it was a thin, ragged carpet, apparently vaguely generalised from memories of seaside lodgings. I reached the pantry door, and here again I had to stop and calm myself. The door opened and a servant appeared, — quite unlike any of my own. This is all I can say, for the excitement of perceiving that I had created a new personage woke me with a shock. The dream was very clear in my mind; I was thoroughly awake; I perceived its great interest to me and I stamped it on my mind — I venture to say — almost exactly as I tell it here. (pp. 241-242)

Although we are usually unaware of the fact that we are dreaming while we are dreaming, at times a remarkable exception occurs, and as in Myers' dream, we become conscious enough to realize that we *are* dreaming. Lucid dreamers (the term derives from Van Eeden, 1913) report being able to remember freely the circumstances of waking life, to think more or less clearly, and to act deliberately upon reflection, all the while experiencing a dream world that seems vividly real (Gackenbach & LaBerge, 1988; Green, 1968; LaBerge, 1985a). Of course, this is all contrary to the characterization of dreams as essentially lacking any reflective awareness or true volition (Rechtschaffen, 1978).

Indeed, the concept of "conscious sleep" can seem so self-contradictory and paradoxical to certain ways of thinking that some theoreticians have considered lucid dreams impossible and even absurd. Probably the most extreme example of this point of view is provided by Malcolm (1959), who argued that if being asleep means experiencing nothing whatsoever, "dreams" are not experiences during sleep at all, but only the reports we tell after awakening. This concept of sleep led Malcolm to conclude that the idea that someone might reason while asleep is "meaningless." From here, Malcolm reasoned that "If 'I am dreaming' could express a judgement it would imply the judgement 'I am asleep,' and therefore the absurdity of the latter proves the absurdity of the former." Thus "the supposed judgement that one is dreaming" is "unintelligible" and "an inherently absurd form of words" (pp. 48-50).

The point of this example is to show the skeptical light in which accounts of lucid dreaming were viewed before physiological proof of the reality of the phenomenon made philosophical arguments moot. As for the occasional reports in which dreamers claimed to have been fully aware that they were dreaming while they were dreaming, up until several years ago the orthodox view in sleep and dream research assumed that anecdotal accounts of lucid dreams must be somehow spurious (see later).

So the question was raised: Under what presumably abnormal or at least exceptional physiological conditions do reports of lucid dreams occur? In the absence of empirical evidence bearing on the question, conjecture largely favored two answers: either wakefulness or NREM sleep. Most sleep researchers apparently agreed with Hartmann's "impression" that lucid dreams were "not typical parts of dreaming thought, but rather brief arousals" (Hartmann, 1975, p. 74; Berger, 1977). Schwartz and Lefebvre (1973) noted that frequent transitory arousals were common during REM sleep and proposed these "micro-awakenings" as the physiological basis for lucid dream reports. Although no evidence for this mechanism had been presented, it seems to have been the received opinion (cf. Foulkes, 1974) until the last few years. A similar view was put forward by Antrobus, Antrobus, and Fisher (1965), who predicted that recognition by the dreamer of the fact that he or she is dreaming would either immediately terminate the dream or continue in NREM sleep. Likewise, Hall (1977) speculated that lucid dreams may represent "a transition from Stage-1 REM to Stage-4 mentation" (p. 312). Only Green (1968) seems to have correctly reasoned that since lucid dreams usually arise from nonlucid dreams, "we may tentatively expect to find lucid dreams occurring, as do other dreams, during the 'paradoxical' phase of sleep" (p. 128).

Empirical evidence began to appear in the late 1970s supporting Green's speculation that lucid dreams occur during REM sleep. Based on standard sleep recordings of two subjects who reported a total of three lucid dreams upon awakening from REM periods, Ogilvie, Hunt, Sawicki, and Mc-Gowan (1978) cautiously concluded that "it *may* be that lucid dreams begin in REM" (p. 165). However, no proof was given that the reported lucid dreams had in fact occurred during the REM sleep immediately preceding the awakenings and reports. Indeed, the subjects themselves were uncertain about when their lucid dreams had taken place. What was needed to determine unambiguously the physiological status of lucid dreams was some sort of behavioral response by the lucid dreamer signaling to the experimenter that the lucid dream was taking place, along the lines pioneered by Antrobus, et al. (1965), who had asked four subjects to signal when they were asleep and dreaming by pressing a microswitch. Although the subjects were able to signal from all stages of sleep, unfortunately they were not awakened after signals and dream reports were only collected at the end of the night. Some of these signals may have been from lucid dreams, but the subjects were not asked whether they were aware of signaling or of dreaming.

LaBerge, Nagel, Dement and Zarcone (1981a) provided the necessary verification by arranging for subjects to signal the onset of a lucid dream immediately upon realizing that they were dreaming by performing specific patterns of dream actions that would be observable on a polygraph (i.e., eye movements and fist clenching). Using this approach, LaBerge et al. reported that the occurrence of lucid dreaming during unequivocal REM sleep had been demonstrated for five subjects. After being instructed in a method of lucid dream induction (see LaBerge, 1980b) the subjects were recorded from 2 to 20 nights each. In the course of the 34 nights of the study, 35 lucid dreams were reported subsequent to spontaneous waking from various stages of sleep as follows: REM sleep 32 times, NREM Stage-1, twice, and during the transition from NREM Stage-2 to REM, once. The subjects reported signaling during 30 of these lucid dreams. After each recording, the reports mentioning signals were submitted along with the respective polysomnograms to a judge uninformed of the times of the reports. In 24 cases (90%), the judge was able to select the appropriate 30-s epoch on the basis of correspondence between reported and observed signals. All signals associated with lucid dream reports occurred during epochs of unambiguous REM sleep scored according to the conventional criteria (Rechtschaffen & Kales, 1968). See Fig. 16.1 for an example of a signal verified lucid dream.

A replication of this study with two additional subjects and 20 more lucid dreams produced identical results (LaBerge, Nagel, et al., 1981b). LaBerge et al. argued that their investigations demonstrated that lucid dreaming usually (though perhaps not exclusively) occurs during REM sleep. This conclusion is supported by research carried out in several other laboratories (Dane, 1984; Fenwick et al., 1984; Hearne, 1978; Ogilvie, Hunt, Kushniruk, and Newman, 1983).

Ogilvie et al. (1983) reported the physiological state preceding 14 spontaneous lucidity signals as unqualified REM in 12 (86%) of the cases; of the remaining two cases, one was "ambiguous" REM and the other appeared to be wakefulness. Hearne and Worsley collaborated on a pioneering study of lucid dreaming in which the latter spent 50 nonconsecutive nights in a sleep laboratory while the former monitored the polygraph. Worsley reported signaling in eight lucid dreams, all of which were described by Hearne (1978) as having occurred during unambiguous REM sleep.

However, demonstrations that signaling of lucid dreams occurs during REM sleep raises other questions: Physiology aside, how do we know that lucid dreamers are "really asleep" when they signal? And what exactly is meant by the assertion that lucid dreamers are "asleep"? If we consider perception of the external world as the essential criterion of being awake (to the external world), the evidence suggests that lucid dreamers are in this sense asleep (to the external world) because although they know they are in the laboratory, this knowledge is a matter of memory, not perception. Upon awakening, they generally report having been totally in the dream world and not in sensory contact with the external world. It might be objected that lucid dreamers might simply not be attending to the environment; rather than being asleep, perhaps they are merely absorbed in their

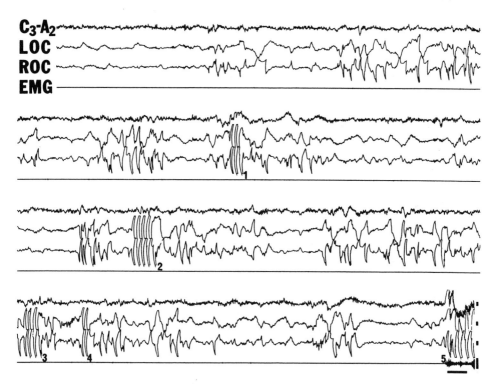

FIG. 16.1 A signal verified lucid dream. The last 8 min of a 30 min REM period are shown. Upon awakening the subject reported having made five eye movement signals (labeled 1–5 in figure). The first signal (1, two pairs of left-right eye movements, LRLR) marked the onset of lucidity. During the following 90 s the subject "flew about" exploring his dream world until he believed he had awakened, at which point he made the signal for awakening (2, LRLRLRLR). After another 90 s, the subject realized he was still dreaming and signaled (3) with three pairs of eye movements. Recognizing that this was too many, he correctly signaled with two pairs (4). Finally, upon awakening 100s later he signaled appropriately (5, LRLRLRLR). [Calibrations are 50 μV and 5 s.]

private fantasy worlds as, for example, when deeply immersed in a novel or daydream. However, according to the reports of lucid dreamers, (LaBerge, 1980a, 1985a) if they deliberately attempt to feel their bedcovers they know they are sleeping in or try to hear the ticking of the clock they know is beside their bed, they fail to feel or hear anything except what they find in their dream worlds. Lucid dreamers are conscious of the *absence* of sensory input from the external world; therefore, on empirical grounds, they conclude that they are asleep. If, in a contrary case, subjects were to claim to have been awake while showing physiological signs of sleep, or vice versa, we might have cause to doubt their subjective reports. However, when the subjective accounts and objective physiological measures are in clear agreement, as in the present case, it would seem unreasonable to suppose that subjects who reported being certain that they were asleep while showing physiological indications of unequivocal sleep were actually awake (cf. LaBerge, et al. 1981a). The conclusion appears unavoidable that lucid dreaming is an experiential and physiological reality; although perhaps paradoxical, it is clearly a phenomenon of sleep.

The preceding studies have shown that lucid dreams typically occur in REM sleep. However, this is not as precise a characterization as we would like. REM sleep is a heterogeneous state exhibiting considerable variations in physiological activity, of which two distinct phases are ordinarily distinguished. In its most active form, REM is dominated by a striking variety of irregular and short-lived events such as muscular twitching, including the rapid eye movements that give the state one of its most common names. This variety of REM is referred to as "phasic," while the relatively quiescent state remaining when rapid eye movements and other phasic events temporarily subside is referred to as "tonic." Thus, to characterize more precisely the physiology of the lucid dream state, it is reasonable to ask whether lucid dreams are more common in tonic or in phasic REM. Pivik (1986) predicted that lucid dreams should be associated with decreased phasic activity. However, research by the Stanford group, which will be detailed, has shown lucid dreaming to be associated with, on the contrary, *increased* phasic activity.

LaBerge, Levitan, and Dement (1986) physiologically analyzed 76 signal-verified lucid dreams (SVLDs) derived from 13 subjects. The polysomno-grams corresponding to each of the SVLDs were scored for sleep stages and every SVLD REM period was divided into 30-s epochs aligned with the lucidity onset signal. Up to 60 consecutive epochs of data from the nonlucid part preceding the SVLD and 15 epochs from the lucid dream were collected. For each epoch, sleep stage was scored and rapid eye movements (EM) were counted; if scalp skin-potential responses were observable as artifacts in the EEG, these were also counted (SP). Heart rate (HR) and respiration rate (RR) were determined for SVLDs recorded with these measures.

For the first lucid epoch, beginning with the initiation of the signal, the sleep stage was unequivocal REM in 70 cases (92%). The remaining six SVLDs were less than 30 s long and hence technically unscorable by the orthodox criteria (Rechtschaffen & Kales, 1968). For these cases, the entire SVLD was scored as a single epoch; with this modification, all SVLDs qualified as REM. The lucid dream signals were followed by an average of 115 s (range: 5 to 490 s) of uninterrupted REM sleep.

Physiological comparison of EM, HR, RR, and SP for lucid versus nonlucid epochs revealed that the lucid epochs of the SVLD REM periods had significantly higher levels of physiological activation than the preceding epochs of nonlucid REM within the same REM period. Similarly, H reflex amplitude was lower during lucid than non-lucid REM (Brylowski, Levitan, & LaBerge, 1989).

Physiological data were also collected for 61 nonlucid REM periods, derived from the same 13 subjects, in order to allow comparison with SVLDs. Mean values for EM and SP were significantly higher for REM periods with lucid dreams than nonlucid control REM periods (RR and HR did not differ).

LaBerge reasoned that if lucid dream probability were constant across time during REM periods, lucid dreams should be observed most frequently in the first few minutes of REM. This can be understood by considering an example: Out of 10 REM periods, there will be nearly 10 min of total REM time for the first min of REM, but less for the second min, and much less for the 20th min (since some REM periods are only a few min in length). So, assuming constant lucid dream probability, lucid dream frequency should be a monotonically decreasing function of time into REM, following the survivor function of mean REM period lengths. Although this survivor function proved to be an excellent predictor of relative lucid dream frequency ($r = .97$, $p < .005$), the data show that relative lucid dream frequency does not reach its maximum before about 5–7 min into REM.

In the light of the findings indicating that lucid dreams reliably occur during activated (phasic) REM, measures of central nervous system activation, such as eye movement density, should partly determine the distribution of lucid dreams. Since it has been reported that eye movement density starts at a low level at the beginning of REM periods and increases until it reaches a peak after approximately 5 to 7 min (Aserinsky, 1971), LaBerge hypothesized that lucid dream probability should follow a parallel development and accordingly found that mean eye movement density correlated positively and significantly with lucid dream probability ($r = .66$, $p < .01$). In a regression of lucid dream probability on eye movement density and the survivor function of mean REM period lengths, both variables entered significantly, giving an adjusted multiple $R = .98$ ($p < .005$), and demonstrating that CNS activation is an important factor in determining when in REM periods lucid dreams are initiated.

As was mentioned, momentary intrusions of wakefulness occur very commonly during the normal course of REM sleep and it had been proposed by Schwartz and Lefebvre (1973) that lucid dreaming takes place during these micro-awakenings. However, LaBerge et al.'s (1981a, 1981b, 1986) data indicate that while lucid dreams do *not* occur during interludes of wakefulness within REM periods, lucidity is sometimes *initiated* from these moments of transitory arousal, with the lucid dreams themselves continuing in subsequent undisturbed REM sleep. The subjects were normally conscious of having been awake before entering this class of lucid dream. More commonly, lucid dreams are initiated from the dream state without an awakening (Green, 1968; LaBerge 1985a).

Since lucid dreams initiated in these two ways would be expected to differ physiologically, the SVLDs were dichotomously classified as either "Wake-initiated" (WILD) or "Dream-initiated" (DILD), depending on whether or not the reports mentioned a transient awakening in which the subject consciously perceived the external environment before (consciously) re-entering the dream state. Fifty-five (72%) of the SVLDs were classified as DILDs and the remaining 21 (28%) as WILDs. For all 13 subjects, DILDs were more common than WILDs (binomial test, $p < .0001$). Compared with DILDs, WILDs were more frequently immediately preceded by physiological indications of awakening (chi-squared $= 38.3$, 1 df, $p < .0001$) establishing the validity of classifying lucid dreams in this manner.

The distributions of DILD and WILD latencies from the onset of REM are significantly different (LaBerge et al., 1986). WILDs do not occur as early or late in REM periods as DILDs (Wald–Wolfowitz, $p < .0015$). This difference may be simply explained: As a matter of definition, a necessary condition for a WILD to occur is a transitory awakening followed by a return to REM sleep. If the awakening were to happen too near the beginning of REM, the REM period might simply be aborted. Similarly, if the awakening were to occur too near the end of the REM period, it is likely that REM might not resume, but that wakefulness would persist or a NREM sleep stage would ensue.

To summarize, an elevated level of CNS activation seems to be a necessary condition for the occurrence of lucid dreams. Were this condition unnecessary, lucid dreams would be found randomly distributed within REM periods and perhaps every stage of sleep. Why then is CNS activation necessary for lucid dreaming? Evidently the high level of cognitive function involved in lucid dreaming requires a correspondingly high level of neuronal activation. In terms of Antrobus's (1986) adaptation of Anderson's (1983) ACT* model of cognition to dreaming, working memory capacity is proportional to cognitive activation, which in turn is proportional to cortical activation. Becoming lucid requires an adequate level of working memory to activate the pre-sleep intention to recognize that one is dreaming. This level of activation is evidently seldom attained during sleep except for during phasic REM.

A common observation has been that lucid dreaming is more likely to occur toward the end of sleep (Aquinas, 1947; Garfield, 1975; Van Eeden, 1913). LaBerge (1979) plotted the times of 212 of his lucid dreams and found their pattern of occurrence closely fit the usual cyclical distribution of REM periods. He suggested that the fact that most REM sleep occurs toward the end of the night provided a plausible explanation for the anecdotal observations. Later, LaBerge (1980a) tested this hypothesis by comparing the temporal distribution of his lucid dreams with that expected on the basis of normative data from Williams, Karacan, and Jursch (1974). A chi-square test indicated that the observed distribution of lucid dreams in the first three REM periods was not significantly different from what would be expected on the basis of mean REM period lengths at different times of the night (however, see the following).

Cohen (1979) argued that the left hemisphere shows a gradual increase in dominance across the night (but see Armitage, Hoffmann, Moffitt, & Shearer, 1985). Since left-hemisphere abstract symbolic functions are undoubtedly crucial for lucid dreaming, Cohen's GILD hypothesis led LaBerge (1985b) to predict that the probability of dream lucidity should increase with time of night.

This hypothesis was tested by LaBerge et al. (1986). For each of their 12 subjects a median split for total REM time was determined; 11 of their subjects had more lucid dreams in the later half of their REM than in the earlier (binomial test; $p < .01$). For the combined sample, relative lucidity probability was calculated for REM periods one through six of the night by dividing the total number of SVLDs observed in a given REM period by the corresponding total time in stage REM for the same REM period. A regression analysis clearly demonstrated that relative lucidity probability was a linear function of ordinal REM period number ($r = .98, p < .0001$). No measure of activation (EM, RR, HR, SP) even approached significance when entered into the regression equation, indicating that the increase in lucid dream probability is not explained by a general increase in CNS activation across the night, as measured by these indexes. These results strongly support the conclusion that lucid dreams are more likely to occur in later REM periods than in earlier ones.

LaBerge (1980a) suggested that the fact that lucid dreamers can remember to perform predetermined actions and signal to the laboratory made possible a new approach to dream research: Lucid dreamers, he proposed, "could carry out diverse dream experiments marking the exact time of particular dream events, allowing the derivation of precise psychophysiological correlations and the methodical testing of hypotheses" (LaBerge et al., 1981a, p. 727). This strategy has been put into practice by the Stanford group in a number of investigations summarized by LaBerge (1985a).

Studies using eye movement signals (Dane, 1984; Fenwick et al., 1984; Hearne, 1978; LaBerge, et al., 1981a; 1981b; Ogilvie, Hunt, Tyson, Lucescu, & Jeakins, 1982) indicate that there is a very direct and reliable relationship between gaze shift reported in lucid dreams and the direction of polygraphically recorded eye movements. It should be noted that the results obtained for lucid dreams are much stronger than the generally weak correlations demonstrated by earlier investigations testing the notion that the dreamer's eyes move with his or her hallucinated dream gaze, which had to rely on the chance occurrence of a highly recognizable eye movement pattern that was readily matchable to the subject's reported dream activity (e.g. Roffwarg, Dement, Muzio, & Fisher, 1962). This would seem to illustrate the methodological advantage of using lucid dreamers as subjects in psychophysiological studies of dreaming. The correspondence between subjective and objective eye movements implies that, to a first approximation, spatial relationships in the dream world are similar to those of the physical world.

A similar result has been found for temporal relationships as well. LaBerge (1980a, 1985a) asked subjects to estimate various intervals of time during their lucid dreams. Signals marking the beginning and end of the subjective intervals allowed comparison with objective time. Time estimates during the lucid dreams were very close to the actual time between signals in all cases (see Fig. 16.2).

In another study, LaBerge and Dement (1982a) tested whether subjects were capable of voluntary control of respiration during lucid dreaming. They recorded three lucid dreamers who were asked to either breathe rapidly or to hold their breath (in their lucid dreams), marking the interval of altered respiration with eye movement signals. The subjects reported successfully carrying out the agreed-upon tasks a total of nine times, and in every case, a judge was able to predict correctly on the basis of the polygraph recordings which of the two patterns had been executed (binomial test, $< .002$).

Evidence of voluntary control of other muscle groups during REM was found by LaBerge et al., (1981a) while testing a variety of lucidity signals. They observed that a sequence of left and right dream-fist clenching resulted in a corresponding sequence of left and right forearm twitches as measured by EMG. However, the amplitude of the twitches bore an unreliable relationship to the subjective intensity of the dreamed action. Since all skeletal muscle groups except those that govern eye movements and breathing suffer a profound loss of tone during REM sleep, it is to be expected that most muscular responses to dreamed movements will be feeble. Nonetheless, it appears that these responses faithfully reflect the motor patterns of the original dream.

Additional support for this conclusion comes from a study (Fenwick et al., 1984) of a single, highly proficient lucid dreamer who carried out a variety of dreamed muscular movements while being polygraphically recorded. In one experiment, the subject executed movements during lucid dreams involving finger, forearm, and shoulder muscle groups (flexors) while EMG was recorded from each area. The results were consistent: The axial muscles showed no measurable EMG activity while the forearm EMG showed lower amplitude and shorter duration, compared with the finger

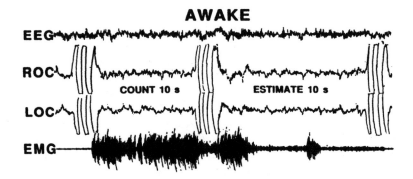

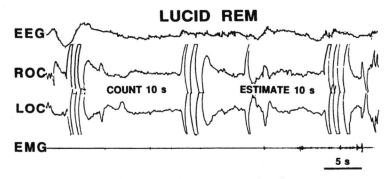

FIG. 16.2 Time estimates during waking and REM lucid dreaming. While awake, (top panel) the subject signaled, estimated 10s by counting, signaled again, estimated 10 s without counting, and signaled a third time. The lower panel shows the subject carrying out the same task in lucid REM sleep. The time estimates are very similar in both states.

EMG. A similar experiment with the lower limbs yielded corresponding results. In addition to the finding that REM atonia shows a central–peripheral gradient with motor inhibition least for the most distal muscles, Fenwick et al. reported that similar experiments comparing EMG response with dreamed arm and leg flexions and extensions suggested that flexors were less inhibited than extensors. In addition to EMG, an accelerometer was utilized in several experiments demonstrating that the subject was able to produce minor movements of his fingers, toes, and feet during REM, though not of his legs. Fenwick et al. also presented the results of a single experiment suggesting that dream speech may be initiated in the expiratory phase of respiration just as it usually is during waking. In still another experiment they demonstrated the voluntary production of smooth pursuit eye movements during a lucid dream. LaBerge (1986) has carried out related experiments in which two subjects tracked the tip of their fingers moving slowly left to right during four conditions: (1) awake, eyes open; (2) awake, eyes closed mental imagery; (3) lucid dreaming; and (4) imagination ("dream eyes closed") during lucid dreaming. The subjects showed saccadic eye movements in the two imagination conditions (2 and 4), and smooth tracking eye movements during dreamed or actual tracking (conditions 1 and 3).

Fenwick et al. (1984) also showed that their subject was able to perceive and respond to environmental stimuli (electrical shocks) without awakening from his lucid dream. This result raises a theoretical issue: If we take perception of the external world to be the essential criterion for wakefulness (LaBerge et al., 1981a; see earlier) then it would seem that Fenwick et al.'s subject must have been at least partly awake. On the other hand, when environmental stimuli are incorporated into dreams without producing any subjective or physiological indications of arousal, it appears reasonable to speak of the perception as having occurred during sleep as we now define it. Furthermore, it may be possible, as LaBerge (1980c) has suggested, for one sense to remain functional and "awake" while others fall "asleep." Similarly, Antrobus, et al. (1965) argued

> [t]hat the question — awake or asleep — is not a particularly useful one. Even though we have two discrete words — sleep and wakefulness — this does not mean that the behavior associated with the words can be forced into two discrete categories. By any variable or operation available to us, not only do sleeping and waking shade gradually into one another but there is only limited agreement among the various physiological and subjective operations that discriminate between sleeping and waking. At a given moment, all systems of the organism are not necessarily equally asleep or awake. (pp. 398-399).

Clearly it will prove necessary to characterize a wider variety of states of consciousness than those few currently distinguished (e.g., "dreaming," "sleeping," "waking," and so on).

Since many researchers have reported cognitive task dependency of lateralization of EEG alpha activity in the waking state, LaBerge and Dement (1982b) undertook a pilot study to determine whether similar relationships would hold in the lucid dream state. The two tasks selected for comparison were dreamed singing and dreamed counting, activities expected to result in relatively greater engagement of the subjects' left and right cerebral hemispheres, respectively.

Left and right temporal EEG (T_3/C_z and T_4/C_z) was recorded on magnetic tape while four subjects sang and counted in their lucid dreams (marking the beginning and end of each task by eye movement signals). The EEG was digitized off-line and Fourier transformed. The results supported the hypothesized lateralization of alpha activity: The right hemisphere was more active (showed less alpha) than the left during singing; during counting the reverse was true. These shifts were similar to those observed during actual singing and counting.

Sexual activity is a rather commonly reported theme of lucid dreams (Garfield, 1979; LaBerge, 1985a). LaBerge, Greenleaf, and Kedzierski (1983) undertook a pilot study to determine the extent to which subjectively experienced sexual activity during REM lucid dreaming would be reflected in physiological responses. Their subject was a highly proficient lucid dreamer who spent the night sleeping in the laboratory. Sixteen channels of physiological data, including EEG, EOG, EMG, respiration, skin conductance level (SCL), heart rate, vaginal EMG (VEMG), and vaginal pulse amplitude (VPA), were recorded. The experimental protocol called for the subject to make specific eye movement signals at the following points: when she realized she was dreaming (i.e., the onset of the lucid dream); when she began sexual activity (in the dream); and when she experienced orgasm. The subject reported a lucid dream in which she carried out the experimental task exactly as agreed upon. Data analysis revealed a significant correspondence between her subjective report and all but one of the autonomic measures; during the 15-s orgasm epoch, mean levels for VEMG activity, VPA, SCL, and respiration rate reached their highest values and were significantly elevated, compared with means for other REM epochs. Surprisingly, there were no significant heart rate increases.

LaBerge (1985a) reports replicating this experiment using two male subjects. In both cases, respiration showed striking increases in rate. Again, there were no significant elevations of heart rate. Although both subjects reported vividly realistic orgasms in their lucid dreams, neither actually ejaculated.

All of these results support the conclusion that the events we seem to experience while asleep and dreaming are the result of brain activity that produces effects on our bodies remarkably similar to those that would occur if we were actually to experience the corresponding events while awake. The reason for this is probably that the multimodal imagery of the dream is produced by the same brain systems that produce the equivalent perceptions (cf. Finke, 1980). Perhaps this explains in part why we usually mistake our dreams for reality: To the functional systems in our brains that build our experiential worlds, dreaming of perceiving or doing something is equivalent to actually perceiving or doing it.

REFERENCES

Anderson, J. R. (1983). *The architecture of cognition*. Cambridge, MA: Harvard University Press.

Antrobus, J. S. (1986). Dreaming: Cortical activation and perceptual thresholds. *Journal of Mind and Behavior, 7,* 193-212.

Antrobus, J. S., Antrobus, J. S., & Fisher, C. (1965). Discrimination of dreaming and nondreaming sleep. *Archives of General Psychiatry, 12,* 395-401.

Armitage, R., Hoffmann, R., Moffitt, A., & Shearer, J. (1985). Ultradian rhythms in interhemispheric EEG during sleep: A disconfirmation of the GILD hypothesis. *Sleep Research, 14,* 286.

Aquinas, St. (1947). *Summa theologica* (Vol. 1). New York: Benziger Brothers.

Aserinsky, E. (1971). Rapid eye movement density and pattern in the sleep of young adults. *Psychophysiology, 8,* 361-375.

Berger, R. (1977). *Psyclosis: The circularity of experience.* San Francisco: W. H. Freeman.

Brylowski, A., Levitan, L., & LaBerge, S. (1989). H-reflex suppression and autonomic activation during lucid REM sleep: A case study. *Sleep, 12,* 374-378.

Cohen, D.B. (1979). *Sleep and dreaming: Origins, nature and functions.* Oxford, England: Pergamon.

Dane, J. (1984). *An empirical evaluation of two techniques for lucid dream induction.* Unpublished doctoral dissertation, Georgia State University.

Fenwick, P., Schatzman, M., Worsley, A., Adams, J., Stone, S., & Baker, A. (1984). Lucid dreaming: Correspondence between dreamed and actual events in one subject during REM sleep. *Biological Psychology, 18,* 243-252.

Finke, R. A. (1980). Levels of equivalence in imagery and perception. *Psychological Review, 87,* 113-132.

Foulkes, D. (1974). [Review of Schwartz & Lefebvre (1973)]. *Sleep Research, 3,* 113.

Gackenbach, J., & LaBerge, S. (1988). *Conscious mind, sleeping brain.* New York: Plenum Press.

Garfield, P. (1975). Psychological concomitants of the lucid dream state. *Sleep Research, 4,* 183.

Garfield, P. (1979). *Pathway to ecstasy.* New York: Holt, Rinehart, & Winston.

Green, C. (1968). *Lucid dreams.* London: Hamish Hamilton.

Hall, J. A. (1977). *Clinical uses of dreams.* New York: Grune & Stratten.

Hartmann, E. (1975). Dreams and other hallucinations: An approach to the underlying mechanism. In R. K. Siegal & L. J. West (Eds.), *Hallucinations* (pp. 71-79). New York: Wiley.

Hearne, K. M. T. (1978). *Lucid dreams: An electrophysiological and psychological study.* Unpublished doctoral dissertation, University of Liverpool.

LaBerge, S. (1979). Lucid dreaming: Some personal observations. *Sleep Research, 8,* 158.

LaBerge, S. (1980a). *Lucid dreaming: An exploratory study of consciousness during sleep.* (Doctoral dissertation, Stanford University, 1980). (University Microfilms International No. 80-24, 691).

LaBerge, S. (1980b). Lucid dreaming as a learnable skill: A case study. *Perceptual and Motor Skills, 51,* 1039-1042.

LaBerge, S. (1980c). Induction of lucid dreams. *Sleep Research, 9,* 138.

LaBerge, S. (1985a). *Lucid dreaming.* Los Angeles: J. P. Tarcher.

LaBerge, S. (1985b). The temporal distribution of lucid dreams. *Sleep Research, 14,* 113.

LaBerge, S. (1986). [unpublished data].

LaBerge, S., & Dement, W. C. (1982a). Lateralization of alpha activity for dreamed singing and counting during REM sleep. *Psychophysiology, 19,* 331-332.

LaBerge, S., & Dement, W. C. (1982b). Voluntary control of respiration during REM sleep. *Sleep Research, 11,* 107.

LaBerge, S., Greenleaf, W., & Kedzierski, B. (1983). Physiological responses to dreamed sexual activity during lucid REM sleep. *Psychophysiology, 20,* 454-455.

LaBerge, S., Levitan, L., & Dement, W. C. (1986). Lucid dreaming: Physiological correlates of consciousness during REM sleep. *Journal of Mind and Behavior, 7,* 251–258.

LaBerge, S., Nagel, L., Dement, W. C., & Zarcone, V., Jr. (1981a). Lucid dreaming verified by volitional communication during REM sleep. *Perceptual and Motor Skills, 52,* 727–732.

LaBerge, S., Nagel, L., Taylor, W., Dement, W. C., & Zarcone, V., Jr. (1981b). Psychophysiological correlates of the initiation of lucid dreaming. *Sleep Research, 10,* 149.

Malcolm, N. (1959). *Dreaming.* London: Routledge.

Myers, F. W. H. (1887). Automatic writing–3. *Proceedings of the Society for Psychical Research, 4(pt.II).*

Ogilvie, R. Hunt, H., Kushniruk, & Newman (1983). Lucid dreams and the arousal continuum. *Sleep Research, 12,* 182.

Ogilvie, R., Hunt, H., Sawicki, C., & McGowan, K. (1978). Searching for lucid dreams. *Sleep Research, 7,* 165.

Ogilvie, R., Hunt, H., Tyson, P. D., Lucescu, M. L., & Jeakins, D. B. (1982). Lucid dreaming and alpha activity: A preliminary report. *Perceptual and Motor Skills, 55,* 795–808.

Pivik, R. T. (1986). Sleep: Physiology and Psychophysiology. In M. G. H. Coles, E. Donchin, & S. Porges (Eds.), *Psychophysiology: Systems, processes, and applications.* New York: Guilford Press. pp. 378–406.

Rechtschaffen, A. (1978). The single-mindedness and isolation of dreams. *Sleep, 1,* 97–109.

Rechtschaffen, A., & Kales, A. (Eds.). (1968). *A manual of standardized terminology, techniques and scoring system for sleep stages of human subjects.* Bethesda, MD: HEW Neurological Information Network.

Roffwarg, H., Dement, W. C., Muzio, J., & Fisher, C. (1962). Dream imagery: Relationship to rapid eye movements of sleep. *Archives of General Psychiatry, 7,* 235–238.

Schwartz, B. A., & Lefebvre, A. (1973). Contacts veille/P.M.O.II. Les P.M.O. morcelees [Conjunction of waking and REM sleep. II. Fragmented REM periods.]. *Revue d'Electroencephalographie et de Neurophysiologie Clinique, 3,* 165–176.

Van Eeden, F. (1913). A study of dreams. *Proceedings of the Society for Psychical Research, 26,* 431–461.

Williams, R., Karacan, I., & Jursch, C. (1974). *Electroencephalography (EEG) of human sleep: Clinical applications.* New York: Wiley.

Author Index

Note: Italicized page numbers refer to bibliography pages.

305

Gopher, D., 34, *43*
Gordon, H. W., 29–30, *43,* 52–53, *61,*
66–69, 75, 77, 80, *83–84,* 96, *97*
Gottman, J. M., 22, *43*
Govin, P., 22, *45*
Graeber, R. C., *43*
Granat, M., 18, *43*
Granieri, B., 279, *287*
Green, C., 291, 296, *302*
Greenberg, J. P., *123,* 130
Greenberg, M. S., 48, 58, *61,* 82, *84,* 100,
118–119, *125*
Greenberg, R., 101, 108, 111, 114, 121,
125, 128, 135, 138
Greenberg, S., 178, *181*
Greenburg, A. G., 22, *45*
Greenleaf, W., 301, *302*
Greenwood, P., 101, *125*
Grindel, O. M., 267, 272, *285*
Grivel, M. L., 22, *43*
Grossi, D., 120, *125*
Grunstein, A. M., 113, *125,* 140
Gruzelier, J., *61, 284, 287*
Guinto, F. C., Jr., 117, *126*
Gur, R. C., 121, *125*

H

Halberg, F., 18, *43*
Halgren, E., 118, *125*
Hall, C. S., 6, *14,* 173, *182*
Hall, J. A., 291, *302*
Hammond, G. R., 80, *85*
Hartmann, E., 249, *250,* 291, *302*
Hartmann, F., 101, *125*
Hartnett, M. B., 79, *83*
Hartwig, P., 3, *13*
Haskel, R., *284*
Hata, T., 5, *14,* 122, *128*
Hauri, P., 159, *182*
Havel, J., 249, *250*
Haynes, C. T., 268–270, 277, *285–287*
Hazout, S., 273–274, *283*
Hearne, K. M. T., 292, 297, *302*
Hebert, J. R., 277, *285*
Hecaen, H., 101, 110, 113, 115–116, *125,*
127
Heilman, K. M., *128*
Heilman, N., 279, *284*
Helfand, R., 172, 252, 258, *261*
Hellige, J. B., 121, *128*

Henkle, V., 204, *214*
Herbert, J. R., 269–270, *284*
Herbert, R., 270, *286*
Herman, J., 8–10, 47–48, *61,* 65, *84,* 89,
97, 110, *125,* 144, *155,* 157, 178, *182,*
251, 253–257, *261–262*
Herrera-Marschitz, M., 231, *245*
Herron, J., 91, *97*
Herscovitch, J., 70, *84*
Herter, G., 273–274, 279, *283*
Hiatt, J. F., 22, *43, 44*
Hinton, G. E., *13,* 177, 179, *182,* 199,
200–205, *214*
Hirshkowitz, M., 27, *43,* 47–48, *61,* 65, *84,*
89, *97*
Hirst, W., 113, *126*
Hishikawa, Y., 110–111, *127*
Hobson, J. A., 4–5, 9–10, *14,* 110, 112,
126, 159–160, 166–167, 169, 172–173,
180, *182,* 200–201, *214,* 217, *224,*
227–228, 231–233, 236–237, *245,* 252,
258, *261–262*
Hoddes, E., 70, *84*
Hoedemaker, F., 23, *43*
Hoffman, H. J., 22, 36, *44*
Hoffman, J., 231, *245*
Hoffman, S., 172, 252, 258, *261*
Hoffmann, R., 1, 7, 17, 20–21, 27–29,
36–39, 41, *42–44,* 47–48, 50, *61,* 65, 81,
84, 266–268, 270–271, 278, 280, *282–283,*
286, 297, *302*
Hollingworth, H. L., 17, *43*
Holmes, D., 111, 274, *285*
Holt, R. R., 17, *43,* 249, *250*
Holtzman, J. D., 82, *83*
Hoppe, K. D., 101, *126*
Horakova, H., 65, *84*
Howard, D., 113, *124*
Hrybyk, M., 268, *287*
Huff, F. J., 117, *126*
Humphreys, G. W., 116, *128*
Humphrey, M. E., 48, *61,* 92, *97, 126,* 133
Hunt, H. T., 167, 170, *182,* 247, 250, 265,
275, 277–278, 280, *285–286, 288,*
291–292, 297, *303*
Hunter, I., 212, *213*

I

Ibba, A., 113, *124*
Ingle, D. J., *128*

314   AUTHOR INDEX

Subject Index